D0917423

3 FREE Minutes
of weather information and save up to 60% on long distance calls!

Let The Weather Channel®️ help you pack! Get all the information you need before you leave.

- Current conditions & forecasts for over 900 cities worldwide
- Severe weather information including winter and tropical storm updates
- Wake-up call complete with your local forecast
- Special interest forecasts featuring ski resort, boating and other outdoor conditions

Remove card and see instructions on back.

Plus:

After selecting any additional payment option, you will receive 5 FREE MINUTES of long distance service!

Easy. Convenient. Fast.

Weather information provided by The Weather Channel. Network Services provided by AT&T. All other services provided by ICN, Ltd. Offer valid only in U.S.

It's The Only Phone Card You Will Ever Need!

During your free call, an automated operator will offer you an option to add $10, $20 or $30 to your phone card using any major credit card.

Use your card to:

- Save 20% on comprehensive weather information!

- Save up to 60% on long distance calls to **anywhere** in the U.S., **anytime**!

- Save 20% on other helpful information including lottery, sports, and more!

Domestic long distance service costs $0.25 per minute and all other options cost $0.75 per minute when using your TWC phone card.

Take the worry out of wondering! Carry the power to access all of these essential services with you in your wallet, wherever **Frommer's** may take you!

No place on Earth has better weather.™

Travel Discount Coupon

This coupon entitles you to special discounts
when you book your trip through the

🍎 *TRAVEL NETWORK* ®
RESERVATION SERVICE

Hotels ♦ Airlines ♦ Car Rentals ♦ Cruises
All Your Travel Needs

Here's what you get: *

♦ A discount of $50 USD on a booking of $1,000** or
  more for two or more people!

♦ A discount of $25 USD on a booking of $500** or more
  for one person!

♦ Free membership for three years, and 1,000 free miles
  on enrollment in the unique Miles-to-Go™ frequent-
  traveler program. Earn one mile for every dollar spent
  through the program. Earn free hotel stays starting at
  5,000 miles. Earn free roundtrip airline tickets starting
  at 25,000 miles.

♦ Personal help in planning your own, customized trip.

♦ Fast, confirmed reservations at any property
  recommended in this guide, subject to availability.***

♦ Special discounts on bookings in the U.S. and around
  the world.

♦ Low-cost visa and passport service.

♦ Reduced-rate cruise packages.

Visit our website at http://www.travnet.com/Frommer or
call us globally at 201-567-8500, ext. 55. In the U.S., call
toll-free at 1-888-940-5000, or fax 201-567-1838. In
Canada, call toll-free at 1-800-883-9959, or fax 416-922-
6053. In Asia, call 60-3-7191044, or fax 60-3-7185415.

---

* To qualify for these travel discounts, at least a portion of your trip must
  include destinations covered in this guide. No more than one coupon discount
  may be used in any 12-month period, for destinations covered in this guide.
  Cannot be combined with any other discount or program.

**These are U.S. dollars spent on commissionable bookings.

***A $10 USD fee, plus fax and/or phone charges, will be added to the cost of
  bookings at each hotel not linked to the reservation service. Customers
  must approve these fees in advance.

Valid until December 31, 1997. Terms and conditions of the Miles-to-
Go™ program are available on request by calling 201-567-8500, ext 55.

LAS123

Frommer's® 97

Las Vegas

by Rena Bulkin

with coverage of southwestern Utah
and Zion National Park
by Don & Barbara Laine

Macmillan • USA

ABOUT THE AUTHORS

Rena Bulkin began her travel-writing career when she set out for Europe in search of adventure. She found it writing about hotels and restaurants for the *New York Times* International Edition. She has since authored 15 travel guides to far-flung destinations.

Don and Barbara Laine have written about and traveled extensively throughout the Rocky Mountains and the Southwest. They are the authors of *Frommer's Utah, Frommer's Colorado,* and *Frommer's Denver, Boulder & Colorado Springs.*

MACMILLAN TRAVEL

A Simon & Schuster Macmillan Company
1633 Broadway
New York, NY 10019

Find us online at **http://www.mgr.com/travel** or
on America Online at Keyword: **Frommer's.**

ISBN 0-02-860917-4
ISSN 0899-3262

Editor: Douglas Stallings
Production Editor: Beth Mayland
Design by Michele Laseau
Digital Cartography by John Decamillis & Ortelius Design
Maps copyright © by Simon & Schuster, Inc.

SPECIAL SALES

Contents

List of Maps

AN INVITATION TO THE READER

In researching this book, we discovered many wonderful places—hotels, restaurants, shops, and more. We're sure you'll find others. Please tell us about them, so we can share the information with your fellow travelers in upcoming editions. If you were disappointed with a recommendation, we'd love to know that, too. Please write to:

Frommer's Las Vegas '97
Macmillan Travel
1633 Broadway
New York, NY 10019

AN ADDITIONAL NOTE

Please be advised that travel information is subject to change at any time—and this is especially true of prices. We therefore suggest that you write or call ahead for confirmation when making your travel plans. The authors, editors, and publisher cannot be held responsible for the experiences of readers while traveling. Your safety is important to us, however, so we encourage you to stay alert and be aware of your surroundings. Keep a close eye on cameras, purses, and wallets, all favorite targets of thieves and pickpockets.

WHAT THE SYMBOLS MEAN

✪ Frommer's Favorites

Hotels, restaurants, attractions, and entertainment you should not miss.

⑤ Super-Special Values

Hotels and restaurants that offer great value for your money.

The following abbreviations are used for credit cards:

AE	American Express	EU	Eurocard
CB	Carte Blanche	JCB	Japan Credit Bank
DC	Diners Club	MC	MasterCard
DISC	Discover	V	Visa
ER	enRoute		

Introducing Las Vegas

Las Vegas is a city designed for overindulgence, an anything-goes kind of place where you're encouraged to eat too much (at lavish low-priced buffets), drink too much (liquor is gratis at gaming tables), spend too much, and sleep too little. Leave your real life back home. In this 24-hour, neon-lit playground, you can leer at sexy showgirls prancing around in topless costumes, hoot and holler at the craps tables, even watch a volcano erupting while you're walking down the street. Traditionally, Las Vegas is the place to let it all hang out. Jimmy Durante—the first performer at the Flamingo—demolished a $1,600 piano on opening night just for kicks. And this was nothing compared to the high jinks of Flamingo owner Bugsy Siegel and his cohorts.

More than Chicago, it's Sinatra's kind of town, offering more superstar entertainment every night of the week than any other city in the world. It would seem that every performer ends up in Las Vegas at some time or other. Even such unlikely people as Noel Coward, Woody Allen, Bob Dylan, Buster Keaton, the Beatles, Luciano Pavarotti, and Orson Welles have played the Strip's showrooms. And Las Vegas audiences have witnessed many great moments in entertainment history. For instance:

In 1962 former President Harry Truman, in town to address the American Legion, joined Jimmy Durante in a piano duet at the Sands.

Elvis and Liberace once appeared together at the Riviera (Elvis played piano, Liberace guitar, and they donned each other's flamboyant costumes for the occasion).

Paul Anka and Wayne Newton surprised pal Tony Orlando by joining him onstage during his opening night at the Riviera in 1977 and belting out his trademark song, "Tie a Yellow Ribbon," for an ecstatic audience.

A year after Gracie Allen retired, Jack Benny—in full drag—performed in her stead one night with George Burns at the Sahara Congo Room.

And it was only years later that audiences realized they had witnessed entertainment history in the making when Judy Garland brought her 9-year-old daughter Liza onstage at the Flamingo in 1957.

Major sporting events take place on a regular basis—from championship boxing matches to championship poker playoffs, not to mention bizarre daredevil feats such as Evel Knievel's near-fatal motorcycle jump over the fountains fronting Caesars Palace.

And then there's gambling. Fortunes are won and lost (usually lost) on a roll of the dice. But we all secretly believe we'll beat the odds and sail out of town with big bucks (preferably in a limo)—like the young bride on her honeymoon who hit the jackpot to the tune of $1 million after playing the slots at Caesars for just 3 minutes! Such stories abound, and even sober folks can contract gambling fever upon hearing them . . . not to mention watching the electronic billboards on the Strip displaying ever increasing multimillion-dollar progressive slot jackpots. A little more than a decade ago $1 slot machines caused a sensation in the casinos. Today—in sumptuous high-roller precincts—you can bet $1,500 on a single pull! On the other hand, you can still find penny slots in some downtown casinos.

But even if you don't want to gamble, you can have a great vacation here. Plush hotels, which charge only about half the amount of their counterparts in other cities, offer numerous resort facilities—immense pools, tennis courts, health clubs, and more. Most shows are reasonably priced. Food is cheap (a full prime-rib dinner can be had for under $5). And many great attractions are within easy driving distance—magnificent desert canyon vistas at Red Rock and Valley of Fire, pine-forested Mount Charleston, Hoover Dam (an awe-inspiring engineering feat even in today's high-tech world), and the recreational pleasures of Lake Mead among them. Or you can just stroll the Strip at night and enjoy the world's most spectacular sound and light show.

It's amazing to think that just 100 years ago all you would have found here was a desert wilderness.

1 Frommer's Favorite Las Vegas Experiences

- **A Stroll on the Strip After Dark:** You haven't really seen Las Vegas until you've seen it at night. This neon wonderland is the world's greatest sound and light show. Begin at Circus Circus, where you'll find circus acts and carnival games, and continue—if your energy holds out—as far as the Luxor for a look at King Tut's Tomb. Make plenty of stops en route to take in the ship battle at Treasure Island, see the Mirage volcano erupt, and enjoy the light, sound, and water show at Bally's.
- **A Creative Adventures Tour:** Char Cruze provides personalized tours that unlock the mysteries of the desert canyons and make regional history come vibrantly alive. I can't think of a better way to spend a day than exploring canyons with her.
- **A Visit to the Magic and Movie Hall of Fame:** This delightful attraction offers hours of solid entertainment for just a few dollars. Following a very good magician/ventriloquist show, you'll tour dozens of fascinating magic-related exhibits enhanced by video clips of actual performances.

- **A Lunch or Dinner Show at Caesars Magical Empire:** This spellbinding magical experience, combined with an excellent meal, is a marvelous way to while away a few hours out of the casino.
- **Fine Dining:** Rather than drop hundreds of dollars in a few hours at Las Vegas casinos, get something for your money. Treat yourself to dinner at one of the city's superb haute cuisine restaurants, such as Emeril's, Gatsby's, or the Coyote Café at the MGM Grand; Fiore at the Rio; and Spago or the Palace Court at Caesars. If you choose Gatsby's or the Palace Court, plan on after-dinner drinks at their adjoining piano bars.
- **An Excursion to Mount Charleston:** Especially in summer, the scenic drive to the mountains, which ends at a charming restaurant nestled in a pine forest, is a delight. Spend the day here hiking, horseback riding, or just kicking back. If you don't feel like going back right away, stay the night at the Mount Charleston Hotel.
- **Riding the Big Shot at the Stratosphere:** This thrilling free-fall ride thrusts you 160 feet in the air along a 228-foot spire at the top of the Stratosphere tower, then plummets you down again. If that seems too terrifying, ascend the tower via elevator and enjoy the view from indoor and outdoor observation decks.
- **Cirque du Soleil:** You haven't really seen Cirque du Soleil until you've seen it at Treasure Island, where the showroom is equipped with state-of-the-art sound and lighting systems, and where Steve Wynn has provided a seemingly infinite budget for sets, costumes, and high-tech special effects. It's an enchantment.
- **An Evening in Glitter Gulch:** Set aside an evening to tour downtown hotels and take in the Fremont Street Experience. Stay on to see *Country Fever* at the Golden Nugget.
- **A Sunday Champagne Brunch:** Especially leisurely and lavish are those featured at Bally's, Caesars Palace, and the Golden Nugget.
- **A Trip to Lake Mead:** Book a night at Lake Mead Lodge, using it as a base to explore Hoover Dam and the 1.5-million-acre Lake Mead National Recreation Area. An engineering marvel in the 1930s, the dam is still damned impressive. After your tour, you can enjoy swimming, boating, fishing, scuba diving, rafting, and canoeing here. Take a scenic lunch or dinner cruise aboard a Mississippi-style paddle wheeler.
- **Catching Your Favorite Headliners:** As soon as you arrive in town, pick up a show guide and see who's playing during your stay. Las Vegas offers an unparalleled opportunity to enjoy your favorite entertainers.
- **Shopping the Forum at Caesars Palace:** This is an only-in-Vegas shopping experience—an arcade replicating an ancient Roman streetscape, with classical piazzas and opulent fountains. The central "Fountain of the Gods" features animatronic statues of Bacchus, Venus, and others. The result is Rodeo Drive meets the Roman Empire.
- **Hiking and Picnicking at Valley of Fire State Park:** More thrilling natural wonders—majestic sandstone canyons, cliffs, rock formations, and Native American petroglyphs—to explore.
- **Seeing Siegfried & Roy:** I'd as soon miss their show at the Mirage as go to India and skip the Taj Mahal.
- **Playing Craps at a Casino:** The most exciting casino action is always at the craps tables, where bettors bond over fast-paced play.

2 The City Today & Tomorrow

Las Vegas is on a roll. Two major new resorts, the Monte Carlo and the Stratosphere Las Vegas, went up in 1996, adding 4,500 new rooms. At this writing, another 11,500 rooms—in five new megaresorts and additions to existing properties—are under construction, and that figure will more than double by the turn of the century (see chapter 5 for details on upcoming hotels). It seems, no matter how many rooms the town builds, tourists just keep arriving to fill them up. Las Vegas's room inventory is already the largest of any city in the nation.

But Las Vegas isn't resting on its laurels. Hoteliers are very aware that if occupancy rates are to keep pace with burgeoning room counts, tourists must be lured to the town. Gone are the days when a hotel could simply offer a casino, a show, and some formula restaurants. Today, each new property has to do something spectacular to garner attention (from rooftop roller coasters to celebrity-chef restaurants), while existing hotels frantically renovate in hopes of competing successfully with sensationalist newcomers.

The phenomenal growth in tourism (the city had about 30 million visitors last year) is paralleled by a population explosion. Las Vegas has had a 26 percent increase in its population over the last 5 years, and between 4,000 and 6,000 people are relocating into the area monthly! While this has been terrific for the local economy, it has caused many problems, such as congested highways and insufficient schools and services. For tourists, the town's all-too-rapid growth is most evident along the Strip, which is totally inadequate to accommodate us in such huge numbers. While monorails and other traffic solutions are under consideration, Strip traffic remains frustratingly bumper-to-bumper at almost all times.

Snarled traffic notwithstanding, the excitement generated by new hotels, restaurants, and sightseeing options easily outweighs the inconveniences. Every year, the Strip undergoes a major change, gaining an erupting volcano here, a towering Eiffel Tower or Empire State Building there. Downtown Las Vegas is also spiffing up, proud of its new look centered on the Fremont Street Experience. As Las Vegas history continues to be written, one can only wonder, "What will they think of next?"

3 A Look at the Past

Dateline

- **Prehistory** Archaeological studies show humans occupying Las Vegas region from **3000** B.C. Hunter-gatherers called the Anasazi ("the ancient ones") have lived here from the 1st century A.D.
- **A.D. 1150** Anasazi leave the area. Nomadic Paiutes become the dominant group.
- **1829** Expedition of Mexican traders camping 100 miles from the present site of Las Vegas send scout Rafael Rivera to explore the

continues

For many centuries the For many centuries the land that would become Nevada was inhabited only by several Native American tribes—the Paiute, Shoshone, and Washoe. It wasn't until 1826 that white men set foot in the future state, and not until 1829 that Rafael Rivera, a scout for Mexican traders, entered a verd ant valley nurtured by desert springs and called it Las Vegas ("the meadows"). From 1831 to 1848 these springs served as a watering place on the Old Spanish Trail for trading caravans plying the route between Santa Fe and the California coast. Explorer, soldier, and pathfinder Col. John C. Frémont (for whom the main thoroughfare Downtown is named) rested near the headwaters of Las Vegas Springs on an overland expedition in 1844. A decade later Congress established a monthly mail route through

Las VegasSprings. And in 1855 Mormon leader Brigham Young sent 30 missionaries to Las Vegas to help expand Mormonism between Salt Lake City and southern California. Just north of what is today downtown (what would these missionaries think if they could see it now?) the Mormon colony built an adobe fort and dwellings. They raised crops, baptized Paiutes, and mined lead in the nearby mountains. However, none of these ventures proved successful, and the ill-fated settlement was abandoned after just 3 years.

The next influx into the area came as a result of mining fever in the early 1860s, but this soon subsided. However, gold prospector Octavius Decatur Gass stayed behind and, in 1865, built the 640-acre Las Vegas Ranch using structures left by the Mormons as his base. Since Gass controlled the valley's water, he finally found "gold" offering services to travelers passing through. Gass planted crops and fruit orchards, started vineyards, raised cattle, established cordial relations with the Paiutes (he even learned their language), and served as a legislator. This became the first significant settlement in the area. By 1900 the Las Vegas valley had a population of 30.

A TENT CITY IN THE WILDERNESS   The city of Las Vegas was officially born in 1905 when the Union Pacific Railroad connecting Los Angeles and Salt Lake City decided to route its trains through this rugged frontier outpost, selected for its ready supply of water and the availability of timber in the surrounding mountains. On a sweltering day in May, 1,200 townsite lots were auctioned off to eager pioneers and real estate speculators who had come from all over the country. The railroad depot was located at the head of Fremont Street (site of today's Amtrak station). Championing the spot was Montana senator William Clark, who had paid the astronomical sum (for that time) of $55,000 for the nearby Las Vegas Ranch and springs. The coming of a railroad more or less ensured the growth of the town. As construction began, tent settlements, saloons, ramshackle restaurants, boardinghouses, and shops gradually emerged. The early tent hotels charged a dollar to share a double bed with a stranger for eight hours! Early businesses flourished serving rail-road men and prospectors from nearby mining operations.

By present-day standards, the new town was not a pleasant place to live. Prospectors' burros roamed

surrounding desert. He discovers a verdant oasis—Las Vegas Springs.

- **1831–48** Artesian spring waters of Las Vegas serve as a watering place on the Old Spanish Trail.

- **1855** Mormon colony of 30 missionaries establishes settlement just north of today's downtown. Unsuccessful in its aims, the colony disbands in 1858.

- **1861** President James Buchanan authorizes formation of the territory of Nevada.

- **1864** President Lincoln proclaims Nevada 36th state of the Union. Las Vegas, however, is still part of the Territory of Arizona.

- **1865** Gold prospector Octavius D. Gass builds Las Vegas Ranch—the first permanent settlement in Las Vegas—on site of the old Mormon fort.

- **1867** Arizona cedes 12,225 square miles to Nevada, which assumes its present shape. Las Vegas is now in Nevada.

- **1880s** Due to mining fever, the population of Nevada soars to more than 60,000 in 1880. The Paiutes are forced onto reservations.

- **1895** San Franciscan inventor Charles Fey creates a three-reel gambling device—the first slot machine.

- **1905** The railroad connecting Salt Lake City and Los Angeles routes its trains through Las Vegas and auctions off 1,200 lots in the official townsite.

- **1907** Fremont Street—the future "Glitter Gulch"—gets electric lights.

- **1909** Gambling is made illegal in Nevada, but Las Vegas pays little heed.

continues

- **1911** William Howard Taft, first American president to pass through Las Vegas, waves at residents from his train.
- **1928** Congress authorizes construction of Hoover Dam 30 miles away, bringing thousands of workers to the area. Later, Las Vegas will capitalize on hundreds of thousands who come to see the engineering marvel.
- **1931** Gambling is legalized once again.
- **1932** The 100-room Apache Hotel opens Downtown.
- **1933** Prohibition is repealed. Las Vegas's numerous speakeasies become legit.
- **1934** The city's first neon sign lights up the Boulder Club downtown.
- **1941** The luxurious El Rancho Las Vegas becomes the first hotel on the Strip. Downtown, the El Cortez opens.
- **1944** Major star Sophie Tucker plays the Last Frontier, which had opened a year earlier.
- **1946** Benjamin "Bugsy" Siegel's Flamingo extends the boundaries of the Strip. Sammy Davis, Jr. debuts at the Last Frontier. Downtown (dubbed "Glitter Gulch") gets two new hotels—the Golden Nugget and the Eldorado.
- **1947** United Airlines inaugurates service to Las Vegas.
- **1948** The Thunderbird becomes the fourth hotel on the Strip.
- **1950** The Desert Inn adds country club panache to the Strip.
- **1951** The first of many atom bombs is tested in the desert just 65 miles from Las Vegas. An explosion of another sort

continues

the streets braying loudly, generally creating havoc and attracting swarms of flies. There were no screens, no air conditioners, no modern showers or baths (the town's bathhouse had but one tub) to ameliorate the fierce summer heat. The streets were rutted with dust pockets up to a foot deep that rose in great gusts as stage coaches, supply wagons, and 20-animal mule teams careened over them. It was a true pioneer town, complete with saloon brawls and shootouts. Discomforts notwithstanding, gaming establishments, hotels, and nightclubs—some of them seedy dives, others rather luxurious—sprang up and prospered in the Nevada wilderness. A red-light district emerged on Second Street between Ogden and Stewart avenues. And gambling, which was legal until 1909, flourished.

THE EIGHTH WONDER OF THE WORLD

For many years after its creation, Las Vegas was a mere whistle-stop town. That all changed in 1928 when Congress authorized the building of nearby Boulder Dam (later renamed Hoover Dam), bringing thousands of workers to the area. In 1931 gambling once again became legal in Nevada, and Fremont Street's gaming emporias and speakeasies attracted workers from the dam. Upon the dam's completion, the Las Vegas Chamber of Commerce worked hard to lure the hordes of tourists who came to see the engineering marvel (it was called "the eighth wonder of the world") to its casinos. Las Vegas was about to make the transition from a sleepy desert town to "a town that never sleeps." But it wasn't until the early years of World War II that visionary entrepreneurs began to plan for its glittering future.

LAS VEGAS GOES SOUTH   Contrary to a popular conception, Bugsy Siegel didn't actually stake a claim in the middle of nowhere—he just built a few blocks south of already existing properties. Development a few miles south of Downtown on Highway 91 (the future Strip) was already underway in the 1930s, with such establishments as the Pair-O-Dice Club and the Last Frontier. And in 1941 El Rancho Vegas, ultra-luxurious for its time, was built on the same remote stretch of highway (across the street from where the Sahara now stands). According to legend, Los Angeles hotelier Thomas E. Hull had been driving by the site when his car broke down. Noticing the extent of passing traffic, he decided to build there. Hull invited scores of Hollywood stars to his grand opening, and El Rancho Vegas soon became the hotel of choice for visiting film stars.

Beginning a trend that still continues today, each new property tried to outdo existing hotels in luxurious amenities and thematic splendor. In 1943 the Last Frontier (the Strip's second hotel) created an authentic western setting by scouring the Southwest in search of authentic pioneer furnishings for its rooms, hiring Zuni craftsmen to create baskets and wall hangings, and picking up guests at the airport in a horse-drawn stagecoach. The Last Frontier also presaged a new era when it brought stage and screen star Sophie Tucker to its showroom for a 2-week engagement in 1944 with much attendant hoopla. Tucker's train was met with a parade, and the "Last of the Red-Hot Mamas" was conveyed to the hotel in a fire truck. Las Vegas was on its way to becoming the entertainment capital of the world.

Las Vegas promoted itself in the 1940s as a town that combined Wild West frontier friendliness with glamour and excitement. As Chamber of Commerce president Maxwell Kelch aptly put it in a 1947 speech, "Las Vegas has the impact of a Wild West show, the friendliness of a country store, and the sophistication of Monte Carlo." Throughout the decade, the city was largely a regional resort—Hollywood's celebrity playground. Clara Bow and Rex Bell (a star of westerns) bought a ranch in Las Vegas where they entertained such luminaries as the Barrymores, Norma Shearer, Clark Gable, and Errol Flynn. The Hollywood connection gave the town glamour in the public's mind. So did the mob connection (something Las Vegas has spent decades trying to live down), which became clear early on when notorious underworld gangster Benjamin "Bugsy" Siegel (with partners Lucky Luciano and Meyer Lansky) built the fabulous Flamingo, a tropical paradise and "a real class joint." Hollywood people found the gangsters glamorous and vice versa—and the public was entranced by both. In 1947 the Club Bingo opened across the street from El Rancho Vegas, bringing a new game to town. The Thunderbird, the fourth hotel on the Strip, opened in 1948.

A steady stream of name entertainers followed Sophie Tucker into Las Vegas, adding to the city's tourist appeal. In 1947 Jimmy Durante opened the showroom at the Flamingo. Other headliners of the 1940s included Dean Martin and Jerry Lewis, comedian Jack Carter, tap-dancing legend Bill "Bojangles" Robinson, the Mills Brothers (who first recorded "Bye-Bye Blackbird"), skater Sonja Henie, Frankie Laine, Vic Damone, and Joe E. Lewis.

takes place when Sinatra debuts at the Desert Inn.

- **1952** The Club Bingo (opened in 1947) becomes the desert-themed Sahara. The Sands' Copa Room enhances the city's image as an entertainment capital.
- **1954** The Showboat pioneers buffet meals and bowling alleys in a new area of Downtown.
- **1955** The Strip gets its first high-rise hotel—the nine-story Riviera—which pays Liberace the unprecedented sum of $50,000 to open its showroom. The Riviera is the ninth hotel on the Strip. A month later, the Dunes becomes the 10th.
- **1956** The Fremont opens downtown, and the Hacienda becomes the southernmost hotel on the Strip.
- **1957** The Dunes introduces bare-breasted showgirls in its *Minsky Goes to Paris* revue. The most luxurious hotel to date, the Tropicana, opens on the Strip.
- **1958** The 1,065-room Stardust opens as the world's largest resort complex with a spectacular show from France, the *Lido de Paris*.
- **1959** The Las Vegas Convention Center goes up, presaging the city's future as a major convention city. Another French production, the still-extant *Folies Bergère*, opens at the Tropicana.
- **1960** The Rat Pack, led by Chairman of the Board Frank Sinatra, holds a 3-week "Summit Meeting" at the Sands. A championship boxing match—the first of many—takes place at the Convention Center. El Rancho Las Vegas, the Strip's first property, burns to the ground.

continues

- **1963** McCarran International Airport opens. Casinos and showrooms are darkened for a day as Las Vegas mourns the death of President John F. Kennedy.
- **1965** The 26-story Mint alters the Fremont Street skyline. Muhammad Ali defeats Floyd Patterson at the Las Vegas Convention Center.
- **1966** The Aladdin, the first new hotel on the Strip in 9 years, is soon eclipsed by the unparalleled grandeur of Caesars Palace. The Four Queens opens Downtown. Howard Hughes takes up residence at the Desert Inn. He buys up big chunks of Las Vegas and helps erase the city's gangland stigma.
- **1967** Elvis Presley marries Priscilla Beaulieu at the Aladdin, the city's all-time most celebrated union.
- **1968** Circus Circus gives kids a reason to come to Las Vegas.
- **1969** The Landmark and the International (today the Hilton) open within a day of each other on Paradise Road. Elvis Presley makes a triumphant return headlining at the latter.
- **1971** The 500-room Union Plaza opens Downtown on the site of the old Union Pacific depot.
- **1973** The ultraglamorous 2,100-room MGM Grand assumes the mantle of "world's largest resort." Superstars of magic, Siegfried & Roy, debut at the Tropicana.
- **1975** A flash flood causes more than $1 million in damages.
- **1976** Fittingly, pioneer aviator Howard Hughes dies aboard a plane en route to a

continues

Future Las Vegas legend Sammy Davis, Jr. debuted at El Rancho Vegas in 1945.

While the Strip was expanding, Downtown kept pace with new hotels such as the El Cortez, the Nevada Biltmore, the Golden Nugget, and the Eldorado Club. By the end of the decade, Fremont Street was known as "Glitter Gulch," its profusion of neon signs proclaiming round-the-clock gaming and entertainment.

THE 1950s: BUILDING BOOMS AND A-BOMBS   Las Vegas entered the new decade as a city (no longer a frontier town) with a population of about 50,000, its future as a tourist mecca ensured by postwar affluence and improved highways. Photographs indicate that Las Vegas was more glamorous in the 1950s than it is today. Men donned suits and ties, women floor-length gowns, to attend shows and even for casino gambling. Hotel growth was phenomenal. The Desert Inn, which opened in 1950 with headliners Edgar Bergen and Charlie McCarthy, brought country club elegance (including an 18-hole golf course and tennis courts) to the Strip. In 1951 the Eldorado Club downtown became Benny Binion's Horseshoe Club, which would gain fame as the home of the annual World Series of Poker. A year later, the Club Bingo entered a new incarnation as the African desert–themed Sahara (with camels guarding its portals), and the Sands emerged to further brighten the star-studded Strip. One of the Sands's major backers was Copacabana nightclub owner Jack Entratter who, being well connected in showbiz, brought major talent and stunning showgirls to its Copa Room. In 1954 the Showboat sailed into a new area east of Downtown. Although people said it could never last in such a remote location, they were wrong. The Showboat not only innovated buffet meals and a bowling alley (106 lanes to date) but offered round-the-clock bingo. In 1955 the Last Frontier became the New Frontier and the Côte d'Azur–themed Riviera became the ninth big hotel to open on the Strip. Breaking the ranch-style mode, it was, at nine stories, the Strip's first high-rise. Liberace, one of the hottest names in show business, was paid the unprecedented sum of $50,000 a week to dazzle audiences in the Riviera's posh Clover Room. The Dunes opened immediately after, topped by a 30-foot fiberglass sultan; the 15-story Fremont Hotel Downtown became the highest building in Las Vegas; and the Hacienda extended the boundaries of the Strip by opening 2 miles south of the nearest resort. Elvis appeared at the New Frontier in 1956 but wasn't a huge success; his fans were too young to fit the Las Vegas tourist mold. In 1957 the Tropicana joined the Hacienda at the far end of Las Vegas Boulevard. Billing itself as "the Tiffany of the Strip," it offered 40 tropically lush acres and a musical extravaganza starring Eddie Fisher. In 1958 the $10-million, 1,065-room Stardust upped the spectacular stakes by importing the famed *Lido de Paris* from the French capital. It became one of the longest running shows ever to play Las Vegas. The Stardust was also the first hotel to bring massive serious neon to the Strip in the form of a 216-foot sign emblazoned with more than 7,000 feet of neon tubing and 11,000 lamps. The year after it opened it absorbed the Royal Nevada next door.

Throughout the 1950s, most of the above-mentioned hotels competed for performers whose followers spent freely in the casinos. The advent of big-name Strip entertainment tolled a death knell for glamorous nightclubs in America; owners simply could not compete with the astronomical salaries paid to Las Vegas headliners. Major '50s stars of the Strip included Rosemary Clooney, Nat King Cole, Peggy Lee, Milton Berle, Judy Garland, Red Skelton, Ernie Kovacs, Abbott and Costello, Ray Bolger, Tommy and Jimmy Dorsey, Fred Astaire and Ginger Rogers, the Andrews Sisters, Zsa Zsa Gabor, Marlene Dietrich, Billy Eckstine, and Gordon McRae. Two performers whose names have ever since been linked to Las Vegas—Frank Sinatra and Wayne Newton—made their debuts there. Mae West not only performed in Las Vegas, but cleverly bought up a half mile of desolate Strip frontage between the Dunes and the Tropicana.

Competition for the tourist dollar also brought nationally televised sporting events such as the PGA's Tournament of Champions to the Desert Inn golf course (the winner got a wheelbarrow filled with silver dollars). In the 1950s the wedding industry helped make Las Vegas one of the nation's most popular venues for "goin' to the chapel." Nevada requires no blood test or waiting period. Celebrity weddings of the 1950s that sparked the trend included singer Dick Haymes and Rita Hayworth, Fernando Lamas and Arlene Dahl, Joan Crawford and Pepsi chairman Alfred Steele, Carol Channing and TV exec Charles Lowe, and Paul Newman and Joanne Woodward.

On a grimmer note, the '50s also heralded the atomic age in Nevada, with nuclear testing taking

Houston hospital. Martin and Lewis make up after a 20-year feud.

- **1978** Leon Spinks dethrones "the Greatest" (Muhammad Ali) at the Las Vegas Hilton. Crime solver Dan Tanna (Robert Urich) makes the streets of "Vega$" safer—and better known.

- **1979** A new international arrivals building opens at McCarran International Airport.

- **1980** McCarran International Airport embarks on a 20-year, $785-million expansion program. Las Vegas celebrates its 75th birthday. A devastating fire destroys the MGM Grand, leaving 84 dead and 700 injured. Bally's takes over the property.

- **1981** Siegfried & Roy begin a record-breaking run in their own show, *Beyond Belief,* at the Frontier.

- **1982** A Las Vegas street is named Wayne Newton Boulevard.

- **1985** Another child-oriented attraction, Wet 'n Wild, opens on the Strip.

- **1989** Steve Wynn makes headlines with his spectacular Mirage, fronted by an erupting volcano. He signs Siegfried & Roy to a 5-year $57-million showroom contract (since extended)!

- **The 1990s** The medieval Arthurian realm of Excalibur opens as the new "world's-largest-resort" title holder with 4,032 rooms, a claim it relinquishes when the MGM Grand's new 5,005-room megaresort/theme park opened in 1994. Other properties to come aboard in the 1990s include the Debbie Reynolds Hotel, Luxor Las Vegas, Treasure Island, The Hard Rock, the Monte Carlo, and the Stratosphere.

place just 65 miles northwest of Las Vegas. A chilling 1951 photograph shows a mushroom-shaped cloud from an atomic bomb test visible over the Fremont Street horizon. Throughout the decade, about one bomb a month was detonated in the nearby desert.

THE 1960S: THE RAT PACK . . .   The very first month of the new decade made entertainment history when the Sands hosted a 3-week "Summit Meeting" in the Copa Room presided over by "Chairman of the Board" Frank Sinatra with Rat Pack cronies Dean Martin, Sammy Davis, Jr., Peter Lawford, and Joey Bishop (all of whom happened to be in town filming *Oceans Eleven)*.

On November 25, 1963, Las Vegas mourned the death of President John F. Kennedy with the rest of the nation. Between 7am and midnight, all the neon lights went off, casinos stood empty, and showrooms were dark.

The building boom of the '50s took a brief respite. The Strip's first property, the El Rancho Vegas, burned down in 1960. And the first new hotel of the decade—the first to be built in 9 years—was the exotic Aladdin in 1966. A year after it opened the Aladdin hosted the most celebrated Las Vegas wedding of all time when Elvis Presley married Priscilla Beaulieu. In 1966 Las Vegas also hailed Caesar—Caesars Palace, that is—a Lucullan pleasure palace whose grand opening was a million-dollar, 3-day Roman orgy with 1,800 guests. Its Carrara marble reproductions of ancient temples, heroic arches, and classical statuary were a radical departure from the more ersatz glitz of earlier Strip hotels. Also in the '60s, the Mint and the Four Queens altered the Downtown skyline.

. . . AND A PACK RAT   During the '60s, negative attention focused—with good reason—on mob influence in Las Vegas. Of the 11 major casino hotels that had opened in the previous decade, 10 were believed to have been financed with mob money. Attorney General Robert Kennedy ordered the Department of Justice to begin serious scrutiny of Las Vegas gaming operations. Then, like a knight in shining armor, Howard Hughes rode into town. He was not, however, on a white horse. Ever eccentric, he arrived (for security rather than health reasons) in an ambulance. The reclusive billionaire moved into a Desert Inn penthouse on Thanksgiving Day 1966 and did not set foot outside the hotel for the next 4 years! It became his headquarters for a $300 million hotel- and property-buying spree, which included the Desert Inn itself (in 1967). Hughes was as "bugsy" as Benjamin Siegel any day, but his pristine reputation helped bring respectability to the desert city and lessen its gangland stigma. People generally believed that if the gaming business was truly shady, Howard Hughes would not be in it. Hughes purchased the Sands along with half a dozen other hotels and casinos, the airport, an airline, and a local TV station. Topless showgirls and hookers were not welcome at his properties, and showroom comedians were warned to "keep it clean." For decades he provided fodder for Strip performers. "You're wondering why I don't have a drink in my hand?" Frank Sinatra asked a Sands audience one night. "Howard Hughes bought it."

Las Vegas became a family destination in 1968 when Circus Circus burst on the scene with the world's largest permanent circus and a "junior casino" comprising dozens of carnival midway games on its mezzanine level. In 1969 the Landmark and the dazzling International (today the Hilton) ventured into a new area of town—Paradise Road near the Convention Center. That same year Elvis made a triumphant return to Las Vegas at the International's showroom and went on to become one of the city's all-time legendary performers. His fans had come of age.

Hoping to establish Las Vegas as "the Broadway of the West," the Thunderbird Hotel presented Rodgers and Hammerstein's *Flower Drum Song.* It was a smash hit.

Soon the Riviera picked up *Bye, Bye, Birdie,* and, as the decade progressed, *Mame* and *The Odd Couple* played at Caesars Palace. While Broadway played the Strip, production shows such as the Dunes's *Casino de Paris* became ever more lavish, expensive, and technically innovative. Showroom stars of the 1960s included "Funny Girl" Barbara Streisand and funny ladies Phyllis Diller and Carol Burnett, Little Richard (who billed himself as "the bronze Liberace"), Louis Armstrong, Bobby Darin, the Supremes, Steve Allen, Johnny Carson, Bob Newhart, the Smothers Brothers, and Aretha Franklin. Liza Minnelli filled her mother's shoes, while Nancy Sinatra's boots were made for walking. And Tom Jones wowed 'em at the Flamingo.

THE 1970S: MERV, MIKE, MGM, & MAGIC In 1971 the 500-room Union Plaza opened at the head of Fremont Street on the site of the old Union Pacific Station. It had what was, at the time, the world's largest casino, and its showroom specialized in Broadway productions. The same year talk show host Merv Griffin began taping at Caesars Palace, taking advantage of a ready supply of local headliner guests. He helped popularize Las Vegas even more by bringing it into America's living rooms every afternoon. Rival Mike Douglas soon followed suit at the Las Vegas Hilton.

The year 1973 was eventful: The Holiday Inn (today Harrah's) built a Mississippi riverboat complete with towering smokestacks and foghorn whistle which was immediately dubbed "the ship on the Strip." Dean Martin headlined in the celebrity room of the magnificent new MGM Grand, named for the movie *Grand Hotel.* More than 800 tons of marble were imported from Italy just for the fountain at the front entrance, and sculptors in three Italian towns were kept busy for 2 years making columns and statues for the property. Facilities included everything from a jai alai fronton to the largest shopping mall in the state. And over at the Tropicana, illusionists extraordinaire Siegfried & Roy began turning women into tigers and themselves into legends in the *Folies Bergére.* Several years later they moved on to *Hallelujah, Hollywood,* and the *Lido de Paris.* Whatever show they were in became (and remains to this day) the hottest ticket in town.

Two major disasters hit Las Vegas in the 1970s. First, a flash flood devastated the Strip, causing more than $1 million in damage. Hundreds of cars were swept away in the raging waters. Second, gambling was legalized in Atlantic City. Las Vegas's hotel business slumped as fickle tourists decided to check out the new East Coast gambling mecca.

On a happier note, audiences were moved when Frank Sinatra helped to patch up a 20-year feud by introducing Dean Martin as a surprise guest on Jerry Lewis's 1976 Muscular Dystrophy Telethon at the Sahara. Martin and Lewis hugged and made up. Who would cross Sinatra?

As the decade drew to a close, Dan Tanna began investigating crime in glamorous *Vega$,* an international arrivals building opened at McCarran International Airport, and dollar slot machines caused a sensation in the casinos. Hot performers of the '70s included José Feliciano, Ann-Margret, Tina Turner, Englebert Humperdinck, Ben Vereen, Bill Cosby, Sonny and Cher, Tony Bennett, the Neils (Diamond and Sedaka), Joel Grey, Mel Tormé, Bobby Darin, Johnny Carson, Gregory Hines (with his brother and dad), Donny and Marie, the Jackson 5, Gladys Knight and the Pips, and that "wild and crazy guy" Steve Martin. Debbie Reynolds introduced her daughter Carrie with a duet performance before a Desert Inn audience. Shirley MacLaine began an incarnation at the Riviera. And country was now cool; the names Johnny Cash, Bobby Gentry, Charlie Pride, and Roy Clark went up in marquee lights.

THE 1980S: THE CITY ERUPTS   Las Vegas was booming once again. McCarran Airport began a 20-year, $785 million expansion program. On a tragic note, in 1980 a devastating fire swept through the MGM Grand, leaving 84 dead and 700 injured. Shortly thereafter, Bally acquired the property and created a cheerful megaresort with so many facilities you need never leave. It billed itself as the "city within a city."

Siegfried & Roy were no longer just the star segment of various stage spectaculars. Their own show, *Beyond Belief,* ran for 6 years at the Frontier, playing a record-breaking 3,538 performances to sellout audiences every night. It became the most successful attraction in the city's history.

In 1989 Steve Wynn made Las Vegas sit up and take notice. His gleaming white and gold Mirage was fronted by five-story waterfalls, lagoons, and lush tropical foliage—not to mention a 50-foot volcano that dramatically erupted, spewing great gusts of fire another 50 feet into the air every 15 minutes after dark! Inside were dolphin and royal white tiger habitats, a rain forest under a 90-foot atrium dome, and a 20,000-gallon simulated coral reef aquarium whose residents included six sharks and 1,000 colorful tropical fish. Wynn gave world-renowned illusionists Siegfried & Roy carte blanche—and more than $30 million—to create the most spellbinding show Las Vegas had ever seen (don't miss it).

Stars of the '80s included Eddie Murphy, Don Rickles, Roseanne Barr, Bob Newhart, Dionne Warwick, Paul Anka, the Captain and Tennille, Donna Summer, Rich Little, George Carlin, David Brenner, Barry Manilow, Bernadette Peters, Flip Wilson, and Diahann Carroll. Country continued to be cool, as evidenced by frequent headliners Willie Nelson, Kenny Rogers, Dolly Parton, Crystal Gale, Merle Haggard, Mickey Gilley, Kris Kristofferson, and Barbara Mandrell. Joan Rivers posed her famous question "Can we talk?" and bug-eyed comic Rodney Dangerfield complained he got "no respect."

THE 1990S: KING ARTHUR MEETS KING TUT   The decade began with a blare of trumpets heralding the rise of a turreted medieval castle fronted by a moated drawbridge and staffed by jousting knights and fair damsels. Excalibur's interior had so many stone castle walls that a Strip comedian quipped "it looks like a prison for Snow White." Like Circus Circus (same owner), it abounds in family attractions—carnival games, puppet shows, jugglers, magicians, high-tech thrill cinemas, and a major show called *King Arthur's Tournament,* which is geared to youngsters. Excalibur reflects the '90s marketing trend to promote Las Vegas as a family vacation destination.

Several sensational megahotels have opened on the Strip since 1993, and they're all running at close to 100% occupancy—as are older properties benefiting from the visitor excitement they've generated. They include the *Wizard of Oz*–themed MGM Grand Hotel, backed by a full theme park (it ended Excalibur's brief reign as the world's largest resort); the Luxor Las Vegas, a gleaming 30-story reflective bronze pyramid, prefaced by a Sphinx and a 191-foot obelisk (inside is a full-scale reproduction of King Tut's tomb); and Steve Wynn's Treasure Island, replicating an 18th-century pirate village overlooking Buccaneer Bay—scene of fierce hourly combat between a British frigate and a pirate vessel.

On October 27, 1993, a quarter of a million people crowded onto the Strip to witness the implosion of the 37-year-old Dunes Hotel. Vegas-style, it went out with a bang. Later that year a unique pink-domed 5-acre indoor amusement park, Grand Slam Canyon, became part of the Circus Circus Hotel. In 1995 the Fremont Street Experience was completed, revitalizing Downtown Las Vegas. Closer to the Strip, rock restaurant magnate Peter Morton opened the Hard Rock Hotel, billed as "the world's first rock-'n'-roll hotel and casino." And 1996 saw the advent of the French

Impressions

Benny often found it necessary to arbitrate business differences with a .45 automatic.
—Article about Benny Binion, founder of Binion's Horseshoe Hotel and Casino,
in *Texas Monthly* (Oct. 1991)

Riviera–themed Monte Carlo and the Stratosphere, its 1,149-foot tower the highest building west of the Mississippi. As the millennium approaches, Las Vegas is flourishing as never before, and the ongoing metamorphosis of the Strip continues to thrill visitors who find a dramatic new streetscape every time they visit.

4 Famous Las Vegans

Andre Agassi (b. 1970)   Consistently ranked among the world's best tennis players, Agassi is probably one of the most famous natives of Las Vegas. A child prodigy, he has been playing tennis since the age of 4. His major titles include wins at the Australian, U.S., and French Opens as well as Wimbledon. Most recently, Agassi won a gold medal for tennis at the 1996 Olympic Summer Games in Atlanta.

Benny Binion (1904–89)   This feisty Texan, who misspent his youth punching cattle, horse trading, running illegal craps games, and bootlegging, came to Las Vegas in 1947 with a suitcase full of money. He bought a casino, renamed it the Horseshoe, and made it famous for the highest limits in town and the annual World Series of Poker. When he died, Binion was a casino czar worth $100 million. The Binion family is still a major player in this town.

Nicholas "Nick the Greek" Dandolos (1893–1966)   America's most famous gambler, Nicholas Andrea Dandolos was a reckless high-stakes player who became a Las Vegas legend. At 18, Nick went to Montreal and—with some inside information—quickly accumulated half-a-million dollars at the racetrack. He blew it just as quickly in Chicago at cards and dice. He is said to have won and lost more than $500 million in his lifetime. He spurned offers of hotel partnerships that would have made him financially independent. Raking in house percentages, he claimed, would have robbed him of the thrill of betting. He died broke.

Las Vegas Advisor

Professional gambler and longtime Las Vegas resident Anthony Curtis, author of *Bargain City: Booking, Betting, and Beating the New Las Vegas,* knows all the angles for stretching your hotel, restaurant and—most important—gaming dollar. His 12-page monthly newsletter, the *Las Vegas Advisor,* is chock-full of insider tips on how to maximize your odds on every game, which slot tournaments to enter, casino promotions that represent money-making opportunities for the bettor, where to obtain the best fun books, which hotel offers a 12-ounce margarita for 99¢ or a steak dinner for $3, what are the best buffet and show values in town, and much, much more. Subscribers get more than $400 worth of coupons for discounts on rooms, meals, show tickets, and car rentals, along with free slot plays, two-for-one bets, and other perks. I recommend it to regular Vegas visitors. A subscription is $45 a year, a single issue $5. To subscribe call **800/244-2224** or send a check to Las Vegas Advisor, 3687 S. Procyon St., Las Vegas, NV 89103.

Jackie Gaughan (b. 1920)   A Nebraskan who ran a bookie joint in an Omaha cigar store, Gaughan started out in Las Vegas by buying a 3 percent interest in the Boulder Club in 1946. In 1951 he bought a 3 percent interest in the Flamingo. He went on to run the city's only race and sports book, the Saratoga, until 1959. In 1963 he bought the El Cortez. He now owns six Downtown Las Vegas properties, including the Gold Spike, the Plaza, Las Vegas Club, the Western Hotel & Bingo Parlor, and the Showboat. His son Michael owns the Barbary Coast and the Gold Coast.

Howard Hughes (1905–76)   Howard Hughes was the man who gave Las Vegas respectability. The richest man in America, he arrived in town in 1966 at a time when the Justice Department had begun focusing on mob involvement in Nevada gaming operations. Eccentric though he was (he hated sunlight and had the windows of his Desert Inn accommodations blacked out), his casino- and hotel-buying spree was a public relations bonanza for Las Vegas. The gambling public trusted him, and they began to trust Las Vegas casinos. During his 4-year residency, he became Nevada's largest employer, putting 8,000 people on his payroll. At one time his seven casinos accounted for 17 percent of the state's gaming revenues.

Kirk Kerkorian (b. 1917)   The self-made son of Armenian immigrants who fled a Turkish massacre by cattle boat, Kerkorian grew up in California, where he dropped out of school in the eighth grade. He was a successful amateur boxer and a World War II army pilot. After the war, he started his own airline, beginning with one used C-47; when he sold the company in 1969 he walked off with $104 million. He built the International Hotel and bought the Flamingo, both of which he eventually sold to Hilton. He went on to build the MGM Grand in the 1970s (today Bally's). In 1993, he made another "grand" statement—the billion-dollar *Wizard of Oz*–themed MGM Grand megaresort and adjacent theme park. Next project; the 2,100-room New York–New York. Kerkorian is also Chrysler Corporation's largest single shareholder.

Thomas "Amarillo Slim" Preston (birth date unknown)   In May 1972 Thomas Preston, a colorful Texas cattle rancher with a slow drawl, loped off with $60,000 at Binion's third World Series of Poker. Preston is a legendary gambler who has made—and won—many bizarre bets. He beat daredevil Evel Knievel at golf using a hammer instead of a club, outplayed Minnesota Fats at pool using a broom handle for a cue, and topped a Ping-Pong champ using a Coke bottle for a paddle.

Benjamin "Bugsy" Siegel (1906–47)   A nefarious underworld kingpin, Siegel opened his dream hotel—the mob-financed $6-million Flamingo—in December 1946. He was gunned down in Los Angeles six months later at the home of his girlfriend, Virginia Hill. Although he was never convicted of any crime (witnesses tended to suffer mysterious deaths), Siegel once boasted to fellow casino owner Del Webb that he had killed 20 men. His suite in the Flamingo had extra-thick walls, a secret trapdoor, and four exits.

They printed a lot of crap about Ben. He just wanted to be somebody. He used to pal around with Clark Gable, Gary Cooper, Cary Grant, and a lot of other big stars. I used to copy a lot of Ben's mannerisms when I played gangsters. Ben and the other tough guys . . . they were like gods to me. Ben had class, he was a real gentleman, and a real pal.

—Movie star George Raft on
his pal Benjamin "Bugsy" Siegel

Steve Wynn (b. 1942)   Wynn, whose father owned a chain of East Coast bingo parlors, first got into Las Vegas real estate by purchasing a small parking lot next to Caesars. Later he sold it back to Caesars and used the money to bankroll his purchase of the Golden Nugget in 1969. In 1989 Wynn's $620-million Mirage revolutionized the Strip with Disneyesque attractions such as dolphin and tiger habitats, an indoor rain forest, and an erupting volcano. In 1993 he followed this up with Treasure Island, another Strip extravaganza property with a swashbuckling pirate theme. And a third Steve Wynn Strip hotel called Bellagio is going up at this writing.

2

Planning a Trip to Las Vegas

Before any trip, you need to do a bit of advance planning. When should I go? Should I take a package deal or make my own hotel and airline reservations? Will there be a major convention in town during my visit? We'll answer these and other questions for you in this chapter, but you might want to read through the sightseeing and excursions chapters (7 and 11) for some ideas on how to spend your time if you tire of gambling.

1 Visitor Information

For advance information call or write the **Las Vegas Convention and Visitors Authority,** 3150 Paradise Rd., Las Vegas, NV 89109 (☎ **800/332-5333**). They can send you a comprehensive packet of brochures, a map, a show guide, an events calendar, and an attractions list; help you find a hotel that meets your specifications; and tell you if a major convention is scheduled during the time you would like to visit Las Vegas. Or stop by when you're in town. They're open daily 8am to 5pm.

Another excellent information source is the **Las Vegas Chamber of Commerce,** 711 E. Desert Inn Rd., Las Vegas, NV 89109 (☎ **702/735-1616**). Ask them to send you their *Visitor's Guide,* which contains extensive information about accommodations, attractions, excursions, children's activities, and more. They can answer all your Las Vegas–related questions, including those about weddings and divorces. They're open Monday to Friday 8am to 5pm.

And for information on all of Nevada, including Las Vegas, contact the **Nevada Commission on Tourism,** Capitol Complex, Carson City, NV 89701 (☎ **800/638-2328**). They send out a comprehensive information packet on Nevada.

If you're surfing the Net, you can get information about Las Vegas from these web sites:

- **The Las Vegas Index:** http://lvindex.com
- **Las Vegas Online:** http://www.infi.net/vegas/vlv/
- **Vegas.net,** an on-line magazine: http://vegasnet.com
- **Where To In Las Vegas** magazine: http://a1-lasvegas-wt.com
- The "Official" Las Vegas Leisure Guide and Resource Directory: http://www.pcap.com

What Things Cost in Las Vegas	U.S. $
Taxi from the airport to the Strip	8–12.00
Taxi from the airport to Downtown	15–18.00
Minibus from the airport to the Strip	3.50
Minibus from the airport to Downtown	4.75
Double at the Desert Inn (very expensive)	175–185.00
Double at the MGM Grand (expensive)	69–119.00
Double at the Maxim (moderate)	49–69.00
Double at Circus Circus (inexpensive)	36–65.00
Five-course tasting menu at Gatsby's without tax or tip (very expensive)	65.00–85.00 with wines
Three-course dinner at Chin's without tax or tip (expensive)	35.00–40.00
Three-course dinner at Stage Deli without tax or tip (moderate)	20.00
Three-course dinner at Chili's without tax or tip (inexpensive)	15.00
All-you-can-eat buffet dinner at Circus Circus	4.99
All-you-can-eat buffet dinner at Caesars Palace	13.95
Bottle of beer	2.50
Coca-Cola	1.50
Cup of coffee	1.50
Roll of ASA 100 Kodacolor film, 36 exposures	4.70
Show ticket for *Country Fever* (including a drink and a basket of chicken tenders; tax and gratuity extra)	22.50
Show ticket for *Enter the Night* (including two drinks; tax and gratuity extra)	29.85
Show ticket for headliners at Caesars (including tax, drinks extra)	45–75.00
Show ticket for *Siegfried & Roy* (including two drinks, tax, souvenir brochure, and gratuity)	83.85

2 When to Go

Since most of a Las Vegas vacation is usually spent indoors, you can have a good time here year-round. The most pleasant seasons, as you'll see from the chart below, are spring and fall, especially if you want to experience the great outdoors. Weekdays are slightly less crowded than weekends. Holidays are always a mob scene accompanied by high hotel prices. Hotel prices also skyrocket when big conventions and special events are taking place. The slowest times of year are June and July, the week before Christmas, and the week after New Year's. If a major convention is to be held during your trip, you might want to change your date.

THE CLIMATE

One thing you'll hear again and again is that even though Las Vegas gets very hot, the dry desert heat is not unbearable. This is true. The humidity averages a low 22%, and even on very hot days there's apt to be a breeze. Also, except on the hottest summer days, there's relief at night when temperatures often drop as much as 20 degrees.

Temperatures (°F) in Las Vegas

	Jan	Feb	Mar	Apr	May	June	July	Aug	Sept	Oct	Nov	Dec
Average	44	50	57	66	74	84	91	88	81	67	54	47
High	55	62	69	79	88	99	105	103	96	82	67	58
Low	33	39	44	53	60	68	76	74	65	53	41	36

LAS VEGAS CALENDAR OF EVENTS

You may be surprised that Las Vegas does not offer as many annual events as most tourist cities. The reason is Las Vegas's very *raison d'être:* the gaming industry. This town wants its visitors spending their money in the casinos, not off at Renaissance fairs and parades. When in town, check the local paper and call the **Las Vegas Convention and Visitors Authority** (☎ 702/892-0711), **Las Vegas Events** (☎ 702/731-2115), or the **Chamber of Commerce** (☎ 702/735-1616) to find out about other events scheduled during your visit.

January
- **The PBA Classic.** The Showboat Hotel, 2800 Fremont St. (☎ 702/385-9150), hosts this major bowling tournament every January.

March
- **The PBA Invitational.** Another major annual bowling tournament, also at the Showboat Hotel.

April
- **The World Series of Poker.** This famed 21-day event takes place at Binion's Horseshoe Casino, 128 Fremont St. (☎ 702/382-1600), in late April and early May, with high-stakes gamblers and show-biz personalities competing for six-figure purses. There are daily events with entry stakes ranging from $125 to $5,000. To enter the World Championship Event (purse $1 million), players must put up $10,000. It costs nothing to go watch the action.

- **TruGreen-ChemLawn Las Vegas Senior Classic.** This 4-day event in mid- to late April or early May takes place at the Tournament Players Club (TPC), The Canyons, 9851 Canyon Run Dr., in nearby Summerlin. For details and driving information, call 702/382-6616.

May
- **Helldorado.** This Elks-sponsored western heritage celebration takes place over a 10-day period in mid-May. It includes a western dress ("be-seen-in-jeans") parade, a vast carnival midway, bull riders, a trail ride, a barbecue, and four major Professional Rodeo Cowboys Association (PRCA) rodeos at the Sam Boyd Stadium, located at Boulder Highway and Russell Road. *Note:* There is some talk at press time of moving this event to a new facility, and possibly even changing the date. For information call the Elks Lodge (☎ 702/870-1221) or check the local papers. The ticket office number is 702/895-3900.

September
- **Oktoberfest.** This boisterous autumn holiday is celebrated from mid-September through the end of October at the Mount Charleston Resort (☎ 800/955-1314

or 702/872-5408) with music, folk dancers, sing-alongs around a roaring fire, special decorations, and Bavarian cookouts.

October

- **PGA Tour Las Vegas Invitational.** This 5-day championship event, played on three local courses, is televised by ESPN. For details call 702/382-6616.

December

○ **National Finals Rodeo.** This is the Super Bowl of rodeos, attended by close to 170,000 people each year. The top 15 male rodeo stars compete in six different events: calf roping, steer wrestling, bull riding, team roping, saddle bronc riding, and bareback riding. And the top 15 women compete in barrel racing. An all-around "Cowboy of the Year" is chosen. In connection with this event, hotels book country stars in their showrooms, and there's a cowboy shopping spree—the NFR Cowboy Christmas Gift Show, a trade show for western gear—at Cashman Field.

    Where: At the 17,000-seat Thomas and Mack Center of UNLV. **When:** For 10 days during the first 2 weeks of the month. **How:** Order tickets as far in advance as possible (☎ **702/895-3900**).

- **Las Vegas Bowl Week.** A championship football event in mid-December pits the winners of the Mid-American Conference against the winners of the Big West Conference. The action takes place at the 32,000-seat Sam Boyd Stadium. Call 702/895-3900 for ticket information.

Major Convention Dates for 1997/1998

Listed below are Las Vegas's major annual conventions with projected attendance figures for 1997, and, where available, for 1998.

Consumer Electronics Show			**Networld/Interop**	
1997: Jan 9–12	91,200		1997: May 5–9	60,000
1998: Jan 8–11	100,000		1998: May 4—8	60,000
World of Concrete Exposition			**International Council of Shopping Centers**	
1997: Jan 21–24	30,000		1997: May 18–20	35,000
Shooting, Hunting, Outdoor Trade Show			**World Educational Congress for Laundering & Dry Cleaning**	
1997: Jan 30–Feb 2	25,000		1997: June 2–5	25,000
Men's Apparel Guild in California (Magic)			**Men's Apparel Guild in California (Magic)**	
1997: Feb 18–21	60,000		1997: Aug 25–28	60,000
1998: Feb 18—21	70,000		**International Baking Industry Exposition**	
Associated Surplus Dealers			1997: Sept 22–26	30,000
1997: Mar 2–6	40,000		**Interbike**	
National Association of Broadcasters			1997: Oct 6–9	30,000
1997: Apr 7–10	85,000		**Specialty Equipment Market Association**	
Air Force Association			1997: Nov 4–7	60,000
1997: Apr 22–25	45,000		1998: Nov 3–6	60,000

- **Western Athletic Conference (WAC) Football Championship.** This collegiate championship event takes place the first week in December. Call 792/731-5595 for ticket information. Tickets prices range from $15 to $100.
- **New Year's Eve.** This is a biggie (reserve your hotel room early). Downtown, Fremont Street is closed to traffic between Third and Main streets, and there's a big block party with two dramatic countdowns to midnight (the first is at 9pm, midnight on the East Coast). Of course, there are fireworks.

  There's also a big New Year's Eve gala at the Mount Charleston Resort (☎ 800/955-1314 or 702/872-5408). Make dinner reservations early and book a cabin for the night. See chapter 11 for details.

3 Tips for Travelers with Special Needs

FOR PEOPLE WITH DISABILITIES Write or call **The Independent Living Program,** Nevada Association for the Handicapped, 6200 W. Oakey Blvd., Las Vegas, NV 89102 (☎ 702/870-7050). They can recommend hotels and restaurants that meet your needs, help you find a personal attendant, advise about transportation, and answer all questions.

In addition, the **Nevada Commission on Tourism,** Capitol Complex, Carson City, NV 89701 (☎ 800/638-2328), offers a free accommodations guide to Las Vegas hotels that includes access information.

Two helpful travel organizations—**Accessible Journeys** (☎ 800/TINGLES or 610/521-0339) and **Flying Wheels Travel** (☎ 800/535-6790 or 507/451-5005)—offer tours, cruises, and custom vacations worldwide for people with physical disabilities; Accessible Journeys can also provide nurses/companions to travelers. **The Guided Tour Inc.** (☎ 800/783-5841 or 215/782-1370) has tours for people with physical or mental disabilities, the visually impaired, and the elderly.

Mobility International USA, P.O. Box 10767, Eugene, OR 97440 (☎ 503/343-1284), offers accessibility and resource information to its members. Membership ($25 a year) includes a quarterly newsletter called *Over the Rainbow.*

There's no charge for help via telephone (accessibility information and more) from the **Travel Information Service,** Moss Rehab Hospital (☎ 215/456-9600). Another organization, the Society for the Advancement of Travel for the Handicapped (SATH), 347 Fifth Ave., Suite 610, New York, NY 10016 (☎ 212/447-7284) charges $5 for sending requested information.

Recommended books: A publisher called **Twin Peaks Press,** Box 129, Vancouver, WA 98666 (☎ 360/694-2462), specializes in books for people with disabilities. Write for their *Disability Bookshop Catalog,* enclosing $5.

Greyhound (☎ 800/752-4841) allows a disabled person to travel with a companion for a single fare. Call at least 48 hours in advance to discuss this and other special needs.

Airlines don't offer special fares to the disabled. When making your flight reservations, ask where your wheelchair will be stowed on the plane and if your guide dog may accompany you.

Fun Fact

In 1995, Don Harrington entered a satellite event at the World Series of Poker for just $220, won his way into the $10,000 buy for the Championship Event, and went on to win the $1 million prize.

FOR SENIORS Always carry some form of photo ID that includes your birth date so you can take advantage of discounts wherever they're offered. And it never hurts to ask.

If you haven't already done so, consider joining the **American Association of Retired Persons** (☎ **800/424-3410** or 202/434-2277). Annual membership costs $8 per person or couple. You must be at least 50 to join. Membership entitles you to many discounts. Write to Purchase Privilege Program, AARP Fulfillment, 601 E St. NW, Washington, DC 20049, to receive their *Purchase Privilege* brochure—a free list of hotels, motels, and car-rental firms nationwide that offer discounts to AARP members.

Elderhostel is a national organization that offers low-priced educational programs for people over 55 (your spouse can be any age; a companion must be at least 50). Programs are generally a week long, and prices average about $355 per person, including room, board, and classes. For information on programs in Nevada call or write Elderhostel headquarters, 75 Federal St., Boston, MA 02110 (☎ **617/426-7788**), and ask for a free catalog.

Greyhound also offers discounted fares for senior citizens. Call your local Greyhound office for details.

FOR FAMILIES Las Vegas in the '90s is doing its utmost to promote itself as a family vacation destination. Kids just adore the place. Everything for them is geared to having fun; nothing is educational. See the "Especially for Kids" suggestions in chapter 7 and the "Family-Friendly" boxes for suggestions for hotels, restaurants, and shows. A few general suggestions to make traveling with kids easier:

If they're old enough, let the kids write to various tourist offices for information and color brochures. If you're driving, give them a map on which they can outline the route. Let them help decide your sightseeing itinerary.

Although your home may be toddler-proof, hotel accommodations are not. Bring blank plugs to cover outlets and whatever else is necessary.

Carry a few simple games to relieve the tedium of traveling. Packing snacks will also help and save money. If you're using public transportation (airlines, bus), always inquire about discounted fares for children.

Children under 12, and in many cases even older, stay free in their parents' rooms in most hotels. Look for establishments that have pools and other recreational facilities (see "Family-Friendly Hotels" in chapter 5).

FOR GAYS & LESBIANS The *Las Vegas Bugle,* a monthly magazine serving the gay community, provides information about bars, workshops, local politics, support groups, shops, events and more. A subscription costs $20 for 12 issues. For details call **702/369-6260.** See also listings for gay bars in chapter 10.

4 Getting There

BY AIR

THE MAJOR AIRLINES

The following airlines have regularly scheduled flights into Las Vegas (some of these are regional carriers, so they may not all fly from your point of origin): **Air Canada** (☎ 800/776-3000), **Air 21** (☎ 800/359-2472), **Alaska Airlines** (☎ 800/426-0333), **America West** (☎ 800/548-8969), **American/American Eagle** (☎ 800/433-7300), **American Trans Air** (☎ 800/543-3708), **Canadian International** (☎ 800/426-7000), **Condor** (☎ 800/524-6975), **Continental** (☎ 800/525-0280), **Delta** (☎ 800/221-1212), **Frontier** (☎ 800/432-1359), **Hawaiian** (☎ 800/

367-5320), **Kiwi** (☎ 800/538-5494), **Midway** (☎ 800/446-4932), **Midwest Express** (☎ 800/452-2022), **Northwest** (☎ 800/225-2525), **Reno Air** (☎ 800/736-6247), **Sky West** (☎ 800/221-1212), **Southwest** (☎ 800/435-9792), **Sun Country** (☎ 800/359-6786), **TriStar** (☎ 800/218-8777), **TWA** (☎ 800/221-2000), **United** (☎ 800/241-6522), **USAir** (☎ 800/428-4322), and **Western Pacific** (☎ 800/930-3030).

FINDING THE BEST AIRFARE

Generally, the least expensive fares (except for special packages and special-promotion discount fares you see announced in newspaper travel sections) are **advance-purchase fares** that involve certain restrictions. For example, in addition to paying for your ticket 3 to 21 days in advance, you may have to leave or return on certain days, stay a maximum or minimum number of days, and so on. Also, advance-purchase fares are often nonrefundable. Nonetheless, the restrictions are usually within the framework of one's vacation plans, and savings of $500 and more are not unusual.

THE LAS VEGAS AIRPORT

Las Vegas is served by **McCarran International Airport,** 5757 Wayne Newton Blvd. (☎ **702/261-5743**), just a few minutes' drive from the southern end of the Strip. It's a big, modern airport, and rather unique in that it includes a casino area with more than 1,000 slot machines. Although these are reputed to offer lower paybacks than hotel casinos (the airport has a captive audience and doesn't need to lure repeat customers), I can never resist throwing in a few quarters while waiting for my luggage to arrive. Lower payback rumors notwithstanding, my first quarter in a slot machine here recently netted me a $50 jackpot—which I erroneously viewed as a good betting omen for the rest of the trip.

Airport Transportation   Getting to your hotel from the airport is a cinch. **Bell Trans** (☎ **702/739-7990**) runs 20-passenger minibuses daily between the airport and all major Las Vegas hotels and motels almost around the clock (4:30am to 2am). Buses from the airport leave about every 10 minutes. For departure from your hotel, call at least 2 hours in advance. The cost is $3.50 per person each way to Strip and Convention Center area hotels, $4.75 to Downtown properties (any place north of the Sahara Hotel and west of I-15).

Even less expensive are **Citizen's Area Transit (CAT)** buses (☎ **702/CAT-RIDE**). The no. 302 bus departs from the airport and stops close to most Strip and Convention Center area hotels. The no. 109 bus goes from the airport to the Downtown Transportation Center at Casino Center Blvd. and Stewart Ave. The fare for the no. 302 is $1.50, 50¢ for seniors and children. *Note:* If you have heavy luggage, you should know that you might have a long walk from the bus stop to your door (even if it's right in front of your hotel).

Renting a Car   All of the major car-rental companies are represented in Las Vegas. I always rent from **Allstate** (☎ **800/634-6186** or 702/736-6148), the least expensive of the airport-based car-rental agencies. Their fleet of more than 1,500 vehicles includes—besides the usual mix—an inventory of 15 passenger vans, four-wheel drives, jeeps, minivans, sports cars, and convertibles. I've always found this local, family-owned company (the largest independent operator in Las Vegas) friendly and competent; they're open 24 hours. And they've agreed to offer my readers a **20% discount off regular rental rates** at any Allstate location (just show the agent your copy of this book). In addition to McCarran Airport, there are Allstate car desks at the

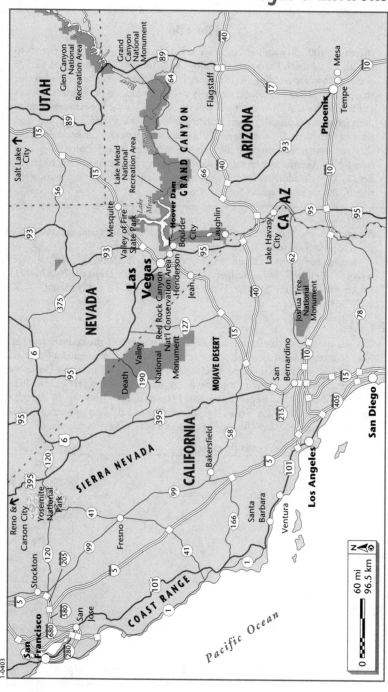

I Do, I Do

More than 100,000 weddings take place in Las Vegas each year. If you feel ready to take the plunge, call **Las Vegas Weddings and Rooms** (☎ **800/488-MATE**), a one-stop shop for wedding services. They'll find a chapel or outdoor garden that suits your taste (not to mention such only-in-Vegas venues as the former mansions of Elvis Presley and Liberace), book you into a hotel for the honeymoon, arrange the ceremony, and provide flowers, a photographer (or videographer), wedding cake, limo, car rental, music, champagne, balloons, and a garter for the bride. Basically they can arrange anything you like. Theme weddings are a specialty. They even have a New Age minister on call who can perform a Native American ceremony. Let Las Vegas Weddings arrange your honeymoon stay—sightseeing tours, show tickets, and meals, as well.

Aladdin, Riviera, Stardust, and Jackie Gaughan's Plaza hotels, and the company offers free pickup anywhere in Las Vegas.

National companies with outlets in Las Vegas include **Alamo** (☎ 800/327-9633), **Avis** (☎ 800/367-2847), **Budget** (☎ 800/922-2899), **Dollar** (800/826-9911), **Enterprise** (☎ 800/325/8007), **Hertz** (☎ 800/654-3131), and **National** (☎ 800/227-7368).

BY CAR

The main highway connecting Las Vegas with the rest of the country is I-15; it links Montana, Idaho, and Utah with southern California. From the East Coast, take I-70 or I-80 west to Kingman, Arizona, and then U.S. 93 north to Downtown Las Vegas (Fremont Street). From the south, take I-10 west to Phoenix and then U.S. 93 north to Las Vegas. From San Francisco, take I-80 east to Reno and then U.S. 95 south to Las Vegas. If you're driving to Las Vegas be sure to read the driving precautions under "By Car" in chapter 4's "Getting Around" section.

Driving Distances to Las Vegas (in miles)

Chicago	1,766
Dallas	1,230
Denver	759
Los Angeles	269
New York City	2,564
Phoenix	286
Salt Lake City	421
San Francisco	586

PACKAGE DEALS

When you make reservations on any airline, also inquire about money-saving packages that include hotel accommodations, car rentals, tours, and so forth with your airfare.

For instance, at press time, a **Delta Dream Vacation** package leaving from New York could cost as little as $337 per person based on double occupancy, including round-trip coach air transportation, two nights at your choice of several major casino hotels, a rental car for 24 hours, airport transfers, and bonus discounts and

Doing It in the Car

The **Little White Chapel,** 1301 Las Vegas Blvd. S. (☎ **800/545-8111** or 702/ 382-5943), is one of numerous well-known Las Vegas wedding chapels. It's been around since 1959. Among the famous folks who've tied the knot here are Bruce and Demi, Patty Duke, Michael Jordan, Ricky Lake, Sally Jessy Raphael, and Joan Collins. What makes The Little White Chapel unique is its drive-in service. Just pull up to the window, ring the bell, present your credentials, and owner Charolette Richards will read you your vows while you're comfortably seated in your car. She's even joined couples perched on motorcycles in holy matrimony. Of course, you can also get married on foot here, and all wedding services (including limo rental) are available. If you request it in advance, I'm sure Charolette could even arrange a burger and fries, giving your wedding a "Little White Castle" theme. Honk if you love each other.

admissions. Prices vary according to the season, seat availability, hotel choice, whether you travel midweek or on the weekend, and other factors. Since even an advance-purchase round-trip fare between New York and Las Vegas can easily be $100 or $200 more than the above-quoted figure, it seems almost insane not to book a less expensive package that includes so many extras. For details on Delta packages, consult your travel agent or call the airline directly (☎ **800/872-7786**).

Similar packages are available from such companies as **American Airlines Fly Away Vacations** (☎ **800/321-2121**), **America West Vacations** (**800/356-6611**), and **USAir Vacations** (☎ **800/455-0123**), all of which also offer packages directly or through a travel agent.

CHARTER FLIGHTS

Similar to airline packages, charter flights are booked by tour operators who buy up all the seats on an airplane and put together packages that include airfare and other features—perhaps accommodations, shows, meals, car rentals, airport transfers, and/ or attractions tickets. The operators then sell these charters through travel agents. It can be worth your while to compare charter offerings to major airline packages. Most travel agents know which tour operators specialize in Las Vegas charters. If yours does not, ask them to investigate packages offered by **Funjet Vacations** (☎ 800/ 558-3050), **Hamilton, Miller, Hudson & Fang** (☎ 800/669-4466), **MLT Vacations** (☎ 800/328-0025), and **Adventure Tours** (☎ 800/638-9040).

3 For Foreign Visitors

This chapter will provide some specifics about getting to the United States as economically and effortlessly as possible, plus some helpful information about how things are done in Las Vegas—from receiving mail to making a local or long-distance telephone call.

1 Preparing for Your Trip

ENTRY REQUIREMENTS

Document Regulations   Canadian citizens may enter the United States without visas; they need only proof of residence.

Citizens of the United Kingdom, New Zealand, Japan, and most other western European countries traveling on valid passports may not need a visa for fewer than 90 days of holiday or business travel to the United States, providing that they hold a round-trip or return ticket and enter the United States on an airline or cruise line that participates in the visa waiver program.

(Note that citizens of these visa-exempt countries who first enter the United States may then visit Mexico, Canada, Bermuda, and/or the Caribbean islands and then reenter the States, by any mode of transportation, without needing a visa. Further information is available from any U.S. embassy or consulate.)

Citizens of countries other than those stipulated above, including citizens of Australia, must have two documents: a valid **passport,** with an expiration date at least six months later than the scheduled end of the visit to the United States; and a **tourist visa,** available without charge from the nearest U.S. consulate. To obtain a visa, the traveler must submit a completed application form (either in person or by mail) with a $1^1/_2$-inch square photo and demonstrate binding ties to a residence abroad.

Usually you can obtain a visa at once or within 24 hours, but it may take longer during the summer rush from June to August. If you cannot go in person, contact the nearest U.S. embassy or consulate for directions on applying by mail. Your travel agent or airline office may also be able to provide you with visa applications and instructions. The U.S. consulate or embassy that issues your visa will determine whether you will be issued a multiple- or single-entry visa and if any restrictions regarding the length of your stay will apply.

Medical Requirements   No inoculations are needed to enter the United States unless you are coming from, or have stopped over in, areas known to be suffering from epidemics, particularly cholera or yellow fever.

If you have a disease requiring treatment with medications containing narcotics or drugs requiring a syringe, carry a valid, signed generic prescription from your physician to allay any suspicions that you are smuggling drugs. The prescription brands you are accustomed to buying in your country may not be available in the United States.

Customs Requirements   Every adult visitor may bring in, free of duty: 1 liter of wine or hard liquor; 200 cigarettes or 100 cigars (but no cigars from Cuba) or 3 pounds of smoking tobacco; and $100 worth of gifts. These exemptions are offered to travelers who spend at least 72 hours in the United States and who have not claimed them within the preceding 6 months. It is altogether forbidden to bring foodstuffs (particularly cheese, fruit, cooked meats, and canned goods) and plants (vegetables, seeds, tropical plants, and so on) into the country. Foreign tourists may bring in or take out up to $10,000 in U.S. or foreign currency with no formalities; larger sums must be declared to customs on entering or leaving.

INSURANCE

Unlike most other countries, the United States does not have a national health system. Because the cost of medical care is extremely high, we strongly advise all travelers to secure health coverage before setting out on their trip. You may want to take out a comprehensive travel policy that covers (for a relatively low premium) sickness or injury costs (medical, surgical, and hospital); loss or theft of your baggage; trip-cancellation costs; guarantee of bail in case you are arrested; and costs of accident, repatriation, or death. Such packages (for example, "Europe Assistance" in Europe) are sold by automobile clubs at attractive rates, as well as by insurance companies and travel agencies.

MONEY

The U.S. monetary system has a decimal base: One American dollar ($1) = 100 cents (100¢). Dollar bills commonly come in $1 (a "buck"), $5, $10, $20, $50, and $100 denominations (the last two are not welcome when paying for small purchases and are usually not accepted in taxis or at subway ticket booths). There are six coin denominations: 1¢ (one cent or "penny"); 5¢ (five cents or "nickel"); 10¢ (ten cents or "dime"); 25¢ (twenty-five cents or "quarter"); 50¢ (fifty cents or "half dollar"); and the rare $1 piece.

Traveler's checks in U.S. dollars are accepted at most hotels, motels, restaurants, and large stores. Sometimes picture identification is required. American Express, Thomas Cook, and Barclay's Bank traveler's checks are readily accepted in the United States. Do not bring traveler's checks denominated in other currencies.

Credit cards are the method of payment most widely used: Visa (BarclayCard in Britain), MasterCard (EuroCard in Europe, Access in Britain, Chargex in Canada), American Express, Discover, Diners Club, JCB, and Carte Blanche, in descending order of acceptance. You can save yourself trouble by using "plastic" rather than cash or traveler's checks in almost all hotels, motels, restaurants, and retail stores. You must have a credit or charge card to rent a car. It can also be used as proof of identity or as a "cash card" enabling you to draw money from automatic-teller machines (ATMs).

If you plan to travel for several weeks or more in the United States, you may want to deposit enough money into your credit-card account to cover anticipated expenses and avoid finance charges in your absence. This also reduces the likelihood of your receiving an unwelcome big bill on your return.

You can telegraph money, or have it telegraphed to you very quickly using the **Western Union** system (☎ **800/325-6000**).

SAFETY

While tourist areas are generally safe, crime is on the increase everywhere, and U.S. urban areas tend to be less safe than those in Europe or Japan. Visitors should always stay alert. This is particularly true of large U.S. cities, including Las Vegas.

Remember also that hotels are open to the public, and in a large hotel, security may not be able to screen everyone entering. Always lock your room door—don't assume that once inside your hotel you are automatically safe and no longer need to be aware of your surroundings. In Las Vegas, many hotels check room keys at the elevators at night, providing some extra security. Many Las Vegas hotels also have in-room safes; if yours doesn't and you're traveling with valuables, put them in a safety-deposit box at the front desk.

DRIVING

Safety while driving is particularly important. Question your rental agency about personal safety, or ask for a brochure of traveler safety tips when you pick up your car. Obtain written directions, or a map with the route marked in red, from the agency showing how to get to your destination. And, if possible, arrive and depart during daylight hours.

Recently more and more crime has involved cars and drivers. If you drive off a highway into a doubtful neighborhood, leave the area as quickly as possible. If you have an accident, even on the highway, stay in your car with the doors locked until you assess the situation or until the police arrive. If you are bumped from behind on the street or are involved in a minor accident with no injuries and the situation appears to be suspicious, motion to the other driver to follow you. Never get out of your car in such situations.

If you see someone on the road who indicates a need for help, do not stop. Take note of the location, drive on to a well-lighted area, and telephone the police by dialing 911. Park in well-lighted, well-traveled areas if possible.

Always keep your car doors locked, whether attended or unattended. Never leave any packages or valuables in sight. If someone attempts to rob you or steal your car, do not try to resist the thief/carjacker—report the incident to the police department immediately.

2 Getting to the United States

For an extensive listing of airlines that fly into Las Vegas, see "Getting There" in chapter 2. Travelers from overseas can take advantage of the advance-purchase fares offered by all the major U.S. and European carriers.

A number of U.S. airlines offer service from Europe to the United States. If they do not have direct flights from Europe to Las Vegas, they can book you straight through on a connecting flight. You can make reservations by calling the following numbers in London: **American** (☎ 0181/572-5555), **Continental** (☎ 4412/9377-6464), **Delta** (☎ 0800/414-767), and **United** (☎ 0181/990-9900).

And of course many international carriers serve LAX and/or San Francisco International Airport. Helpful numbers to know include **Virgin Atlantic** (☎ 0293/747-747 in London), **British Airways** (☎ 0345/222-111 in London), and **Aer Lingus** (☎ 01/844-4747 in Dublin or 061/415-556 in Shannon). **Quantas** (☎ 008/177-767 in Australia) has flights from Sydney to Los Angeles and San Francisco; you can also take United from Australia to the West Coast. **Air New Zealand** (☎ 0800/737-000 in Auckland or 643/379-5200 in Christchurch) also offers service to LAX. Canadian readers might book flights on **Air Canada** (☎ in Canada 800/268-7240 or 800/361-8620), which offers direct service from Toronto, Montreal, Calgary, and Vancouver to San Francisco and Los Angeles.

The visitor arriving by air, no matter what the port of entry, should cultivate patience and resignation before setting foot on U.S. soil. Getting through immigration control may take as long as 2 hours on some days, especially summer weekends, so have your guidebook or something else to read handy. Add the time it takes to clear customs and you will see you should make a very generous allowance for delay in planning connections between international and domestic flights—figure on 2 to 3 hours at least.

In contrast, for the traveler arriving by car or by rail from Canada, the border-crossing formalities have been streamlined to the vanishing point. And for the traveler by air from Canada, Bermuda, and some places in the Caribbean, you can sometimes go through customs and immigration at the point of departure, which is much quicker.

3 Getting Around the United States

On their transatlantic or transpacific flights, some large U.S. airlines (for example, TWA, American, Northwest, United, and Delta) offer travelers special discount tickets under the name **Visit USA,** allowing travel between U.S. destinations at minimum rates. They are not on sale in the United States and must be purchased before you leave your point of departure. This system is the best, easiest, and fastest way to see the United States at low cost. You should obtain information well in advance from your travel agent or the office of the airline concerned, since the conditions attached to these discount tickets can be changed without advance notice.

International visitors—except Canadians and Mexicans—can also buy a **USA Railpass,** good for 15 or 30 days of unlimited travel on Amtrak trains throughout the U.S. or Canada. The pass is available through many foreign travel agents. At press time, prices for a 15-day pass were $245 off-peak, $355 peak; a 30-day pass cost $350 off-peak, $440 peak (peak is June 17 to August 21). (With a foreign passport, you can also buy passes at some Amtrak offices in the United States, including locations in San Francisco, Los Angeles, Chicago, New York, Miami, Boston, and Washington, D.C.) Even cheaper are **regional USA Railpasses** allowing unlimited travel through a specific section of the U.S. Reservations are generally required and should be made for each part of your trip as early as possible.

With a few notable exceptions (for instance, the Northeast Corridor line between Boston and Washington, D.C.), train service is rarely up to European standards: Delays are common, routes are limited and often infrequently served, and fares are rarely significantly lower than discount airfares. Thus, cross-country train travel should be approached with caution.

Currently, Amtrak has no regularly scheduled service to Las Vegas. **Bus travel** in the United States can be both slow and uncomfortable; however, it can also be quite inexpensive. **Greyhound,** the sole nationwide bus line, offers an **Ameripass** for unlimited travel throughout the United States. At press time, prices were $179 for 7 days, $289 for 15 days, $399 for 30 days, and $559 for 60 days. Though bus stations are often located in undesirable neighborhoods, the one in Las Vegas is conveniently located in a safe part of downtown.

FAST FACTS: For the Foreign Traveler

Automobile Organizations   Auto clubs will supply maps, suggested routes, guide-books, accident and bail-bond insurance, and emergency road service. The major auto club in the United States, with 955 offices nationwide, is the **American Automobile Association (AAA).** Members of some foreign auto clubs have recipro-cal arrangements with the AAA and enjoy its services at no charge. If you belong to an auto club, inquire about AAA reciprocity before you leave. The AAA can pro-vide you with an **International Driving Permit** validating your foreign license, although drivers with valid licenses from most home countries don't really need this permit. You may be able to join the AAA even if you are not a member of a reciprocal club. To inquire, call 800/AAA-HELP. In addition, some automobile rental agencies now provide these services, so you should inquire about their avail-ability when you rent your car.

Automobile Rentals   To rent a car you need a major credit or charge card. A valid driver's license is required, and you usually need to be at least 25 years old. Some companies do rent to younger people but add a daily surcharge. Be sure to return your car with the same amount of gas you started out with; rental companies charge excessive prices for gasoline. For car-rental companies in Las Vegas, see "Renting a Car" in chapter 2.

Business Hours   Offices are usually open weekdays from 9am to 5pm. Banks are open weekdays from 9am to 3pm or later, although there's 24-hour access to the automatic tellers (ATMs) at most banks and other outlets. In Las Vegas, money is also available around the clock at casino cages. Shops, especially those in shop-ping complexes, tend to stay open late: until about 9pm weekdays and until 6pm weekends.

Climate   See "When to Go" in chapter 2.

Currency   See "Preparing for Your Trip" earlier in this chapter.

Currency Exchange   The "foreign-exchange bureaus" so common in Europe are rare in the United States. They're at major international airports, and there are a few in most major cities, but they're nonexistent in medium-size cities and small towns. Try to avoid having to change foreign money, or traveler's checks denomi-nated other than in U.S. dollars, at small-town banks, or even at branches in a big city; in fact leave any currency other than U.S. dollars at home (except the cash you need for the taxi or bus ride home when you return to your own country); other-wise, your own currency may prove more nuisance to you than it's worth.

Las Vegas casinos can exchange foreign currency, usually at a good rate.

Drinking Laws   The legal age to drink alcohol is 21.

Electric Current   The United States uses 110–120 volts, 60 cycles, compared to 220–240 volts, 50 cycles, as in most of Europe. Besides a 100-volt converter, small appliances of non-American manufacture, such as hair dryers or shavers, will re-quire a plug adapter with two flat, parallel pins. The easiest solution to the power struggle is to purchase dual-voltage appliances that operate on both 110 and 220 volts and then all that is required is a U.S. adapter plug.

Embassies/Consulates   All embassies are located in Washington, D.C. Listed here are the West Coast consulates of the major English-speaking countries. The Australian Consulate is located at 611 N. Larchmont, Los Angeles, CA 90004 (☎ 213/469-4300). The Canadian Consulate is at 300 South Grand Ave., Suite 1000, Los Angeles, CA 90071 (☎ 213/346-2700). The Irish Consulate is located at 655 Montgomery St., Suite 930, San Francisco, CA 94111 (☎ 415/392-4214). The New Zealand Consulate is at 12400 Wilshire Blvd., Los Angeles, CA 90025 (☎ 310/207-1605). Contact the U.K. Consulate at 11766 Wilshire Blvd., Suite 400, Los Angeles, CA 90025 (☎ 310/477-3322).

Emergencies   Call **911** for fire, police, and ambulance. If you encounter such traveler's problems as sickness, accident, or lost or stolen baggage, call Traveler's Aid, an organization that specializes in helping distressed travelers. In Las Vegas, there is an office in McCarran International Airport (☎ 702/798-1742), which is open daily from 8am to 5pm. Similar services are provided by Help of Southern Nevada, 953 E. Sahara Ave., Suite 23B, at Maryland Parkway in the Commercial Center on the northeast corner (☎ 702/369-4357). Hours are Monday to Friday, from 8am to 4pm.

Holidays   On the following national legal holidays, banks, government offices, post offices, and many stores, restaurants, and museums are closed: January 1 (New Year's Day), third Monday in January (Martin Luther King Jr. Day), third Monday in February (Presidents' Day), last Monday in May (Memorial Day), July 4 (Independence Day), first Monday in September (Labor Day), second Monday in October (Columbus Day), November 11 (Veterans Day/Armistice Day), fourth Thursday in November (Thanksgiving Day), and December 25 (Christmas Day). The Tuesday following the first Monday in November is Election Day.

Legal Aid   If you are stopped for a minor infraction (for example, of the highway code, such as speeding), never attempt to pay the fine directly to a police officer; you may be arrested on the much more serious charge of attempted bribery. Pay fines by mail, or directly into the hands of the clerk of the court. If accused of a more serious offense, it is best to say and do nothing before consulting a lawyer. Under U.S. law, an arrested person is allowed one telephone call to a party of his or her choice. Call your embassy or consulate.

Mail   You may receive mail c/o General Delivery at the main post office of the city or region where you expect to be. The addressee must pick it up in person, and must produce proof of identity (driver's license, credit card, passport).

Mailboxes are blue with a red-and-white logo, and carry the inscription U.S. MAIL. Within the United States, it costs 20¢ to mail a standard-size postcard. Letters that weigh up to 1 ounce cost 32¢, plus 23¢ for each additional ounce. A postcard to Mexico costs 30¢, a ¹/₂-ounce letter 35¢; a postcard to Canada costs 30¢, a 1-ounce letter 40¢. A postcard to Europe, Australia, New Zealand, the Far East, South America, and elsewhere costs 40¢, while a letter is 50¢ for each ¹/₂ ounce. In Las Vegas, the main post office is behind the Stardust Hotel at 3100 Industrial Rd., between Sahara Avenue and Spring Mountain Road (☎ 800/297-5543). It's open Monday to Friday from 8:30am to 5pm. You can also mail letters and packages at your hotel, and there's a full-service U.S. Post Office in the Forum Shops in Caesars Palace.

Medical Emergencies   See "Emergencies" above.

Taxes   In the United States there is no VAT (value-added tax) or other indirect tax at a national level. There is a $10 customs tax, payable on entry to the United States, and a $6 departure tax. Sales tax is levied on goods and services by state and local governments, however, and is not included in the price tags you'll see on merchandise. These taxes are not refundable.

Telephone and Fax   Pay phones can be found on street corners, as well as in bars, restaurants, public buildings, stores and at service stations. Some accept 20¢, most are 25¢. If the telephone accepts 20¢, you may also use a quarter (25¢) but you will not receive change.

In the past few years, many American companies have installed "voice-mail" systems, so be prepared to deal with a machine instead of a receptionist if calling a business number. Listen carefully to the instructions (you'll probably be asked to dial 1, 2, or 3 or wait for an operator to pick up); if you can't understand, sometimes dialing zero will put you in touch with an operator within the company. It's frustrating even for locals!

For long-distance or international calls, it's most economical to charge the call to a telephone charge card or a credit card; or you can use a lot of change. The pay phone will instruct you how much to deposit and when to deposit it into the slot on the top of the telephone box.

For long-distance calls in the United States, dial 1 followed by the area code and number you want. For direct overseas calls, first dial 011, followed by the country code (Australia, 61; Republic of Ireland, 353; New Zealand, 64; United Kingdom, 44; and so on), and then by the city code (for example, 71 or 81 for London, 21 for Birmingham, 1 for Dublin) and the number of the person you wish to call.

Before calling from a hotel room, always ask the hotel phone operator if there are any telephone surcharges. There almost always are, and they often are as much as 75¢ or $1, even for a local call. These charges are best avoided by using a public phone, calling collect, or using a telephone charge card.

For reversed-charge or collect calls and for person-to-person calls, dial 0 (zero, not the letter "O") followed by the area code and number you want; an operator will then come on the line, and you should specify that you are calling collect, or person-to-person, or both. If your operator-assisted call is international, immediately ask to speak with an overseas operator.

Telephone Directory   The local phone company provides two kinds of telephone directories. The general directory, called the "white pages," lists businesses and personal residences separately, in alphabetical order. The first few pages are devoted to community-service numbers, including a guide to long-distance and international calling, complete with country codes and area codes.

The second directory, the "yellow pages," lists all local services, businesses, and industries by type, with an index at the back. The listings cover not only such obvious items as automobile repairs by make of car, or drugstores (pharmacies), often by geographical location, but also restaurants by type of cuisine and geographical location, bookstores by special subject and/or language, places of worship by religious denomination, and other information that a visitor might otherwise not readily find. The yellow pages also include city plans or detailed area maps, often showing postal ZIP codes and public transportation.

For local directory assistance ("Information"), dial 411; for long-distance information dial 1, then the appropriate area code and **555-1212.**

Most hotels have fax machines available for their customers and there is usually a charge to send or receive a facsimile. You will also see signs for public faxes in the windows of small shops.

Time Nevada is on Pacific time, which is 3 hours earlier than on the U.S. East Coast. For instance, when it is noon in Las Vegas, it is 3pm in New York and Miami; 2pm in Chicago, in the central part of the country; and 1pm in Denver, Colorado, in the midwestern part of the country. Nevada, like most of the rest of the United States, observes daylight saving time during the summer; in late spring, clocks are moved ahead 1 hour and then are turned back again in the fall. This results in lovely long summer evenings, when the sun sets as late as 8:30 or 9pm.

Tipping Some rules of thumb: bartenders, 10–15%; bellhops, at least 50¢ per bag, or $2–$3 for a lot of luggage; cab drivers, 10% of the fare; chambermaids, $1 per day; checkroom attendants, $1 per garment; hairdressers and barbers, 15–20%; waiters and waitresses, 15–20% of the check; valet parking attendants, $1; showroom maitre d's, see chapter 10 for details; casino dealers, a few dollars if you've had a big win.

Getting to Know Las Vegas

Located in the southernmost precincts of a wide, pancake-flat valley, Las Vegas is the biggest city in the state of Nevada. Treeless mountains form a scenic backdrop to hotels awash in neon glitter. For tourism purposes, the city is quite compact.

1 Orientation

VISITOR INFORMATION

All major Las Vegas hotels provide comprehensive tourist information at their reception and/or sightseeing and show desks. Other good information sources are: the **Las Vegas Convention and Visitors Authority,** 3150 Paradise Rd., Las Vegas, NV 89109 (☎ **702/ 892-0711,** daily 8am to 5pm); the **Las Vegas Chamber of Commerce,** 711 E. Desert Inn Rd., Las Vegas, NV 89109 (☎ **702/ 735-1616,** Monday to Friday 8am to 5pm), and, for information on all of Nevada, including Las Vegas, the **Nevada Commission on Tourism,** Capitol Complex, Carson City, NV 89710 (☎ **800/ 638-2328**).

FOR TROUBLED TRAVELERS

The **Traveler's Aid Society** is a social-service organization geared to helping travelers in difficult straits. Their services might include re-uniting families separated while traveling, feeding people stranded without cash, or even emotional counseling. If you're in trouble, seek them out. In Las Vegas there is a Traveler's Aid office at McCarran International Airport (☎ **702/798-1742**). It's open daily from 8am to 5pm. Similar services are provided by **Help of Southern Nevada,** 953 E. Sahara Ave. (suite 23B), at Maryland Parkway in the Commercial Center at the northeast corner (☎ **702/369-4357**). Hours are Monday to Friday 8am to 4pm.

CITY LAYOUT

Nothing could be simpler than the layout of Las Vegas—especially the three areas of interest to tourists.

THE STRIP

The Strip is probably the most famous $3^1/_2$-mile stretch of highway in the nation. Officially Las Vegas Boulevard South, it contains most of the top hotels in town and offers almost all of the major showroom entertainment. It extends from just below Tropicana Avenue at the

Las Vegas at a Glance

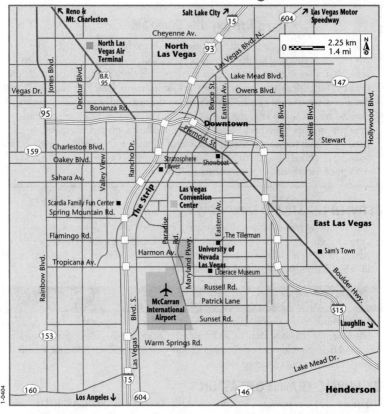

southernmost end—where you'll find the Luxor, Excalibur, Tropicana, and MGM Grand hotels—to Sahara Avenue, where the Sahara hotel anchors the northern boundary.

CONVENTION CENTER

This area east of the Strip has grown up around the Las Vegas Convention Center. Las Vegas is one of the nation's top convention cities, attracting more than 2.9 million conventioneers each year. The major hotel in this section is the Las Vegas Hilton, but in recent years Marriott has built Residence Inn and Courtyard properties here, and the Debbie Reynolds and Hard Rock hotels have opened. You'll find many excellent smaller hotels and motels southward along Paradise Road. All of these offer close proximity to the Strip.

DOWNTOWN

Also known as "Glitter Gulch" (narrower streets make the neon seem brighter), Downtown Las Vegas, which is centered on Fremont Street between Main and 9th Streets, was the first section of the city to develop hotels and casinos. With the exception of the Golden Nugget, which looks like it belongs in Monte Carlo, this area has traditionally been more casual than the Strip. But with the advent of the revitalizing Fremont Street Experience (see chapter 7 for details), Downtown is becoming more upscale. Las Vegas Boulevard runs all the way into Fremont Street downtown (about a 5-minute drive).

Driving: The Down Side

Las Vegas is booming. All of the exciting new hotels that have opened in the past few years are attracting hordes of tourists. As a result, traffic on the Strip is often—make that almost always—bumper-to-bumper. And since just about all the action is on the Strip, there aren't many alternate routes you can take. Best bet: Use Paradise Road, which runs parallel to the Strip on the east, and cross back to the Strip close to the hotel you're visiting. Also keep in mind that with increased tourism valet parking lots sometimes fill up. Between traffic tie-ups and the specter of self parking (which sometimes means you'll have to walk a city block or more from your car to a hotel), be sure to leave plenty of time when you're driving if you have restaurant reservations or show tickets.

BETWEEN THE STRIP & DOWNTOWN

The area between the Strip and Downtown is a seedy stretch dotted with tacky wedding chapels, bail-bond operations, pawnshops, and cheap motels. However, the advent in 1996 of the new 1,149-room Stratosphere Tower on this blighted stretch may be a harbinger of future development.

2 Getting Around

I can't think of any tourist destination that is easier to navigate than Las Vegas. The hotels are the major attractions and they're clustered in two different areas—on and around the Strip/Convention Center area and Downtown. Even first-time visitors will feel like natives after a day or two.

BY PUBLIC TRANSPORTATION

The no. 301 bus operated by **Citizens Area Transit** (☎ 702/CAT-RIDE) plies a route between the Downtown Transportation Center (at Casino Center Boulevard and Stewart Avenue) and a few miles beyond the southern end of the Strip. The fare is $1.50 for adults, 50¢ for seniors (62 and older) and children 5 to 17, and free for those under 5. CAT buses run 24 hours a day and are wheelchair-accessible. Exact change is required, but dollar bills are accepted.

Or you can hop aboard a classic streetcar replica run by **Las Vegas Strip Trolley** (☎ 702/382-1404). These old-fashioned dark-green vehicles have interior oak paneling and are comfortably air-conditioned. Like the buses, they run northward from Hacienda Avenue, stopping at all major hotels en route to the Sahara, and then looping back via the Las Vegas Hilton. They do not, however, go to the Stratosphere Tower or Downtown. Trolleys run about every 15 minutes daily between 9:30am and 2am. The fare is $1.30 (under 5 free), and exact change is required.

BY CAR

Although it is possible to get around in Las Vegas without a car, I love to have one at my disposal. Parking is usually a pleasure, since all casino hotels offer valet service. That means that for a mere $1 tip you can park right at the door. And in sweltering summer heat, the valet will bring back your car with the air-conditioning already turned on. Furthermore, though bus tours are available to nearby attractions, a car lets you explore at your own pace rather than according to a tour schedule. See "Renting a Car" in chapter 2 for information and toll-free numbers of companies with offices in Las Vegas.

Since driving on the outskirts of Las Vegas—for example, coming from California—involves desert driving, you must take certain precautions. It's a good idea to check your tires, water, and oil before leaving. Take at least 5 gallons of water in a clean container that can be used for either drinking or the radiator. Pay attention to road signs that suggest when to turn off your car's air conditioner. And don't push your luck with gas—it may be 35 miles, or more, between stations. If your car overheats, do not remove the radiator cap until the engine has cooled, and then remove it only very slowly. Add water to within an inch of the top of the radiator.

BY TAXI

Since cabs line up in front of all major hotels, an easy way to get around town is by taxi. Cabs charge $2.20 at the meter drop and 30¢ for each additional one-fifth of a mile. A taxi from the airport to the Strip will run you $8 to $12, from the airport to Downtown $15 to $18, and between the Strip and Downtown about $7 to $10. You can often save money by sharing a cab with someone going to the same destination (up to five people can ride for the same fare).

If you want to call a taxi, any of the following companies can provide one: **Desert Cab Company** (☎ 702/376-2688), **Whittlesea Blue Cab** (☎ 702/384-6111), and **Yellow/Checker Cab/Star Company** (☎ 702/873-2000).

FAST FACTS: Las Vegas

Ambulances   See "Emergencies," below.

Area Code   702

Babysitters   Contact **Around the Clock Child Care** (☎ 800/798-6768 or 702/365-1040). In business since 1985, this reputable company clears its sitters with the Health Department, the sheriff, and the FBI and carefully screens references. Charges are $38 for 4 hours for one or two children, $7.50 for each additional hour, with surcharges for additional children and on holidays. Sitters are on call 7 days a week, 24 hours a day, and they will come to your hotel. Call at least 2 hours in advance.

Banks   Banks are generally open 9 or 10am to 3pm, and most have Saturday hours. See also "Cash and Credit," below.

Car Rentals   See "Getting Around," above.

Cash and Credit   It's extremely easy—too easy—to obtain cash in Las Vegas. Most casino cashiers will cash personal checks and can exchange foreign currency, and just about every casino has a machine that will provide cash on a wide variety of credit cards.

Climate   See "When to Go" in chapter 2.

Convention Facilities   Las Vegas is one of America's top convention destinations. Much of the action takes place at the Las Vegas Convention Center, 3150 Paradise Rd., Las Vegas, NV 89109 (☎ 702/892-0711). The largest single-level convention center in the world, its 1.3 million square feet includes 89 meeting rooms. And this immense facility is augmented by the Cashman Field Center, 850 Las Vegas Blvd. N., Las Vegas, NV 89101 (☎ 702/386-7100). Under the same auspices, Cashman provides another 98,100 square feet of convention space.

Currency Exchange   Most Las Vegas hotels can exchange foreign currency. There's also a currency exchange desk run by Travelex in the ticketing area on the first level of McCarran International Airport.

Dentists and Doctors   Hotels usually have lists of dentists and doctors should you need one. In addition, they are listed in the Centel Yellow Pages.

For dentist referrals you can also call the Clark County Dental Society (☎ 702/ 255-7873), weekdays 9am to noon and 1 to 5pm; when the office is closed, a recording will tell you whom to call for emergency service.

For physician referrals, call Desert Springs Hospital (☎ 800/842-5439 or 702/ 733-6875). Hours are Monday to Friday 8am to 5pm.

Drugstores   Sav-on is a large 24-hour drugstore and pharmacy close to the Strip at 1360 E. Flamingo Rd., at Maryland Pkwy. (☎ 702/731-5373 for the pharmacy, 702/737-0595 for general merchandise). White Cross Drugs, 1700 Las Vegas Blvd. S. (☎ 702/382-1733), open daily 7am to 1am, will make pharmacy deliveries to your hotel during the day.

Emergencies   Dial 911 to contact the police or fire departments or to call an ambulance.

Emergency services are available 24 hours a day at University Medical Center, 1800 W. Charleston Blvd., at Shadow Lane (☎ 702/383-2661); the emergency room entrance is on the corner of Hastings and Rose streets. Sunrise Hospital & Medical Center, 3186 Maryland Pkwy., between Desert Inn Road and Sahara Avenue (☎ 702/731-8080), also has a 24-hour emergency room.

Highway Conditions   For recorded information, call 702/486-3116.

Hot Lines   The Rape Crisis Center (☎ 702/366-1640), Suicide Prevention (☎ 702/731-2990), Poison Emergencies (☎ 702/732-4989).

Information   See "Visitor Information" earlier in this chapter.

Libraries   The largest in town is the Clark County Library branch at 1401 Flamingo Rd., at Escondido Street, on the southeast corner (☎ 702/733-7810). Hours are Monday to Thursday 9am to 9pm, Friday and Saturday 9am to 5pm, Sunday 1 to 5pm.

Liquor and Gambling Laws   You must be 21 to drink or gamble. There are no closing hours in Las Vegas for the sale or consumption of alcohol, even on Sunday.

Newspapers and Periodicals   There are two Las Vegas dailies—the *Las Vegas Review Journal* and the *Las Vegas Sun*. The *Review Journal's* Friday edition has a helpful "Weekend" section with a comprehensive guide to shows and buffets. And at every hotel desk, you'll find dozens of free local magazines, such as *Vegas Visitor, What's On in Las Vegas, Showbiz Weekly,* and *Where To in Las Vegas,* that are chock-full of helpful information.

Parking   Valet parking is one of the great pleasures of Las Vegas and well worth the dollar tip (given when the car is returned) to save walking a city block from the far reaches of a hotel parking lot, particularly when the temperature is over 100°. Another summer plus: the valet will turn on your air-conditioning, so you don't have to get in an "oven on wheels."

Police   For non-emergencies call 702/795-3111. For emergencies call 911.

Post Office   The most convenient post office is immediately behind the Stardust Hotel at 3100 Industrial Rd., between Sahara Avenue and Spring Mountain Road (☎ 800/297-5543). It's open Monday to Friday 8:30am to 5pm. You can also mail letters and packages at your hotel, and there's a full-service U.S. Post Office in the Forum Shops in Caesars Palace.

Safety   In Las Vegas, vast amounts of money are always on display, and criminals find many easy marks. Don't be one of them. At gaming tables and slot machines, men should keep wallets well concealed and out of the reach of pickpockets, and women should keep handbags in plain sight (on laps). Outside casinos, popular spots for pickpockets and thieves are restaurants and outdoor shows, such as the volcano at Mirage or at the Treasure Island pirate battle. Stay alert. Unless your hotel room has an in-room safe, check your valuables in a safety-deposit box at the front desk.

Show Tickets   See chapter 10 for details on obtaining show tickets.

Taxes   Clark County hotel room tax is 8%; the sales tax is 7%.

Taxis   See "Getting Around—By Taxi" earlier in this chapter.

Time Zone   Las Vegas is in the Pacific time zone, 3 hours earlier than the East Coast, 2 hours earlier than the Midwest.

Weather and Time   Call 702/248-4800.

Weddings   Las Vegas is one of the easiest places in the world to tie the knot. There's no blood test or waiting period, the ceremony and license are inexpensive, chapels are open around-the-clock, and your honeymoon destination is right at hand. More than 101,000 marriages are performed here each year. Get a license Downtown at the Clark County Marriage License Bureau, 200 S. 3rd St., at Bridger Avenue (☎ 702/455-3156). Open 8am to midnight Monday to Thursday and from 8am Friday through midnight Sunday. On legal holidays they're open 24 hours. The cost of a marriage license is $35, the cost of the ceremony, another $35.

Wedding chapels abound, and there's something for every taste (yes, you can have an Elvis impersonator perform your wedding) and pocketbook. The most romantic settings are at Mount Charleston or on a boat on Lake Mead (see chapter 7). One of the most popular chapels is the historic Candlelight Wedding Chapel, 2855 Las Vegas Blvd. S. (☎ 800/962-1818 or 702/735-4179). The Candlelight, along with most other Las Vegas wedding chapels, can meet requests (with enough advance notice) to stage your wedding in a limousine, a hot-air balloon, in a nearby canyon, or in almost any eccentric setting you can think of. A service called Las Vegas Weddings and Rooms (☎ 800/488-MATE) can give you a full rundown on the various options.

5 Accommodations in Las Vegas

About 15 percent of Las Vegas's 93,997 hotel and motel rooms have been built since 1993; another 11,500 rooms are currently under construction; and by a conservative estimate, more than 15,000 additional rooms are planned by the turn of the century. Why this unprecedented building boom? Although Las Vegas has substantially more rooms than any other American tourist city, its annual occupancy rate (88%) is also far higher than the national average. And as America's top convention site, it frequently fills existing hotels to the bursting point. Booking well in advance is recommended.

If the current room boom could be traced to a single source, it might be the genius of one man: Steve Wynn. His lavish Strip hotels—the Mirage (opened in 1989) and Treasure Island (opened in 1993)—gave the city a hefty booster shot and set spectacular new standards for Vegas hotels. Since then, both existing and new resorts have been frantically scrambling to match Wynn's boldly sensational ventures, and several legendary old timers—the Dunes, Sands, and Hacienda hotels, all Strip residents of four decades or more—have bitten the dust. Locals vainly decry the loss of historic properties in this current excess-or-exit climate (even Bugsy Siegel's vast suite at the Flamingo, complete with trap door escape routes and tunnels, has been demolished), but the process is unstoppable.

THE HOTEL SCENE TODAY

Two major new properties came on board in 1996: the chic Monte Carlo, a joint venture of Steve Wynn's Mirage Resorts and Circus Circus Enterprises, and the skyline-altering Stratosphere, the first major venture in the former no-man's-land between the Strip and Downtown. Numerous expansions are planned at hotels all over town, and brand-new projects include the following:

- **New York, New York,** a joint venture of the MGM Grand and Primadonna Resorts, the 2,035-room hotel is well underway and will probably be open by the time you read this. The hotel consists of 12 towers in the form of landmark skyscrapers (approximately a third of the size of the originals). A major attraction will be a Coney Island–style midway with rides and carnival games.
- On a smaller scale is the French Quarter–themed **Orleans Hotel and Casino,** under the same auspices as the Barbary Coast, which will be open soon. This 840-room hotel will contain a 70-lane bowling alley and offer a Branson, Missouri–style country music

---

Important Information about Las Vegas Hotel Rates

You'll notice quoted rates vary dramatically. For instance, the Mirage lists its standard room rates as $79 to $399! The reason: Rates soar during holidays and when major conventions are in town. If you have some flexibility in planning the dates of your vacation, you can save quite a bit. Call the **Las Vegas Convention and Visitors Authority** (☎ **800/332-5334**) to find out if an important convention is scheduled at the time of your planned visit; if so, you might want to change your date. Some of the most popular conventions are listed in under "When to Go" in chapter 2.

Another anomaly here: While in many cities hotels offer reduced weekend rates, in Las Vegas rates are lower Sunday to Thursday.

---

production show. And the Orleans will be off the Strip at Tropicana Avenue, just west of I-15.

- Bally's 2,900-room **Paris Casino Resort,** scheduled for completion in 1998, will re-create the "City of Lights" at the turn of the century, including a 540-foot replica of the Eiffel Tower.
- Mirage Resort's upscale **Bellagio** is inspired by the eponymous Italian village that overlooks Lake Como, and also scheduled to open in 1998. Occupying the former site of the Dunes, the property will feature a 12-acre lake, the setting for water-ballet extravaganzas.
- Finally, the ITT Corporation (owner of Caesars and the Desert Inn, as well as Planet Hollywood International) recently announced plans for **Planet Hollywood** casino resort here adjacent to the Desert Inn. Budgeted at $830 million, this 3,200-room hotel is scheduled for completion in 1998. Look out, Hard Rock!

Extravagant themes, by the way, are only part of what makes this city's accommodations profile unique. Here the hotel norm is a 24-hour megaresort (10 of the 11 largest hotels in the world are located in Las Vegas) with restaurants, lavish entertainment showrooms and lounges, shopping arcades, fully equipped health clubs, swimming pools, and—most important—vast casinos. The good news for tourists is that these megaresorts charge considerably less for rooms than do equivalent properties in other major cities. The price of a room in a deluxe Las Vegas hotel is close to what you would pay at a moderate hotel in any other destination. The reason: The casino is the resort's raison d'être; inexpensive hotel rooms are the lure.

GETTING THE MOST FOR YOUR HOTEL DOLLAR

When the town is overflowing with visitors, top rates are charged, and there's little you can do about it. However, when business isn't quite so brisk, you can cut deals—possibly even lower than the rack rates quoted in these listings. Call around to the various toll-free numbers and ask reservations clerks if they can do better than the first rates quoted. Often, they will. A hotel makes nothing on an empty room. Hence, though they don't bruit it about (for obvious reasons), most hotels would rather reduce rates than leave a room unoccupied. Whatever rate you agree upon, ask for a confirmation number (written or faxed confirmation if possible) and check the rate again when you register at the hotel. Also, always inquire about reduced-price packages when you reserve.

If you're willing to chance it, an especially advantageous time to secure reduced rates is late in the afternoon or early evening on the day of your arrival, when a hotel's likelihood of filling up with full-price bookings is remote. But don't try this tactic on weekends, especially on Saturdays when you might find it difficult to get a hotel room at all.

RESERVATIONS SERVICES

If you get harried when you have to haggle, use a free service offered by **City-Wide Reservations,** 2929 E. Desert Inn Rd., Suite 20, Las Vegas, NV 89121-3604 (☎ **800/733-6644** or 702/794-4481; or connect on line at **CWRes@AOL.com**). They'll find you a hotel room in your price range meets your specific requirements. Because they book rooms in volume, they are able to get discounted rates. Not only can they book rooms, but they can arrange packages (including meals, transportation, tours, show tickets, car rentals, and other features) and group rates.

The **Las Vegas Convention and Visitors Authority** also runs a room reservations hot line (☎ **800/332-5334**), which can be helpful. They can apprise you of room availability, quote rates, contact a hotel for you, and tell you when major conventions will be in town.

WHAT THE PRICE CATEGORIES MEAN

The following price categories represent the average rack rate you can expect to be quoted for a double room on an average night (i.e., *not* when the Consumer Electronics Show is in town, *not* on New Year's Eve). Your *actual* rate may be a little less than this if you stay only Sunday through Thursday and a little more than this if you stay Friday and Saturday.

Very Expensive	More than $100
Expensive	Between $75 and $100
Moderate	Between $50 and $75
Inexpensive	$50 and under

Of course, you can expect significant savings if you book a money-saving package deal, like those described in chapter 2. And on any given night when business is slow, you might be able to stay at a "very expensive" hotel for a "moderate" price.

1 Best Bets

- **Best for Conventioneers/Business Travelers:** The **Las Vegas Hilton,** adjacent to the Las Vegas Convention Center and the setting for many on-premises conventions, offers extensive facilities along with helpful services such as a full business center.
- **Best Elegant Hotel:** Country club elegance is the keynote of the **Sheraton Desert Inn.** In its European-style casino, gaming tables are comfortably spaced, the glitzy glow of neon is replaced by the glitter of crystal chandeliers, and the scarcity of slot and video poker machines eliminates the usual noisy jangle of coins. Extensive facilities are complemented by attentive personal service. This is the most prestigious hotel address in town.
- **Best Archetypically Las Vegas Hotel:** **Caesars Palace** continues to embody the excess and excitement that is Las Vegas—from the overstated magnificence of its classical Roman facade to the orgiastic ambience of its Bacchanal Room. Catering to a sophisticated, upscale clientele, Caesars houses a spectacular Rodeo Drive–style shopping arcade and an impressive roster of restaurants. Its extensive facilities are matched by classy service: Once, when I was standing in a long line at the registration desk, gratis champagne was served.

- **Best Swimming Pool:** Almost every Las Vegas hotel has a stunning pool area. The **Flamingo Hilton** boasts a 15-acre Caribbean landscape with five pools, Jacuzzis, water slides, swan- and duck-filled ponds, a grove of 2,000 palms, waterfalls, fountains, lagoons, and islands of flamingos and African penguins. Similarly lush is the **Tropicana,** where you'll also find a swim-up bar/blackjack table.
- **Best Health Club:** Like sumptuous swimming pools, deluxe state-of-the-art health clubs are the rule in Las Vegas hotels. Most exclusive (fee is $18 per visit) and extensively equipped is the club at the **Mirage,** offering a full complement of machines—some with individual TVs (headphones are supplied), free weights, private whirlpool rooms as well as a large whirlpool and saunas, a thoroughly equipped locker room, and comfortable lounges in which to rest up after your workout. An adjoining salon offers every imaginable spa service. Steve Wynn works out here almost daily, as do many celebrity guests.
- **Best Hotel Dining/Entertainment:** Food aficionados will be thrilled with the nationally renowned celebrity chefs at the **MGM Grand.** You'll find restaurants by Mark Miller, Emiril Lagasse, and Wolfgang Puck, as well as the hotel's posh gourmet room, Gatsby's. There's also a re-creation of Hollywood's famed Brown Derby here.
- **Best for Twentysomethings Through Baby Boomers:** The **Hard Rock Hotel,** billing itself as the world's "first rock-'n'-roll hotel and casino" and "Vegas for a new generation," sent out invitations to its opening on casino chips bearing the image of Jimi Hendrix. Need I say more?
- **Best Interior:** I love walking into the verdant tropical rain forest at the **Mirage.** A massive coral-reef aquarium behind the registration desk and the on-premises tiger habitat further enhance this property's natural ambience, and well-designed paths make the casino extremely easy to navigate.
- **Best for Families:** The centrally located and low-priced **Circus Circus** has almost unlimited activities for kids—ongoing circus acts, a vast video-game arcade, a carnival midway, and a full amusement park.
- **Best Rooms:** The **Rio's** tropically themed and spacious suites are the most beautiful in town. Decorated in resort hues with half-canopy beds, they offer large dressing rooms, gorgeous baths, wraparound sofas, and upholstered chaise longues. Picture windows provide panoramic views of the Strip. Many people consider the Rio the most appealing hotel in Las Vegas.
- **Best Non-Casino Hotel:** The very upscale **Alexis Park Resort** is the choice of many visiting celebrities and headliners. Many of its rooms have working fireplaces and/or Jacuzzis, and guests are cosseted with can-do concierge service.
- **Best Casinos:** My favorite places to gamble are the **Mirage** (lively, beautiful, and not overwhelming), the **Sheraton Desert Inn** (where the intimate casino is reminiscent of sophisticated European gaming houses), and the **Hard Rock** (where you can bet to a beat).
- **Best Downtown Hotel:** The **Golden Nugget,** evoking an elegant resort on the French Riviera, is exceptionally appealing in every aspect—from its sun-dappled interior to its opulent, European-style casino.
- **Best Views:** From high-floor rooms at the **Stratosphere** you can see the entire city.

2 Choosing a Hotel

There are basically three areas of town of interest to visitors: the Strip, Convention Center and Paradise Road (both east of the Strip), and Downtown. Since it's only a

5-minute ride by car between Downtown and Strip hotels (the Convention Center is more or less in between), there's no such thing as a bad location if you have access to a car. If money is no object, a $10 cab ride separates the Strip from Downtown.

For those of you depending on public transportation: while the bus ride between Downtown and the Strip is short in distance, it can be long in time stuck in traffic. You should also be aware that the buses become quite crowded once they reach the Strip and may pass by a bus stop if no one signals to get out and the driver does not wish to take on more passengers. Without a car, your ease of movement between areas of town is, therefore, limited.

Personally, I like to stay on the Strip (or close by in the Convention Center area), but others prefer the more casual Downtown ambience. If you've never seen Las Vegas before, I'd suggest staying on the Strip and checking out Downtown for possible future visits.

Another factor in your choice is whether to stay at a casino or non-casino hotel. A casino hotel, especially a major one, is a kind of city-within-a-city that offers nonstop gaming, shows, and excitement. You'll be in the heart of the action. The down side: casino hotels want you downstairs placing bets, not lounging up in your room; hence, you'll probably have a smaller-than-average TV with limited cable stations, and you won't enjoy standard hotel services such as daily newspaper delivery. If you'd rather visit the action but then retire to more tranquil surroundings at night, choose a non-casino hotel. The hotel that gives you the best of both worlds is the Desert Inn—a refined casino hotel with a country-club atmosphere.

HOTELS BY LOCATION
ON OR NEAR THE STRIP

Algiers (No Casino, *I*)
Bally's (Casino, *VE*)
Barbary Coast (Casino, *M*)
Caesars Palace (Casino, *VE*)
Carriage House (No Casino, *VE*)
Center Strip Inn (No Casino, *I*)
Circus Circus (Casino, *I*)
Desert Inn (Casino, *VE*)
Excalibur (Casino, *M*)
Flamingo Hilton (Casino, *E*)
Harrah's (Casino, *M*)
Holiday Inn Casino Boardwalk (Casino, *M*)
Imperial Palace (Casino, *M*)
La Quinta Motor Inn (No Casino, *M*)
Las Vegas International Hostel (No Casino, *I*)
Luxor Las Vegas (Casino, *M*)
Maxim (Casino, *M*)
MGM Grand (Casino, *E*)
Mirage (Casino, *E*)
Monte Carlo (Casino, *E*)
Rio (Casino, *E*)
Riviera (Casino, *E*)
Sahara (Casino, *M*)
Stardust (Casino, *M*)
Stratosphere (Casino, *M*)
Treasure Island at the Mirage (Casino, *E*)
Tropicana (Casino, *E*)
Vagabond Inn (No Casino, *M*)
Westward Ho (Casino, *I*)

NEAR THE CONVENTION CENTER/ EAST OF THE STRIP

Alexis Park (No Casino, *VE*)
Best Western Mardi Gras Inn (Casino, *M*)
Courtyard Marriott (No Casino, *VE*)
Debbie Reynolds (No Casino, *M*)
Emerald Springs Holiday Inn (No Casino, *M*)
Fairfield Inn by Marriott (No Casino, *M*)
Hard Rock Hotel (Casino, *VE*)
La Quinta Inn (No Casino, *E*)
Las Vegas Hilton (Casino, *VE*)

Key to abbreviations: *I*=Inexpensive; *M*=Moderate; *E*=Expensive; *VE*=Very Expensive.

Motel 6 (No Casino, *I*)
Residence Inn by Marriott
    (No Casino, *E*)
Super 8 (Casino, *I*)

EAST LAS VEGAS

Sam's Town (Casino, *M*)

DOWNTOWN

California (Casino, *I*)
Days Inn (Casino, *M*)
El Cortez (Casino, *I*)

Golden Nugget
    (Casino, *E*)
Fitzgerald's (Casino, *M*)
Four Queens (Casino, *M*)
Jackie Gaughan's Plaza
    (Casino, *I*)
Lady Luck
    (Casino, *I*)
Sam Boyd's Fremont
    (Casino, *I*)
Showboat (Casino, *I*)

3 On or Near the Strip—Hotels with Casinos

VERY EXPENSIVE

Bally's Las Vegas

3645 Las Vegas Blvd. S., at Flamingo Rd., Las Vegas 89109. ☎ **800/634-3434** or 702/739-4111. Fax 702/794-2413. 2,549 rms, 265 suites. A/C TV TEL. $95–$135 single or double; concierge floor $35 additional (including breakfast); $300–$2,500 suite. Extra person $15. Children 18 and under stay free in parents' room. AE, CB, DC, JCB, MC, V. Free parking (self and valet).

Bally's recently completed a $72-million renovation, which included the construction of a monorail that whisks passengers from its downstairs shopping level (a bit of a hike from the casino) to the MGM Grand. More noticeable is its elaborate new facade—a plaza containing four 200-foot people movers that transport visitors to and from the Strip via a neon-lit arch surrounded by cascading waters and lush landscaping. Light, sound, and water shows take place here every 20 minutes after dark.

You'll notice that Bally's is one of the most cheerful hotels on the Strip the minute you step from its glittering entranceway into its light and airy casino. A whimsical mural of Las Vegas scenes backs the registration desk. A virtual "city within a city," Bally's offers a vast array of casino games, superb restaurants, entertainment options, shops, and services. During your Las Vegas stay, you'll never need to step outside.

Large rooms are decorated in teal, mauve, and earth tones. All have sofas. TVs offer video checkout, not to mention credit card cash-advance capability. The 22nd floor is a concierge level.

Dining/Entertainment: Seasons, its interior modeled after a grand salon at Versailles, is an ornate setting of crystal chandeliers, gilded plasterwork and trellises, and elegantly draped private alcoves backed by gilt-framed mirrors. Cuisine is continental. Dinner only; most entrees $22.75 to $29.95.

Bally's Steakhouse exudes an aura of substantial comfort. Gleaming brass chandeliers are suspended from a gorgeous oak-and-mahogany ceiling, and diners are ensconced in leopard-skin booths and black leather armchairs. A traditional steak and seafood menu is complemented by an extensive wine list. Dinner only; entrees $17.50 to $28.50.

Al Dente has an expanse of marble flooring and art-deco maple and black lacquer columns where planters of greenery create intimate dining areas. Its menu offers delicious pastas, thin-crust pizzas with California-style toppings, and other Italian entrees. Dinner only; entrees $14.75 to $26.95 (most pastas under $15, pizzas $8.75 to $12).

Las Olas is a charming candlelit Mexican eatery fronted by a lounge with a tiered fountain. The dining area, its walls hung with rugs and embroideries, displays Mexican statuary and pottery in wall niches. Dinner entrees $8.50 to $17.95. Las Olas also serves Mexican and American breakfasts and lunches.

There's also a bright and cheerful 24-hour coffee shop, and food outlets in the shopping mall include a branch of New York's Stage Deli.

The mermaid-themed Bubbles Bar serves the casino. In addition, On the Rocks, a poolside bar with a lovely terrace cooled by ceiling fans, specializes in tropical drinks and wines by the glass. And the Terrace Café, a seasonal poolside eatery, offers light fare during the day. See also "Buffets and Sunday Brunches" in chapter 6.

Services: 24-hour room service, guest-services desk, shoeshine, foreign-currency exchange.

Facilities: Casino, tour and show desks, car-rental desk, small video-game arcade, shopping arcade (see chapter 9), wedding chapel, men's and women's hair salons, state-of-the-art health spa and fitness center, eight night-lit tennis courts and pro shop (lessons available), two basketball courts. A gorgeous palm-fringed sundeck surrounds an Olympic-size swimming pool—one of the most beautiful in Las Vegas. There's a whirlpool, and guests can rent private cabanas with stocked refrigerators, TVs, ceiling fans, rafts, and private phones for $60 to $85 a day.

✪ Caesars Palace

3570 Las Vegas Blvd. S., just north of Flamingo Rd., Las Vegas, NV 89109. ☎ **800/634-6661** or 702/731-7110. Fax 702/731-6636. 1,305 rms, 190 suites. A/C TV TEL. $115–$190 double, $450–$7,500 suite. Extra person $20. Children under 12 stay free in parents' room. AE, CD, DC, DISC, MC, V. Free parking (self and valet).

Designed to reflect the decadent grandeur of ancient Rome, Caesars has been a major player on the Strip since it opened in 1966. This world-class resort is a Roman pleasure palace where guests are greeted by gladiators and centurions, classical Roman statuary adorns public areas, and cocktail waitresses are costumed as goddesses. Its several entrances are graced by 18 spectacular fountains (Evel Knievel once attempted to jump over them on a motorcycle), Roman temples, heroic arches, golden charioteers, and elegant driveways lined by 50-foot Italian cypresses. Caesars pioneered the "people mover" concept, using moving walkways to convey visitors from the Strip into the hotel. Today there are four of these conveyances, leading to the casino, the hotel, the OMNIMAX™ Theatre, and The Forum Shops—a Rodeo Drive–style shopping complex.

Accommodations occupy three towers, and there are too many decorator schemes to describe here. You'll likely enjoy a lavish bath with marble floor, European fixtures, and oversized marble tubs (about half are Jacuzzis). Art in the rooms keeps to the Greco-Roman theme (some have classical sculptures in niches), furnishings tend to neoclassic styles; Roman columns, pilasters, and pediments are common. Many rooms have four-poster beds with mirrored ceilings, and all are equipped with three phones (bedside, bath, and desk) and cable TVs with HBO, a gaming instruction channel (with cameo appearances by hotel headliners like Natalie Cole and Johnny Mathis), and in-house information stations. All rooms have private safes.

At press time, Caesars was in the midst of a $900-million renovation and expansion, so some of what you read here will have changed. With its typical panache, this classy resort turned ongoing construction work in its casino into a fun event with superb circus acts performed by clowns and acrobats (some of them former Cirque du Soleil performers) at frequent intervals.

In the works are 2,150 new guest rooms, an additional 50,000 square feet of casino space, a new Circus Maximus (with an entrance on the Strip) featuring themed

Accommodations on the Strip & Paradise Rd.

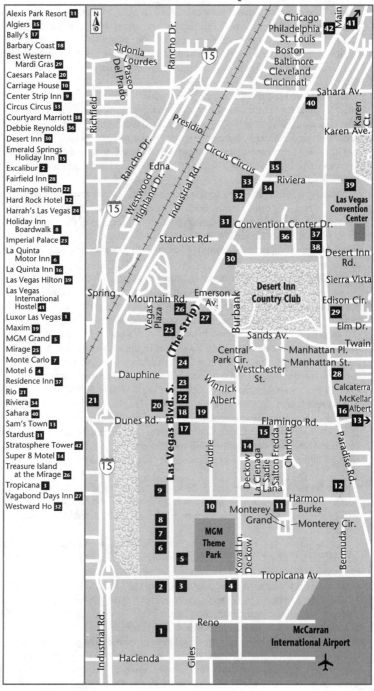

Alexis Park Resort 11
Algiers 35
Bally's 17
Barbary Coast 18
Best Western
  Mardi Gras 29
Caesars Palace 20
Carriage House 10
Center Strip Inn 9
Circus Circus 33
Courtyard Marriott 38
Debbie Reynolds 36
Desert Inn 30
Emerald Springs
  Holiday Inn 15
Excalibur 2
Fairfield Inn 28
Flamingo Hilton 22
Hard Rock Hotel 12
Harrah's Las Vegas 24
Holiday Inn
  Boardwalk 8
Imperial Palace 23
La Quinta
  Motor Inn 6
La Quinta Inn 16
Las Vegas Hilton 39
Las Vegas
  International
  Hostel 41
Luxor Las Vegas 1
Maxim 19
MGM Grand 5
Mirage 25
Monte Carlo 7
Motel 6 4
Residence Inn 37
Rio 21
Riviera 34
Sahara 40
Sam's Town 13
Stardust 31
Stratosphere Tower 42
Super 8 Motel 14
Treasure Island
  at the Mirage 26
Tropicana 3
Vagabond Days Inn 27
Westward Ho 32

47

1-0405

entertainment, a menagerie of performing wild animals, an outdoor arena, and a covered "Roman hill" covered with more restaurants and retail spaces. Yet another Strip entrance will go into a completely remodeled pool area with an 8-story waterfall, a 21,400-square-foot spa/health club, and 113,000 square feet of meeting space. In addition, The Forum Shops will be adding 250,000 square feet of additional retail space.

Dining/Entertainment: Caesars has a well-deserved reputation for superior in-house restaurants. There are nine in the hotel, plus dining facilities in The Forum shopping area. All are highly recommended. Well worth checking out are the $29.95 prix-fixe early-bird menus featured at several major restaurants here.

The hotel's premier restaurant, the exquisite **Palace Court,** and **Bacchanal,** which re-creates a multicourse Roman feast, are both described in chapter 6 along with the hotel's food court and buffets.

Neros, specializing in prime aged steaks and fresh seafood at dinner, has an extensive wine list. It's lunch menu features international contemporary fare. The restaurant's octagonal design is a contemporary interpretation of the Spanish Madejar style, with an eight-pointed star radiating from the ceiling and tiered copper walls forming a gleaming inverse pyramid. Entrees $8 to $15 at lunch, $21.50 to $44.50 at dinner.

Just off the casino is the elegant Japanese restaurant, **Ah'So,** fronted by an oak-floored terrace lit by paper lanterns. Inside, seating areas under pine and cherry trees are divided by arched bridges that span flower-bordered streams, and a waterfall cascades over faux lava rock. Fixed-price multicourse dinners are $54.50 per person.

The pretty crystal-chandeliered **Primavera,** with a wall of Palladian windows overlooking the pool, seats diners amid ficus trees in big terra-cotta pots for homemade pasta and specialties from all regions of Italy. Alfresco terrace seating under white canvas umbrellas is especially lovely at night when poolside trees are lit by tiny lights. Open for all meals. Lunch entrees $9.95 to $18.95, dinner $15.95 to $32.95.

Empress Court, fronted by a two-story double-balustraded staircase encircling a koi pond, is aquatically themed from its coral reef aquarium to its etched-glass fish-motif room dividers. Chinese dulcimer music enhances the ambience. The menu offers first-rate Cantonese cuisine and specializes in fresh seafood. Dinner only; entrees $8.50 to $60 (many selections are under $20); multicourse fixed-price dinners $40 to $55 per person.

Cafe Roma, Caesars' comfortable 24-hour casual-dining venue, offers international buffets and a menu that runs the gamut from filet mignon to chicken quesadillas, as well as burgers, salads, and sandwiches. A Chinese menu is available from 5pm to 1:15am.

Restaurants in The Forum Shops arcade include **Spago** (Wolfgang Puck's famed establishment), **The Palm, Planet Hollywood,** and the **Stage Deli**—all discussed in chapter 6.

There are several casino lounges, among them the Olympic Lounge and La Piazza Lounge offering nightly live entertainment in the Olympic Casino. The **Palace Court Terrace** (an ultra-elegant, romantic piano bar) is one of my favorite Las Vegas nightspots. See also **Cleopatra's Barge** (a nightclub).

Services: 24-hour room service, shoeshine, complimentary gaming lessons.

Facilities: Three casinos, tennis courts/pro shop, two extensive shopping arcades (see chapter 9), state-of-the-art video arcade, American Express office, full-service unisex salon, tour and show desks, car-rental desk.

Caesars' swimming pool area, which was already magnificent, is being completely remodeled at this time in an elaborate classical Roman theme, with pediments, columns, and temple-like structures. The Roman Tower health spa offers extensive workout equipment as well as a steam room, sauna, whirlpool, tanning beds, massage, aromatherapy, facials, and a sun deck.

✪ Desert Inn Country Club Resort & Casino

3145 Las Vegas Blvd. S., between Desert Inn Rd. and Sands Ave., Las Vegas, NV 89109. ☎ **800/634-6906** or 702/733-4444. Fax 702/733-4744. 566 rms, 136 suites/minisuites. A/C TV TEL. $175–$185 single or double, $215–$225 minisuite, $350–$555 suite. Extra person $35. Children under 12 stay free in parents' room. AE, CB, DC, DISC, JCB, MC, V. Free parking (self and valet).

Since 1995 both Caesars and the Desert Inn have been under the auspices of ITT, and like Caesars, the DI is currently undergoing a massive renovation. Always the most upscale of Las Vegas hotels, it's now aiming at five-star status. In the works are a 12,000-square foot ballroom; upgraded health spa, rooms, restaurants, and entertainment lounge; an expanded casino; a new accommodations tower; and a stunning new 10-story skylit atrium entrance. Much was in flux at press time, and not many details were available, so some of the copy below might be out of date by the time you read this. I can promise that everything will be first class and fabulous.

Many people consider the Desert Inn the most prestigious address on the Strip, among them serious golfers. *Golf Digest* calls the Desert Inn's verdant, palm-studded 18-hole facility one of America's top resort courses (more about this in chapter 7). Even if it had no casino or golf course, the Desert Inn could function as a luxury spa retreat, offering water-therapy programs (there are hot, warm, and cool tubs), private whirlpools with recliner seats, tanning beds, steam rooms, and sauna, and all the treatments one would expect in a world-class spa. It's not all pampering. The cardiovascular fitness center has a range of machines, free weights, a small pool and sun deck, aerobics classes, and a jogging parcourse with exercise stations. You can relax, post-workout, in a TV lounge. The hotel has a large swimming pool in a garden setting with adjoining whirlpool, poolside snack/cocktail bar, and pool sundries shop. And there are five tournament-class tennis courts—all lit for night play; expert instruction and practice ball machines are available.

Country-club elegance is the keynote here: The emphasis is on extensive leisure facilities, fine restaurants, and first-rate service; when you reserve a room here, you can arrange restaurant reservations and show tickets anywhere in town, car rentals, golf times, and more in the same phone call. The property occupies 200 exquisitely landscaped acres of rock gardens, flower beds, duck ponds, waterfalls, and tree-shaded lawns. Strolling the grounds is almost like visiting a botanical garden or arboretum. The hotel opened in 1950, with Edgar and Charlie McCarthy premiering in the showroom. Howard Hughes (and later his estate) owned the hotel from 1967 to 1988, and he lived here in the late 1960s. It is my favorite Las Vegas hotel.

Stunning rooms and suites—named for famous golf courses and tennis stadiums—offer substantial comfort. Lack of information about the current renovation makes it impossible for me to describe rooms in detail. Many have spacious marble baths with Jacuzzi tubs and large dressing rooms. The Wimbledon Building's duplex suites—the choice of headliners, high rollers, and other well-heeled folks—have private pools or 4,000-square-foot penthouses. And a luxurious new 98-suite tower houses 12 poolside lanai suites. All Desert Inn rooms offer superior bath toiletries, and you'll find an iron and full-sized ironing board in the closet. Cable TVs feature pay-movie options as well as gaming instruction and hotel-information channels.

Dining/Entertainment: See chapter 6 for details on the opulent **Monte Carlo Room.**

Portofino, previously a Northern Italian restaurant, is being remodeled. It will feature upscale Mediterranean cuisine with many dinners priced for two.

At **Ho Wan,** an upscale Cantonese/Szechuan restaurant, a traditional Chinese interior is currently undergoing total renovation to a more contemporary Asian decor, and a new menu is also in the works.

Terrace Pointe, a delightful plant-filled 24-hour coffee shop with a windowed wall overlooking the pool, offers an American/continental à la carte menu along with Asian specialties and buffet breakfasts and lunches. An omelet station is featured every morning, and, at lunch, there's a carving station.

A posh new steakhouse is also in the works. The newly remodeled Starlight Theatre, a plush casino lounge, features name entertainment at night; it's a romatic setting for cocktails and dancing, one of two casino bars.

Services: 24-hour room service, concierge, shoeshine.

Facilities: Golf course, five tennis courts, full-service spa and health club, swimming pool (some suites have private swimming pools).

Other facilities include a casino, tour and show desks, car-rental desk, beauty salon/barbershop, business center, shops, including golf and tennis pro shops.

EXPENSIVE

Flamingo Hilton

3555 Las Vegas Blvd. S., between Sands Ave. and Flamingo Rd., Las Vegas, NV 89109. ☎ **800/ 732-2111** or 702/733-3111. Fax 702/733-3353. 3,642 rms, 176 suites, 201 time-share units. A/C TV TEL. $69–$205 single or double, $250–$580 suite. Extra person $16. Children 18 and under stay free in parents' room. Inquire about packages and time-share suites. AE, CB, DC, DISC, JCB, MC, V. Free parking (self and valet).

The Flamingo has changed a great deal since Bugsy Siegel opened his 105-room oasis "in the middle of nowhere" in 1946. It was so luxurious for its time that even the janitors wore tuxedos. Jimmy Durante was the opening headliner, and the wealthy and famous flocked to the tropical paradise of swaying palms, lagoons, and waterfalls. While the Flamingo is a senior citizen on the Strip with a colorful history, a fresh, new look—enhanced by a recent $130-million renovation and expansion—has made Siegel's "real class joint" better than ever.

For those planning some leisure time outside the casino, the Flamingo's exceptional pool area, spa, and tennis courts are a big draw.

Rooms—occupying six towers—are variously decorated. Some are done up in soft blues and peach for a resort look enhanced by pretty fabrics, light painted-wood furnishings, and lovely watercolors of tropical scenes. Others utilize soft earth tones, forest green, or coral. All accommodations offer in-room safes; TVs have in-house information and gaming-instruction stations, a keno channel, video checkout, message retrieval, and account review.

Dining/Entertainment: The Old West-themed **Beef Baron,** heralded by golden steer heads and a mural of a cattle roundup, bills itself as "a steakhouse forged in the spirit of our first great cattle ranchers." Dinner only; entrees $14.25 to $27.

Fronted by a tiered terra-cotta fountain, **Alta Villa** is designed to suggest an Italian village, with a vaulted ceiling, a trellised grape arbor under a painted sky, and grapevine-motif carpeting. A pretty ceramic-tiled exhibition kitchen is a focal point. A traditional Italian menu is featured. Dinner only; entrees $11.50 to $20 (pastas and pizzas $5.50 to $11).

Peking Market's interior simulates an open marketplace in a bustling Chinese city. A central wood-burning brick oven casts a warm glow. Dinner only; entrees mostly $11 to $17.50. A full egg roll to fortune cookie dinner is $15.75 per person.

The candlelit **Flamingo Room**—adorned with murals of flamingos, flamingo sculptures, and glass etched with flamingos—offers piano-bar music at dinner. One of the draws here is an extensive salad bar supplemented by smoked whitefish and salmon, crab and shrimp salads, and much more ($9.95 alone, $4.25 with an entree). The menu highlights steak and seafood dishes; full American breakfasts are also served here. Dinner entrees $18.50 to $22.50.

Hamada of Japan is a softly lit, teak-beamed restaurant centered by a small rock garden. Some of the seating is at teppanyaki grill tables, and there's also a sushi bar. Come by for a Japanese breakfast of fish, raw egg, sticky beans, rice, soup, pickles, vegetables, and seaweed ($12, including tax and tip). Open for all meals; lunch entrees $7.50 to $19.50, dinner entrees $7.50 to $26.50 (full teppanyaki dinners $13.95 to $42).

Lindy's Deli, a pleasant and spacious 24-hour coffee shop, offers appetizing smoked fish platters (salmon, whitefish, sturgeon) with bagels and cream cheese, corned beef and pastrami sandwiches, matzo ball soup, and other traditional Jewish deli items in addition to typical Las Vegas coffee-shop fare.

Bugsy's Deli, highlighting sandwiches on fresh-baked breads, is a casual self-service eatery just off the casino. The **Pool Grille** serves up light fare, and a **snack bar** serves the race and sports book area. Bugsy's Bar, festooned with orange and pink neon flamingo feathers, occupies a central position in the casino. And the **Rainbow Bar,** off the casino, has a wall of windows overlooking palm trees and waterfalls. The Flamingo's **Paradise Garden Buffet** is described in chapter 6.

Services: 24-hour room service, guest services desk, translation services (interpreters are available for more than 35 languages; gaming guides are available in six languages).

Facilities: Casino, car-rental desk, tour and show desks, full-service beauty salon/barber shop, wedding chapel, four night-lit championship tennis courts with pro shop and practice alley (tennis clinics and lessons are available), shopping arcade (see chapter 9 for details). Five gorgeous swimming pools—along with two Jacuzzis, water slides, and a kiddie pool—are located in a 15-acre Caribbean landscape amid lagoons, meandering streams, fountains, waterfalls, a rose garden, and islands of live flamingos and African penguins. Ponds are filled with ducks, swans, and koi, and a grove of 2,000 palms graces an expanse of lawn. A health club offers a variety of Universal machines, treadmills, stair machines, free weights, sauna, steam, a TV lounge, and hot and cold whirlpools. Exercise tapes are available, and spa services include massage, soap rub, salt glow, tanning beds, and oxygen pep-up.

✪ MGM Grand Hotel/Casino

3799 Las Vegas Blvd. S., at Tropicana Ave., Las Vegas, NV 89109. ☎ **800/929-1111** or 702/891-7777. Fax 702/891-1112. 4,254 rms, 751 suites. A/C TV TEL. $69–$119 single or double, concierge floor $79–$129 single or double with breakfast, $99–$2,500 suite. Extra person $10. Children under 12 stay free in parents' room. AE, DC, DISC, MC, V. Free parking (self and valet).

Sprawling over 112 acres, Kirk Kerkorian's billion-dollar *Wizard of Oz*–themed megaresort is the world's largest—an immense emerald-green monolith fronted by a towering MGM lion. Visitors enter into a vast white-marble-floored lobby (the most impressive in town), where the registration desk is backed by the world's largest video wall comprised of eighty 42-inch TV monitors apprising registering guests of hotel happenings. The casino—which includes a seven-story replica of Emerald City, with 75-foot green crystal spires—is the size of four football fields.

And the hotel's "backyard" is a 33-acre theme park (see chapter 7). A monorail connects this property with Bally's (see details in that hotel's listing above), and pedestrian skywalks link it with the Tropicana, Luxor, and Excalibur; it will also join up with the soon-to-open New York, New York.

Although the current incarnation of the MGM Grand is only a few years old, the resort has already embarked on a $250-million renovation, which will transform the restaurant arcade into a "City of Entertainment" promenade marked by Hollywood landmarks. A new "liquid gold" six-story lion flanked by 80-foot entertainment walls (featuring multimedia and light shows) will be erected over the Tropicana Avenue Strip entrance, the main entranceway will be upgraded, and existing walkways across the Strip and Tropicana Avenue will be extended to enter the property at a new mezzanine level. The casino's current Emerald City attraction will be replaced by a new casino area, with its own themed restaurants and nightclub. Additional plans call for a 300,000-square-foot convention center and an entertainment/retail complex of equal size, the latter with plenty of new nightclub entertainment and restaurants. Finally, the theme park is due for some exciting new rides.

Since some visitors have found the MGM's massive interior overwhelming, one of the renovation's aims is to create more intimate enclaves. Many of these changes will already be in place as you read this.

Rooms in the Grand's quartet of 30-story towers are decorated in four distinct motifs. Most glamorous are the Hollywood rooms furnished in two-tone wood pieces (bird's-eye maple on cherry), with gold-flecked walls (hung with gilt-framed prints of Humphrey Bogart, Marilyn Monroe, and Vivien Leigh as Scarlett), gilded moldings, and beds backed by mirrors. Oz-themed rooms have emerald-green rugs and upholstery, silver and gold star-motif wallpaper, bright poppy-print bedspreads, and tassled green drapes; walls are hung with paintings of Dorothy and friends. In the Casablanca rooms—decorated in earth tones with shimmery fabrics and pecan/walnut furnishings and moldings—artworks depict Moroccan scenes such as an Arab marketplace. And the cheerful Old South rooms feature 18th-century-style furnishings and faux-silk beige damask walls hung with paintings of southern belles and scenes from *Gone with the Wind*. All rooms offer gorgeous marble baths.

Dining/Entertainment: MGM houses the most prestigious assemblage of dining rooms of any hotel in town. Four cutting-edge stars in the Las Vegas culinary galaxy—the **Wolfgang Puck Café,** Emiril Lagasse's **New Orleans Fish House, Gatsby's,** and Mark Miller's **Coyote Café**—along with buffet offerings, are described in chapter 6. The **Oz Buffet** is described in chapter 6. In addition, the following dining facilities comprise a restaurant row between the casino and the theme park.

Heralding the restaurant area's new Hollywood theme is the plush and luxurious **Brown Derby,** modeled after the legendary Los Angeles celebrity haunt where Louella Parsons and Hedda Hopper held court in the 1940s. Like the original, its walls are lined with caricatures of celebrities (a caricaturist on the premises draws customers for a fee), and signature dishes on its largely steak/chops/seafood menu include Cobb salad and grapefruit cake. A handsome mahogany-paneled bar adjoins. Lunch entrees $9 to $15, dinner $15.50 to $39.75 (with a few exceptions, such as a 42-ounce porterhouse steak for $96.50!).

Another new facility here consists of two distinct dining areas, **La Scala** and **Tre Visi.** Both serve regional Italian fare. The very elegant La Scala (named for the famed Milan opera house), has walls hung with opera posters and antique musical instruments. It's open for dinner only. Fronted by an imposing Doric colonnade suggestive of a Roman ruin—with columned archways inside framing scenes of ancient Rome—the more casual Tre Visi serves lunch and dinner. Entrees at La Scala mostly $28 to $38. Tre Visi lunch entrees $7.50 to $15, dinner $9 to $18.

Dragon Court is an elegant restaurant with textured gold wall coverings and purple and gold fleur-de-lis pattern carpeting. Eclectic Chinese fare is featured. Dinner only; entrees $7.50 to $24 (many under $15).

The inviting circus-themed One-Liners Food Court—with seating under an orange-and-yellow tent top—houses McDonald's, Hamada's Orient Express, Mamma Ilardo's Pizzeria, Nathan's (hot dogs and fries), and a Häagen-Dazs ice cream outlet that also features espresso and cappuccino. It is conveniently near the video-game arcade/carnival midway.

The Stage Deli Express, a cafeteria-style offshoot of the New York original, serves up traditional deli sandwiches; seating overlooks race and sports book action. **Benninger's,** off the casino, provides gourmet coffees and scrumptious fresh-baked pastries (great bear claws here). In addition, there are many restaurants and fast-food places in the theme park.

The **Center Stage** and **Betty Boop** lounges offer entertainment nightly. The circular Flying Monkey Bar and the **Santa Fe Lounge** offer live music. A talking robotic horse and jockey spout sports data at the Turf Club Lounge in the race and sports book area.

Services: 24-hour room service, foreign-currency exchange, guest-relations desk, shoeshine (in men's rooms).

Facilities: World's largest casino; MGM Grand Adventures Theme Park; full-service health spa and health club; full-service unisex hair/beauty salon; four night-lit tennis courts with pro shop (lessons available); huge, beach-entry swimming pool with waterfall; a vast sundeck area with a Jacuzzi, pool bar, and cabanas equipped with cushioned chairs and towels that rent for $20 per day; a 30,000-square-foot video arcade (including virtual-reality games); carnival midway with 33 games of skill; business center; florist; shopping arcade; two wedding chapels (in the theme park); show/sports event ticket desks; car-rental desk; sightseeing/tour desks; America West airline desk.

The **MGM Grand Youth Center,** a first-rate facility for children ages 3 to 16, has separate areas for different age groups. The center has a playhouse and tumbling mats for toddlers, a game room, extensive arts and crafts equipment, video games, a dining area, and a large-screen TV/VCR for children's movies. Accompanied by professional counselors, youngsters can visit the theme park or the swimming pool, take excursions to nearby attractions, have meals, and participate in all sorts of entertainment and activities (☎ 702/891-3200 for details and prices).

✪ Mirage

3400 Las Vegas Blvd. S., between Flamingo Rd. and Sands Ave., Las Vegas, NV 89109. ☎ **800/627-6667** or 702/791-7111. Fax 702/791-7446. 3,044 rms, 279 suites. A/C TV TEL. Single or double $79–$399 Sun–Thurs, $159–$399 Fri–Sat and holidays; $250–$3,000 suite. Extra person $30. AE, CB, DC, DISC, MC, V. Free parking (self and valet).

Steve Wynn's gleaming white and gold Mirage redefines the word "spectacular" in a town where spectacular is a way of life. Occupying 102 acres, it's fronted by more than a city block of cascading waterfalls and tropical foliage centering on a very active "volcano," which, after dark, erupts every 15 minutes, spewing fire 100 feet above the lagoons below. Step inside the hotel and you're in a verdant rain forest—a 90-foot domed atrium where paths meander through palms, banana trees, waterfalls, and serene pools. And behind the front desk is a 53-foot, 20,000-gallon simulated coral reef aquarium stocked with more than 1,000 colorful tropical fish, including six sharks.

In addition, the hotel has a habitat for rare white tigers belonging to performers Siegfried & Roy, and another for seven Atlantic bottle-nose dolphins (the site of fascinating educational tours). The Mirage corporation has been active in protesting fishing practices harmful to dolphins and serves only "dolphin-safe" tuna in its restaurants. Nor are furs sold in Mirage boutiques.

Mirage rooms, among the most aesthetically tasteful in town, are decorated in subtle earth tones with upscale furnishings and lovely prints (botanicals and others) gracing the walls. Beds have shuttered backboards framed by curtains; dressing areas offer lighted cosmetic mirrors; and luxurious marble baths are equipped with hair dryers. Oak armoires house 25-inch TVs, and phones are equipped with fax and computer jacks. Further up the price scale are super-deluxe rooms with whirlpool tubs.

Dining/Entertainment: The **Noodle Kitchen,** a very authentic Asian restaurant, and the **Mirage Buffet** are detailed in chapter 6.

Kokomo's, situated in the tropical rain forest atrium, offers seating under bamboo-thatched roofing and trellised bougainvillea vines. Some tables overlook lagoons and waterfalls. The menu highlights steaks, chops, prime rib, and seafood. All meals are served; lunch entrees $7.50 to $22.50, dinner $17 to $42.

Mikado, under a starlit sky, offers diners a candlelit setting with a sunken tropical rock garden, lotus pond, and sheltering pines. Teppanyaki cooking is featured along with à la carte Japanese specialties and a sushi bar. Dinner only; entrees mostly $16 to $30.

At **Moongate,** also under the stars, seating is in an open courtyard defined by classical Chinese architectural facades and tiled roof-lines. White doves perch on cherry tree branches, and intricately hand-carved walls frame a moongate tableau. The menu offers Cantonese and Szechuan specialties. Dinner only; entrees $16 to $42.

A cobblestone passage evoking a European village street leads to **Restaurant Riva,** a very pretty dining room. Candlelit at night, its walls are hung with gilt-framed still-life paintings and its windows with swagged draperies. Sophisticated northern Italian fare is served. Dinner only; entrees $14 to $32.

Off the same quaint street is the **Bistro,** a charming belle époque setting with rich mahogany paneling, Toulouse-Lautrec–style murals, and pink-cloth-covered tables lit by shaded brass oil lamps. Fare is French/continental, dinner only; entrees mostly $22.50 to $37.50.

A branch of **California Pizza Kitchen,** under a thatch-roofed dome, is in the center of the casino overlooking the race and sports book. A bank of video monitors lets you follow the action while dining on oak-fired pizzas with toppings ranging from duck sausage to goat cheese. Calzones, salads, and pasta dishes here, too. All entrees under $11.

The Caribe Café, a festive 24-hour coffee shop, adheres to the tropical theme. It's designed to suggest an open-air Caribbean village. Additional food and beverage facilities include an ice-cream parlor; the Paradise Café, an alfresco terrace with umbrella tables overlooking the pool (drinks and light fare are served); the Lagoon Saloon in the rain forest, specializing in tropical drinks and offering live music for dancing until 1am Sunday to Wednesday; the Baccarat Bar, where a pianist entertains nightly (jackets required for men); the poolside Dolphin Bar, and the Sports Bar in the casino.

Services: 24-hour room service, overnight shoeshine on request, morning newspaper delivery.

Facilities: Casino, car-rental desk, shops (*Siegfried & Roy* and *Cirque du Soleil* merchandise and others), unisex hairdresser and salon offering all beauty services, state-of-the-art video-game arcade, business-services center. A free tram travels between the Mirage and Treasure Island almost around the clock.

Supercalafragilisticexpialadocious!
　　　　　—Governor Bob Miller's reaction upon first visiting the Mirage

The Mirage health club is the most extensive hotel facility in town, offering a large selection of machines, Gravitron, free weights, sauna, steam, whirlpool, and massage.

Waterfalls cascade into the hotel's immense swimming pool (it has a quarter-mile shoreline) in a lush tropical setting where lagoons link palm-lined islands. Kids will enjoy the big pool slides. Free swimming lessons and water aerobics classes take place daily. Private poolside cabanas (equipped with phones, TVs, free snacks and soft drinks, refrigerators, misting systems, rafts, and radios) can be rented for $85 a day.

Monte Carlo Resort & Casino

3770 Las Vegas Blvd. S., between Flamingo Rd. and Tropicana Ave., Las Vegas, NV 89109. ☎ **800/311-8999** or 702/730-7777. Fax 702/730-7250. 2,759 rms, 255 suites. A/C TV TEL. Single or double $69–$199 Sun–Thurs, $99–$269 Fri–Sat. Suites $139–$339. Extra person $10. Children under 13 stay free in parents' room. AE, CB, DC, DISC, MC, V. Free parking (self and valet).

The newest resort on the Strip, the massive Monte Carlo is the world's seventh-largest hotel. It's fronted by Corinthian colonnades, triumphal arches, splashing fountains, and allegorical statuary, with an entranceway opening not on a bustling casino but a splendiferous marble-floored, crystal-chandeliered lobby evocative of a European grand hotel. Palladian windows behind the registration desk overlook a salient feature: the hotel's 20,000-acre pool area, a lushly landscaped mini–water park with a 4,800-foot wave pool, a surf pond, waterfalls, and a "river" for tubing. Also notable is the Monte Carlo's spa, offering extensive workout facilities, hot and cool whirlpools, steam and sauna, and numerous services (massage, facials, sea-salt scrubs, seaweed wraps, and more). Workout clothing and toiletries are provided.

Spacious rooms—with big marble baths—exude a warmly traditional European feel. Striped tan wallpapers with fleur-de-lis friezes create a neutral backdrop for rich cherrywood furnishings and vivid floral-print fabrics and carpeting. Cable TVs are equipped with hotel-information channels, keno, and pay-movie options. A concierge level is currently in the works on the 32nd floor.

Dining/Entertainment: The Monte Carlo's **Pub & Brewery, Dragon Noodle Company,** and buffet room are described in chapter 6.

A wall of stained-glass windows, beveled mirrors, rich mahogany paneling, plush leather booths, and elegantly appointed tables lit by shaded candle lamps set an opulent tone at **Blackstone's Steak House.** Dinner only; entrees such as mesquite-grilled steaks, seafood, prime rib, and roast duck Grand Marnier are $14.95 to $23.95.

At the **Market City Caffe,** a tempting antipasto bar (with dozens of items ranging from roasted potato salad to mussels marinara, a good deal at $7.95, $4.95 with an entree), a display kitchen housing an oak-burning pizza oven, and wooden bins overflowing with eggplants, tomatoes, lemons, and potatoes create a warmly colorful interior. Lunch and dinner daily; entrees $6.95 to $12.95.

The plant-filled, sky-ceilinged 24-hour café has a whimsical magic/fantasy theme; delightful murals depict clowns, court jesters, and harlequins. Additional venues include a food court (with branches of Nathan's, McDonald's, Sbarro, Häagen-Dazs, and a first-rate bagel bakery), a pool-area snack bar, and several lounges, most notably the plush Houdini's, it's magic theme honoring illusionist Lance Burton, who headlines at the hotel's showroom.

Services: 24-hour room service, foreign currency exchange, shoeshine, limo rental.

Facilities: Casino, car-rental desk, four tennis courts, sightseeing/tour/show desk, barber/beauty salon, vast swimming pool, kiddie pool, whirlpool, water attractions (see above), wedding chapel, full business center, large video-game arcade, large shopping arcade.

✪ Rio Hotel & Casino

3700 W. Flamingo Rd., at I-15, Las Vegas, NV 89103. ☎ **800/752-9746** or 702/252-7777. Fax 702/252-0080. 1,555 suites. A/C TV TEL. Single or double $85 Sun–Thurs, $103–$150 Fri–Sat and holidays. Extra person $15. Children under 12 stay free in parents' room. Inquire about golf packages. AE, CB, DC, MC, V. Free parking (self and valet).

The Rio's gorgeous palm-fringed facade heralds a luxurious tropical resort—an ongoing "carnivale" enhanced by Brazilian music emanating from the Ipanema Bar. Casino carpeting is strewn with Rio resort motifs—confetti, maracas, streamers, and seashells—and there's a sandy "beach" out back. You won't miss the Strip at this lively casino hotel, and, in any case, it's just a few minutes away.

The Rio's spacious suites (each one is at least 600 square feet) are, unequivocally, the most stunning accommodations in town. The original suites are decorated in resort hues (peach, mauve, turquoise, coral) with splash-of-color accents; they feature bamboo furnishings, half-canopy beds, paintings of parrots and toucans, and tropical-motif floral prints. Tower suites—done up in teal and burgundy, with handsome teak furnishings and lovely chintz fabrics—are equally appealing. Each suite has a large dressing room, a stunning bath (with full-length mirror and cosmetic lighting), big closets, a wraparound sofa, and an upholstered chaise longue. Picture windows provide panoramic views of the Strip. As for in-room amenities, you'll find a safe, marble-topped refrigerator, and coffeemaker. Some suites are equipped with two phones.

At press time, a new 41-story tower, with 1,025 additional suites, is under construction. Also in the works: expanded gaming areas (500 slots, 27 table games), an expanded pool and beach area, and 60,000 square feet of new retail and entertainment space. The Rio has also purchased 22 adjacent acres on which it plans to erect another hotel and casino in the future.

Dining/Entertainment: Restaurants here are notably excellent. **Fiore** (the Rio's premier restaurant), the **All American Bar & Grille,** and the hotel's first-rate buffet are all described in chapter 6.

In the elegant **Antonio's,** an Italian restaurant, the centerpiece of the room is a marble-columned rotunda in which a crystal chandelier is suspended from a recessed Mediterranean-sky ceiling. Other focal points are an exhibition kitchen and a magnificent marble display table brimming with tempting antipasto selections. Dinner only; most entrees $17.95 to $24.95 (less for pasta).

Buzio's Seafood Restaurant overlooks a palm-fringed pool. Massive alabaster chandeliers and flowering plants are suspended from a lofty canvas-tent ceiling, and a marble counter faces an exhibition kitchen. Lunch and dinner daily; entrees mostly $8.95 to $14.95 at lunch, $11.95 to $21.95 at dinner (lobster dishes are higher).

Fun Fact

In Martin Scorsese's movie *Casino*, starring Robert De Niro, Joe Pesci, and Sharon Stone, the Riviera stood in for the fictional Tangiers.

👫 Family-Friendly Hotels

Circus Circus *(see p. 71).*   Centrally located on the Strip, this is my first choice if you're traveling with the kids. The hotel's mezzanine level offers ongoing circus acts daily from 11am to midnight, dozens of carnival games, and an arcade with more than 300 video and pinball games. And behind the hotel is a full amusement park.

Excalibur *(see p. 62).*   Also owned by Circus Circus, Excalibur features a whole floor of midway games, a large video-game arcade, crafts demonstrations, free shows for kids (puppets, jugglers, magicians), and thrill cinemas. It has child-oriented eateries and shows (details in chapter 10).

Luxor Las Vegas *(see p. 66).*   Another Circus Circus property. Kids will enjoy VirtuaLand—an 18,000-square-foot video-game arcade that showcases Sega's latest game technologies. Another big attraction here is the "Secrets of the Luxor Pyramid"—a high-tech adventure/thrill ride utilizing motion simulators and IMAX™ film.

The MGM Grand Hotel, Casino & Theme Park *(see p. 51).*   This *Wizard of Oz*–themed resort is backed by a 33-acre theme park and houses a state-of-the-art video-game arcade and carnival midway. A unique offering here is a youth center for hotel guests ages 3 to 16, with separate sections for different age groups. Its facilities range from a playhouse and tumbling mats for toddlers to extensive arts and crafts equipment for the older kids.

The **Beach Café,** also overlooking the pool and sandy beach, is the Rio's tropically festive 24-hour facility. Besides regular coffee-shop fare, it features Mexican, Italian, and Polynesian/Chinese specialties. Delicious fresh-baked desserts are a plus.

Toscano's Deli, off the casino, not only looks like a New York delicatessen but serves up a creditable pastrami or corned beef on rye. It also features pizza, pastas, and a wide array of first-rate fresh-baked breads, cakes, and pastries.

The **Ipanema Piano Bar** features live music Sunday through Friday. **Mambo's Entertainment Lounge** in the casino has dancing from 9pm to 3am (except Sunday). Another casino bar is under a fantasy coral reef with fish swimming overhead. Drinks, tropical and otherwise, are available poolside from the open-air Coco-Bana or a service window off Buzio's.

Services: 24-hour room service, guest-services desk, foreign-currency exchange, shoeshine, complimentary shuttle bus to/from the MGM and the Forum Mall.

Facilities: Casino, tour and show desks, unisex hair salon (all beauty services, including massage and facials), small video-game arcade, fitness room (stair machine, rowing machine, Lifecycle, four-station exercise machine), shops (gifts, clothing for the entire family, logo merchandise). The Rio has two swimming pools, one shaped like an angelfish, the other a nautilus shell with a sand bottom (extending to a beach) and a waterfall. Three whirlpool spas nestle amid rocks and foliage, there are two sand volleyball courts, and blue-and-white-striped cabanas (equipped with rafts and misting coolers) can be rented for $8 per hour or $25 per day.

Riviera Hotel & Casino

2901 Las Vegas Blvd. S., at Riviera Blvd., Las Vegas, NV 89109. ☎ **800/834-6753** or 702/734-5110. Fax 702/794-9451. 1,978 rms, 158 suites. A/C TV TEL. $59–$95 single or double, $125–$500 suite. Extra person $20. Inquire about "Gambler's Spree" packages. AE, CB, DC, MC, V. Free parking (self and valet).

Opened in 1955 (Liberace cut the ribbon and Joan Crawford was official hostess of opening ceremonies), the Riviera is styled after the luxurious casino resorts of the Côte d'Azur. Its original nine stories made it the first "high-rise" on the Strip. Several towers later, the present-day Riviera is as elegant as ever.

Accommodations are richly decorated with handsome mahogany furnishings and burgundy or teal bedspreads with matching gold-tasseled drapes. Half the rooms offer pool views. Amenities include in-room safes and cable TVs with pay-movie options and in-house information stations.

Dining/Entertainment: Kristofer's, an elegant tropically themed steak and sea-food restaurant overlooking the pool, offers prix-fixe dinners from $19.95 to $25.95. The adjoining lounge serves poolside fare. Dinner only.

Ristorante Italiano, a romantic setting under a simulated starlit sky, has a win-dow wall backed by murals of Venice. Classic Italian specialties are featured. Dinner only; most entrees $10.95 to $23.50 (veal and lobster dishes are pricier).

Kady's is the Riviera's very cheerful 24-hour restaurant, with a wall of windows overlooking the pool as well as outdoor patio seating. Along with the usual coffee-shop fare, Kady's menu offers Jewish deli specialties.

Rik' Shaw (don't ask me what the punctuation means) features Chinese fare in an elegant candlelit room with crystal chandeliers and mirrored columns. The fan-shaped menu lists traditional Cantonese specialties. Dinner only; entrees $9.50 to $22.95 (most under $15).

An excellent choice for families is the Mardi Gras Food Court which, unlike most of its genre, is extremely attractive. White canvas umbrella tables and Toulouse-Lautrec–style murals create a comfortable French café ambience. Food choices are wide-ranging, including burgers, pizza, gyros, falafel, and Chinese fare. The food court is adjacent to the video-game arcade, so you can relax over espresso while the kids run off and play. Open daily 10:30am to midnight.

See also the buffet listings in chapter 6. There are two casino bars, the Splash Bar and Le Bistro Lounge; the latter offers nightly live entertainment.

Services: 24-hour room service, shoeshine.

Facilities: Casino (one of the world's largest), large arcade with carnival and video games, well-equipped health club (full complement of cardio and weight machines, free weights, steam, sauna, tanning, facials, salt/soap rubs, massage), Olympic-size swimming pool and sundeck, wedding chapel, beauty salon/barbershop, comprehen-sive business-services center, America West airlines desk, tour and show desks, car-rental desk, shops (see chapter 9 for details), two Har-Tru tennis courts lit for night play. A unique feature here: a wine-tasting booth operated by Nevada's only winery.

✪ Treasure Island at the Mirage

3300 Las Vegas Blvd. S., at Spring Mountain Rd., Las Vegas, NV 89109. ☎ **800/944-7444** or 702/894-7111. Fax 702/894-7446. 2,688 rms, 212 suites. A/C TV TEL. Single or double $69–$149 Sun–Thurs, $129–$269 Fri–Sat; $109–$500 suite. Extra person $30. Inquire about packages. AE, CB, DC, DISC, JCB, MC, V. Free parking (self and valet).

In 1989 Steve Wynn brought a lava-spewing volcano to the Strip to front his spec-tacular Mirage. What could he possibly do for an encore? Everyone found out in 1993, when he lowered the gangplank to unveil Treasure Island, a resort in the form of an 18th-century Caribbean pirate village. The Strip in front of the hotel has been transformed into a long wooden dock overlooking Buccaneer Bay, where live sea battles between two full-scale ships—the pirate vessel *Hispaniola* (its prow adorned with a pair of fierce-looking dragons) and the proud but battle-scarred British frig-ate HMS *Britannia*—take place at regular intervals. The facade behind the bay is made up of a village of ramshackle waterfront structures. Towering above is the hotel itself—a 36-story peach and stucco building with white-shuttered windows. Within, public areas all maintain the pirate theme.

Rooms are decorated in soft hues (there are five different color schemes). Nautically themed prints, maps, and astrological charts adorn the walls, and floor-to-ceiling windows provide great views of the Strip, pool, or mountains. Especially desirable are corner rooms with windows on two sides.

Dining/Entertainment: The hotel's premier restaurant, the **Buccaneer Bay Club,** is described in chapter 6, as are its buffet offerings.

Madame Ching's—luxurious, romantically lit (red silk globe lights are suspended from lotus medallions), and adorned with Chinese paintings, ceramics, sculpture, and lacquer screens—is a good choice for intimate dining.

The regional Chinese fare is excellent, and Western pastries are a dessert option. Dinner only; entrees mostly $12.95 to $21.50. Madame Ching, by the way, was a notorious 19th-century female pirate.

The Plank, designed on the unlikely theme of a pirate's library, comprises a warren of cozy rooms where books and curios are displayed in leaded-glass cases. Its ambience is a mix of gleaming brass, polished burl, and musty leather-bound volumes. The menu features seafood and mesquite-grilled steaks and prime rib. Dinner only; entrees $13.50 to $45.

The Black Spot Grille, its name notwithstanding, is an Italian "sidewalk café" set off from the shopping arcade by lacy iron grillwork. Its Italian village ambience is reflected in a Venetian *putti* (cherub) fountain, festival lanterns strung overhead, and faux bougainvillea draped from terra-cotta eaves. Lunch and dinner; almost all menu items are under $10.

The very comfortable **Lookout Café,** Treasure Island's 24-hour coffee shop, has an arched beamed ceiling suggestive of a ship's underdeck. Walls are hung with muskets, daggers, and pirate booty from the seven seas, and amber broken-bottle sconces provide soft lighting. From 4pm to midnight, a full prime rib dinner is $9.95.

Just across from Mutiny Bay (the video-game arcade) is Sweet Revenge, an ice-cream/frozen yogurt parlor. The Quarterdeck Deli, a cafeteria off the casino, serves items ranging from pastrami to potato pancakes. And the Island Snack Bar offers light fare and non-alcoholic specialty drinks by the pool.

Captain Morgan's Lounge is a piano bar that overlooks the casino. The Battle Bar, in the casino near the race and sports book, airs athletic events on TV monitors overhead and offers live music nightly except Monday. More importantly, it provides patio seating overlooking Buccaneer Bay; for the best possible view of the ship battle, arrive at least 45 minutes prior to the show and snag a table by the railing. The ornate, crystal-chandeliered Swashbuckler's specializes in ice cream drinks and a 24-ounce rum concoction served in a skull mug; you can play progressive video poker while imbibing. And in the pool area is the simpatico Island Bar offering frozen specialty drinks; it's cooled by a misting system in summer.

Services: 24-hour room service, limo rental, foreign currency exchange, shoeshine (in men's room in the lobby and casino).

Facilities: Casino, tour and sightseeing desks, car-rental desk, travel agency, Mutiny Bay (an 18,000-square-foot, state-of-the-art video game arcade and carnival midway; one highlight is a full-size Mazda Miata motion-simulator ride), two wedding chapels, full-service unisex salon (days of beauty are an option), and a shopping arcade (for details, see chapter 9). A full-service spa and health club with a complement of machines, exercise bikes, and free weights; sauna, steam, whirlpools, and massage; on-site trainers; TVs and stereos with headsets; and anything else you might need. A free tram travels between Treasure Island and the Mirage almost around the clock.

A large free-form swimming pool with a 230-foot loop slide has a beautifully landscaped sundeck area amid palms and flower beds. There's a kiddie pool and whirlpool, and cabanas (equipped with overhead fans, small refrigerators, phones, cable TVs, rafts, tables, and chairs) can be rented for $75 a day.

Tropicana Resort & Casino

3801 Las Vegas Blvd. S., at Tropicana Ave., Las Vegas, NV 89109. ☎ **800/634-4000** or 702/739-2222. Fax 702/739-2469. 1,884 rms, 130 suites (for high rollers only). A/C TV TEL. $65–$95 single or double. Extra person $10. Children under 18 stay free in parents' room. AE, CB, DC, MC, V. Free parking (self and valet).

This long-time denizen of the Strip is looking great since a major renovation in 1995. The entranceway is now a colorful Caribbean-village facade; there are nightly laser light shows on the Outer Island corner facing the Strip; pedestrian skywalks link the Trop with the MGM Grand, the Excalibur, and the Luxor; and the resort's resident bird and wildlife population has dramatically increased. The Trop today comprises a lush landscape of manicured lawns, towering palms, oleanders, weeping willows, and crepe myrtles. There are dozens of waterfalls, thousands of exotic flowers, lagoons, aquariums, and koi ponds. And flamingos, finches, black swans, mandarin ducks, African crown cranes, cockatoos, macaws, toucans, and Brazilian parrots live on the grounds. There's even a wildlife walk (home to pygmy marmosets, boa constrictors, and others) inside the resort itself.

Rooms in the Paradise Tower are traditional, with French provincial furnishings and turn-of-the-century-look wallpapers. Island Tower rooms, more befitting a tropical resort, are decorated in pastel colors like pale pink and seafoam green, with splashy print bedspreads and bamboo furnishings; some have beds with mirrored walls and ceilings. All Trop rooms have sofas and safes; TVs offer Spectravision movies, account review, video checkout, and channels for in-house information.

Dining/Entertainment: Mizuno's, a beautiful teppanyaki dining room, is detailed in chapter 6, as are the Trop's buffet offerings.

El Gaucho is an elegantly rustic Argentine steak house, with rough-hewn log beams overhead and pecky-pine walls hung with cowhides, antlers, serapes, branding irons, and gaucho gear. Steaks, chops, prime rib, and seafood come with traditional accompaniments. Dinner only; entrees $19.50 to $33.95.

Bella Roma's, a charming candlelit Italian ristorante, has oak-shuttered windows overlooking the treetops of the lushly landscaped pool area. Traditional Italian fare is served along with steaks. Dinner only; entrees $11.50 to $21.95.

Impressions

There was a magic in this place. It was like stepping back into the frontier. Casino owners were king. They owned the town. They were glamorous. They had beautiful women and lots of money.

—Steve Wynn, on Las Vegas when he visited as a boy

Shifting Sands: Tribute to a Las Vegas Legend

The Sands Hotel, closed this year, has been a Las Vegas landmark since 1952. It was the seventh resort to open on the Strip. New York show producer and Copacabana nightclub owner Jack Entratter was one of its original backers, and he used his showbiz contacts to bring superstar entertainment and gorgeous showgirls to the Copa Room stage. Danny Thomas was the room's opening headliner; Jimmy Durante, Red Skelton, Debbie Reynolds, and Jerry Lewis were among those who made regular appearances; and Louis Armstrong and Metropolitan Opera star Robert Merrill performed together for a memorable two weeks in 1954. Entrater's efforts not only put the Sands on the map, but helped establish Las Vegas as America's entertainment capital.

However, the Sands was probably most famous as the home of the notorious Rat Pack (Frank Sinatra, Sammy Davis Jr., Dean Martin, Peter Lawford, and Joey Bishop) and the site of their 3-week "Summit Meeting" in January of 1960. No other Las Vegas show tickets have ever been more coveted or difficult to obtain. One night Sinatra picked up Sammy Davis, Jr. bodily and said, "Ladies and gentlemen, I want to thank you for giving me this valuable NAACP trophy." He then dropped Davis into the lap of a man in a ringside seat who happened to be Senator John F. Kennedy. Davis looked up and quipped, "It's perfectly all right with me, Senator, as long as I'm not being donated to George Wallace or James Eastland." The Rat Pack returned to the Copa stage in 1961 for an onstage birthday party for Dean Martin with a 5-foot-high cake in the shape of a whiskey bottle. Martin threw the first slice, and a food fight ensued. The riotous clan kept Las Vegas amused during most of the decade. By the way, Frank Sinatra and Mia Farrow were married at the Sands several eons ago.

Papagayo's is a colorful Mexican eatery behind a wrought-iron gate, where cream stucco walls are adorned with Mexican rugs and Diego Rivera prints. At lunch, an extensive Mexican buffet is $6.95; dinner entrees $7.95 to $15.95.

Calypso's, the Trop's 24-hour coffee shop, is the most cheerful in town. Decorated in bright island colors, it has a wall of windows overlooking waterfalls, weeping willows, and palm-fringed ponds filled with ducks and flamingos. Traditional (and very tasty) coffee-shop fare is augmented by interesting items ranging from Caribbean shrimp sate to bacon-stuffed cheese quesadillas. An extensive Chinese menu is available nightly from 6pm to midnight.

The **Players Deli,** sandwiched between the casino and the pool, is a unique cafeteria-cum-gaming room where slot and video poker machines are equipped with handy pullout dining ledges. Gamblers can also snack here at poker tables or in a small keno lounge or sports book. Hot and cold sandwiches, salads, and snack fare (nachos, chicken wings) are featured. Open daily from 10am to 10pm.

Down a level from the casino, in the Atrium Shopping area, is a Baskin-Robbins ice-cream parlor. The Atrium Lounge in the casino offers a variety of live music nightly after 5pm. The Coconut Grove Bar serves the pool area, and the Tropics Bar is between the two towers on the wildlife walk.

Services: 24-hour room service, shoeshine.

Facilities: Casino, health club (a range of machines, treadmills, exercise bikes, steam, sauna, Jacuzzi, massage, and tanning room), video-game arcade, tour and show desks, wedding chapel, car-rental desk, beauty salon and barbershop, business center, travel agent, shops (jewelry, chocolates, women's footwear, logo items, women's fashions, sports clothing, gifts, newsstand).

Three swimming pools (one Olympic size) and three whirlpool spas are located in a 5-acre garden with 30 splashing waterfalls, lagoons, and lush tropical plantings. One pool has a swim-up bar/blackjack table.

MODERATE

Barbary Coast Hotel & Casino

3595 Las Vegas Blvd. S., at Flamingo Rd., Las Vegas, NV 89109. ☎ **888/227-2297** or 702/737-7111. Fax 702/737-6304. 200 rms. A/C TV TEL. Single or double $39–75 Sun–Thurs, $100 Fri–Sat and holidays. Extra person $10. Children under 12 stay free in parents' room. AE, CB, DC, DISC, JCB, MC, V. Free parking (self and valet).

Evoking the romantic image of turn-of-the-century San Francisco, the Barbary Coast enjoys a terrific Strip location. The casino is adorned with $2 million worth of magnificent stained-glass skylights, and the extremely charming Victorian-style rooms make for an opulent setting. The latter, decorated in shades of rose and gray, have half-canopied brass beds, gaslight-style lamps, lace-curtained windows, and pretty floral carpets. All accommodations include little sitting parlors with entrances framed by floral chintz curtains.

Dining/Entertainment: Michael's, the Barbary Coast's premier restaurant, is flamboyantly Victorian—an intimate dining room with white marble floors, red satin damask wall coverings, plush red velvet booths, and a gorgeous stained-glass dome overhead. The menu highlights steaks and seafood. Dinner only; entrees $30 to $70.

The **Victorian Room,** open 24 hours, is another attractive turn-of-the-century venue. Its extensive menu runs the gamut from burgers to broiled Alaskan crab legs; in addition, Chinese entrees are offered at lunch and dinner.

Two bars serve the casino.

Services: 24-hour room service, shoeshine.

Facilities: Casino, Western Union office, tour and show desks, gift shop.

Excalibur

3850 Las Vegas Blvd. S., at Tropicana Ave., Las Vegas, NV 89109. ☎ **800/937-7777** or 702/597-7777. Fax 702/597-7040. 4,032 rms. A/C TV TEL. For up to 4 people: $49–$69 Sun–Thurs, $59–$89 Fri–Sat. Children under 18 stay free in parents' room, children over 18 pay $10 weekends only. Rates may be higher during holidays and convention periods. AE, CB, DC, MC, V. Free parking (self and valet).

One of the largest resort hotels in the world, Excalibur (aka "the Realm") is a gleaming white turreted castle complete with moat, drawbridge, battlements, and lofty towers. Within this Arthurian fantasy world, the casino is festooned with armor and heraldic banners, and knights, jesters, madrigal singers, and dancing "bears" roam the premises. The second floor comprises the hotel's Medieval Village—site of Excalibur's restaurants and quaint shops along winding streets and alleyways. On the Village's Jester's Stage, jugglers, puppeteers, and magicians delight guests with free 20-minute performances throughout the day. Another unique Excalibur feature is the Fantasy Faire, below the casino level, housing a large video-game arcade, dozens of medieval-themed carnival games, and two "magic motion machine" theaters featuring high-tech visual thrills; the thrills include simulated roller coaster and runaway train adventures and an outer space demolition derby directed by George Lucas—enhanced by hydraulically activated seats that synchronize with the on-screen action. There's enough to entertain kids for hours while mom and dad enjoy the casino.

The rooms maintain the Arthurian-legend motif with walls papered to look like stone castle interiors. Oak furnishings are heraldically embellished, mirrors are flanked by torchier sconces, bedspreads have a fleur-de-lis theme, and prints of jousting knights adorn the walls.

Dining/Entertainment: Camelot, Excalibur's fine dining room, offers continental fare in a rustic castle setting, with murals of Camelot's pristine lakes and verdant forests forming an idyllic backdrop. Dinner only; entrees $14.95 to $22.95.

Sir Galahad's, a prime rib restaurant, occupies a candlelit "castle" chamber with massive oak beams and wrought-iron candelabra chandeliers overhead. The specialty is prime rib, carved tableside and served with soup or salad, mashed potatoes, creamed spinach, and Yorkshire pudding. Dinner only; entrees $13.95 to $17.95.

Wild Bill's, a western-themed restaurant and dance hall, has beveled-glass doors punctured by "bullet holes," walls adorned with rodeo murals, and booths separated by large wagon wheels. A rustic bar nestles in one corner. Country music is played during the day; at night there's live music for dancing. Entrees include steak, ribs, catfish, and burgers. Dinner only; entrees $10.95 to $21.95 (burgers and sandwiches $7.95 to $9.95). Sundays a $5.99 breakfast buffet is served from 9am to 1pm.

Lance-a-Lotta Pasta replicates a flamboyant Italian village, complete with strolling guitarists. The menu lists pizzas and pastas, subs and hero sandwiches. Dinner only; entrees $11.95 to $15.95 (a wide choice of pastas is under $10). Café Expresso, a window operation off Lance-a-Lotta Pasta, serves espresso, cappuccino, and pastries. It has several tables in the Medieval Village.

The **Sherwood Forest Cafe,** its entrance guarded by a sentry of lavender dragons (kids love to climb on them), is Excalibur's 24-hour facility. A low-priced children's menu is a plus.

Another heraldic dining room, the **Round Table Buffet,** is described in chapter 6. Other facilities include three snack bars named Robin Hood (in the Medieval Village), Hansel & Gretel (in Fantasy Faire), and Little John's (in the casino). The Village Pub is an Alpine-themed bar in the Medieval Village; the Minstrel's Theatre Lounge offers live entertainment nightly (during the day, movies and sporting events are shown on a large-screen TV); there are several bars in the casino (most interesting of these is King George's, featuring international beers and microbrews); and a snack and cocktail bar serves the North pool.

Services: 24-hour room service, free gaming lessons, shoeshine, foreign-currency exchange.

Facilities: Casino, tour and show desks, state-of-the-art video-game arcade, wedding chapel (you can marry in medieval attire), unisex hairdresser, car-rental desk, a parking lot that can accommodate RVs, shops (see chapter 9). There are two large, beautifully landscaped swimming pools complete with waterfalls and water slides and an adjoining 16-seat whirlpool spa.

⑤ Harrah's Las Vegas

3475 Las Vegas Blvd. S., between Flamingo and Spring Mountain rds., Las Vegas, NV 89109. ☎ **800/634-6785,** 800/HARRAHS, or 702/369-5000. Fax 702/369-5008. 1,675 rms, 36 suites. A/C TV TEL. $50–$250 single or double. Extra person $15. Children 12 and under stay free in parents' room. AE, CB, DC, DISC, MC, V. Free parking (self and valet).

Since 1973, Harrah's glittering Mississippi riverboat facade has been a Las Vegas landmark. That ship has now sailed off the Strip. In its place will soon be a dramatic new facade, part of a $150-million expansion and renovation based on a brand-new Mardis Gras/ *Carnaval* theme. A 35-story tower, already in the works, will add 671 rooms and 28 suites. There will also be 22,000 additional square feet of casino space, six new restaurants (including a lofty steak house that will offer diners scenic views of the Strip), a Brazilian-themed lounge, and a festive, palm-fringed shopping/ entertainment plaza where strolling entertainers will perform.

My favorite Harrah's rooms, in the 35-story Captain's Tower, are decorated in peach and teal with bleached oak furnishings and verdigris accents. Prints of works by Renoir, Van Gogh, and Degas hang in the hallways—a rare note of culture in this town. Spacious mini-suites in this section, offering large sofas and comfortable armchairs, are especially desirable. In the 23-story Riverboat Tower, the carpets are gray or teal, the furnishings mahogany, with print bedspreads adding a splash of color. In all rooms, TVs offer hotel-information and keno channels, pay movies, Nintendo, and video account review and checkout.

Dining/Entertainment: The plush **Claudine's Steak House** is a romantic turn-of-the-century setting for steak and seafood meals. After you dine, relax over drinks in the adjoining piano bar lounge. Dinner only; most entrees $17.95 to $24.95.

An "old salt" mannequin guards the entrance to **Joe's Bayou,** a Creole/seafood restaurant. The nautical theme continues inside, with amber ship's lanterns suspended over candlelit tables, riverboat paintings, fishnets, and racks of oars. Dinner only; entrees $8.95 to $15.95.

The garden-themed **Veranda,** Harrah's 24-hour coffee shop, has an extensive menu listing all the expected Las Vegas coffee-shop fare.

All That Jazz simulates a French Quarter street. Its walls reproduce the facades of shuttered New Orleans townhouses, and jazz emanates from a player piano at night. The price of your breakfast entree includes selections from a fruit, cereal, and pastry bar; Italian dinner entrees ($5.95 to $7.95) include soup, salad bar, and dessert bar.

Similar in decor is the Court of Two Gators, a bar/lounge off the casino with ivied walls and a lofty skylight ceiling. Its dance floor is popular at night when live bands play jazz and oldies. In the lobby are a TCBY and a cappuccino/espresso/pastry cart for quick breakfasts. And, finally, there's a Race & Sports Book Bar with an adjoining snack bar called the Derby Deli. See also the buffet listings in chapter 6.

Services: 24-hour room service (including a special pizza and pasta menu), complimentary gaming lessons.

Facilities: Casino, car-rental desk, tour and show desks, nice sized video-game arcade, coin-op laundry, shops (see chapter 9 for details), unisex hair salon.

Harrah's has a beautiful Olympic-size swimming pool and sun deck area with a whirlpool, kids' wading pool, cocktail and snack bar, and poolside shop selling T-shirts and sundries. The hotel's health club is one of the better facilities on the Strip, offering Lifecycles, treadmills, stair machines, rowing machines, lots of Universal equipment, free weights, whirlpool, steam, sauna, and massage; there are two TVs and a VCR for which aerobic exercise tapes are available.

Holiday Inn Casino Boardwalk

3750 Las Vegas Blvd. S., between Harmon and Tropicana aves., Las Vegas , NV 89109. ☎ **800/ HOLIDAY,** 800/635-4581, or 702/735-2400. Fax 702/730-3166. 630 rms, 12 suites. A/C TV TEL. Single or double $69–$125 Sun–Thurs, $89–$149 Fri–Sat; suites $300–$900. Extra person $15. Rates may be higher during special events. Children 19 and under stay free in parents' room. AE, CB, DC, DISC, JCB, MC, V. Parking (free self and valet).

You can't miss this Holiday Inn. Its unique new midway facade, fronted by a 100-foot sign, replicates New York's Coney Island, complete with a roller coaster, Ferris wheel, and parachute jump, all with screaming mannequin passengers (it's for display only; there are no actual rides here). A midway clock runs backwards, a jack-in-the-box pops up 30 feet every couple of minutes, and Jocko, a 50-foot clown, caps the casino entrance. This is a small, friendly property, with a very convenient Strip location. I enjoy perusing public areas here, which display numerous black-and-white photographs of Las Vegas in days gone by (e.g., Liza Minnelli and mom Judy Garland onstage at the Flamingo in 1957), vintage movie posters, and historic newspaper headlines. Rooms—most of them in a new 16-story tower—are decorated in vibrant colors with cherrywood furnishings and prints of Coney Island adorning the walls. Older units are pleasantly done up in soft pastels with blond wood furnishings. All offer cable TVs with pay-movie options.

Dining/Entertainment: A big draw is the **Cyclone Coffee Shop,** a 24-hour facility decorated with murals of the Coney Island boardwalk and adorable roller-coaster-motif lighting fixtures. Well worth a visit even if you're staying elsewhere, it has some of the best bargain meals in town (see chapter 6 for details). Coney's, totally replicating the feel of a beach restaurant, serves boardwalk fare: fresh roasted corn on the cob, fresh-cut fries, pizza, and cheesesteak sandwiches. Other facilities include a 24-hour deli in the casino, an ice cream/yogurt parlor, and two casino bars; a buffet room is under construction.

Services: 24-hour room service, shoeshine.

Facilities: Casino, two small swimming pools, shops, coin-op washers/dryers, video-game arcade and shooting gallery, sightseeing/show/tour desk, car rental desk. Guests can use health club facilities nearby.

Imperial Palace

3535 Las Vegas Blvd. S., between Sands Ave. and Flamingo Rd., Las Vegas, NV 89109. ☎ **800/ 634-6441** or 702/731-3311. Fax 702/735-8578. 2,412 rms, 225 suites. A/C TV TEL. $49–$99 single or double, $79–$149 "luv tub" suite, $159–$499 other suites. Extra person $15. Inquire about packages. AE, DC, DISC, MC, V. Free parking (self and valet).

The blue pagoda–topped Imperial Palace, its shoji-screen facade patterned after Japanese temple architecture, is one of the larger hotels in Vegas. Its Asian theme continues inside, with a dragon-motif ceiling and giant wind-chime chandeliers in the casino. A unique feature here is the Imperial Palace Auto Collection of more than 800 antique, classic, and special-interest vehicles spanning a century of automotive history (details in chapter 7).

Rooms, decorated in soft earth tones, with bamboo-motif beds and furnishings, are perked up by bright, tropical curtains and paintings. TVs offer in-house information channels, video message review and checkout, and pay-per-view movies. If you so desire, you can rent a "luv tub" suite with an enormous faux-marble bath (ample for two) and a canopied bed with a mirrored ceiling.

Dining/Entertainment: Embers, the Imperial Palace's plush gourmet room, has burgundy silk-covered walls, spacious candlelit booths, and a smoked-mirror ceiling with recessed pink neon. The menu features steak and seafood entrees, along with pasta dishes; flambé desserts are a specialty. Dinner only; entrees $10.95 to $28 (most under $18).

The Ming Terrace, fronted by a bamboo ricksha, achieves additional Eastern ambience from Chinese screens and painted fans. The menu features Mandarin, Cantonese, and Szechuan specialties. Dinner only; most entrees $8.75 to $20.95.

The Rib House is a rustic setting with exposed-brick walls and heavy oak dividers defining seating areas. A warm, cozy glow emanates from frosted-glass sconces, candlelit tables, and a working fireplace. Barbecued ribs and chicken are specialties. Dinner only; entrees $9.95 to $16.95.

The Seahouse, a casual nautically themed restaurant softly lit by ship's lanterns, features fresh seafood; if you're not a fish fancier you might order filet mignon béarnaise or charbroiled chicken breast with sautéed mushrooms. Dinner only; entrees mostly $11.95 to $16.95.

The 24-hour pagoda-like **Teahouse** offers (in addition to the usual burgers, salads, sandwiches, and full entrees) buffet brunches weekdays ($5.95) and champagne Sunday brunches ($6.50) from 8am to 3pm. A prime rib and champagne dinner is featured nightly from 5 to 10pm for $7.95.

Pizza Palace—a cheerful eatery with red-and-white checkered tablecloths and big tufted-leather booths—serves regular and deep-dish pizzas, Italian sandwiches, and pasta dishes. An antipasto salad bar is a plus. Open 11am to midnight; entrees $3.75 to $10.30, the latter for a large pizza with three toppings.

The **Emperor's Buffet,** on the third floor, has a South Seas decor composed of thatched roofing, bamboo and rattan paneling, and Polynesian carvings. Breakfast is served 7 to 11am ($4.99), lunch 11am to 4pm ($5.99), dinner 5 to 10pm ($6.99).

Betty's Diner, in the shopping arcade, serves sandwiches, pizza, nachos, hot dogs, malts, and ice-cream sundaes. Burger Palace is attractively decorated with sports-themed murals. Adjoining it is the Sports Bar where you can follow the races over cocktails. There are a total of 10 cocktail bars/lounges in the hotel, including the Mai Tai Lounge on the main floor and the Poolside Bar (both specializing in exotic Polynesian drinks), and the Ginza, Geisha, Sake, and Kanpai bars serving the casino.

Services: 24-hour room service, free gaming lessons, shoeshine in casino.

Facilities: Casino, health club (machines, free weights, sauna, steam, massage, tanning, TV lounge), show and tour desks, car-rental desk, travel agency, unisex hairdresser, wedding chapel, video-game arcade, shopping arcade. An Olympic-size swimming pool is backed by a rock garden and waterfalls, and its palm-fringed sun deck area also has a Jacuzzi.

✪ Luxor Las Vegas

3900 Las Vegas Blvd. S., between Reno and Hacienda aves., Las Vegas, NV 81119. ☎ **800/288-1000** or 702/262-4000. Fax 702/262-4452. 3,986 rms, 488 suites. Single or double $49–$259 Sun–Thurs, $99–$299 Fri–Sat. Concierge level $179–$279, Jacuzzi suite $99–$329, other suites $500–$800. Extra person $10. Children under 12 stay free in parents' room. AE, CB, DC, DISC, MC, V. Free parking (self and valet).

The Luxor is perfectly suited to its desert setting. A 30-story bronze pyramid, it's fronted by an ornately carved 191-foot obelisk and guarded by a 10-story replica of the Sphinx of Giza. Throughout the property, ornamentation authentically replicates paintings, hieroglyphics, and artifacts from historic Egyptian sites, and murals trace 4,000 years of Egyptian history. High-speed "inclinator" elevators run on a 39-degree angle, making the ride up to your room a bit of a thrill. At night, holographic images appear on a water screen on the Karnak Lagoon, and "Re," a 315,000-watt light beam (the most powerful on earth) searches the heavens from the pyramid's apex (ancient Egyptians believed that their souls would climb the sides of a pyramid and ascend to the afterlife on a beam of light).

At press time, the Luxor is completing a $240-million expansion, which will include two pyramid-shaped towers (bringing the room count to the above-mentioned figures), two new dining rooms (a steak house and an Italian restaurant), a 1,200-seat showroom, a wedding chapel, a 12,000-square-foot spa, and a major $35-million water attraction (no details available yet, but rumor has it they're planning something on the order of Pirates of the Caribbean).

The Luxor's rooms are among the most appealing in town. Handsome faux-marquetry furnishings of mahogany- and amber-stained maple are painted with cartouches (symbolic signatures of Cleopatra and Alexander the Great) and hieroglyphics, walls are decorated with Egyptian friezes and bas-relief art, and attractive Egyptian-motif print fabrics complement deep teal carpeting. Sloped window walls remind you you're in a pyramid. *Note:* Most baths have showers only—no tubs. Especially desirable are a group of suites with glamorous art-deco elements, private sitting rooms, refrigerators, and—notably—Jacuzzis by the window (enabling you to soak under the stars at night). Floors 28 through 30 comprise a concierge level (though not all accommodations on those floors offer concierge services).

Dining/Entertainment: The Luxor's **Manhattan Buffet** is discussed in chapter 6.

To enter **Isis,** a gourmet room, you'll pass through a colonnade of caryatid statues. Within, replicas of artifacts from King Tutankhamen's tomb are on display in glass cases, and a golden statue of Osiris forms a visual centerpiece. A harpist plays during dinner. The classic continental menu features items such as braised breast of pheasant filled with foie gras and pistachio. Dinner only; entrees $17 to $24.

The **Sacred Sea Room** has gold walls adorned with murals and hieroglyphics depicting fishing on the Nile. Turquoise mosaic tiles on the ceiling suggest ocean waves, and the dining-at-sea ambience is further enhanced by a central ship's hull and mast. Fresh- and saltwater seafood arrives daily from both coasts. Dinner only; entrees mostly $14 to $21.

Papyrus, a Trader Vic's–like tropical setting, seats diners in high-backed bamboo and rattan chairs amid lush palms, Polynesian sculptures, native spears, and colorful stuffed birds. A rear wall replicates a Mayan ruin. The cuisine is eclectic Asian/Pacific Rim. Dinner only; entrees $8.75 to $14.75.

The futuristic **Millennium High-Energy Café** on the attractions level—decorated in bold patterns and colors with red and blue neon tubing and faux-industrial finishes—serves space-age-monikered light fare such as "Molecular Fusion Fajitas." Beer, wine, and a vast selection of specialty drinks are available. Open daily 11am to 11pm; entrees $5.50 to $9.25.

The 24-hour **Pyramid Café**—its booths flanked by palm trees and foliage—replicates the interior of a pyramid. Like the decor, the menu has an Egyptian theme with a small nod to Middle Eastern cuisine. Most menu items, however, are of the predictable Las Vegas hotel coffee-shop genre. A $2.99 late-night breakfast of sirloin steak, eggs, hash browns, and toast is served daily except Wednesday from 11pm to 6am.

Other venues are a deli off the casino and a **Swensen's Ice Cream** shop on the attraction level.

The plush Nefertiti's Lounge features live bands for dancing nightly; off-hours sporting events are aired on a large-screen TV. The Obelisk Bar and Anteroom Lounge serve the casino. Tut's Hut specializes in Polynesian drinks and Otemanu Hot Rock samplers (seafood, tenderloin, chicken, pork, or vegetables grilled at your table and served with plum, peanut, mustard, and teriyaki dipping sauces). The Sportsbook Lounge, adjoining the race and sports book, airs sports action on TV monitors overhead. And the Oasis Terrace & Bar provides poolside food and drinks.

Services: 24-hour room service, foreign-currency exchange, shoeshine.

Facilities: Casino; full-service unisex hair salon; complete spa and health club (with a full range of machines, free weights, steam, sauna, and Jacuzzi; massage, facials, herbal wraps, and other beauty treatments available); VirtuaLand, an 18,000-square-foot video arcade that showcases Sega's latest game technologies; car-rental desk; tour/show/sightseeing desks.

The hotel has an immense palm-fringed swimming pool (palms even grow right in the pool) with outdoor whirlpool, kiddie pool, pool-accessories shop, and luxurious cabanas (cooled by misting systems and equipped with rafts, cable TVs, phones, ceiling fans, tables and chairs, chaise longues, and refrigerators stocked with juices and bottled water) that rent for $75 a day.

Maxim

160 E. Flamingo Rd., between the Strip and Koval Lane, Las Vegas, NV 89109. ☎ **800/ 634-6987** or 702/731-4300. Fax 702/735-3252. 757 rms, 38 suites. A/C TV TEL. Single or double $49–$69, Sun–Thurs, $75–$98 Fri–Sat; $175–$305 suite. Extra person $10. Children under 4 stay free in parents' room. AE, DC, MC, V. Free parking (self and valet).

Just a short walk from the heart of the Strip, the Maxim is a friendly property that has doubled in size since its 1977 opening. The rooms and public areas are currently undergoing a multimillion-dollar renovation. Most accommodations already sport a new southwestern resort look. The older rooms, decorated in earth tones, have sienna ultrasuede walls and photomurals of Las Vegas behind the beds. All offer TVs with pay-movie options and in-house information channels. If you prefer, you can rent a "players suite" with a whirlpool tub in the bedroom and a separate living room with wet bar.

Dining/Entertainment: A major new restaurant is in the planning stage at this writing, though no details were available at press time.

The Treehouse is the Maxim's 24-hour coffee shop, a dimly-lit facility (it's a bit claustrophobic actually) with many tables overlooking the casino. In addition to the requisite coffee-shop fare, it features daily specials such as a New York steak or prime rib dinner for $4.95.

More cheerful is **Jack's Colossal Deli,** a plant-filled self-service "sidewalk cafe" with a window wall and red-and-green-striped booths under an awning. There's also an interior room. Light fare (fresh-baked breakfast pastries, tacos, chili, salads, sandwiches, homemade soups) is served daily from 7am to 9pm.

The **Grand Buffet,** served on the mezzanine level, is rather elegant, especially at dinner when tables are candlelit and a pianist entertains on a baby grand. Dinner ($6.95) is served nightly 4 to 10pm, weekday brunch buffet ($5.49) 10am to 3pm, Saturday and Sunday champagne brunch ($7.95) 9am to 3pm.

There are two casino cocktail lounges, the **Waterfall** and Cloud Nine.

Services: Room service, shoeshine.

Facilities: Casino, car-rental desk, tour and show desks, small video-game arcade, gift shop (it also carries resort wear, liquor, luggage, jewelry, and logo items), beauty salon/barbershop, pool and sun deck with seasonal poolside bar.

Sahara Hotel & Casino

2535 Las Vegas Blvd. S., at E. Sahara Ave., Las Vegas, NV 89109. ☎ **800/634-6666** or 702/ 737-2111. Fax 702/791-2027. 1,945 rms, 90 suites, A/C TV TEL. $55–$85 single or double, $200 suite. Extra person $10. Children under 14 stay free in parents' room. AE, CB, DC, MC, V. Free parking (self and valet).

The Sahara's come a long way since it opened in 1952 on the site of the old Club Bingo. It's gone from 200 to 2,000 rooms with lofty towers, a major showroom, and an impressive array of restaurants, shops, and services. For decades—until the recent advent of the Stratosphere—it was the northernmost major hotel on the Strip.

In recent years, the Sahara was beginning to seem, if not exactly down at the heels, insufficiently unique to keep up with the magnificent new megaresorts. At press time, it is in the process of a multi-million-dollar transition into an exotic Moroccan-motif resort with an impressive domed entranceway. Since not many details were available, what you read here may be subject to change. Rooms are being redecorated to reflect the Moroccan look, and grounds will be enhanced by lush tropical landscaping. Also in the works: Moroccan-themed attractions, new restaurants and shops, a gorgeous new pool area, and the expansion of the casino to 75,000 square feet.

Dining/Entertainment: The House of Lords is a plush continental restaurant with a suit of armor in its entrance foyer and a stunning mahogany ceiling within. You'll dine on fancy fare with sorbet served between courses and complimentary petit fours as a finale. Dinner only; entrees $12.95 to $29.50.

La Terrazza, an Italian restaurant, is an intimate bilevel grotto with a wall of windows overlooking the pool and tables lit by silk-shaded candle lamps. Dinner only; entrees $12.95 to $29.95.

The Mexican Village—housed in a room that was originally the exotic setting for a Polynesian dinner show—still has a few private dining gazebos that used to comprise VIP seating. Ask for them when you reserve if you have at least three in your party. Fare is Mexican. Dinner only; entrees $8.95 to $12.95. The adjoining Acapulco Cantina, backed by a tropical aquarium, serves margaritas, Mexican beers, and light fare.

The **Caravan Coffee Shop,** a 24-hour facility off the casino with windows overlooking the pool, serves all the requisite coffee-shop fare. A steak and lobster dinner with salad, potato, and vegetable is just $7.77. A steak and eggs breakfast served from 11pm to 6am is $2.95.

The **Turf Club Deli,** next to the Race and Sports Center, features Jewish deli fare—homemade matzo ball soup, lox and bagels, pickled herring, and pastrami on rye. Open 10am to 8pm; everything on the menu is under $6.

Bar/lounges include two 24-hour casino bars (the Safari Bar and the Sports Book Bar), plus the Casbah Lounge offering top-notch live entertainment daily from 2pm to 6pm and 7pm to 4am. The Oasis Buffet is detailed in chapter 6.

Services: 24-hour room service.

Facilities: Casino, beauty salon/barbershop, car-rental desk, tour and show desks, shops (see chapter 9), video-game arcade. The Sahara has a large swimming pool and sun deck with a pool shop and poolside bar in nearby thatched-roof structures. A smaller pool shares the same courtyard setting.

Stardust Resort & Casino

3000 Las Vegas Blvd. S., at Convention Center Dr., Las Vegas, NV 89109. ☎ **800/634-6757** or 702/732-6111. Fax 702/732-6257. 2,271 rms, 160 suites. A/C TV TEL. Single or double Tower room $75–$150 Sun–Thurs, $75–$300 Fri–Sat; Villa room $40–$70 Sun–Thurs, $60–$100 Fri–Sat; Motor Inn room $24–$36 Sun–Thurs, $45–$65 Fri–Sat; $150–$500 suite. Extra person $10. Children 12 and under stay free in parents' room. AE, CB, DC, MC, V. Free parking (self and valet).

Opened in 1958, the Stardust is a longtime resident of the Strip, its 188-foot starry sign one of America's most recognized landmarks. Today, fronted by a fountain-splashed exterior plaza, the Stardust has kept pace with a growing city. In 1991, it added a 1,500-room tower and a 35,000-square-foot state-of-the-art meeting and conference center—part of a comprehensive $300-million expansion and renovation project. In the 1990s the Stardust is still a brightly shining star on the Strip.

Rooms in the 32-story West Tower are decorated in rich earth tones with black accents and bedspreads and drapes in bold abstract prints. East Tower rooms (my favorites) are light, airy, and spacious, with peach carpeting and attractive sea-foam green floral-print bedspreads, upholstered headboards, and draperies. You can rent an adjoining parlor room with a sofa bed, Jacuzzi tub, refrigerator, and wet bar—a good choice for families. Also quite nice are Villa rooms in two-story buildings surrounding a large swimming pool. Decorated in soft southwestern pastels, they have private shaded patios overlooking the pool. The least expensive rooms are in the Stardust's Motor Inn—four two-story white buildings with shuttered windows set far back on the property. They've been cheerfully decorated in southwestern resort colors, and if you don't mind being a block from the casino, they represent good value. Motor Inn guests can park at their doors. All Stardust accommodations offer in-room safes, and TVs have Spectravision movie options and in-house information channels.

Dining/Entertainment: William B's is an elegant steak-and-seafood restaurant fronted by a handsome bar/lounge. Flambé desserts are a house specialty. Dinner only; entrees $15.95 to $27.95.

Tres Lobos is an attractive restaurant designed to resemble the open courtyard of a hacienda. A plush adjoining lounge specializes in many-flavored margaritas. *Las Vegas Review Journal* readers recently voted this the city's best Mexican restaurant. Dinner only; entrees $6.95 to $11.95.

Toucan Harry's Coffee Shop, the Stardust's 24-hour facility, is a lushly tropical setting under a tented fabric ceiling. In addition to a vast array of sandwiches, salads, and full entrees (including many low-fat, low-cholesterol items), Harry's features a full Chinese menu with more than 50 dishes.

Ralph's Diner reflects America's current nostalgia craze. Fifties rock-'n'-roll tunes emanate from an old-fashioned jukebox, and waitresses garbed in classic white diner uniforms sometimes dance to the music. It's not a quiet place. All-American fare is served, an old-fashioned soda fountain turns out desserts, and low-priced blue-plate specials are offered daily. Open 7am to 10pm; everything is under $10 (most are under $7).

Tony Roma's, which you may know from other locations, has a home at the Stardust; more about it—and the Stardust's **Warehouse Buffet**—in chapter 6. The Short Stop is a snack bar in the race and sports book area of the casino. There are eight bars and cocktail lounges in the hotel, including the Terrace Bar in the casino with an alfresco seating area overlooking the pool and the Starlight Lounge, featuring live music nightly.

Services: 24-hour room service, shoeshine.

Facilities: Casino, beauty salon/barbershop, video-game arcade, car-rental desk, tour and show desks, shops (gifts, candy, clothing, jewelry, logo items, liquor). There are two large swimming pools, one in the Villa section, the other between the East and West Towers. Both have attractively landscaped sun decks and poolside bars; the Towers pool area has three whirlpool spas. Guests can use the Las Vegas Sporting House directly behind the hotel, a state-of-the-art, 24-hour health club; its extensive facilities are detailed in chapter 7.

Stratosphere Las Vegas

2000 Las Vegas Blvd. S., between St. Louis St. and Baltimore Ave., Las Vegas, NV 89104. ☎ **800/99-TOWER** or 702/380-7777. Fax 702/383-5334. 1,278 rms, 222 suites. A/C TV TEL. Sun–Thurs $39–$93 single or double, Fri–Sat $59–$129; suites $69–$400. Extra person $15. Children 18 and under stay free in parents' room. Rates may be higher during special events. AE, CB, DC, DISC, JCB, MC, V. Free parking (self and valet).

When the Stratosphere opened in 1996, it altered the city skyline (at 1,149 feet, it's the tallest building west of the Mississippi) and added a number of thrilling options for Las Vegas visitors. These include not only panoramic vistas from a revolving rooftop restaurant, but the world's highest roller-coaster (it careens around the outer rim of the tower 909 feet—108 stories—above ground) and the Big Shot, a fabulous free-fall ride that thrusts passengers up and down the tower at speeds of up to 45 miles per hour. For the less adventurous, indoor and outdoor observation decks offer stunning city views; you're so high up that other Strip properties look like Monopoly hotels. Notably good restaurants and shows are also pluses here, as are rooms furnished in handsome Biedermeier-style cherrywood pieces with black lacquer accents. Enhanced by bright abstract paintings, they offer TVs with in-house information channels and pay-movie options, safes, phones with modem ports, and hair dryers and cosmetic mirrors in the bath. Ask for a high floor when you reserve to optimize your view. At this writing, 1,000 additional rooms are in the works.

Dining/Entertainment: Three notable restaurants here—the revolving **Top of the World,** featuring panoramic vistas of Las Vegas from 800 feet; **Big Sky,** offering all-you-can-eat barbecue dinners; and the rollicking **Roxy's Diner**—are described in chapter 6, where you'll also find details about the hotel's buffet room.

At the delightful **Ferraro's,** sky-painted ceilings, trompe l'oeil effects, and stunning murals create the illusion that you're dining in an Italian courtyard. Most entrees $11.95 to $18.95.

The 24-hour **Sister's Cafe & Grille,** its corrugated tin roofing and bayou murals designed to suggest a rustic Louisiana fishing camp, adds Cajun/Creole specialties to the more traditional Las Vegas coffee shop fare.

A Nathan's, McDonald's, and Rainforest Cafe are in the Tower Shops area, along with a pizzeria, Jitters (a gourmet coffee shop), and a Häagen-Dazs outlet.

Bars and lounges include the Images Cabaret; the L'Isles Bar featuring live Caribbean/reggae music and tropical drinks; a cocktail lounge on the 107th floor; and the Big Sky Lounge adjacent to the restaurant, which features country music nightly after 8pm.

Services: 24-hour room service, foreign currency exchange.

Facilities: Casino, guest services desk, tour and show desk, video-game arcade, shopping arcade, three wedding chapels (offering incredible views from the 103rd floor), car-rental desk. An exercise facility, child care center, and vast resort-style pool and sundeck are in the works.

INEXPENSIVE

⑤ Circus Circus Hotel/Casino

2880 Las Vegas Blvd. S., between Circus Circus Dr. and Convention Center Dr., Las Vegas, NV 89109. ☎ **800/444-CIRC,** 800/634-3450, or 702/734-0410. Fax 702/734-2268. 2,674 rms, 126 suites. A/C TV TEL. For up to 4 people $36–$40 Sun–Thurs, $50–$55 Fri–Sat, $65 holidays; suite $46 Sun–Thurs, $65 Fri–Sat, $85–$100 holidays and convention times; two-bedroom parlor suite $129. AE, CB, DC, DISC, MC, V. Free parking (self and valet).

A 123-foot clown (his name is Lucky) and a festive pink-and-white circus tent beckon visitors to Circus Circus, a hotel that revolutionized Las Vegas tourism by offering a wealth of entertainment for kids. The midway level features dozens of carnival games, a large arcade (more than 300 video and pinball games), trick mirrors, and ongoing circus acts under the big top from 11am to midnight daily. The world's largest permanent circus according to the *Guinness Book of World Records,* it features renowned trapeze artists, stunt cyclists, jugglers, magicians, acrobats, and high-wire daredevils. Spectators can view the action from much of the midway or get up close and comfy on benches in the performance arena. There's a "be-a-clown" booth where kids can be made up with washable clown makeup and red foam rubber noses. They can grab a bite to eat in McDonald's (also on this level), and since the mezzanine overlooks the casino action, they can also look down and wave to mom and dad. Circus clowns wander the midway creating balloon animals and cutting up in various ways. Sometimes they even work the front desk.

At this writing, a 35-story tower is nearing completion; it will add 1,000 new rooms to the property. With it will come additional shops, an Italian restaurant, a third round-the-clock coffee shop, and a food court.

The thousands of rooms here occupy sufficient acreage to warrant a free Disney World–style aerial shuttle (another kid pleaser) and minibuses connecting its many components. Tower rooms, decorated in an attractive, contemporary mode, offer safes, and TVs are equipped with in-house information and gaming-instruction stations. The Manor section comprises five white, three-story buildings out back fronted by rows of cypresses. Manor guests can park at their doors, and a gate to the complex that can be opened only with a room key assures security. All sections of this vast property have their own swimming pools; additional casinos serve the main tower and Skyrise buildings; and both towers provide covered parking garages.

Dining/Entertainment: Highly esteemed by locals, **The Steak House** is elegant and candlelit, its cherry-paneled walls hung with gilt-framed oil landscapes. Shelves of books and green glass chandeliers create a clubby look. A plush lounge adjoins. Open for dinner and Sunday brunch. Dinner entrees $13.95 to $23.95; brunch $24.95 adults, $14.95 children 6 to 12, under 6 free.

The very reasonably priced **Pink Pony** is Circus Circus's cheerful bubble-gum pink and bright red 24-hour eatery, with big paintings of clowns on the walls and pink pony–motif carpeting. It offers a wide array of coffee-shop fare, including a number of specially marked "heart-smart" (low-fat, low-cholesterol) items.

The **Skyrise Dining Room,** another festive 24-hour facility in the Skyrise Tower, has walls hung with old-fashioned circus posters. Its menu is similar to the Pink Pony's. A 16-ounce prime rib or New York steak dinner here is just $6.95.

The brass-railed Pizzeria is in the main casino. Latte Express, featuring gourmet coffees, adjoins. Two 24-hour eateries—the **Westside Deli** (in the Main Tower's casino) and the Skyrise Snack Bar (near the race and sports book)—round out food options here.

In addition there are seven casino bars throughout the Circus Circus complex, notably the carousel-themed Horse-A-Round Bar on the midway level. The Circus Buffet is discussed in chapter 6.

Services: Limited room service (continental breakfast and drinks only), shoeshine.

Facilities: Three casinos, wedding chapel, tour and show desks, car-rental desk, unisex hairdresser, two swimming pools, two video-game arcades, shops (see chapter 9), Grand Slam Canyon Theme Park (see chapter 7).

Adjacent to the hotel is **Circusland RV Park,** with 384 full-utility spaces and up to 50-amp hookups. It has its own 24-hour convenience store, swimming pools, saunas, Jacuzzis, kiddie playground, fenced pet runs, video-game arcade, and community room. The rate is $12 Sunday to Thursday, $16 Friday and Saturday, $18 holidays.

Westward Ho Hotel & Casino

2900 Las Vegas Blvd. S., between Circus Circus Dr. and Convention Center Dr., Las Vegas, NV 89109. ☎ **800/634-6803** or 702/731-2900. 656 rms, 121 suites. A/C TV TEL. $36.90 to $56 double, $76 suite. Extra person $10. MC, V. Free parking at your room door.

Centrally located on the Strip (right next door to Circus Circus), the Westward Ho is fronted by a vast casino, with rooms in two-story buildings that extend out back for several city blocks. In fact, the property is so large that a free bus shuttles regularly between the rooms and the casino 24 hours a day. There are three swimming pools and three whirlpool spas to serve all areas.

The rooms are clean and adequately furnished motel units. A good buy here: two-bedroom suites with 1 1/2 baths, living rooms with sofa beds, and refrigerators that sleep up to six people.

There's a 24-hour restaurant in the casino under a stained-glass skylight dome. It serves a buffet breakfast ($4.95), brunch ($4.95), and dinner ($6.95), as well as an à la carte menu featuring traditional coffee-shop fare. Other facilities include a tour desk, free airport shuttle, a gift shop, a casino lounge where a three-piece country band entertains Monday to Saturday from 7pm to 1am, and a deli in the casino serving sandwiches, ribs, and half-pound extra-long hot dogs.

4 On or Near the Strip—Hotels without Casinos

VERY EXPENSIVE

Carriage House

105 E. Harmon Ave., between Las Vegas Blvd. S. and Koval Lane, Las Vegas, NV 89109. ☎ **800/ 221-2301** or 702/798-1020. Fax 702/798-1020, ext. 112. 154 suites. A/C TV TEL. $115 studio suite for 1 or 2, $145 one-bedroom suite condominium for up to 4, $345 two-bedroom condominium for up to 6. Inquire about lower-priced packages. AE, CB, DC, DISC, MC, V. Free parking (self).

Housed in a nine-story stucco building fronted by palm trees, this friendly, low-key resort hotel has a loyal repeat clientele. It's entered via a large, comfortably furnished lobby where guests enjoy a complimentary Monday afternoon manager's reception with hors d'oeuvres and wine. And the hotel caters to kids with welcome bags of cookies at check-in and gratis VCRs and movies on request; the front desk maintains a nice-sized movie library.

Attractive suites, with brass-trimmed lacquer or bleached-oak furnishings, have small sitting areas and fully equipped kitchenettes (most with dishwashers). One-bedroom units have full living rooms and dining areas, with phones, radios, and TVs in both rooms. Two-bedroom/two-bath condominiums have a king-size bed in each bedroom and a queen sleeper sofa in the living room. Both the rooms and the public areas are immaculate. Free local phone calls are a plus.

Dining/Entertainment: Kiefers, perched on the ninth floor, offers a romantic, candlelit setting and superb skyline views via a wall of windows. Tuesday through Saturday a pianist entertains in an adjoining lounge with a small dance floor. The menu highlights steak, seafood, and pasta dishes. Breakfast and dinner only; dinner entrees $12.95 to $18.95.

Services: Complimentary transportation 7am to 10:30pm to/from airport and major Strip hotels.

Facilities: Tour and show desks, coin-op washers/dryers, Har-Tru tennis court lit for night play (no charge for play, balls, or racquets), swimming pool/sundeck, whirlpool.

MODERATE

La Quinta Motor Inn

3782 Las Vegas Blvd. S., between Tropicana and Harmon aves., Las Vegas, NV 89109. ☎ **800/ 531-5900** or 702/739-7457. Fax 702/736-1129. 114 rms. A/C TV TEL. $65–$85 double. Extra person $10. Rates include continental breakfast. Children 18 and under stay free in parents' room. AE, CB, DC, DISC, MC, V. Free self parking.

Like many of this chain's properties, the La Quinta Motor Inn can be easily recognized by its terra-cotta roof and mission-style exterior architecture. Rooms are also southwestern in decor, with Aztec-motif paintings and fabrics. In-room amenities include TVs with pay-movie options.

There's a nice-sized pool and sun deck, and a big, comfortable 24-hour Carrows Restaurant adjoins. Carrows serves everything from breakfast burritos to USDA choice steaks, Italian pastas, and southern fried chicken. Oven-fresh pies here, too. A complimentary breakfast (juice, fruit, muffins, and coffee) is served each morning in La Quinta's pleasant lobby, and there's free transportation to/from the airport. Excalibur and MGM Grand restaurants and casino action are both a block away, and the Monte Carlo is right next door.

Vagabond Inn

3265 Las Vegas Blvd. S., just south of Sands Avenue, Las Vegas, NV 89109. ☎ **800/828-8032**, 800/522-1555, or 702/735-5102. Fax 702/735-0168. 126 rms. A/C TV TEL. Double $42–$95 Sun–Thurs, $52–$110 Fri–Sat; king rooms $65–$125 Sun–Thurs, $72–$150 Fri–Sat. Rates include continental breakfast. AE, CB, DC, DISC, MC, V. Free self parking.

A central location just across the street from Treasure Island—plus clean, nicely decorated basic motel rooms—make this a viable choice. One-third of the rooms have patios or balconies, and all offer cable TVs with pay-movie options. King rooms have wet bars and refrigerators. A wide selection of complimentary bath amenities is available at the front desk, and free coffee is served in the lobby around the clock, as is a daily continental breakfast of juice, fruit, and pastries. Facilities include coin-op washers and dryers. There's a swimming pool but no restaurant. A gratis airport shuttle and free local calls are pluses.

INEXPENSIVE

Algiers Hotel

2845 Las Vegas Blvd. S., between Riviera Blvd. and Sahara Ave., Las Vegas, NV 89109. ☎ **800/732-3361** or 702/735-3311. Fax 702/792-2112. 103 rms, 2 suites. A/C TV TEL. Single or double $35–$45 Sun–Thurs; $49.95–$89.95 Fri–Sat, holidays, and special events. Extra person $10. Children under 12 stay free in parents' room. AE, CB, DC, DISC, MC, V. Free self parking at your room door.

A venerable denizen of the Strip, the Algiers opened in 1953. However, a recent multi-million dollar renovation—including landscaping (note the lovely flower beds out back) and a new facade with a 60-foot sign—brought rooms and public areas up to date. There's no casino here, though you can play video poker in the bar. Neat two-story, aqua-trimmed peach stucco buildings house nice sized rooms (with dressing areas) that are clean and spiffy looking. Free local calls are a plus. Facilities include a medium-sized pool and palm-fringed sun deck.

The cozy Algiers Restaurant & Lounge is a local hangout frequented by state and city politicians and journalists. It has a copper-hooded fireplace and walls hung with historic Las Vegas photographs of pre-tower Strip hotels (Dunes, Sands, Flamingo), Liberace cutting the ribbon at the opening of the Riviera, Clara Bow and Joey Adams with the owner of the now-defunct Thunderbird, and many more. A glassed-in cafe overlooks the pool. The restaurant serves all meals, including many steak and seafood specialties, barbecued baby back ribs, and low-calorie dishes. There are souvenir shops, a jeweler, and a car-rental office out front. Also on the premises is the famed Candlelight Chapel, where many celebrities have tied the knot over the last three decades.

The Algiers is a good choice for families—right across the street from Circus Circus with its many child-oriented facilities and a half block from Wet 'n' Wild. It's also within walking distance of the Las Vegas Convention Center and the new Stratosphere Tower.

Center Strip Inn

3688 Las Vegas Blvd. S., at Harmon Ave., Las Vegas, NV 89109. ☎ **800/777-7737** or 702/739-6066. Fax 702/736-2521. 105 rms, 51 suites. A/C TV TEL. Sun–Thurs $39.95–$49.95 double; Fri–Sat and holidays $49.95–$199.95 single or double. Suites (for up to 4): $69 Sun–Thurs, $89–$249 Fri, Sat, and special events. Rates include continental breakfast. Mention you read about the Center Strip in Frommer's for a $5 discount Sun–Thurs. AE, DC, DISC, MC, V. Free parking at your room door.

This centrally located little motel is owned and operated by Robert Cohen, who is usually on the premises making sure guests are happy. He's a bit of an eccentric, and his hotel doesn't fit into any expected budget-property pattern. For example, the rooms have video-cassette players, and a selection of about 1,000 movies can be rented for just $2 each. Local calls and use of a fax machine are free. Breakfast consists of bagels, danish, juice, and coffee, and free coffee is available in the lobby all day. Also available at the front desk: irons, hair dryers, and gratis bath amenities.

The rooms, situated in two-story white stucco buildings, are standard motel units equipped with small refrigerators and safes. Suites offer kitchenettes, tubs with whirl-pool jets, and steam rooms.

There's no on-premises restaurant, but a 24-hour Denny's adjoins, numerous hotel restaurants are within easy walking distance, and you can have pizza delivered to your room. You'll also get a coupon for an all-you-can-eat $5.95 buffet for two at the Aladdin across the street. Facilities include a swimming pool and sun deck and a car-rental desk; the front desk can arrange tours.

Cohen also operates two Downtown properties—**The Crest Budget Inn** (207 N. 6th St., Las Vegas, NV 89101. ☎ **800/777-1817** or 702/382-5642) and **The Downtowner** (129 N. 8th St., Las Vegas, NV 89101. ☎ **800/777-2566** or 702/384-1441). If you mention this book, you'll pay just $24.95 a night Sunday to Friday, $39.95 Saturday.

5 Convention Center & Paradise Road

HOTELS WITH CASINOS
VERY EXPENSIVE

✪ The Hard Rock Hotel and Casino

4455 Paradise Rd., at Harmon Ave., Las Vegas, NV 89109. ☎ **800/473-ROCK** or 702/693-5000. Fax 702/693-5010. 316 rms, 24 suites. A/C TV TEL. Double $85–$250 Sun–Thurs, $135–$300 Fri–Sat, $250–$350 suite. Extra person $25. Children 12 and under stay free in parents' room. AE, DC, DISC, MC, V. Free parking (self and valet).

Owner Peter Morton, who bills his Hard Rock Hotel and Casino as "Vegas for a new generation," sent out invitations to the property's March 1995 opening inscribed on casino chips bearing the image of Jimi Hendrix. Dozens of celebrities—Kevin Costner, Rob Lowe, Patty Smyth, Sandra Bernhard, Stephen Baldwin, Christy Turlington, Jason Patric, Jack Nicholson, Pamela Anderson, and Jon Lovitz, among them—flew in for the festivities, which included concerts by the Eagles and Sheryl Crow. Everything here is rock-themed, from the Stevie Ray Vaughan quote over the entrance ("When this house is a rocking, don't bother knocking, come on in.") to the vast collection of music memorabilia displayed in public areas. The house is always "a rocking" (the pulsating beat emanates from hundreds of speakers through-out the property), and the cheerful casino features piano-shaped roulette tables and guitar-neck-handle slot machines. Even the walls of the bell desk are lined with gold records.

Large, attractive rooms, decorated in earth tones with photographs of rock stars adorning the walls, have beds with leather headboards and French windows that actually open to fresh air (a rarity in Las Vegas). Uncharacteristically large 27-inch TVs (most hotel sets are smaller since they want you in the casino, not staring at the tube) offers pay movie options and special music channels.

Dining/Entertainment: The Hard Rock's premier restaurant, **Mortoni's,** is a beauty. Parchment-yellow walls are hung with vintage photographs such as a

The Smithsonian of Rock 'n' Roll

Fronted by a 90-foot Fender Stratocaster guitar, the Hard Rock is a rock 'n' roll museum displaying a massive collection of rock-legend memorabilia. Some of the exhibits you'll see here include:

- Elvis' gold lamé jacket.
- Guitars from Nirvana, ZZ Top, Bruce Springsteen, Bill Haley (from the movie *Rock Around the Clock*), Eric Clapton, and many others.
- James Brown's shoeshine stand (where he wrote songs when he was a kid) and his "King of Soul" cape and crown.
- The dresses the Supremes wore on the *Ed Sullivan Show.*
- A piece of the plane that carried Otis Redding to his death in the late '60s.
- Pete Townshend's smashed guitar from the *Late Night With David Letterman* show.
- The artist-formerly-known-as-Prince's handwritten lyrics for a song from *Purple Rain.*
- "Maestro of Love" Barry White's Lifetime Achievement Award.
- The white suit worn by Mick Jagger when he was released from a UK jail in the late '60s.
- Greg Allman's favorite biker jacket.
- A collection of surfboards belonging to the Beach Boys.
- An XXL jacket worn on tour by Meat Loaf.
- Las Vegas hotel menus signed by Elvis and Jimi Hendrix.
- Over 500 merchandising items manufactured with the Beatles' images.
- The piano on which Al Green composed "Take Me to the River."
- "I Hope I Die Before I Get Old"—a poem written by Pearl Jam's Eddie Vedder after Kurt Cobain's suicide.

tuxedoed James Dean at a Hollywood party; Humphrey Bogart, Frank Sinatra, and Grace Kelly at Chasen's in the 1940s; and stills from Las Vegas movies. Furnishings are butter-soft plush red leather. Large windows overlook the pool area, where, weather permitting, you can dine outdoors at umbrella tables. The fare is Italian, and portions are vast. Dinner only; entrees $12.95 to $23.95 (pastas and pizzas mostly $9 to $14).

At **Mr. Lucky's 24/7**—the hotel's round-the-clock coffee shop displaying rock memorabilia and old Las Vegas hotel signs—California-style entrees and pizzas are offered in addition to the usual Las Vegas menu.

The **Hard Rock Café** (details in chapter 6) is adjacent to the hotel.

The Center Bar in the casino is under a glowing purple dome, from which a globe inscribed with the words "One Love, One World" is suspended. The Beach Club Bar serves light fare and frozen drinks poolside. And the Viva Las Vegas Lounge, off the casino, has a video wall where four monitors display rapid-paced rock footage.

Services: 24-hour room service, concierge.

Facilities: Small video-game arcade, gift/sundry shop and immense Hard Rock retail store, show desk (for **The Joint** only; tickets to other shows can be arranged by the concierge), health club (offering a full complement of Cybex equipment, stair machines, treadmills, massage, and steamrooms).

The Hard Rock has one of the most gorgeous pool areas in Las Vegas, complete with a palm-fringed sandy beach, grassy expanses of lawn, a vast free-form sand-bottomed pool with a water slide and 150 speakers providing underwater music, several whirlpools, and raft rentals. Luxurious poolside cabanas (equipped with TVs, phones, misters, and refrigerators) can be rented for $55 to $85 a day.

✪ Las Vegas Hilton

3000 Paradise Rd., at Riviera Blvd., Las Vegas, NV 89109. ☎ **800/732-7117** or 702/732-5111. Fax 702/732-5805. 2,900 rms, 274 suites, A/C TV TEL. $89–$269 double, $310–$1,520 suite. Extra person $25. Children of any age stay free in parents' room. Off-season rates may be lower, subject to availability. Inquire about attractively priced golf and other packages. AE, CB, DC, DISC, JCB, MC, V. Free parking (self and valet).

Its 375-foot tower dominating the desert horizon, this dazzling megahotel—fronted by a laser fantasy fountain—occupies 80 acres overlooking the blue lakes and manicured lawns of an adjacent 18-hole golf course. Barbra Streisand and Cary Grant presided at the hotel's 1969 opening, and Elvis Presley made a dramatic return to live performances at the Hilton Showroom the same year. The Hilton is simply magnificent—from its lobby and casino glittering with massive Austrian crystal chandeliers to its comprehensive resort facilities, showroom, and distinguished restaurants—not to mention the largest hotel convention and meeting facilities in the world. A new Star Trek attraction will be opening here Spring 1997 (the available details are in chapter 7).

Rooms are decorated in muted southwestern hues with verdigris accents and bleached oak furnishings. Paintings of cacti enhance this motif. Some rooms have sofas and/or dressing rooms; most contain safes. All offer TVs (cached in handsome armoires) with HBO, On-Command pay-movie options, an in-house information channel, and video checkout capability.

Dining/Entertainment: Bistro Le Montrachet is reviewed in chapter 6.

Most dramatic of the Hilton's restaurants is Benihana Village, a pagoda-roofed Oriental fantasyland with cascading waterfalls and meandering streams, spanned by quaint wooden bridges. You'll enjoy dancing water displays and fiber-optic fireworks while you dine. The Village houses three restaurants and a lounge. On one side of the central waterway is the **Garden of the Dragon,** its entrance presided over by a fiery-eyed dragon atop a pagoda. The menu offers regional Chinese specialties. Dinner only; most entrees $14 to $19 (less for rice, noodle, and vegetable dishes).

Across the stream is the **Seafood Grille,** fronted by a colorful Asian marketplace aclutter with barrels of eggs (above which are animated hens in wooden cages) and displays of fish, fruits, and vegetables. Seating is under a pagoda eave, walls are hung with fishing nets, and wooden columns are embellished with Chinese kites. Dinner only; entrees $13.75 to $34.50 (most under $20). At the far end, occupying two dining levels, is a branch of **Benihana,** with a restrained Japanese shoji-screen decor and teppanyaki-grill tables. Dinner only; entrees $14.95 to $25.95; combination dinners $28.50 to $30.50.

Near the entrance to this exotic restaurant complex is the **Kabuki Lounge,** an inviting setting for cocktails.

The **Hilton Steakhouse,** which also serves seafood and chops, offers a warmly intimate wood-paneled interior with candlelit tables. Dinner only; entrees $19 to $29.95.

Another beef eatery is the **Barronshire Room,** where an English club ambience is created by high-backed burgundy leather booths and armchairs, crystal chandeliers and sconces, and walls hung with gilt-framed oil paintings. The restaurant is patterned after the renowned Barronshire Inn in southern England. Dinner only; entrees $18 to $24.95.

At the simpatico **MargaritaGrille,** Mexican music, pots of cacti, and displays of papier-mâché birds and pottery combine to create a south-of-the-border ambience. The Grille's bar is quite popular for cocktails and Mexican appetizers. Dinner only; entrees $8.25 to $15.50.

Andiamo, a charming Italian *ristorante,* seats diners amid planters of ficus trees and terra-cotta columns. Above the brass- and copper-accented exhibition kitchen is a colorful display of Italian food products. All pasta served here is made fresh on the premises. Dinner only; entrees $13.50 to $25.25.

Finally there's **The Coffee Shop,** a southwestern-motif 24-hour facility where lush faux foliage, including hibiscus draped from driftwood beams overhead, gives the room a cheerful ambience. Traditional Las Vegas coffee-shop fare is supplemented by Mexican specialties.

Additional facilities include a branch of TCBY and a cappuccino and pastry cart in the lobby. There are seven bar/lounges at the Hilton. In addition, the Garden Snack Bar serves the pool deck; the Paddock Snack Bar in the race and sports book features pizza, sandwiches, and other light fare items (not oats); and the Nightclub, a first-rate casino lounge, which features live entertainment nightly. See also the buffet listings in chapter 6. *Note:* Children 12 and under dine in any Hilton restaurant for half the listed menu prices.

Services: 24-hour room service, foreign-currency exchange.

Facilities: Casino, car-rental desk, tour desk, travel agency, shops (upscale clothing, shoes, logo items, gifts, candy), small video-game arcade, business service center, multiservice beauty salon/barbershop, jogging trail, 18-hole golf course.

The third-floor roof comprises a beautifully landscaped 8-acre recreation deck with a large swimming pool, a 24-seat whirlpool spa, six Har-Tru tennis courts lit for night play, Ping-Pong, and a putting green. Also on this level is a luxurious, 17,000-square-foot, state-of-the-art health club offering Nautilus equipment, Lifecycles, treadmills, rowing machines, three whirlpool spas, steam, sauna, massage, and tanning beds. Guests are totally pampered: all toiletries are provided; there are comfortable TV lounges; complimentary bottled waters and juices are served in the canteen; and beauty services include facials, oxygen pep-up, and spa body treatments.

MODERATE

Best Western Mardi Gras Inn

3500 Paradise Rd., between Sands Ave. and Desert Inn Rd., Las Vegas, NV 89109. ☎ **800/ 634-6501** or 702/731-2020. Fax 702/733-6994. 315 minisuites. A/C TV TEL. $40–$125 single or double. Extra person $8. Children 18 and under stay free in parents' room. AE, CB, DC, DISC, JCB, MC, V. Free parking at your room door.

Opened in 1980, this well-run little casino hotel has a lot to offer. A block from the convention center and close to major properties, its three-story building sits on nicely landscaped grounds with manicured lawns, trees, and shrubbery. There's a gazebo out back where guests can enjoy a picnic lunch.

Accommodations are all spacious queen-bedded minisuites with sofa-bedded living room areas and eat-in kitchens, the latter equipped with wet bars, refrigerators, and coffeemakers. All are attractively decorated and offer TVs with HBO and pay-movie options. Staying here is like having your own little Las Vegas apartment.

Dining/Entertainment: A pleasant restaurant/bar off the lobby, open from 6:30am to 11pm daily, serves typical coffee-shop fare; a 12-ounce prime rib dinner here is just $8.95.

Services: Free transportation to/from airport and major Strip hotels.

Facilities: Small casino (64 slots/video poker machines), small video-game arcade, car-rental desk, tour and show desks, coin-op washers/dryers, unisex hairdresser, gift shop, RV parking. The inn has a large swimming pool with a duplex sundeck and whirlpool.

INEXPENSIVE

Super 8 Motel

4250 Koval Lane, just south of Flamingo Rd., Las Vegas, NV 89109. ☎ **800/800-8000** or 702/794-0888. 294 rms, 6 suites. A/C TV TEL. Sun–Thurs $41–$43 double; Fri–Sat $56–$58 double. Extra person $8. Children 12 and under stay free in parents' room. Pets $5 per night. AE, CB, DC, DISC, MC, V. Free parking (self).

Billing itself as "the world's largest Super 8 Motel," this friendly property occupies a vaguely Tudor-style stone and stucco building. Coffee is served gratis in a pleasant little lobby furnished with comfortable sofas and wing chairs. Rooms are clean and well maintained. Some have safes, and TVs offer free movie channels.

Dining/Entertainment: The nautically themed **Ellis Island Restaurant,** open 24 hours, offers typical coffee-shop fare at reasonable prices. In the adjoining bar—a library-like setting with shelves of books and green marble tables—sporting events are aired on TV monitors. There's also a bar in the casino with a karaoke machine.

Services: 24-hour room service, free airport transfer.

Facilities: Casino (race book and 50 slot/poker/21 machines), small kidney-shaped pool/sundeck and adjoining whirlpool, car-rental desk, coin-op washers/dryers.

HOTELS WITHOUT CASINOS
VERY EXPENSIVE

✪ Alexis Park Resort

375 E. Harmon Ave., between Koval Lane and Paradise Rd., Las Vegas, NV 89109. ☎ **702/796-3300** or 800/453-8000. Fax 702/796-4334. 600 suites. A/C MINIBAR TV TEL. $105–$250 one-bedroom suite, $175–$400 one-bedroom loft suite, $350–$1,500 larger suite. Extra person $15. Children 18 and under stay free in parents' room. AE, CB, DC, DISC, JCB, MC, V. Free parking (self and valet).

A low-key atmosphere, luxurious digs, and superb service combine to make Alexis Park the hotel choice of many showroom headliners and visiting celebrities. Alan Alda, Alec Baldwin, Whitney Houston, Robert de Niro, Dolly Parton, and Garth Brooks are just a few of the superstars who've chosen this resort's discreet elegance over the seemingly more glitzier Strip hotels. It's the kind of place where you can get a phone at your restaurant table or your suit pressed at 3am.

You'll sense the difference the moment you approach the palm-fringed entranceway, fronted by lovingly tended flower beds and a rock waterfall. The elegant lobby has comfortable sofas amid immense terra-cotta pots of ferns, cacti, and calla lilies, and there's notably fine artwork throughout the public areas.

Spacious suites are decorated in light resort colors with taupe lacquer furnishings. Loft suites have cathedral ceilings. All are equipped with refrigerators, wet bars, two-line phones (one in each room of your suite) with computer jacks, and TVs (also one in each room) with HBO and pay-movie options. More than a third of the suites have working fireplaces and/or Jacuzzi tubs.

Dining/Entertainment: Pegasus, an exquisite award-winning gourmet dining room, is described in chapter 6.

The **Pisces Bistro,** under a 30-foot domed ceiling with planters of greenery cascading from tiers overhead, provides live entertainment Tuesday through Saturday nights (see chapter 10) and serves drinks, pizzas, salads, sandwiches, a few full entrees (steak, seafood, pasta), and desserts—both inside and on a patio overlooking the pool.

Services: 24-hour room service, concierge.

Facilities: Gift shop, unisex hair salon, health club (including a good complement of workout equipment, whirlpool, massage, steam, and sauna).

Behind the hotel are beautifully landscaped grounds with palm trees and pines, streams and ponds spanned by quaint bridges, gazebos, rock gardens, flower beds, and oleanders. Here you'll find a large fountain-centered swimming pool, two smaller pools, cabana bars, three whirlpool spas, umbrella tables, table tennis, and a nine-hole putting green.

Courtyard Marriott

3275 Paradise Rd., between Convention Center Dr. and Desert Inn Rd., Las Vegas, NV 89109. ☎ **800/321-2211** or 702/791-3600. Fax 702/796-7981. 137 rms, 12 suites. A/C TV TEL. Per-room rates are $109 Sun–Thurs, $119 Fri–Sat; suites $119–$129. AE, CB, DC, DISC, MC, V. Free parking at your room door.

Housed in three-story terra-cotta-roofed stucco buildings, in an attractively landscaped setting of trees, shrubbery, and flower beds, the Courtyard is a welcome link in the Marriott chain. The concept for these limited-service, lower-priced lodgings (though not especially low priced for Las Vegas) developed in the 1980s, and this particular property opened in 1989. Although the services are limited, don't picture a no-frills establishment. This is a beautiful hotel, with a pleasant, plant-filled lobby and very nice rooms indeed.

Like its public areas, the rooms—most with king-size beds—still look spanking new. Decorated in shades of gray-blue, mauve, and burgundy, with sofas and handsome mahogany furnishings (including large desks), they offer TVs with multiple On-Command movie options. All rooms have balconies or patios.

Dining/Entertainment: Off the lobby is a light and airy plant-filled restaurant with glossy oak paneling and tables. It serves buffet breakfasts, as well as à la carte lunches (mostly salads and sandwiches); light fare is available from 5 to 10pm. Adjoining is a comfortable lobby lounge with plush furnishings, a large-screen TV, and a working fireplace. Drinks are served here from 4 to 10pm. You can also enjoy breakfast in this lounge and catch a morning TV news show.

Services: Room service 4 to 10pm, complimentary airport shuttle.

Facilities: Small exercise room, medium-size swimming pool with adjoining whirlpool, picnic tables and barbecue grills, coin-op washers/dryers.

EXPENSIVE

La Quinta Inn

3970 Paradise Rd., between Twain Ave. and Flamingo Rd., Las Vegas, NV 89109. ☎ **800/531-5900** or 702/796-9000. Fax 702/796-3537. 228 rms, 51 suites. A/C TV TEL. Executive rooms $89 Sun–Thurs, $99 Fri–Sat; double queen rooms $85 Sun–Thurs, $95 Fri–Sat; $99–$200 suite. Rates include continental breakfast; inquire about seasonal discounts. AE, CB, DC, DISC, MC, V. Free parking (self).

Its four mission-style buildings forming a U around a large courtyard, this La Quinta offers a tranquil alternative to the razzle-dazzle of Strip hotels. Although you're just a minute (and a gratis shuttle ride) from major casinos, you'll feel like you're staying in a countryside retreat. Lovely grounds, with manicured lawns, lovingly tended flower beds, and a charming stone fountain, offer rustic benches, lawn games (croquet, badminton, volleyball), barbecue grills, and picnic tables.

Accommodations are immaculate and attractive. Executive rooms feature one queen-size bed, a small refrigerator, a wet bar, and a microwave oven. Double queens are larger but have no kitchen facilities. And spacious one- and two-bedroom suites contain large living rooms (some with sofa beds), dining areas, and full kitchens. Most accommodations have patios or balconies, and all feature baths with oversized whirlpool tubs. TVs offer satellite channels and HBO.

Dining/Entertainment: Complimentary continental breakfast (juice, bagels, cereal, muffins, fresh fruit, beverages) is served daily in the Patio Café.

Facilities: Car rentals/tours arranged at the front desk, coin-op washers/dryers, medium-size swimming pool and adjoining whirlpool. A free 24-hour shuttle offers pickup and return to and from the airport and several Strip casino hotels.

✪ Residence Inn by Marriott

3225 Paradise Rd., between Desert Inn Rd. and Convention Center Dr., Las Vegas, NV 89109. ☎ **800/331-3131** or 702/796-9300. 144 studios, 48 penthouses. A/C TV TEL. $89–$169 studio (for 1 or 2; extra person $10), $109–$219 penthouse (for up to 5). Rates include continental breakfast. AE, CB, DC, DISC, MC, V. Free parking (self).

Staying here is like having your own apartment in Las Vegas. The property occupies seven acres of perfectly manicured lawns, tropical foliage, and neat flower beds. It's a great choice for families and business travelers.

Accommodations, most with working fireplaces, are housed in condo-like, two-story wood and stucco buildings, fronted by little gardens. Studios have adjoining sitting rooms with sofas and armchairs, dressing areas, and fully equipped eat-in kitchens complete with dishwashers. Every guest receives a welcome basket of microwave popcorn and coffee. TVs offer visitor-information channels and VCRs (you can rent movies nearby), and all rooms have balconies or patios. Duplex penthouses, some with cathedral ceilings, add an upstairs bedroom (with its own bath, phone, TV, and radio) and a full dining room.

Dining/Entertainment: A big continental buffet breakfast (fresh fruit, yogurt, cereals, muffins, bagels, pastries) is served each morning in the gatehouse, a delightful cathedral-ceilinged lobby lounge with a working fireplace. There's comfortable seating amid planters of greenery. Daily papers are set out here each morning; there's a large-screen TV and a stereo for guest use; and a selection of toys, games, and books is available for children. Weekday evenings from 5:30 to 7pm, complimentary buffets with beverages (beer, wine, coffee, soda), fresh popcorn, and daily varying fare soup/salad/sandwiches, tacos, Chinese, barbecue, spaghetti, and so on) are served in the gatehouse. This cocktail-hour spread affords an opportunity to socialize with other guests—a nice feature if you're traveling alone.

Services: Local restaurants deliver food, and there's also a complimentary food-shopping service. Maids wash your dishes.

Facilities: Car-rental desk, barbecue grills, coin-op washers/dryers, sports court (paddle tennis, volleyball, basketball). There's a good-size swimming pool and whirlpool with a sundeck. Guests can use the health club next door at Courtyard Marriott (details below).

MODERATE

Debbie Reynolds Hotel/Casino/Hollywood Movie Museum

305 Convention Center Dr., between Las Vegas Blvd. S. and Paradise Rd., Las Vegas, NV 89109. ☎ **800/633-1777** or 702/734-0711. Fax 702/734-2954. 197 rms, 7 suites. A/C TV TEL. Single

or double $49–$69 Sun–Thurs, $59–$79 Fri–Sat. Rates can go as high as $175 during conventions and peak seasons. Extra person $10. AE, DC, DISC, MC, V. Free parking (self and valet).

Note: This was originally designed as a casino hotel, and it has a large space set aside for gaming. Debbie is temporarily without a gaming license, but she may have it by the time you read this.

In 1993, America's sweetheart—musical-comedy star Debbie Reynolds—took over the 12-story Paddlewheel Hotel, transforming its signature paddlewheel facade into a neon-lit revolving film reel and inserting color photographs of Hollywood icons into the frames. Why did Debbie buy a hotel? Ever the vivacious entertainer, she had long dreamed of creating a performance space to her own specifications as well as a museum to house her massive collection of Hollywood memorabilia (see chapter 7). Her Hollywood-glamour concept is an exciting one. Not only does she perform in the showroom, but she has created an after-hours lounge where Strip entertainers (many of whom are her friends) can unwind—and take the stage—after their shows.

The lobby here is a mini-museum of Hollywood memorabilia: The Baccarat crystal chandeliers overhead are from the film *The Great Waltz,* the marble-topped console tables were used on the sets of *Camille* and *Marie Antoinette,* and a teak opium bed and side chairs from *The Good Earth* are on display. You can even sit down (an unusual feature for a Las Vegas hotel lobby) on a high-backed burgundy brocade ottoman from the 1932 movie *Grand Hotel.*

Large rooms offer great views of the Strip from picture windows. All have sizable dressing areas, TVs with Spectravision movie options, and phones with call waiting. Some accommodations also offer refrigerators, hair dryers, and coffeemakers. In keeping with the hotel's Hollywood theme, walls are hung with large black-and-white photographs of movie legends (perhaps Gable and Lombard will be watching over you). The top three floors house luxurious time-share units; call for details.

Dining/Entertainment: The 24-hour Celebrity Café serves as both a hotel coffee shop and a lounge where Debbie and her Strip entertainer friends can hang out and perform until the wee hours on weekend nights.

And Bogie's Bar, its back wall lined with Bogart movie stills, serves the casino.

Services: 24-hour room service.

Facilities: Large swimming pool with bilevel sun deck, whirlpool, saunas, gift shop, sightseeing/show/tour desk. A large shopping center—with a drugstore/pharmacy, a post office, a dry cleaner, and a coin-op laundry—is just across the street. Guests can enjoy health club privileges nearby.

Emerald Springs Holiday Inn

325 E. Flamingo Rd., between Koval Lane and Paradise Rd., Las Vegas, NV 89109. ☎ **800/ 732-7889** or 702/732-9100. Fax 702/731-9784. 132 rms, 18 suites. A/C TV TEL. Single or double $69–$99 for studio, $99–$129 Jacuzzi suite, $129–$175 hospitality suite. Extra person $15. Children 18 and under stay free in parents' room. AE, CB, DC, DISC, MC, V. Free parking (self).

Housed in three mauve-trimmed peach stucco buildings, Emerald Springs offers a friendly, low-key alternative to the usual glitz and glitter. It's entered via a charming marble-floored lobby with a waterfall fountain and lush, faux tropical plantings under a domed skylight. Off the lobby is a comfortably furnished lounge with a large-screen TV and working fireplace. Typical of the inn's hospitality is a bowl of apples for the taking at the front desk. And weeknights from 10:30pm to midnight you can "raid the icebox" at the Veranda Café, which offers complimentary cookies, peanut butter and jelly sandwiches, and coffee, tea, or milk. Although your surroundings here are serene, you're only two blocks from the heart of the Strip.

Public areas and rooms here are notably clean and spiffy. Pristine hallways are hung with nice abstract paintings and have small seating areas on every level, and rooms are beautifully decorated in teal and mauve with bleached-oak furnishings. Even the smallest accommodations (studios) offer small sofas, desks, and armchairs with hassocks. You also get two phones (desk and bedside), an in-room coffeemaker (with gratis coffee), and a wet bar with refrigerator. TVs (concealed in an armoire) have HBO and pay-movie options; VCRs are available on request. There's a separate dressing room and a hair dryer in the bath. Suites add a living-room area with a large-screen TV to the above, an eat-in kitchenette with a microwave oven, a larger dressing room, and a Jacuzzi tub. Hospitality suites feature sitting room areas and dining tables.

Dining/Entertainment: Just off the lobby (you can hear the splashing of the fountain and waterfall), the **Veranda Café** offers both indoor and alfresco dining, the latter on a covered patio overlooking the pool. It serves buffet breakfasts and à la carte lunches (burgers, salads, deli sandwiches) and dinners (light fare plus entrees). A comfortable bar/lounge with video poker games adjoins.

Services: Concierge, complimentary limousine transportation to and from the airport and nearby casinos between 6:30am and 11pm (van service available 11pm to 6:30am), room service, business services, gratis newspapers available at the front desk.

Facilities: Fitness room, nice sized pool/sun deck and whirlpool in an attractively landscaped setting.

Fairfield Inn by Marriott

3850 Paradise Rd., between Twain Ave. and Flamingo Rd., Las Vegas, NV 89109. ☎ **800/ 228-2800** or 702/791-0899. Fax 702/791-0899. 129 rms. A/C TV TEL. $56–$70 for up to 5 people. Rates include continental breakfast. AE, CB, DC, DISC, MC, V. Free parking (self).

This pristine property, opened in 1990, is a pleasant place to stay. It has a comfortable lobby with sofas and armchairs—a simpatico setting in which to plan your day's activities over a cup of coffee, tea, or hot chocolate (provided gratis all day).

Rooms are cheerful. Units with king-size beds have convertible sofas, and all accommodations offer well-lit work areas with desks; TVs have free movie channels as well as pay-movie options. Local calls are free.

Breakfast pastries, fresh fruit, juice, and yogurt are served in the lobby each morning, and many restaurants are within easy walking distance. Facilities include a pool/ whirlpool and sun deck with umbrella tables. A free shuttle goes to and from the airport every 30 minutes between 6am and midnight. Car rentals and tours can be arranged. The front desk proffers warm hospitality.

INEXPENSIVE

⑤ Motel 6

195 E. Tropicana Ave., at Koval Lane, Las Vegas, NV 89109. ☎ **800/4-MOTEL-6** or 702/ 798-0728. Fax 702/798-5657. 602 rms. A/C TV TEL. For 1 person, Sun–Thurs $32.99, Fri–Sat $49.99. Extra person $6. Children under 17 stay free in parents' room. AE, CB, DC, DISC, MC, V. Free parking at your room door.

Fronted by a big neon sign, Las Vegas's Motel 6 is the largest in the country, and it happens to be a great budget choice. Most Motel 6 properties are a little out-of-the-way, but this one is quite close to major Strip casino hotels (the MGM is adjacent). It has a big, pleasant lobby, and the rooms, in two-story cream stucco buildings, are clean and attractively decorated. Some rooms have showers only, others, tub/shower baths. Local calls are free and your TV offers HBO.

Three restaurants (including a pleasant 24-hour family restaurant called **Carrows;** see description in listing for La Quinta Motor Inn on page 00) adjoin. On-premises facilities include a large well-stocked gift shop, vending machines, a tour desk, two nice-size swimming pools in enclosed courtyards, a whirlpool, and coin-op washers/ dryers.

6 East Las Vegas: A Hotel with Casino

✪ Sam's Town Hotel & Gambling Hall

5111 Boulder Hwy., at Flamingo Rd., Las Vegas, NV 89122. ☎ **800/634-6371** or 702/ 456-7777. Fax 702/454-8014. 617 rms, 33 suites. A/C TV TEL. Single or double $50–$135 Sun-Thurs, $75–$135 Fri–Sat; suites $160–$270. Extra person $5. AE, CB, DC, DISC, MC, V. Free parking (self and valet).

Just five miles from the Strip and Western-themed, Sam's Town is immensely popular with locals and tourists alike. Its friendly atmosphere and nightly laser shows make it a good choice for families. The property occupies 58 acres, with accommodations surrounding one of its biggest selling points: Mystic Falls—a lush 25,000-square-foot indoor park under a nine-story skylight. Here, amid leafy trees, fern gullies, fountains, and flower beds, are meandering streams, rock waterfalls, and wildlife, both real (including a dam-building beaver) and animatronic (chirping birds). Lovely year round, the park is an especially welcome setting in summer when 100°-plus temperatures make it impossible to spend any time outdoors; in this controlled setting, it's always a comfortable 70 degrees. There are chairs and benches, as well as a log pagoda where you can sit in tranquil comfort and read a book, a novelty in this town.

Large, high-ceilinged accommodations—overlooking the park or mountains—are also notably appealing, with rustic light-wood furnishings, Native American-motif carpeting, cowhide-shaded lighting fixtures, and Western art on the walls. Each room has a large desk and a cable TV offering pay-movie options, keno, and a hotel-information channel. At night the park is lit by lanterns, and trees are strung with thousands of tiny lights.

Dining/Entertainment: Papamios and **The Great Buffet** are described in chapter 6.

Diamond Lil's, an opulent Old West/Victorian crystal-chandeliered gourmet room, seats diners in plush booths lit by fringe-shaded oil lamps. Dinner only; steaks, prime rib, and seafood items $13.95 to $18.95 (more for lobster). A bar/lounge adjoins.

At **Billy Bob's Steak House & Saloon**—also highlighting steak, prime rib, and seafood—log and stone walls are hung with rusty farm implements and paintings of the Old West. A waterwheel in one room creates a pleasant splashy backdrop. Dinner only; entrees $14.95 to $19.95. The Silver Dollar Bar, embellished by a display of animal horns, adjoins.

Willy & Jose's—a "Mexican cantina" with fading wallpapers and neon beer signs over the bar—serves traditional Mexican (not Tex-Mex) fare. Twelve-ounce margaritas are 95¢. Dinner only; entrees $6.25 to $11.95.

Mary's Diner, open for all meals, conforms to the traditions of its genre, complete with counter seating and small jukeboxes adjoining its comfortable red leatherette booths. The menu includes Yankee pot roast, meat loaf with real mashed potatoes, homemade chili, and the like; everything but a T-bone steak is under $5.

Smokey Joe's Cafe & Market—another Western setting with knotty-pine booths, faux windows overlooking a cowboy town mural, and walls hung with washboards and antique farm implements—is the hotel's 24-hour facility. Coffee shop fare is supplemented by a full Chinese menu. Great deals here include inexpensive buffets at breakfast and terrific all-you-can-eat salad bars at lunch and dinner—not to mention graveyard specials such as three eggs, a ³/₄-pound ham steak, hash browns, and toast served from 11pm to 11am for $2.95.

Another 24-hour facility is the Final Score Sports Bar, where you'll find pool tables, darts, pinball, air hockey, and a basketball cage; sporting events are aired on more than 30 TV monitors, and there's occasionally live music for dancing. Light fare (burgers, wings, nachos) is available, and there's patio seating overlooking the pool.

Roxy's Saloon, one of 13 bars on the premises, offers live entertainment (C&W) for dancing daily from noon to the wee hours. Rounding out facilities here are: a deli in the race and sports book area, a bowling alley snack bar, a food court, an ice cream parlor, and a rotating bar in the park.

Services: Room service, foreign currency exchange, shoeshine; free shuttle bus to/from the Stardust, MGM, Bally's, Fremont, and California hotels.

Facilities: Casino, two RV parks ($14 a night with complete hook-up), 56-lane bowling alley open 24 hours, 25,000-square-foot Western shop, dance hall, gift/logo shop, sand volleyball court, country dance hall.

7 Downtown (All Accommodations with Casinos)
EXPENSIVE

✪ Golden Nugget

129 E. Fremont St., at Casino Center Blvd., Las Vegas, NV 89101. ☎ **800/634-3454** or 702/385-7111. Fax 702/386-8362. 1,805 rms, 102 suites. A/C TV TEL. Single or double $59–$159 Sun–Thurs, $99–$259 Fri–Sat, $275–$475 suite. Extra person $20. AE, CB, DC, DISC, MC, V. Free parking (self and valet).

Gleaming white and gold in the Las Vegas sun, its surrounding streets lined with tall swaying palms, the Golden Nugget looks more like a luxurious Côte d'Azur resort than a Downtown hotel. And it is. Opened in 1946, it was the first building in Las Vegas constructed specifically for casino gambling. When Steve Wynn acquired the property in 1973, it had a plush Old West/Victorian decor. Over the next decade, Wynn took down all the neon signs, western art, and turn-of-the-century furnishings and created a magnificent, first-class European-style resort with a stunning chandeliered white-marble lobby (no casino games in view), mirrored ceiling, gleaming brass accents, and lavish floral arrangements gracing public areas. The Nugget's sun-dappled interior spaces are a welcome change from the Las Vegas tradition of dim lighting.

Resort-style rooms are fittingly charming—light and airy, with valanced beds, Indian batik-look bedspreads and draperies, and gilt-framed prints of 19th-century Rangoon and botanicals adorning the walls. Large desks are a plus for business travelers, and baths offer vanity tables with cosmetic mirrors. Cable TVs feature in-house information stations and pay-movie options.

Dining/Entertainment: The **Carson Street Cafe,** the Nugget's 24-hour restaurant, and its superb buffets and 24-hour Sunday brunch are described in chapter 6.

Stefano's, off a gorgeous marble-floored courtyard, offers a festive setting for northern Italian cuisine, complete with singing waiters. Murals of Venice behind trellised "windows" are designed to look like scenery, and baroque elaboration includes cupids, ornate columns, and gilt-framed mirrors. Dinner only; entrees $9.95 to $27.25.

The opulent **Lillie Langtry's** is adorned with beveled and gilt-framed mirrors, gilded wood flowers, Chinese art, and a lovely painting of swans. It's a lovely setting, softly lit and enhanced by a backdrop of piano and harp music. The menu is Chinese. Dinner only; entrees $9 to $14.75 (more for lobster dishes).

This branch of the **California Pizza Kitchen** is a plush precinct with an exhibition kitchen housing an oak-burning pizza oven. In addition to pizzas with trendy toppings the menu offers calzones, salads, pasta, and other entrees. Open for lunch and dinner daily; all entrees under $10.

In addition, a 24-hour snack bar in the casino offers deli sandwiches, pizza, and light fare, and there are four casino bars including the elegant **Claude's** and the 38 Different Kinds of Beer Bar.

Services: 24-hour room service, shoeshine, concierge.

Facilities: Casino, car-rental desk, full-service unisex hair salon, shops (gifts, jewelry, designer fashions, sportswear, logo items), video-game arcade.

The Nugget's top-rated health club offers a full line of Universal equipment, Lifecycles, StairMasters, treadmills, rowing machines, Gravitron, free weights, steam sauna, tanning beds, and massage. Salon treatments include everything from leg waxing to seaweed-mask facials. The spa's opulent Palladian-mirrored foyer is modeled after a salon in New York's Frick Museum.

The entrance to the hotel's immense swimming pool and outdoor whirlpool spa is graced by elegant marble swans and bronze fish sculptures. Fountains, palm trees, and verdant landscaping create a tropical setting, and a poolside bar serves the sundeck.

MODERATE

Days Inn Downtown
707 E. Fremont St., at 7th St., Las Vegas, NV 89101. ☎ **800/325-2344**, 800/325-2525, or 702/388-1400. Fax 702/388-9622. 140 rms, 7 suites. A/C TV TEL. $40–$65 for a one-bed room, $45–$80 for a two-bed room. Rates for up to 4 people; may be higher during special events. "Super Saver" rate ($39 Sun–Thurs, $50 Fri–Sat, single or double) if you reserve 30 days in advance via the toll-free number 800/325-2525 (subject to availability). AE, CB, DC, DISC, MC, V. Free parking (self).

Opened in 1988, this Days Inn still looks quite new. Rooms, in a U-shaped three-story building, are cheerfully decorated and have TVs offering pay movies. On-premises facilities comprise a rooftop pool and sundeck, a few video games, and the Culinary Restaurant, serving coffee-shop fare at all meals.

Fitzgeralds Casino Holiday Inn
301 Fremont St., at 3rd St., Las Vegas, NV 89101. ☎ **800/274-LUCK** or 702/388-2400. Fax 702/388-2181. 648 rms, 14 suites. A/C TV TEL. Single or double $48–$68 Sun–Thurs, $65–$105 Fri–Sat. Extra person $10. Children under 19 stay free in parents' room. AE, CB, DC, DISC, MC, V. Free parking (self and valet).

At 34 stories Fitzgeralds used to be the tallest casino hotel in Nevada. The theme is Irish, with pieces of the actual Blarney stone from County Cork at various places in the casino (rub them for luck) and a four-leaf clover logo. Out front, the hotel's mascot, Mr. O'Lucky, is depicted in a 45-foot neon sign amid cascading coins and a vast rainbow. In 1996 the property came under the auspices of the Holiday Inn chain and underwent a total renovation and upgrade. Recently remodeled rooms are nicely decorated in "lucky shades of green," with oak furnishings and pretty prints on the walls. All offer safes and 25-inch TVs with pay-movie options. Corner rooms provide dazzling two-sided views of the Fremont Street Experience, and 34 units have Jacuzzis and sofas. Another 650 rooms will be added by 1998.

Dining/Entertainment: Several new facilities are under construction at this writing. **Limericks,** an upscale Irish pub open for dinner only, will highlight steaks, seafood, lamb, and pasta dishes. Also in the works are a moderately priced Italian/

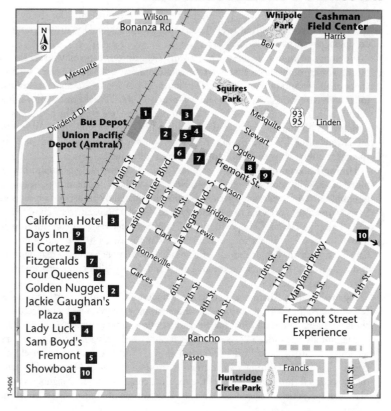

California Hotel **3**
Days Inn **9**
El Cortez **8**
Fitzgeralds **7**
Four Queens **6**
Golden Nugget **2**
Jackie Gaughan's
  Plaza **1**
Lady Luck **4**
Sam Boyd's
  Fremont **5**
Showboat **10**

Fremont Street
Experience

1-0406

seafood restaurant called **Vincenzo's** and an ice cream/liqueur/coffee bar with out-door cafe seating on Fremont Street.

Molly's Country Kitchen & Buffet is an attractive 24-hour coffee shop with planters of greenery creating intimate seating areas. Meals here are inexpensive, with many specials such as a complete roast turkey dinner for $4.95. Molly's also offers buffets at all meals ($4.99 for breakfast and lunch, $7.99 for dinner); on Saturday and Sunday an unlimited-champagne brunch is $5.99.

The balcony of the second-floor Lookout Lounge (featuring Irish drinks) is a good vantage point for viewing the Fremont Street Experience. A **McDonald's** (with windowed walls overlooking Fremont Street) and three bars are on the casino floor.

Services: Room service 6am to 2pm and 5 to 11pm, complimentary gaming lessons.

Facilities: Casino, tour and show desks, car-rental desk, gift shop, jewelry shop.

Ⓢ Four Queens

202 Fremont St., at Casino Center Blvd., Las Vegas, NV 89101. ☎ **800/634-6045** or 702/385-4011. Fax 702/387-5133. 700 rms, 38 minisuites. A/C TV TEL. Single or double $54–$79 Sun–Thurs, $65–$79 Fri–Sat; minisuite $99–$125. Extra person $10. Children under 2 stay free in parents' room. AE, CB, DC, DISC, MC, V. Free parking (self and valet).

Opened in 1966 with a mere 120 rooms, the Four Queens (named for the owner's four daughters) has evolved over the decades into a major Downtown property occupying an entire city block.

Notably nice rooms are located in 19-story twin towers. Especially lovely are the North Tower rooms, decorated in a southwestern motif and, in most cases, offering views of the Fremont Street Experience. South Tower rooms are done up in earth tones with dark wood furnishings and wallpapers in small floral prints. Mini-suites, decorated in traditional styles, have living rooms (separated from the bedrooms by a trellised wall) and dining areas, double-sink baths, and dressing areas. All accommodations offer TVs with in-house information and pay-movie channels. Some rooms are equipped with small refrigerators and coffeemakers.

Dining/Entertainment: Hugo's Cellar, a plush continental restaurant, has exposed brick walls hung with gilt-framed landscape and still-life paintings. Seating is in upholstered armchairs and spacious booths illuminated by amber-bulbed sconces. Every woman receives a red rose as she is seated. Dinner only; entrees $20 to $32.

At **Lailani's Island Café,** a whimsical Hawaiian cafeteria with colorful tropical murals on its walls, diners are entertained by island music, a 3-foot talking macaw, dancing flowers in dugout canoes, a five-headed totem pole with eyes that light up, and a fiber-optic light show overhead. Lunch and dinner; all menu items are under $7, most under $5.

Pastina's Italian Bistro is somewhat more traditional, though it, too, has a vaulted fiber-optic ceiling with shooting stars and swirling galaxies. The menu features a choice of pastas and traditional Italian entrees. Dinner only; entrees $4.95–$8.50.

Magnolia's Veranda, a 24-hour dining facility overlooking the casino, has three sections—a casual plant-filled cafe, an adjoining "courtyard," and a rather elegant crystal-chandeliered dining area adorned with murals of New Orleans. The same menu is offered throughout. Besides the requisite coffee-shop fare, Magnolia's offers Hawaiian specialties. A great deal here is the $4.95 prime rib dinner served from 6pm to 2am.

Hugo's has a cozy lounge with a working fireplace, and two bars serve the casino. **Services:** 24-hour room service.

Facilities: Gift shop, car-rental desk, tour and show desks, small video-game arcade, small fitness room.

INEXPENSIVE

California Hotel/Casino & RV Park

12 Ogden Ave., at 1st St., Las Vegas, NV 89101. ☎ **800/634-6255** or 702/385-1222. Fax 702/388-2660. 781 rms, 74 suites. A/C TV TEL. Single or double $40 Sun–Thurs, $50 Fri–Sat, $60 holidays. Extra person $5. Children 12 and under stay free in parents' room. AE, CB, DC, DISC, MC, V. Free parking (self and valet).

This is a hotel with a unique personality. California-themed, it markets mostly in Hawaii, and since 85% of the guests are from the "Aloha State," it offers Hawaiian entrees in several of its restaurants and even has an on-premises store specializing in Hawaiian foodstuffs. You'll also notice that dealers are wearing colorful Hawaiian shirts. Of course, everyone is welcome to enjoy the aloha spirit here.

The rooms, however, reflect neither California nor Hawaii. Decorated in contemporary-look burgundy/mauve or apricot/teal color schemes, they have mahogany furnishings and attractive marble baths. In-room safes are a plus, and TVs offer pay-per-view movies and keno channels.

Dining/Entertainment: With its redwood paneling and massive stone fireplace, the **Redwood Bar & Grill**—featuring steak and seafood—looks like an elegant ski lodge. A noteworthy special: a 16-ounce porterhouse steak dinner for $12.95. There's piano bar entertainment in the adjoining lounge. Dinner only; most entrees $12.95 to $18.95.

The **Pasta Pirate,** themed to suggest a coastal cannery warehouse, has a corrugated-tin ceiling and exposed overhead pipes. Walls are hung with neon signs and historic pages from the *San Francisco Chronicle.* Italian, steak, and seafood entrees are featured. Dinner only; most entrees $10.95 to $13.95 (pasta dishes mostly $7.95 to $8.95).

Also evoking San Francisco is the rather charming Market Street Café, a 24-hour facility. The menu lists all the expected coffee-shop fare, as well as Hawaiian items and specially marked "heart-smart" choices. The **Cal Club Snack Bar,** a casual cafeteria/ice-cream parlor, serves sundaes, along with Hawaiian soft drinks (flavors like guava and island punch) and Chinese/Japanese snack fare.

There are two 24-hour casino bars—the Main Street Bar and the San Francisco Pub. Dave's Aloha Bar on the mezzanine level is a tropical setting for exotic cocktails, liqueur-spiked coffees and ice-cream drinks, and international beers.

Services: Room service (breakfast only).

Facilities: Casino, car-rental desk, car wash, small rooftop pool, small video-game arcade, shops (gift shop, chocolates). A food store carries items popular with Hawaiians and there are several umbrella tables outside where these snacks can be eaten.

El Cortez Hotel & Casino

600 Fremont St., between 6th and 7th Sts., Las Vegas, NV 89101. ☎ **800/634-6703** or 702/385-5200. 107 rms, 200 minisuites. A/C TV TEL. $23–$28 single or double. $32–$40 minisuite. Extra person $3. AE, CB, DC, DISC, JCB, MC, V. Free parking (self and valet).

This small hotel is popular with locals for its casual, "just-folks" Downtown atmosphere and its frequent big-prize lotteries (up to $50,000) based on Social Security numbers. The nicest accommodations are the enormous minisuites in the newer 14-story tower. Some are exceptionally large king-bedded rooms with sofas; others have separate sitting areas with sofas, armchairs, and tables, plus small dressing areas. The rooms in the original building are furnished more traditionally and with less flair, and they cost less. Local calls are just 25¢.

Roberta's Café is an elegant candlelit restaurant featuring charbroiled steaks and seafood. Dinner only; most entrees $5.95 to $10.95.

There's also a large 24-hour coffee shop called the **Emerald Room,** where you can enjoy a bacon-and-eggs breakfast with hash browns, toast, and coffee for $1. A "soup-to-nuts" 18-ounce porterhouse steak dinner is $6.45 here; many other full dinners are $4 to $6, and Mexican combination platters are also available. Four bars serve the casino.

On-premises facilities include a small video-game arcade, beauty salon, gift shop, and barbershop.

Under the same ownership is **Ogden House,** just across the street, with rooms that go for just $18 a night.

Jackie Gaughan's Plaza Hotel/Casino

1 Main St., at Fremont St., Las Vegas, NV 89101. ☎ **800/634-6575** or 702/386-2110. Fax 702/382-8281. 876 rms, 161 suites. A/C TV TEL. $40 Sun–Thurs, $50–$75 Fri–Sat; $60–$150 suite. Extra person $8. Children under 12 stay free in parents' room. AE, DISC, MC, V. Free parking (self and valet).

Built in 1971 on the site of the old Union Pacific Railroad Depot, the Plaza, a double-towered, three-block-long property, permanently altered the Downtown skyline. Las Vegas's Amtrak station is right in the hotel, and the main Greyhound terminal adjoins it.

Accommodations are spacious and attractively decorated, with king rooms offering plush sofas.

Dining/Entertainment: The **Center Stage Restaurant,** offering fabulous views of Glitter Gulch and the Fremont Street Experience, is described in chapter 6. The '50s-motif **Plaza Diner,** open 24 hours a day and agleam with chrome, features red leatherette booths and a Wurlitzer-style jukebox stocked with oldies. Typical diner fare is featured—everything from a BLT to a stack of hotcakes. A noteworthy special is the full roast prime rib dinner for $5.95, available from 10am to midnight (midnight to 10am it's just $4.95).

At the **Back Stage,** comfortable leather booths, walls hung with still-life oil paintings, stained-glass windows, and brass candelabra chandeliers combine to create a warmly inviting ambience. Open for breakfast and lunch, the latter featuring sandwiches, salads, and Cajun specialties. Nothing on the menu is more than $9.25, and an 18-ounce porterhouse steak is just $8.95.

Other food and beverage facilities include an ice-cream parlor, Coffee & Cravings for gourmet coffees and fresh-baked goods, a 24-hour casino snack bar, several casino cocktail bars, and the Omaha Lounge offering live entertainment in the casino almost around the clock.

Services: Guest-services desk (also handles in-house shows), tour desk.

Facilities: Casino, car-rental desk, shops, a wedding chapel, beauty salon/barbershop. There's a sports deck with a nice-sized swimming pool, a $1/4$-mile outdoor jogging track, and four Har-Tru tennis courts.

Lady Luck Casino Hotel

206 N. 3rd St., at Ogden Ave., Las Vegas, NV 89101. ☎ **800/523-9582** or 702/477-3000. Fax 702/477-7021. 630 rms, 162 suites. A/C TV TEL. $45–$55 Sun–Thurs, $55–$90 Fri–Sat; junior suite $55–$75 Sun–Thurs, $70–$105 Fri–Sat. Extra person $8. AE, CB, DC, DISC, MC, V. Free parking (self and valet).

What is today Lady Luck opened in 1964 as Honest John's—a 2,000-square-foot casino with five employees, five pinball machines, and 17 slots. Today that casino occupies 30,000 square feet, and the hotel—including sleek 17- and 25-story towers—is a major Downtown player taking up an entire city block. What it retains from earlier times is a friendly atmosphere—one that has kept customers coming back for decades. Eighty percent of Lady Luck's clientele is repeat business.

Tower rooms are decorated in a variety of attractive color schemes, mostly utilizing muted southwestern hues and handsome oak furnishings. All are equipped with small refrigerators and TVs with pay-per-view movie options. Junior suites in the West Tower have parlor areas with sofas and armchairs, separate dressing areas, and baths with whirlpool tubs. The original Garden Rooms are a little smaller and less spiffy looking in terms of decor; on the plus side, they're right by the pool.

Dining/Entertainment: The **Burgundy Room** evokes Paris in the 1930s, with plush velvet-upholstered booths and a display of period art including lithographs and original prints by Erté, Poucette, and Salvador Dali. Elegantly appointed tables are lit by Venetian hurricane lamps. The menu highlights steak, pasta, and fresh seafood. Dinner only; entrees $10.95 to $19.95.

The **Emperor's Room** is also enhanced by museum-quality paintings, sculpture, and screens from the owner's collection, including an exact replica of a work called "Soldiers of Xian" dating from 2000 B.C. It's an elegant setting, with candlelit tables and a Persian rug on the floor. Cantonese, Mandarin, and Szechuan entrees are offered. Dinner only; most entrees $6.25 to $11.25.

At the southwestern-themed, 24-hour **Winners' Café,** a basic coffee-shop menu is augmented by Mexican and Polynesian specialties.

In addition, there are daily buffets (details in chapter 6), and ESPN sports are aired on three TV monitors in the Casino Bar.

Services: 24-hour room service, multilingual front desk, and complimentary airport shuttle.

Facilities: Casino, tour and show desks, car-rental desk, gift shop, swimming pool and sundeck.

Sam Boyd's Fremont Hotel & Casino

200 E. Fremont St., between Casino Center Blvd. and 3rd St., Las Vegas, NV 89101. ☎ **800/ 634-6182** or 702/385-3232. Fax 702/385-6229. 428 rms, 24 suites. A/C TV TEL. Single or double $30–$44 Sun–Thurs, $55–$80, Fri–Sat, $60–$80 holidays. Extra person $8. Children under 12 stay free in parents' room. AE, CB, DC, DISC, JCB, MC, V. Free parking (valet).

When it opened in 1956, the Fremont was the first high-rise in downtown Las Vegas. Wayne Newton got his start here, singing in the now-defunct Carousel Showroom. Rooms offer safes and TVs with in-house information channels and pay-movie options.

Dining/Entertainment: The Fremont boasts a gorgeous oak-paneled art deco restaurant called the **Second Street Grill.** Diners are comfortably ensconced in plush leather booths and oversized chairs at candlelit tables. A handsome bar adjoins. The menu, highlighting steaks and seafood, is contemporary American with international overtones. Dinner only; entrees $14.50–$25.95.

A branch of **Tony Roma's, A Place for Ribs,** offers scrumptious barbecued chicken and smoky, fork-tender baby back ribs, juicy charbroiled steaks, and fresh seafood. A children's menu is a plus. The walls of this handsome plant-filled restaurant are hung with historic photographs of Las Vegas. Dinner only; entrees $5.95–$14.95.

The **Lanai Cafe** is a comfortable 24-hour coffee shop, with a wide-ranging American and Chinese menu. Specials here include a full prime/rib dinner ($5.95) or a steak and lobster tail dinner ($9.99). The Lanai Express, a tiny cafeteria also featuring American and Chinese fare, adjoins.

The Fremont also has great buffets (see chapter 6 for details). There are bars in the casino, race and sports book, and keno lounge.

Services: Room service at breakfast only.

Facilities: Casino, 24-hour gift shop. Guests can use the swimming pool and RV park at the nearby California Hotel, another Sam Boyd enterprise.

✪ Showboat

2800 Fremont St., between Charleston Blvd. and Mojave Rd., Las Vegas, NV 89104. ☎ **800/ 826-2800** or 702/385-9123. Fax 702/383-9283. 451 rms, 4 suites. A/C TV TEL. $30–$65 Sun–Thurs, $30–$85 Fri–Sat, $85 holidays; $130–$195 suite. Extra person $10. Children under 12 stay free in parents' room. AE, CB, DC, DISC, MC, V. Free parking (self and valet).

Despite its slightly off-the-beaten-track location, this New Orleans–themed hotel is quite popular for its extensive facilities, friendliness, and totally delightful interior. The Showboat welcomes guests into a charming lobby adorned with flower boxes, murals of Mississippi plantations and riverboats, and stunning Venetian-glass chandeliers. Everything's looking great after a recent $18-million renovation.

The Showboat has a long history in this town. Opened in 1954, it was the first hotel to offer buffet meals and bingo—not to mention bowling alleys. Today its gorgeous 24-hour bingo parlor is famous, both for its flower garden murals and for the highest payouts in town. And the bowling alley—North America's largest—hosts major PBA tournaments.

Spacious, cheerfully decorated rooms, have dressing areas equipped with cosmetic mirrors. You'll find a hair dryer and extra phone in the bath, and TVs offer pay-movies and hotel-information stations.

Dining/Entertainment: The **Plantation** keeps to the garden theme. One room evokes a veranda with white porch railings backed by exquisite botanical murals; the other is more elegant, with Palladian windows and ornate Victorian chandeliers. Together they comprise a lovely setting in which to enjoy mesquite-grilled steaks and seafood specialties. Dinner only; entrees $5.95 to $13.95.

DiNapoli diverges from the New Orleans theme with Roman frescoes, columns, and classical statuary. The menu features California-inspired southern Italian cuisine as well as seafood specialties. Dinner only; most entrees $5.95 to $14.95.

And the delightful 24-hour Mardi Gras-themed Showboat Coffee Shop extends into the casino with cafe seating.

There's also a very good buffet here (details in chapter 6), and a snack bar and a bar/lounge are located in the Bowling Center. Several bars serve the casino, including the Mardi Gras Room, which features quality lounge acts and occasional bigger names such as Juice Newton, Sha Na Na, Chubby Checker, and Lacy J. Dalton. When headliners appear, there's a two-drink minimum.

Services: 24-hour room service, shoeshine.

Facilities: Casino, gift shop, beauty salon/barbershop, 24-hour Bowling Center with 106 lanes, bowling pro shop, video-game arcade; Olympic-size swimming pool in a courtyard setting. A plus for parents is the in-house babysitting center for children age 2 to 7 (with no charge for up to three hours a day). Equipped with TV tapes, a slide, toys, art supplies, and games, its staff members play with the kids and read them stories.

8   A Hostel

Las Vegas International Hostel

1208 Las Vegas Blvd. S., between Charleston and Oakey blvds., Las Vegas, NV 89104. ☎ **702/ 385-9955.** Capacity: 60 people. A/C. $14 for a bed in a dorm room with shared bath accommodating 4 people, $20–28 for a private room with shared bath. There's a $2 surcharge for one-night stays on weekends. AYH and AAIH members receive discounted rates. No credit cards. Free parking (self).

This American Association of International Hostels (AAIH) facility—the only legitimate hostel in town—houses clean but spartan rooms in a two-story building. Upstairs rooms are a tad nicer, with balconies and polished pine floors (ceramic tile downstairs). You get a free sheet and pillowcase and pay $1 for a top sheet, blanket, and towels. Gratis coffee, tea, and lemonade are available in the lounge throughout the day. There are two lounges offering TVs, VCRs (and tapes), stereos, books, and games. Other facilities include barbecue grills, picnic tables, and chaise longues out back; coin-op washers/dryers; a fully equipped kitchen; and bicycle racks and lockup. The host arranges excursions to Hoover Dam; Red Rock Canyon; Mount Charleston; Valley of Fire; and Bryce, Zion, and Grand canyons, and the friendly staff is knowledgeable about local sights and restaurants.

July and August are the busiest months for the hostel, though these are the slowest months elsewhere in town. Hence, if you want to stay here because you like hosteling as a way of life, reserve several weeks in advance. On the other hand, if you're considering a hostel only to save money, try bargaining with Strip hotels in their off-season; you might be able to obtain very low rates.

Note: Although conveniently located (the Sahara Hotel is just a few blocks away), this stretch of Las Vegas Boulevard South is rather seedy. It may not be a good choice for women traveling alone; and it's not wise for anyone to walk around the area alone at night.

Dining in Las Vegas 6

Many people consider Las Vegas a great restaurant town. It all depends on your point of view. From the vantage point of value for your money it's unbeatable. You can enjoy veritable food orgies at low-priced buffets, many of them consisting of incredible arrays of good, fresh food, creatively prepared and attractively displayed. At weekend brunch buffets, champagne flows freely as well.

Nor are buffets the only game in town. At many casino-hotel restaurants full steak or prime rib dinners are well under $10, especially late at night. To locate budget fare, see the box below and check local newspapers (especially Friday editions) and free magazines (such as *Vegas Visitor* and *What's On in Las Vegas*) which are given away at hotel reception desks (sometimes these sources also yield money-saving coupons).

Now for the negatives. In terms of sophisticated dining—though there are glimmers of hope—Las Vegas is still barely a player. Basically this is a steak and potatoes kind of town, where bastions of haute cuisine serve everything flambé in cognac cream sauce and still feature cherries jubilee for dessert. Culinary concepts that took hold in close-by California decades ago are just beginning to make a dent in the dining scene here. And the low-priced ethnic eateries you find in most big towns are sparse. Not that I really mind. Las Vegas dining rooms are gorgeous and plushly comfortable, service is gracious, and let's face it, there are many worse things than cognac cream sauce or a really good steak.

But the times they are a-changing. In 1994 L.A. restaurateur Wolfgang Puck (of Spago) opened two establishments here and another noted American chef, Mark Miller, installed a Coyote Cafe at the MGM Grand. Fiore's at the Rio is superb; San Francisco's critically acclaimed Fog City Diner arrived in town in 1996; and the MGM Grand has two cutting-edge restaurants—Gatsby's and Emeril's New Orleans Fish House (under the auspices of the brilliant Emeril Lagasse). The exquisite Charlie Trotter's (recently replaced by Gatsby's at MGM) will relocate to Bellagio when it opens in 1998. The future for foodies is looking brighter.

The following establishments comprise a mix of exceptional hotel dining rooms and noteworthy freestanding restaurants. Among the latter, Las Vegas has far fewer cheap eateries than other cities; they simply can't compete with casino hotels that try to attract gamblers by offering inexpensive food. Las Vegas visitors tend to eat in hotels, and in the hotel section of this book (chapter 5), you'll find dozens of additional restaurants briefly described, at all price levels. Many larger hotels have food courts (the one at Caesars Palace is especially nice).

The restaurants in this chapter are arranged first by location, then by the following price categories (based on the average cost of a dinner entree): **Very Expensive,** more than $20; **Expensive,** $15 to $20; **Moderate,** $10 to $15; **Inexpensive,** under $10 (sometimes well under). In expensive and very expensive restaurants, expect to spend no less than twice the price of the average entree for your entire meal with a tip; you can usually get by on a bit less in moderate and inexpensive restaurants. Buffets and Sunday brunches are gathered in a separate category at the end of this chapter.

1 Best Bets

- **Best Buffet:** For variety, ambience, overall food quality, and reasonable price, the **Rio's Carnival World Buffet** is the best deal in town.
- **Best Sunday Champagne Brunch:** Bally's lavish Sterling Sunday Brunch, where display tables embellished with floral arrangements and ice sculptures are laden with everything from mounds of fresh shrimp to sushi and sashimi, and fancy entrees include the likes of roast duckling with black-currant and blueberry sauce.
- **Best Graveyard Dinner Deal: Binion's Horseshoe** offers a complete New York steak dinner served with potato, roll, and salad for just $3 from 10pm to 5:45am.
- **Best Cheap Breakfast:** Make your first stop of the day the **Cyclone Coffee Shop** at the Holiday Inn Casino Boardwalk, where a $1.29 breakfast includes two eggs, bacon or sausage, hash browns and toast. It's served around the clock.
- **Best Decor:** Most exquisitely elegant is the Beidermeier interior at **Gatsby's.**
- **Best Spot for a Romantic Dinner:** The warmly elegant **Fiore,** with its gorgeous interior and arched windows overlooking the palm-fringed pool, is the most simpatico setting for a leisurely romantic dinner. Brilliant cuisine, a great wine cellar, and superb service combine to create a memorable evening.
- **Best Spot for a Celebration: Mizuno's** teppanyaki grills are ideal for small parties, with the chef's theatrics comprising a tableside show.
- **Best Free Show at Dinner:** At Treasure Island's **Buccaneer Bay Club** everyone rushes to the window when the ship battle begins.
- **Best Wine List:** The distinguished cellar at **Gatsby's** houses 600 wines in all price ranges and has a friendly master sommelier on hand to guide you in your selections.
- **Best View:** See all of Las Vegas from the revolving **Top of the World,** at the Stratosphere, 106 stories up.
- **Best California Cuisine:** Wolfgang Puck's **Spago**—the very essence of California chic—is always thrilling. I could lunch every day on his signature Chinois chicken salad.
- **Best Chinese Cuisine: Chin's**—where piano bar music enhances an ambience of low-key elegance—offers scrumptious and authentic Cantonese fare, including some original creations such as deep-fried battered chicken served with strawberry sauce and fresh strawberries.
- **Best Deli:** There is the New York transplant—the **Stage Deli**—and there is nothing else.
- **Best Dim Sum:** Chinatown's **Plum Tree Inn,** quite simply, has the best dim sum I've ever discovered—which says a lot, since I live in New York and have written extensively about California restaurants.

- **Best Italian Cuisine:** The northern Italian culinary creations at **Fiore** are unparalleled and sublime, as is the setting in which you'll enjoy them.
- **Best New Orleans Cuisine:** One of Las Vegas' newest celebrity chef venues, **Emeril's New Orleans Fish House** at the MGM Grand, offers total authenticity combined with culinary brilliance.
- **Best Southwestern Cuisine:** The fact that it's the only notable southwestern restaurant in town doesn't make the **Coyote Cafe** any less impressive. Superstar Santa Fe chef Mark Miller brings contemporary culinary panache to traditional southwestern cookery, and the results are spicy and spectacular.
- **Best Steak and Seafood:** Power-dining precinct **Morton's of Chicago** serves up prime succulent steaks in a comfortable, convivial, and often celebrity-studded setting. And you'll enjoy nothing but the best cuts of beef and the freshest seafood at **The Tillerman,** a gorgeous restaurant with candlelit tables amid an indoor grove of ficus trees and tree-trunk pillars.

2 Restaurants by Cuisine

AMERICAN

All-American Bar & Grille (Rio Hotel, On/Near the Strip, *M*)

Binion's Horseshoe Coffee Shop (Binion's Horseshoe, Downtown, *I*)

Carson Street Café (Golden Nugget, Downtown, *I*)

Center Stage (Jackie Gaughan's Plaza, Downtown, *I*)

Country Star (On/Near the Strip, *M*)

Dive! (Fashion Show Mall, On/Near the Strip, *M*)

Fog City Diner (East Las Vegas/ Flamingo Road, *M*)

Hard Rock Café (Convention Center/Paradise Road/Sahara Avenue, *M*)

Hippo & the Wild Bunch (Convention Center/ParadiseRoad/ Sahara Avenue, *I*)

Roxy's Diner (Stratosphere, On/Near the Strip, *I*)

AMERICAN/CONTINENTAL

Buccaneer Bay Club (Treasure Island, On/Near the Strip, *VE*)

Top of the World (Stratosphere, On/Near the Strip, *VE*)

BAGELS

Einstein Bros. Bagels (East Las Vegas/Flamingo Road, *I*)

BARBECUE

Big Sky (Stratosphere, On/Near the Strip, *I*)

Tony Roma's (Stardust, On/Near the Strip, *M*)

BUFFETS/SUNDAY BRUNCHES

Bally's Big Kitchen Buffet (On/Near the Strip, *M*)

Bally's Sterling Sunday Brunch (On/Near the Strip, *VE*)

Caesars Palace Palatium Buffet (On/Near the Strip, *M*)

Circus Circus Buffet (On/Near the Strip, *I*)

Excalibur's Round Table Buffet (On/Near the Strip, *I*)

Flamingo Hilton Paradise Garden Buffet (On/Near the Strip, *I*)

Golden Nugget Buffet (Downtown, *M*)

Harrah's Galley Buffet (On/Near the Strip, *I*)

Lady Luck Banquet Buffet (Downtown, *I*)

Key to abbreviations: *I*=Inexpensive; *M*=Moderate; *E*=Expensive; *VE*=Very Expensive

Las Vegas Hilton Buffet of Champions (Convention Center/Paradise Road/Sahara Avenue, *M*)

Luxor Buffet (On/Near the Strip, *I*)

MGM Grand Oz Buffet (On/Near the Strip, *M*)

Mirage Buffet (On/Near the Strip, *M*)

Monte Carlo Buffet (On/Near the Strip, *I*)

Rio's Carnival World Buffet (On/Near the Strip, *I*)

Sahara Oasis Buffet (On/Near the Strip, *I*)

Sam Boyd's Fremont Paradise Buffet (Downtown, *I* to *M*)

Sam's Town Great Buffet (East Las Vegas/Flamingo Road, *I*)

Showboat Captain's Buffet (Downtown, *I*)

Stardust Warehouse Buffet (On/Near the Strip, *I*)

Stratosphere Buffet (On/Near the Strip, *I*)

Treasure Island Buffet (On/Near the Strip, *I*)

Tropicana Island Buffet (On/Near the Strip, *I*)

Tropicana Sunday Brunch Buffet (On/Near the Strip, *E*)

CALIFORNIA

Planet Hollywood (Caesars Palace, On/Near the Strip, *M*)

Spago (Caesars Palace, On/Near the Strip, *VE*)

Wolfgang Puck Café (MGM Grand, On/Near the Strip, *M*)

CHINESE

Chin's (Fashion Show Mall, On/Near the Strip, *E*)

Dragon Noodle Co. (Monte Carlo Resort, On/Near the Strip, *M*)

The Noodle Kitchen (Mirage Hotel, On/Near the Strip, *M*)

Plum Tree Inn (Chinatown, *M*)

CONTINENTAL

Bacchanal (Caesars Palace, On/Near the Strip, *VE*)

Pegasus (Alexis Park, Convention Center/Paradise Road/ Sahara Avenue, *VE*)

DELI

Stage Deli (Caesars Palace, On Near the Strip, *M*)

EURASIAN

Gatsby's (MGM Grand, On/Near the Strip, *VE*)

FOOD COURT

La Piazza (Caesars Palace, On/Near the Strip, *I*)

FRENCH

Andre's (Downtown, *VE*)

Bistro Le Montrachet (Las Vegas Hilton, Convention Center/ Paradise Road/ Sahara Avenue, *VE*)

The Monte Carlo Room (Sheraton Desert Inn, On/Near the Strip, *VE*)

Palace Court (Caesars Palace, On/Near the Strip, *VE*)

Pamplemousse (Convention Center/Paradise Road/Sahara Avenue, *E*)

GERMAN

The Rathskeller (Convention Center/Paradise Road/Sahara Avenue, *I*)

ITALIAN

Fiore (Rio Hotel, On/Near the Strip, *VE*)

Papamios (Sam's Town, (East LasVegas/FlamingoRoad, *M*)

Romano's Macaroni Grill (Convention Center/Paradise Road/Sahara Avenue, *M*)

JAPANESE

Ginza (Convention Center/
Paradise Road/Sahara
Avenue, *M*)
Mizuno's (Tropicana, On/Near the
Strip, *E*)

MEDITERRANEAN

Mediterranean Café and
Market (East Las Vegas/
Flamingo Road, *I*)

MEXICAN

Ricardo's (East Las Vegas/
Flamingo Road, *M*)

NEW ORLEANS

Emeril's New Orleans Fish
House (MGM Grand, On/
Near the Strip, *VE*)

PUB FARE

Monte Carlo Pub & Bre-
wery. (Monte Carlo Resort,
On/Near the Strip, *I*)

SOUTHWESTERN

Chili's (Convention Center/
Paradise Road/Sahara
Avenue, *I*)
Coyote Cafe (MGM Grand,
On/Near the Strip, *VE*)
Z Tejas Grill (Convention Cen-
ter/Paradise Road/Sahara
Avenue, *M*)

STEAK/SEAFOOD

Morton's of Chicago (Fashion Show
Mall, On/Near the
Strip, *VE*)
The Palm (Caesars Palace, On/Near
the Strip, *VE*)
The Tillerman (East Las Vegas/
Flamingo Road, *E*)

SWISS/GERMAN

Alpine Village Inn (Convention
Center/Paradise Road/Sahara
Avenue, *M*)

3 On or Near the Strip

VERY EXPENSIVE

Bacchanal

Caesars Palace, 3570 Las Vegas Blvd. S., just north of Flamingo Rd. ☎ **702/731-7110.**
Reservations essential. Fixed-price $69.50, plus tax and gratuity. AE, CB, DC, DISC, MC, V. Tues–
Sat 6–11pm with seatings at 6 and 9:30pm. ROMAN ORGY/CONTINENTAL.

Its pedimented doorways guarded by golden lions, Bacchanal is an archetypal Las
Vegas experience—an imperial Roman feast with comely "wine goddesses" performing sinuous belly dances, decanting wine from shoulder height into ornate silver
chalices, and—believe it or not—massaging male diners and feeding them grapes!
When not performing, the goddesses repose gracefully around a fountained pool centered on a bronze Venus. The setting is palatial: White-columned walls are backed
by murals of ancient Rome; an azure ceiling suggests an open sky, with a grape arbor looping from beam to beam and crystal torches provide romantic lighting. The
dramatic focus of the evening is a thunder and lightning storm produced by Zeus to
announce the arrival of Caesar and Cleopatra. Caesar makes a short speech, and the
royal pair tour the room greeting diners. Abandon all reality, ye who enter here.

Dinner is a sumptuous multicourse feast, including unlimited wine and champagne. The menu changes a bit seasonally. On my last visit, it began with a selection
of crudités served with creamy roasted garlic-chive dip. This was followed by a
smoked Roma tomato soup and a salad of field greens with champagne vinaigrette

dressing. A choice of five entrees ranged from roast rack of lamb to oven-roasted wild salmon filet. The dramatic finale—a flaming dessert of vanilla ice cream topped with liqueur-soaked fresh fruits—was accompanied by petits fours and tea or coffee. The food falls short of haute gourmet standards, but there's plenty of it, and the elaborate presentation (not to mention the wine) justifies the price.

Buccaneer Bay Club

Treasure Island, 3300 Las Vegas Blvd. S. ☎ **702/894-7350.** Reservations recommended. Main courses $14.95–$25.50. AE, CB, DC, DISC, JCB, MC, V. Nightly 5–10:30pm. AMERICAN/ CONTINENTAL.

Its serpentine interior comprising a series of intimate dining nooks, Buccaneer Bay Club is a posh pirate lair, with mullioned windows overlooking the bay, a low beamed ceiling, and rustic stucco walls adorned with daggers and pistols. Treasure chests are displayed in wall niches along with a museum's worth of international plunder that ranges from a cane once owned by a maharajah (a gift to Steve Wynn) to a Spanish conquistador's helmet. Steve Wynn often drops by with celebrity pals such as Diana Ross, Tom Selleck, Don Johnson, Robin Williams, Steven Spielberg, or Tom Hanks. And, just like everyone else, they rush to the windows when the ship battle begins below. It's part of the fun of dining here.

Begin your meal with an appetizer of chilled lobster medallions with a piquant brandied Louis sauce. My favorite entree here is roast rack of lamb—four tender, juicy chops in a balsamic *jus reduction* with sautéed shallots. Also noteworthy: duckling à l'orange, spit-roasted in Grand Marnier, and crisp-crusted prime rib served with creamy horseradish sauce. All of the above come with potatoes and haricots verts. For dessert order a taster's platter of goodies such as flourless chocolate cake, cappuccino mousse, and a crème brûlée tart.

✪ Coyote Cafe

The MGM Grand, 3799 Las Vegas Blvd. S. ☎ **702/891-7349.** Reservations recommended for the Grill Room, not accepted for the Cafe. Grill Room main courses $15–$32. Cafe main courses $7.50–$17.50 (many are under $10). AE, CB, DC, DISC, JCB, MC, V. Grill Room daily 5:30– 10pm. Cafe daily 9am–11pm. MODERN SOUTHWESTERN.

In a town where restaurant cuisine often seems stuck in a 1950s time warp, Mark Miller's Coyote Cafe evokes howls of delight. His robust regional cuisine combines elements of traditional Mexican, Native American, Creole, and Cajun cookery with cutting-edge culinary trends. The main dining room is fronted by a lively cafe/bar, in which an exhibition-cooking area houses a *cazuela* (casserole) oven and *comal* grill under a gleaming ceramic tile hood. The adobe-walled Grill Room offers a more tranquil setting. Tables are candlelit, etched-glass partitions by Santa Fe artist Kit Carson depict whimsical scenes (such as a coyote and a horse dining in a restaurant), and a warm glow emanates from innovative sconces that filter light through multi-colored Japanese rice paper.

The Grill Room menu changes monthly. On a recent visit, I began with a heavenly "painted soup"—half garlicky black bean, half beer-infused smoked Cheddar— "painted" with chipotle cream and garnished with salsa fresca and de árbol chili powder. My main course was a salmon fillet crusted with ground pumpkin seeds and corn tortillas topped with roasted chile/pumpkin-seed sauce; it was presented on a bed of spinach-wrapped spaghetti squash studded with pine nuts, corn kernels, scallions, and morsels of sun-dried tomato. Dessert was a chocolate banana torte served on banana crème anglaise and topped with a scoop of vanilla ice cream. The wine list includes many by-the-glass selections, including champagnes and sparkling wines, which nicely complement spicy southwestern fare; Brazilian daiquiris are a house specialty.

Dining on the Strip & Paradise Road

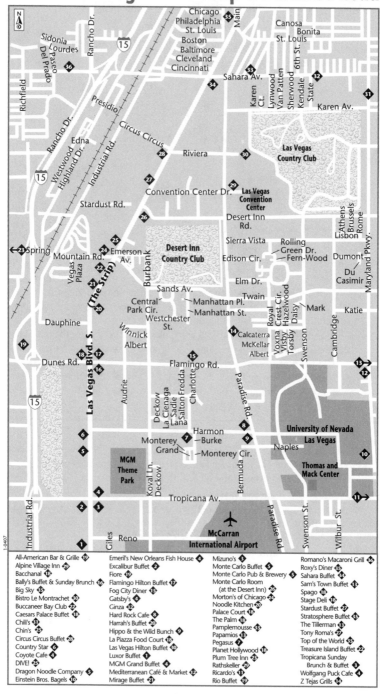

All-American Bar & Grille 🔵12
Alpine Village Inn 🔵25
Bacchanal 🔵18
Bally's Buffet & Sunday Brunch 🔵16
Big Sky 🔵13
Bistro Le Montrachet 🔵30
Buccaneer Bay Club 🔵22
Caesars Palace Buffet 🔵18
Chili's 🔵8
Chin's 🔵23
Circus Circus Buffet 🔵28
Country Star 🔵6
Coyote Cafe 🔵4
DIVE! 🔵23
Dragon Noodle Company 🔵5
Einstein Bros. Bagels 🔵10

Emeril's New Orleans Fish House 🔵4
Excalibur Buffet 🔵2
Fiore 🔵19
Flamingo Hilton Buffet 🔵17
Fog City Diner 🔵13
Gatsby's 🔵1
Ginza 🔵3
Hard Rock Cafe 🔵8
Harrah's Buffet 🔵23
Hippo & the Wild Bunch 🔵9
La Piazza Food Court 🔵18
Las Vegas Hilton Buffet 🔵30
Luxor Buffet 🔵3
MGM Grand Buffet 🔵4
Mediterranean Café & Market 🔵12
Mirage Buffet 🔵23

Mizuno's 🔵3
Monte Carlo Buffet 🔵5
Monte Carlo Pub & Brewery 🔵5
Monte Carlo Room
   (at the Desert Inn) 🔵26
Morton's of Chicago 🔵32
Noodle Kitchen 🔵23
Palace Court 🔵18
The Palm 🔵16
Pamplemousse 🔵31
Papamios 🔵13
Pegasus 🔵31
Planet Hollywood 🔵18
Plum Tree Inn 🔵24
Rathskeller 🔵25
Ricardo's 🔵31
Rio Buffet 🔵19

Romano's Macaroni Grill 🔵36
Roxy's Diner 🔵45
Sahara Buffet 🔵33
Sam's Town Buffet 🔵13
Spago 🔵18
Stage Deli 🔵18
Stardust Buffet 🔵27
Stratosphere Buffet 🔵35
The Tillerman 🔵13
Tony Roma's 🔵27
Top of the World 🔵35
Treasure Island Buffet 🔵22
Tropicana Sunday
   Brunch & Buffet 🔵3
Wolfgang Puck Cafe 🔵4
Z Tejas Grills 🔵13

99

A Frommer's Exclusive

I was so taken with Emeril's delicious Fall River clam chowder, I asked for permission to share the recipe with readers. Here it is:

$^1/_2$ pound unsalted butter

2 cups all-purpose flour

$^1/_2$ pound bacon, medium diced (1/3" squares)

2 cups chopped leeks (about a pound)

2 cups chopped yellow onions

2 cups clam juice

6 cups heavy cream

2 pounds littleneck clams, shucked and chopped

3 bay leaves

1 tablespoon chopped fresh thyme

2 tablespoons finely chopped parsley

salt and pepper

In a sauté pan, melt the butter over medium heat. Stir the flour into the melted butter until smooth. Cook for 6 to 8 minutes to create a blond roux, stirring occasionally. Remove from the heat and set aside. In a stock pot, over medium heat, render the diced bacon for about 5 minutes or until crispy. Add the leeks and onions. Sauté for 3 to 4 minutes or until vegetables are wilted. Stir in the clam juice and cream. Bring the liquid to a simmer. Add the bay leaves and fresh thyme. Season with salt and pepper. Stir in $^1/_2$ cup of the roux at a time, until all the roux is incorporated and the soup is smooth. Simmer for 20 minutes. Stir in the chopped clams and cook for 2 minutes. Add the parsley, and re-season if necessary. Yields about 8 to 10 servings (about 1 gallon).

The Cafe menu offers similar but somewhat lighter fare. Southwestern breakfasts ($5.95 to $9.50) range from *huevos rancheros* to blue-corn pancakes with toasted pine nuts, honey butter, and real maple syrup.

✪ Emeril's New Orleans Fish House

The MGM Grand, 3799 Las Vegas Blvd. S. ☎ **702/891-7374.** Reservations suggested. Main courses $12–$18 lunch, $18–$28 dinner (more for lobster). AE, CB, DC, DISC, MC, V. Daily lunch 11am–3pm, dinner 5:30–10:30pm. CONTEMPORARY NEW ORLEANS.

You may know eccentric celebrity chef Emeril Lagasse from his famed New Orleans restaurant or from his wacky Food Network show, *The Essence of Emeril.* His Las Vegas restaurant—a thrilling development for foodies here—is fronted by a horseshoe–shaped raw bar and has a cigar-friendly, brick-walled indoor "courtyard" (the restaurant maintains a recherché humidor). The oak-floored dining room itself has a high-tech minimalist/industrial decor, with bolted, galvanized-steel columns and wire-mesh sconces. Candlelight, ochre and sienna stucco walls, and large black-and-white photographs of Louisiana farmers and fisherfolk add rusticity and warmth.

Though the setting is casual, the food and wine are just about flawless. Every dish is an occasion for ecstasy. Start off with the shrimp parfait (layered with lettuces, tomato, and avocado in piquant remoulade sauce) or with Emeril's creamy Fall River clam chowder—easily the apogee of its genre, with apple-smoked bacon adding flavor and crunch. Presentations are exquisite. A bass entree, for instance, nuanced with Dijon mustard, was served over Louisiana lump crabmeat crowned by a delicate crispy potato nest; accompanied by wild mushroom relish, it rested on a roasted red pepper coulis marbleized with green herb vinaigrette. Great desserts here, too, including a definitive banana cream pie drizzled with caramel. The carefully crafted wine list is extensive; consult the sommelier for suggestions.

✪ Fiore

Rio Suite Hotel, 3700 W. Flamingo Rd., at I-15. ☎ **702/252-7702.** Reservations recommended. Main courses $21–$36. AE, CB, DC, DISC, MC, V. Nightly 5pm–11pm. NORTHERN ITALIAN/ PROVENÇAL.

Fiore offers a deliciously simpatico setting for the brilliantly innovative cuisine of chef Kolachai Ngimsangaim. In his spacious, mahogany-ceilinged dining room, with arched windows overlooking a palm-fringed pool, tables are exquisitely appointed with fine silver, flowers, and Villeroy and Boch china in diverse floral patterns. Flower- and fruit-motif carpeting furthers the "fiore" motif, while an exhibition kitchen aglow with wood-burning pizza ovens (nine different hardwoods are used for grilling here) adds warmth and theatricality. I love the interior space, but it's also tempting to dine alfresco on the flower-bordered flagstone terrace (heated in winter, mist-cooled in summer). Light jazz provides a pleasant musical backdrop.

Ngimsangaim's seasonally changing menus complement the culinary elegance of northern Italy with the earthy exuberance of southern France. I began a recent dinner here with sautéed herb-crusted prawns in a buttery mustard/anise sauce. It was followed by an entree of barbecued Atlantic salmon in honeyed hickory sauce, served with grilled polenta, Portobello mushrooms, roasted Roman tomatoes, and grilled asparagus spears. Fiore's thoughtful list of more than 400 wines—in several price ranges—is international in scope and includes 45 premium by-the-glass selections. Consult knowledgeable sommelier Barrie Larvin for suggestions. Dine slowly and consider including a cheese course—excellent cheeses are served with seasonal fruits. But do save room for dessert—perhaps a warm chocolate torte on crème anglaise embellished with raspberry stars and chocolate hearts. In addition to an extensive listing of cognacs, ports, and dessert wines, hand-rolled cigars—elegantly presented in a mahogany humidor—are a postprandial option on the terrace.

✪ Gatsby's

The MGM Grand, 3799 Las Vegas Blvd. S. ☎ **702/891-7337.** Reservations suggested. Jackets suggested for men. Main courses $28.95–$58. Degustation (tasting) menu $65, $85 with selected wines accompanying each course. AE, CB, DC, DISC, MC, V. Wed–Mon 6–10:30pm. EURASIAN.

Though I moaned and groaned when informed that Gatsby's had replaced the stellar Charlie Trotter's here, my despair soon turned to delight. Trotter has not disappeared forever (it will return to a new Las Vegas home, the Bellagio, in 1998), and Gatsby's is at the very pinnacle of fine dining. Food, ambience, service, and wines are all impeccable. The restaurant's luxe Biedermeier interior—its organic curvatures as richly sinuous as a Stradivarius violin's—is an aesthetic tour de force, utilizing contrasting woods, Axminster floral-patterned carpeting, and alabaster chandeliers and sconces. Columned credenzas framing a central promenade display lavish flower arrangements. A harpist entertains during dinner, and there's a plush lounge (for pre- or post-dinner drinks and cigars) as well as a piano bar with a dance floor. Plan to make a night of it.

Brilliant chef Terence Fong learned Chinese and Japanese cooking in his native Hawaii, adding classic French cuisine to his repertoire during a long stint at Caesars' deluxe Palace Court. He is complemented by a very talented pastry chef, Melanie Bonanno, and user-friendly master sommelier/maître d' Angelo Tavernaro. I strongly suggest opting for Fong's nightly changing degustation menu, comprised of five exquisitely complex courses. On a recent visit, such a dinner began with a trio of pre-menu appetizers—an onion tartlet with mango chutney, an eggplant pancake topped with balsamic and bell peppercorns, and a cucumber cup filled with salmon mousse. It was succeeded by tender macadamia-crusted abalone served atop curried basmati rice studded with toasted orzo and wheatberries with roasted garlic vinaigrette. A warm potato- and leek-wrapped terrine stuffed with squab and roasted bell pepper arrived next, with haricots verts and a red pepper sauce. Mesquite-grilled Hawaiian yellowtail was accompanied by bean ragout, roasted corn-tortilla sauce, and mixed field greens. A sorbet refreshed the palate for the final course: a fan of tender grilled Louisiana ostrich with wild mushroom risotto, steamed spring vegetables, and truffle-infused red wine sauce. The grand finale was a chocolate/cappuccino terrine wrapped in flourless chocolate cake and embellished with white chocolate sauce and shards of bubbled chocolate. Gilding the lily were glazed strawberries and chocolate truffles. Appropriate wines, including a dessert port, accompanied each course. If you order à la carte, be sure to consult Angelo. His distinguished international cellar (highlighting French and California wines) contains more than 600 selections in all price ranges, including 30 wines available by the glass.

The Monte Carlo Room

Desert Inn, 3145 Las Vegas Blvd. S., between Desert Inn Rd. and Sands Ave. ☎ **702/733-4444.** Reservations recommended. Main courses $26–$37. Fixed-price dinner $37. AE, CB, DC, DISC, JCB, MC, V. Thurs–Mon 6–11pm. FRENCH.

The delightful Monte Carlo Room is equally renowned for its sublime setting and fine French cuisine. The romantic main dining—with charming murals of Greek youths and nymphs lolling in a classical setting framed by rose bowers—has Palladian windows overlooking the palm-fringed pool. The ceiling is painted with cupids frolicking amid fluffy clouds. Diners are comfortably ensconced in tapestried banquettes at tables illuminated by white taper candles or pink-shaded crystal lamps.

Excellent appetizer choices include seafood ravioli with champagne-caviar sauce or a terrine of fresh goose liver. I also love the thick, velvety, cognac-laced lobster bisque, full of rich flavor, served in a scooped-out round loaf of bread. For your entree, consider a classic French entrecôte au poivre or duck à l'orange served with apple- and pine nut–studded wild rice. A mélange of vegetables and a potato dish (perhaps pommes soufflés) accompany entrees. There's an extensive wine list; consult the sommelier for suggestions. Flaming tableside preparations are a specialty, including desserts such as crêpes Suzette and cherries jubilee.

✪ Morton's of Chicago

3200 Las Vegas Blvd. S., in the Fashion Show Mall (take Spring Mountain Rd. off the Strip, make a right at Fashion Show Dr. and follow the signs). ☎ **702/893-0703.** Reservations recommended. Main courses $16.95–$29.95. AE, CB, DC, JCB, MC, V. Mon–Sat 5:30–11pm, Sun 5–10pm. STEAK/SEAFOOD.

This famous gourmet steak house has a warm club-like interior. Ecru walls are hung with LeRoy Neiman prints and photographs of celebrity diners (a keynote of every Morton's is a star-studded clientele), rich mahogany paneling adds a note of substantial elegance, and much of the seating is in roomy, gold leather booths. An exhibition kitchen gleams with copper pots, and wines are stored in a brick-walled rack. Frequent power diners here include most hotel/casino owners as well as Strip entertainers Siegfried and Roy. Robert de Niro and Joe Pesci came in frequently during the filming of *Casino*, and, one night, Tony Curtis joined the waitstaff in singing "Happy Birthday" to a guest.

Start off with an appetizer—perhaps a lump crabmeat cocktail with mustard-mayonnaise sauce. Entree choices include succulent prime midwestern steaks prepared to your exact specifications, plus lemon oregano chicken, lamb chops, Sicilian veal, grilled swordfish, whole baked Maine lobster, and prime rib with creamed horseradish. Side orders such as flavorfully fresh al dente asparagus served with hollandaise, or hash browns are highly recommended. Portions are bountiful; plan to share. A loaf of warm onion bread on every table is complimentary. Leave room for dessert—perhaps a Grand Marnier soufflé. There's an extensive wine list, and you may want to retreat to a sofa in the cozy mahogany-paneled bar/lounge for after-dinner drinks.

✪ Palace Court

Caesars Palace, 3570 Las Vegas Blvd. S., just north of Flamingo Rd. ☎ **702/734-7110.** Reservations essential. Main courses $29–$55. AE, MC, V. Nightly 6–11pm; there are specified seatings every half hour from 6pm. FRENCH.

Reached via a crystal-ceilinged bronze elevator—or a brass-balustraded spiral staircase—the circular Palace Court is as opulent as a Venetian palazzo. The centerpiece of the room—a towering stained-glass domed skylight, 36 feet in diameter—shelters a grove of ficus trees flanked by classical statuary and flower beds. White-lattice windows draped with peach balloon curtains overlook the hotel's swimming pool and the mountains beyond. On the opposite wall is a charming mural of the French countryside. Tables are elegantly appointed (with gold and white Lenox china, vermeil flatware, and hand-blown crystal) and softly lit by shaded brass candle lamps.

Menus change seasonally. A recent one offered appetizers of poached champagne-glazed Long Island oysters (embellished with beluga caviar, smoked salmon, and julienned leeks) and ravioli stuffed with minced pink prawns, mushrooms, and truffles in lobster bisque sauce. Sorbets are served between courses in frosted glass lilies. Among the entrees, Maine lobster was served with coral (lobster roe) butter and steamed broccoli, and chateaubriand came with peppery red wine/game sauce, a mousseline of spinach, poached pears, and dauphinois potatoes.

There's an extensive wine list, with 12 by-the-glass selections; consult the sommelier for assistance.

Petit-fours and chocolate truffles are served gratis at the conclusion of your meal. However, that doesn't mean you should forgo dessert. Choices include ambrosial soufflés and a totally satisfying flourless chocolate truffle cake topped with homemade hazelnut ice cream. *Note:* A prix-fixe pre-theater special (soup or salad, entree, and dessert) is served Sunday to Thursday from 6 to 7pm; it costs $34.50.

End your evening over après-dinner drinks in the romantic adjoining piano bar/lounge. Overlooking the pool, this plushly furnished venue has a stained-glass skylight that retracts for a view of open starlit sky. Off the lounge is an intimate crystal-chandeliered European-style casino for high-stakes players only.

✪ The Palm

The Forum Shops at Caesars Palace, 3500 Las Vegas Blvd. S. ☎ **702/732-7256.** Reservations recommended. Main courses $8.50–$14 lunch, $15–$29 dinner. AE, CB, DC, MC, V. Daily 11:30am–11pm. STEAK/SEAFOOD.

Grandsons of New York's original Palm owners John Ganzi and Pio Bozzi have parlayed the family business into a nationwide restaurant empire. Hence, this Las Vegas branch. In the Palm tradition, signature pine-wainscoted ecru walls are plastered with celebrity caricatures of everyone from Wayne Newton to Walt Kelly's Pogo. Diners are comfortably seated in roomy mahogany booths upholstered in dark green leather. A star-studded clientele includes everyone from Tony Curtis (who celebrated a birthday here) to George Foreman (who got a standing ovation from fellow diners).

Another Palm tradition is a bare-bones menu that austerely offers up appetizers (such as shrimp cocktail, clams casino, melon and prosciutto) and entrees (filet mignon, lamb chops, salmon fillet, broiled crabcakes, linguine with clam sauce, prime rib of beef) without descriptive frills. By contrast, a listing for string beans aglio e olio (in garlic and oil) seems positively lyrical. Food preparation is simple (nothing is drizzled, infused, or nuanced here). Rather, the emphasis is on fresh fish and seafood, top-quality cuts of meat, and salads using the ripest, reddest, and juiciest tomatoes—all served up in satisfying hungry-man portions. Side dishes of cottage fries and creamed spinach are recommended. The wine list nicely complements the menu, and desserts include big wedges of cheesecake and chocolate pecan pie. At lunch you can choose a $12 fixed-price meal, which includes an entree (perhaps prime rib or batter-fried shrimp), salad, cottage fries, and tea or coffee.

✪ Spago

The Forum Shops at Caesars Palace, 3500 Las Vegas Blvd. S. ☎ **702/369-6300.** Reservations recommended for the dining room; not accepted at the cafe. Dining Room: Main courses $14–$28. Cafe: Main courses $8.50–$16.50. AE, CB, DC, DISC, MC, Optima, V. Dining Room: Sun–Thurs 6–10:30pm, Fri–Sat 5:30–11pm. Cafe: Daily 11am–1am. ASIAN/ITALIAN-INFLUENCED CALIFORNIAN.

The galaxy of Las Vegas restaurants acquired a bright new star in 1994, when legendary California chef Wolfgang Puck's movable feast traveled east. Puck hired noted restaurant designer Adam Tihany to create an enchanting interior, which is fronted by a high-energy casual-chic cafe/bar overlooking the Forum Shops' classical Roman piazza. Sunday afternoons, a jazz quartet performs at this convivial cafe. I love the cafe, but the theatrical multi-level main dining room is simply breathtaking. Its visual centerpiece, an outer-space-themed painting by James Rosenquist, accentuates an alluring otherworldly ambience. To the right is a grand, whimsically railed Brazilian cherrywood staircase—scene of many a dramatic descent. And lighting plays a stellar role, bouncing off lofty copper columns and enhancing the shimmer of cookware in a 50-foot exhibition kitchen. Most impressive is the play of light on two glossy wood mezzanine-level doors, transforming them into golden panels. Needless to say, Spago is Las Vegas's numero uno celebrity haunt.

The dining room menu changes nightly, but ambrosial appetizers have included such dishes as a quartet of tuna sashimi atop blocks of Japanese rice studded with tiny morsels of cucumber and peppers. Puckish pasta entrees are always divine, but the pièce de résistance when I last dined here was tender moist, crisp-skinned roast Chinese duck, marinated in red wine vinegar and soy sauce and stuffed with pears and ginger. It was served with a doughy steamed bun filled with julienned vegetables, plum wine sauce enlivened by an infusion of other fruits, and a garnish of grapefruit slices. Pastry chef Mary Bergin's desserts—such as a caramelized espresso pot de crème textured with coarsely ground espresso beans—make fitting finales. Equally impressive is the extensive and expertly researched wine list. Cafe specialties include Puck's signature Chinois chicken salad and a superb mesquite-fried salmon served with a tangy toss of soba noodles and cashews in a coconut-sesame-chili paste vinaigrette nuanced with lime juice and Szechuan mustard.

Top of the World

Stratosphere Las Vegas Hotel, 2000 Las Vegas Blvd. S., between St. Louis St. and Baltimore Ave. ☎ **702/380-7711.** Reservations required. Main courses $13–$21 lunch, $21–$29 dinner. AE, CB, DC, DISC, JCB, MC, V. Lunch daily 11am–3:45pm; dinner Sun–Thurs 4–11pm, Fri–Sat 4pm–midnight. AMERICAN/CONTINENTAL.

In a city filled with high-rise hotel towers, you'd think there'd be dozens of restaurants offering breathtaking views. There aren't—and the few that do exist can't begin to match the panoramic vistas visible from this revolving dining room, 800 feet above the Strip on the 106th floor of the Statrosphere. The jewel-toned interior is fittingly elegant, with comfortable seating at tables lit by shaded lamps, but the glorious exterior scenery is more to the point. Plan to arrive in time to see the sunset, and stay on to see the Strip brilliantly aglitter in neon light.

Dinner here proved there was more to this restaurant than the view. An excellent meal started off with crispy spring rolls served atop a mound of thin-sliced Asian cucumber salad in a sweet vinaigrette; it came with a piquant peanut/coconut dipping sauce. Another Asian appetizer, chicken satay, was also noteworthy. The stellar entree was a moist 10-ounce filet of almond-crusted salmon, laced with lemon dill butter and served with yummy mashed potatoes and an array of sautéed al dente baby vegetables. There are terrific desserts, such as the towering vacherin—layers of hazelnut meringue filled with Bavarian cream, garnished with fresh berries, and served with crème anglaise and kiwi and raspberry sauces. The wine list is extensive, and the lunch menu adds sandwiches and burgers to your options.

EXPENSIVE

✪ Chin's

3200 Las Vegas Blvd. S., in the Fashion Show Mall (turn at the Frontier sign). ☎ **702/ 733-8899.** Reservations recommended. Main courses $9.95–$11.95 lunch, $12–$29.50 dinner. AE, MC, V. Mon–Sat 11:30am–10pm, Sun noon–10pm. CANTONESE.

Chin's offers a tranquil contrast to the neon overkill of the Strip. Its understated decor, with bare white walls, is almost stark. During the day a single flower in a vase graces each table; at night this flower is removed and replaced by a glass oil candle. Other than that, a narrow band of recessed pink lighting is virtually the only adornment. Tuesday through Saturday nights, a pianist plays mellow classics— Cole Porter and the like. I believe you'll find, as I did, that what at first seems a too-cool setting is actually aesthetically refined and soothing.

Chin's cuisine is as pleasing as its ambience. Not-to-be-missed appetizers—served with a trio of sauces—include crispy spring rolls; heavenly deep-fried shrimp puffs (stuffed with minced shrimp and mildly curried cream cheese); and a crunchy salad of crisp-fried chicken strips tossed with lettuce, rice noodles, sesame seeds, and coriander in a light dressing with a tang of mustard. At lunch this scrumptious salad is offered as a main course. There are many highly recommended dinner entrees, among them barbecued pork fried rice—here a culinary masterpiece comprising a mound of savory rice studded with morsels of pork, crisp scallions, peas, and finely chopped carrots and onions. Also excellent: tender chunks of orange roughy wok-fried in black pepper sauce with onions and red and green peppers. A small, but carefully chosen, wine list features French and California wines that complement Chinese cooking. Order crispy pudding for dessert—a refreshing batter-dipped egg custard splashed with Midori, a melon liqueur.

Mizuno's

Tropicana Resort & Casino, 3801 Las Vegas Blvd. S. ☎ **702/739-2222.** Reservations suggested. Full Samurai dinners mostly $14.95–$19.95, Shogun combination dinners $24.95–$38.95. AE, CB, DC, MC, V. Daily 5–10:30pm. JAPANESE TEPPANYAKI.

This stunning marble-floored restaurant is filled with authentic Japanese artifacts, among them an ancient temple bell, a 400-year-old vase from Tokyo, and antique scrolls and shoji screens. One of the latter depicts the restaurant's theme—the exchange of cultures between the East and West as exemplified by the silk and tea trade. A meandering glass "stream" is lit by tiny twinkling lights to suggest running water, and cut-glass dividers are etched with graceful cherry blossoms, irises, and plum trees.

Food is prepared at marble teppanyaki grill tables where you're seated with other patrons; together you comprise the "audience" for a highly skilled chef, who, wielding cooking knives with the panache of a samurai swordsman, rapidly trims, chops, sautés, and flips the food onto everyone's plates. This being Las Vegas, his dazzling display of dexterity is enhanced by a flashing light show over the grill.

Entrees comprised of tasty morsels of New York strip steak, filet mignon, shrimp, lobster, chicken, or shrimp and vegetable tempura—and various combinations of the above—come with miso soup or consommé (get the tastier miso), salad with ginger dressing, an array of crispy flavorful vegetables stir-fried with sesame seeds and spices, steamed rice, and tea. Though it's a lot of food, an appetizer of shrimp and mushrooms sautéed in garlic butter with lemon soy sauce merits consideration. And a bottle of warm sake is recommended. Ginger or red bean ice cream make for a fittingly light dessert. A great bargain here: a full early-bird dinner served from 5 to 6pm for just $9.95.

MODERATE

See also the listings for **Coyote Cafe** (p. 98) and **Spago** (p. 104), upscale restaurants that are fronted by more inexpensive cafes.

All-American Bar & Grille

Rio Suite Hotel, 3700 W. Flamingo Rd., at I-15. ☎ **702/252-7767.** Reservations not accepted. Main courses $5.95–$13.75 at lunch (most under $10), $11.95—$23.95 at dinner. AE, CB, DC, DISC, MC, V. Daily llam–11pm. AMERICAN.

This warmly inviting balconied restaurant has two themes: sports and Americana. Mahogany-paneled walls are hung with snowshoes, golf clubs, oars, and croquet mallets; there's a portrait of George Washington and a torch-bearing Statue of Liberty; vintage American flags fly from lofty mahogany rafters; and the waitstaff is in flag-motif shirts. You can also eat in a lively sunken bar area filled with athletic memorabilia (Roger Staubach's football jersey, and the like), while watching sporting events aired on eight TV monitors.

At lunch, the menu features burgers, salads, and sandwiches. Dinner options include steaks, seafood, and a choice of 27 domestic beers and selected wines by the glass.

A typical meal here might begin with an order of Blue Point oysters, followed by filet mignon and lobster tails (served with soup or salad, warm sourdough bread and butter, grilled vegetables, and a baked potato), with a finale of peach cobbler topped with homemade vanilla ice cream.

Country Star

3724 Las Vegas Blvd. S., at Harmon Ave. ☎ **702/740-8400.** Reservations for large parties only. Main courses $5.95–$21.95 (most under $14). AE, CB, DC, DISC, MC. V. Mon–Thurs 11am–midnight, Fri–Sun 11am–1am. AMERICAN COWBOY COOKING.

It's been called the hillbilly Hard Rock. Country Star opened with a celebrity-studded bash in July 1996 attended by country-music luminaries, among them restaurant principals Reba McEntire, Vince Gill, Tracy Lawrence, Neal McCoy, Lorianne Crook, and Charlie Chase. Like the Hard Rock (or Planet Hollywood), it's a vast establishment filled with music memorabilia (Merle Haggard's boots, a Minnie Pearl hat with dangling price tag, Dolly Parton's wedding dress, gold records, Grand Ole Opry posters). And though it's both lower key and friendlier than its rock- and movie-themed competitors, like its forebears, Country Star was conceived as a Las Vegas home for visiting C&W performers. Dozens of video monitors—including several embedded in the entranceway floor—play nonstop C&W music videos. Dining areas include an Elvis Room. And since there's a dance floor, a fully equipped

Do Some Dim Sum

Most people don't know that Las Vegas has a Chinatown—not on the scale of New York's or San Francisco's, but nevertheless a fun place to visit and a great place to eat. It centers on the pretty pagoda-roofed **Chinatown Plaza**, a two-level complex of restaurants and shops at Spring Mountain Road between Wynn Road and Arville Street. The complex also functions as a Chinese cultural center and, this being Las Vegas, houses a wedding chapel and trade-exhibit center.

It's fun to browse the shops (which include an Asian supermarket and bakery as well as jewelry and furniture stores), but for me the big lure is the ✪ **Plum Tree Inn** (☎ 702/873-7077) on the Plaza's upper level. This restaurant's dim sum—its authenticity affirmed by a 95 percent Chinese clientele—is peerless and the setting for it—a discreetly lit contemporary Asian/minimalist dining room backed by a large tropical aquarium—most pleasant. Dim sum is served daily from 10am to 3pm. Servers, who speak little English, wheel carts to your table laden with delicious little dishes: chicken and sticky rice wrapped in lotus leaves (one of my favorites), fried shrimp balls covered with crunchy toasted almonds, steamed black bean spare ribs, chopped shrimp wrapped in rice noodles served with a slightly sweet soy sauce, steamed buns stuffed with tangy barbecued pork, and many others. Select only what really appeals to you; more is on the way. The Plum Tree Inn also offers a very moderately priced Cantonese/Mandarin menu from 10am to 10pm Sunday to Thursday, 10am to 11pm Friday and Saturday. There's a full bar. Reservations are suggested. Accepted credit cards: AE, MC, V. *Note:* Though Plum Tree Inn is not to be missed, the other restaurants in the complex, including the Vietnamese Pho Vietnam, also merit a visit. If you don't have a car, there are free shuttle buses between Chinatown and the MGM Grand and Mirage hotels.

stage, and a great sound system, there will be frequent live music (line-dancing lessons, too).

Noted cowboy chef Layne Wootten (his zesty rattlesnake barbecue sauce is on every table) often comes out of the kitchen to schmooze with customers. His specialties include award-winning "bowls of red" served with homemade cornbread; barbecued beef or pork ribs (consider a platter of both, with hickory-smoked chicken, salad, barbecued beans, fries, and cornbread); a homemade sausage platter with similar side dishes; and a pulled pork sandwich on hamburger roll served with fries and corn slaw. There's peanut butter pie for dessert. The bar pours only premium labels and features specialty drinks such as Texas Longhorn Tea—a vodka, rum, and gin concoction.

Dive!

3200 Las Vegas Blvd. S., in the Fashion Show Mall. ☎ **702/369-DIVE.** Reservations not accepted. $6.95–$13.95. AE, CB, DC, DISC, MC. V. Sun–Thurs 11:30am–10pm, Fri–Sat 11:30am–11pm. AMERICAN.

This exuberant restaurant-cum-entertainment concept was the creation of (among others) power visionaries Jeffrey Katzenberg and Steven Spielberg. DIVE!'s exterior is designed as a whimsical yellow submarine crashing through a 30-foot wall of water which cascades into an oversized pool erupting with depth-charge blasts. Its gunmetal-gray interior replicates the hull of a submarine with vaulted cylindrical ceilings, porthole-shaped (albeit neon-accented since this is Vegas) windows, exposed conduits that burst with steam, sonar screens, and working periscopes. Every hour

---

👪 Family-Friendly Dining

Buffets *(see p. 123)*   Cheap meals for the whole family. The kids can choose what they like, and there are sometimes make-your-own sundae machines.

DIVE! *(see p. 107)*   Housed in a submarine and featuring a zany high-tech show every hour projected on a video wall, this is the most fun family-oriented spot of all.

Hard Rock Cafe *(see p. 116)*   Kids also adore this restaurant, which throbs with excitement and is filled with rock memorabilia.

Hippo & The Wild Bunch *(see p. 116)*   A cartoon-like decor and wild party atmosphere (sometimes balloon artists are on hand making hats and animals for diners) makes this a favorite with kids. Adults will be thrilled with the high food quality.

Planet Hollywood *(see p. 109)*   This popular chain houses a veritable museum of movie memorabilia, and the action on numerous video monitors keeps kids from getting bored.

Pink Pony *(see p. 71)*   This bubble-gum pink circus-motif 24-hour coffee shop at Circus Circus will appeal to kids. And mom and dad can linger over coffee while the kids race upstairs to watch circus acts and play carnival games.

Roxy's Diner *(see p. 113)*   Diner food, rock 'n' roll, and a performing waitstaff make this a fun family choice.

Sherwood Forest Cafe *(see p. 62)*   Kids love to climb on the lavender dragons fronting this 24-hour coffee shop at Excalibur, and they also enjoy numerous child-oriented activities while you're on the premises.

---

a high-tech show projected on a 16-cube video wall (and 48 additional monitors throughout the restaurant) simulates a fantasy submarine dive, with special effects ranging from vibrating seats to flashing safety lights. And overhead, a luxury ocean liner, a manta ray research vessel, exotic fish, a fighting shark, and model subs circumnavigate the room on a computerized track. A DIVE! Gear retail shop is on the premises.

For all the hoopla, DIVE! keeps the focus on food. You can get a very good meal here, and portions are immense. There are, of course, "sub" sandwiches (such as grilled shrimp with smoked peppered bacon, lettuce, and mayonnaise), as well as delicious pasta dishes and pizzas, the latter on thin, lavash-like crusts. Other menu choices include hefty burgers on brioche onion rolls, wood oven-roasted herbed chicken (served with grilled corn on the cob, horseradish-whipped mashed potatoes, and an array of about seven other roasted vegetables), and a slab of barbecued baby back ribs. For dessert order crème brûlée garnished with fresh berries.

Dragon Noodle Co.

Monte Carlo Resort, 3770 Las Vegas Blvd. S., between Flamingo Rd. and Tropicana Ave. ☎ **702/730-7777.** Main courses $5.50–$16.95 (many items under $10). Sun–Thurs 11am–11pm, Fri–Sat 11am–midnight. AE, CB, DC, DISC, MC, V. ASIAN FUSION.

Dragon Noodle was designed according to the complex principles of Feng Shui (pronounced fung shway), the ancient Chinese art of geomancy used in planning building interiors to maximize prosperity and positive energy. At its opening, a Buddha Lion (harbinger of good luck) danced among the diners accompanied by drums, gongs, and crashing cymbals, while exploding firecrackers drove away evil spirits. What can I say? The owners are from L.A. The resulting casual, minimalist interior suggests a marketplace, with displays of Asian foodstuffs and sacks of rice on the floor. Along the back wall is a noteworthy exhibit of Asian teapots and other kitchen antiques. Classical piano music creates a soothing audio backdrop.

Order up a platter of pan-seared potstickers and create your own dipping sauce by mixing hoisin sauce, hot sauce, and vinegar. Other notable dishes here are spicy, wok-seared Mongolian beef served over crispy rice-stick noodles with scallion shreds, crisp-skinned roast duck, and Thai-style barbecued chicken scented with lemongrass, ginger, hot chili, and a hint of curry (it's served with spicy peanut and shallot sauces). With any of the above, I like to order steamed buns and make little sandwiches; try it. Dragon Noodle's extensive selection of teas (equivalent to a carefully crafted wine list) are served in exquisite pots. Other beverage options include more than a dozen wines by the glass, Asian beers, specialty iced teas, and fresh-squeezed juices. Among the Asian-nuanced desserts is a rich coconut cake layered with cream cheese frosting and topped with toasted coconut.

The Noodle Kitchen

Mirage, 3400 Las Vegas Blvd. S., between Flamingo Rd. and Sands Ave. ☎ **702/791-6362.** Reservations not accepted. Main courses $7.95–$22.75 (many under $10). AE, CB, DC, DISC, MC, V. Daily 11am–4am. CANTONESE.

The Mirage designed The Noodle Kitchen to serve its sizable clientele of Asian high rollers—a clientele desirous of authentic, non-Americanized Chinese fare. Most of the diners here are Asian, but American and European food aficionados will also appreciate the Kitchen's high-quality cuisine. It's really not so much a separate establishment as a section of the hotel's lushly tropical Caribe Café.

Start off with clear soup, flavored with Chinese cilantro and replete with thin egg noodles and dumplings filled with minced shrimp and ear mushrooms. A combination plate of soy chicken slices, roast pork, and tender crisp-skinned roast duck with plum sauce makes a marvelous entree choice, especially when accompanied by delicious al dente steamed vegetables (Chinese broccoli or choy sum) in oyster sauce. If you like to spice things up, you'll find three hot sauces on the table. There are Asian desserts (such as red bean ice delight), but as these are an acquired taste, you might prefer fresh-baked cakes and pies from the Caribe Café menu. Or skip dessert altogether in favor of sweet Vietnamese iced coffee mixed with condensed milk, coconut milk, and shaved ice. All bar drinks, including Chinese and Japanese beers, are available.

Planet Hollywood

Forum Shops at Caesars Palace, 3500 Las Vegas Blvd. S. ☎ **702/791-STAR.** Reservations not accepted. Main courses $7.50–$17.95 (most under $13). AE, DC, MC, V. Sun–Thurs 11am–midnight, Fri–Sat 11am–1am. CALIFORNIAN.

This famous celebrity-owned (Arnold, Sly, Bruce, and Demi) restaurant has an exuberant, cluttery two-level interior jam-packed with a veritable museum of Hollywood memorabilia—Clint Eastwood's pistol from *A Fistful of Dollars,* Marlon Brando's *Guys and Dolls* costume, Barbara Eden's genie bottle, James Bond's moon buggy from *Diamonds are Forever,* Clayton Moore's Lone Ranger tunic, chariot wheels from *Ben Hur,* the side of beef Stallone sparred with in *Rocky,* the *Star Trek* control tower, and much, much more. Touring the premises is part of the fun. Video monitors abound; while you dine, you can watch trailers for soon-to-be-released movies, themed video montages, and footage of Planet Hollywood grand openings around the world. The restaurant is also the scene of frequent autograph signings (Luke Perry, Cindy Crawford, and many others), memorabilia presentations (such as George Clooney's donation of his *ER* scrubs), and parties (ranging from a benefit for the Agassi

Foundation for Youth—Brooke and Andre hosted—to a season premiere party for *Melrose Place*). Background music is from movie soundtracks.

There are delicious appetizers such as Texas nachos or blackened shrimp served with Creole mustard sauce. Creole pizza topped with blackened shrimp, andouille sausage, chicken, onions, fresh plum tomatoes, Monterey Jack, and cheddar is excellent. Ditto linguine tossed with Thai shrimp, peanuts, and julienned vegetables in spicy sweet chili sauce. Other options include fajitas, burgers, and platters of smoked ribs. There's a full bar, not to mention thick malts and shakes. For dessert, try white chocolate bread pudding drenched in whiskey sauce and topped with white chocolate ice cream. There's a walkway here directly from the Strip, and three Planet Hollywood merchandise shops are on the premises. Arrive off hours to avoid a wait for seating.

Stage Deli
Forum Shops at Caesars Palace, 3500 Las Vegas Blvd. S. ☎ **702/893-4045.** Reservations accepted for large parties only. Main courses $9.95–$13.95, sandwiches $5.95–$12.95. AE, DC, DISC, JCB, MC, V. Sun–Thurs 8am–11pm, Fri–Sat 8am–midnight. KOSHER-STYLE DELI.

New York City's Stage Deli—a legendary hangout for comedians, athletes, and politicians—has been slapping pastrami on rye for more than half a century. Its Las Vegas branch retains the Stage's brightly lit Big Apple essence. Walls are embellished with subway graffiti and hung with Broadway theater posters, bowls of pickles grace the white Formica tables, and, in the New York tradition, comics like Buddy Hackett and Henny Youngman drop by whenever they're in town.

Most of the fare—including fresh-baked pumpernickel and rye, meats, chewy bagels, lox, spicy deli mustard, and pickles—comes in daily from New York. The Stage dishes up authentic 5-inch-high sandwiches stuffed with pastrami, corned beef, brisket, or chopped liver. (I like the soup, half sandwich, and potato salad combo.) Other specialties here include matzo ball soup, knishes, kasha varnishkes, cheese blintzes, kreplach, pirogen, and smoked fish platters accompanied by bagels and cream cheese. Or you might prefer a full meal consisting of pot roast and gravy, salad, homemade dinner rolls, potato pancakes, and fresh vegetables. Desserts run the gamut from rugelach cheesecake to Hungarian-style apple strudel, and available beverages include wine and beer, milk shakes, Dr. Brown's sodas, and chocolate egg creams.

Tony Roma's—A Place for Ribs
Stardust Resort & Casino, 3000 Las Vegas Blvd. S., at Convention Center Dr. ☎ **702/732-6111.** Reservations not accepted. Main courses $8.25–$12.95. Children's portions $4.95. AE, CB, DC, DISC, MC, V. Sun–Thurs 5–11pm, Fri–Sat 5pm–midnight. BARBECUE.

Tony Roma's is a deservedly popular national chain, and the company has voted this Stardust location the very best of its 140 franchises in terms of service, food quality, and cleanliness. It's a comfortable eatery, and a tub with brass faucets sits outside, so you can wash your sticky fingers on exiting.

This is a great choice for family dining. The house specialty is meaty, fork-tender baby back ribs barbecued in tangy sauce, but you can also order big, juicy beef ribs, honey-and-molasses-basted, Carolina-style pork ribs, or spicy Cajun ribs. A sampler plate is available. There are also hearty platters of barbecued shrimp or chicken, burgers, the catch of the day, steaks, and salads. Do try a side order of onion rings (served in a loaf). Entrees come with cole slaw and a choice of baked potato, french fries, or ranch-style beans. The children's menu lists a choice of four meals in a basket—ribs, burgers, chicken fingers, or chicken drumstick and thighs, all served with fries. For dessert there are fresh-baked chocolate, coconut, and banana cream pies, and all bar drinks are available.

✪ Wolfgang Puck Café

MGM Grand, 3799 Las Vegas Blvd. S. ☎ **702/895-9653.** Reservations not accepted. Main courses $9–$14.95. MC, V. Sun–Thurs 11am–11pm, Fri–Sat 11am–midnight. ASIAN/ITALIAN-INFLUENCED CALIFORNIAN.

Lucky Las Vegas has two Wolfgang Puck restaurants—the scintillating Spago at Caesars Forum Shops (see lengthy paean above) and this delightfully whimsical cafe in MGM's massive casino. Puck's wife and partner, Barbara Lazaroff, designed the interior, imprinting her signature pizza-slice logo on chair backs and embedding vibrantly colorful mosaics into walls and glossy granite tables. Black-and-white accents bring unity to this riot of zigzaggy shapes and pulsating color. A large counter seating area faces a display kitchen with an oak-burning brick pizza oven.

One of my favorite dishes is Puck's signature Chinois chicken salad tossed with crispy fried wontons, julienned carrots, cabbage, and green onions in a piquant Chinese honey-mustard sauce. Pizzas are also a signature item; constructed on crusts topped with fontina and mozzarella cheeses, they're brushed with pesto and layered with embellishments such as spicy jalapeño-marinated sautéed chicken, leeks, and cilantro. Also highly recommended is tortellini stuffed with sautéed shiitakes, herbs, and parmesan cheese served with a rich wild mushroom/white wine sauce. Wine and beer are available, but I often prefer Puck's fruity tropical iced tea instead. Desserts include pineapple upside-down cake with hot buttered rum sauce.

INEXPENSIVE

Ⓢ Big Sky

Stratosphere Las Vegas Hotel, 2000 Las Vegas Blvd. S., between St. Louis St. and Baltimore Ave. ☎ **702/780-7777.** All-you-can-eat dinner $12.99, free for children under 6. AE, CB, DC, DISC, JCB, MC, V. Sun–Thurs 5–11pm, Fri–Sat 5pm–midnight. PRIME RIB/BARBECUE.

Food bargains abound in Las Vegas, and this is one of the best. Big Sky—with its murals depicting the Old West, oil paintings of cowboys, log handrails, lasso-motif carpeting, and cashier housed in a chuck wagon—offers a suitably rustic setting for hearty all-you-can-eat family-style feasts. Country music helps set the tone, and service is down home and friendly.

Entree choices include prime rib with creamed horseradish sauce and a barbecue combination (beef brisket, St. Louis ribs, Carolina pulled pork, and fried chicken). At press time, there was talk of adding steaks as well. Whatever you select, it will come with a huge salad, scrumptious corn muffins (don't fill up on them; there's lots more food coming), corn on the cob, seasoned steak fries, cole slaw, Texas toast, and baked beans with pork. And when you've eaten your fill, you can waddle over to the dessert table and help yourself to apple cobbler, fresh berries and cream, and bread pudding with rum sauce. There's a full bar.

La Piazza Food Court

Caesars Palace, 3570 Las Vegas Blvd. S., just north of Flamingo Rd. ☎ **702/731-7110.** Complete meals are $5–$10. AE, DC, DISC, MC, V. Sun–Thurs 8:30am–11pm, Fri–Sat 9am–midnight. FOOD COURT.

Essentially an upscale version of a cafeteria, this is a great choice for families. Food stations are located along an attractive arched walkway lit by pink neon, and the brass-railed dining area, under massive domes, is rather elegant, with gold-topped columns and comfortable upholstered seating. The food is top quality—terrific deep-dish pizzas, an excellent salad bar, fresh-baked pies and cakes, sushi, smoked fish, immense burritos, Chinese stir-fry, deli, Häagen-Dazs bars, and a selection of beverages that includes herbal teas, wine, beer, espresso, and cappuccino. There's something

Ten Great Meal Deals

In the intro to this chapter, I alluded to the abundance of rock-bottom-budget meals and graveyard specials available at casino hotel restaurants. For your convenience, I've assembled some of the best buys below. You'll find addresses and phone numbers for these hotels in chapter 5. You might also want to check out **Big Sky** at the Stratosphere and **Binion's Horseshoe Coffee Shop.**

- **The El Cortez, Emerald Room**: A soup-to-nuts dinner with an 18-ounce porterhouse steak is $6.45, and a dollar will buy a breakfast of bacon and eggs with hash browns, toast, and coffee, both 24 hours.
- **Fitzgeralds, Molly's Country Kitchen:** Round the clock, enjoy a roast turkey dinner with sage dressing and giblet gravy, soup or salad, and choice of potato for $4.95.
- **Golden Nugget, Carson City Cafe:** From 4 to 11pm, a 10-ounce prime rib dinner (with baked potato and a vegetable) is $9.95. And from 11pm to 7am an 8-ounce grilled ham steak with eggs, hash browns and toast costs $3.95.
- **Holiday Inn Casino Boardwalk, Cyclone Coffee Shop:** Round-the-clock standouts include a hearty hobo stew of beef, potatoes, carrots, and gravy served in a pound loaf of freshly baked bread for $2.99; an all-you-can-eat fish fry with cole slaw and fries for $2.49; and a breakfast of two eggs, bacon or sausage, hash browns and toast for $1.29 (the same price will buy you all the pancakes you can eat!). Wednesdays from 4 to 10pm, an 8-ounce prime rib dinner is $3.49.
- **Imperial Palace, Teahouse:** An all-you-can-eat prime rib buffet dinner (including five other hot entrees, salad bar, dessert, coffee, and unlimited champagne) is $7.95 from 5 to 10pm.
- **Jackie Gaughan's Plaza, Plaza Diner:** Between 11pm and 11am, a graveyard special features a 16-ounce ham steak with two eggs, hash browns, toast, and coffee for $1.95.
- **The Luxor, Pyramid Café:** A sirloin steak and eggs breakfast with hash browns and toast is $2.99 Thursday to Tuesday from 11pm to 6am.
- **The Rio, Beach Café:** A 10-ounce T-bone steak with eggs, potatoes, and toast is $2.99 between 11pm and 7am.
- **Sam Boyd's Fremont, Lanai Cafe:** Specials here include a full prime rib dinner (with baked potato, vegetable, and salad) for $5.95, served 4pm to 2am; a steak-and-lobster-tail dinner (same side dishes) for $9.99, served 9pm to 2am; and a pound of Alaskan crab legs with rice and cole slaw for $7.77, served 11pm to 6am.
- **Sam's Town, Smokey Joe's Cafe:** From 11pm to 11am, a hearty breakfast including a ¾-pound ham steak, 3 eggs, hash browns, and toast is $2.95, for the same meal with steak instead of ham you'll pay $3.95.

for every dining mood. Waffle cones are baked on the premises, creating a delicious aroma.

Monte Carlo Pub & Brewery

Monte Carlo Resort, 3770 Las Vegas Blvd. S., between Flamingo Rd. and Tropicana Ave. ☎ **702/730-7777.** Main courses $5.95–$7.95. AE, CB, DC, DISC, MC, V. Sun–Thurs 11am–1am, Fri–Sat 11am–3am. PUB FARE AND BREWS.

When the Monte Carlo opened in the summer of 1996, this large and lively pub immediately became a favorite lunch spot and after-work hangout for local businesspeople. A working microbrewery (you can view the copper holding tanks and vats through large windows), it has a high-ceilinged warehouse/industrial interior, with exposed-brick and rusty corrugated-tin walls, track lighting, and a network of exposed pipes overhead. An ornate mahogany backbar with beveled mirrors adds a note of elegance. The Pub is cigar friendly (maintaining a humidor), and rock videos blare forth from a large screen and 40 TV monitors around the room. This is no place for a romantic rendezvous.

The menu features somewhat sophisticated versions of pub fare, doled out in enormous portions. I like the pizza topped with lamb, grilled eggplant, and goat cheese. Other choices include penne pasta with wild mushrooms in garlic cream sauce, a sample platter of sausages served with warm potato salad and whole-grain mustard, sandwiches, burgers, and barbecued baby back ribs. A microbrew with your meal (or a sampler of five) is de rigueur. Desserts include bread pudding with butterscotch rum sauce and creamy peanut butter pie. After 9pm, only pizza is served and dueling pianos provide dance music and entertainment.

Roxy's Diner

Stratosphere Las Vegas Hotel, 2000 Las Vegas Blvd. S., between St. Louis St. and Baltimore Ave. ☎ **702/780-7777.** Main courses $3.99–$8.99. AE, CB, DC, DISC, JCB, MC, V. Sun–Thurs 11am–11pm, Fri–Sat 11am–midnight. AMERICAN.

Art deco diners like Roxy's are springing up everywhere these days, catering to a nation nostalgic for simpler times. This one is typical of its retro genre, with shiny plastic booths that look like they came from a Thunderbird convertible, gleaming chrome trim, a black and white checkerboard floor, cove ceilings aglow with red neon, and a juke box stocked with oldies. What sets it apart is a very talented staff of waiters and waitresses who do comic routines and renditions of famous '50s songs like "Leader of the Pack." It's great fun; a good choice for family dining.

The menu features typical diner fare: a meat loaf sandwich on a toasted roll with fries, bacon-and-eggs breakfasts, burgers, po' boys, and blue-plate specials such as fresh oven-roasted turkey served over white bread with real mashed potatoes, fresh vegetables, turkey gravy, and cranberry sauce. Desserts run the gamut from rich chocolate layer cake with creamy fudge icing to butterscotch sundaes, and shakes and malts are among your beverage options.

4 Convention Center/Paradise Road/Sahara Avenue

VERY EXPENSIVE

Bistro Le Montrachet

Las Vegas Hilton, 3000 Paradise Rd. ☎ **702/732-5111** or 702/732-5651. Reservations suggested. Main courses $23–$46. AE, CB, DC, DISC, JCB, MC, V. Wed–Mon 6–10:30pm. FRENCH.

This ultra-elegant French restaurant seats diners under a dome bathed in a flattering pink light, an effect enhanced by the discreet glow emanating from shaded Chinese lamps. The room centers on a temple-like circle of massive walnut columns wherein a large floral arrangement graces an ornate marble table. Rich mahogany-paneled walls are hung with landscapes and still-life paintings; a crystal chandelier and beveled mirrors add sparkle.

Dishes are exquisitely presented and prepared. You might begin with chilled duck foie gras served on toast points. Also noteworthy are creamy lobster bisque and the salad "Le Montrachet"—a refreshing mélange of Belgian endive, watercress, julienned beets, and enoki mushrooms in a Gorgonzola/walnut oil dressing. Entree choices range from roasted breast of Muscovy duck (served with white and black beans and currants in a crème de cassis sauce) to broiled live Maine lobster removed from the shell and served atop herbed Moroccan couscous with crab dressing and drawn butter. Among desserts, I'm partial to the rich crème brûlée complemented by seasonal fruits, berries, and petits fours. The restaurant's wine cellar stocks more than 400 wines from vineyards spanning the globe.

Pegasus

Alexis Park Resort, 375 E. Harmon Ave., between Koval Lane and Paradise Rd. ☎ **702/ 796-3300.** Reservations recommended. Main courses $13.50–$39. AE, DC, MC, V. Nightly 6– 11pm. CONTINENTAL.

This low-key luxury resort attracts many visiting celebrities and Strip headliners, and its premier restaurant is a fitting venue for such an upscale clientele. Its splashing fountains and mist of diffused lighting playing on etched mirrors make me feel like I'm dining in an underwater kingdom. Planters of greenery, pots of ferns, and a large floral centerpiece further beautify this serene setting, as does a wall of arched windows overlooking a fountain-splashed rock garden.

Flambé dishes are featured, and sorbets are served between courses. You might begin with a quail egg and mandarin orange salad tossed with sweet mustard dressing. Among the soups, a splendid choice is the velvety cognac-laced lobster bisque. And fresh-shucked oysters Rockefeller here elevate this dish to its delicate apogee. The featured entree is Maine lobster sautéed with black truffles in a Madeira/bordelaise sauce; crowned with almond meringue baked to a golden brown, it is dramatically presented in a flaming veil of fire. A daily game special is offered each evening— perhaps ostrich with fresh seared foie gras. Desserts include bananas Foster and cherries jubilee along with pastries and cakes from the cart. There's an extensive wine list (mostly French and Californian) with choices in varying price ranges.

EXPENSIVE

Pamplemousse

400 E. Sahara Ave., between Santa Paula and Santa Rita drives, just east of Paradise Rd. ☎ **702/ 733-2066.** Reservations essential. Main courses $17.50–$24.50. AE, CB, DC, DISC, MC, V. Two seatings nightly at 6–6:30pm and 9–9:30pm. FRENCH.

Evoking a cozy French countryside inn, Pamplemousse is a catacomb of low-ceilinged rooms and intimate dining nooks with rough-hewn beams. Copperware and provincial pottery adorn the walls; candlelit tables, beautifully appointed with Villeroy & Boch show plates and fresh flowers, are draped in pale-pink linen; and classical music or light jazz plays softly in the background. It's all very charming and un-Vegasy. There's additional seating in a small garden sheltered by a striped tent. The restaurant's name, which means grapefruit, was suggested by the late singer Bobby Darin, one of the many celebrity pals of owner Georges La Forge. Strip headliners Wayne Newton, Robert Goulet, Siegfried & Roy, and Englebert Humperdinck are regulars.

The menu, which changes nightly, is recited by your waiter. The meal always begins with a large complimentary basket of crudités (about 10 different crisp, fresh vegetables), a big bowl of olives, and—a nice country touch—a basket of hard-boiled eggs. From there, you might proceed to an appetizer of lightly floured bay scallops sautéed in buttery grapefruit sauce, followed by an entree of crispy duck breast and banana in a sauce of orange honey, dark rum, and crème de banane. Filet mignon, New York steak, and rack of lamb are always featured. For dessert, perhaps there'll be homemade dark chocolate ice cream with pralines in a sabayon sauce. An extensive, well-rounded wine list complements the menu.

MODERATE

§ Alpine Village Inn

3003 Paradise Rd., between Riviera Blvd. and Convention Center Dr. ☎ **702/734-6888.** Reservations recommended. Fixed-price dinners $9.95–$19.50; children's portions (under 12 only) about half price. AE, CB, DC, DISC, MC, V. Sun–Thurs 5–10pm, Fri–Sat 5–11pm. SWISS/GERMAN.

A Las Vegas tradition since 1950, this extremely popular family restaurant doesn't subscribe to the less-is-more theory of interior design. Walls are painted with murals of snowy Alpine scenery, an effect echoed by snow-covered chalet roofing, twinkling Christmas tree lights, and miniature ski lifts on cables strung across the ceiling. There are Swiss and Austrian cowbells, mounted deer heads, and window boxes filled with geraniums. And the very efficient waitstaff is in Tyrolean costume.

Dinner is a multicourse feast beginning with a big pewter bowl of crudités served with herbed cottage cheese dip. A steaming bowl of savory Bavarian chicken soup is followed by a salad, and a basket of fresh-baked breads includes scrumptious hot cinnamon rolls. For your entree, I recommend the roast duckling with sausage stuffing served over wild and brown rice (it comes with orange and cherry sauces) or roast tender chicken with chestnut stuffing. These are accompanied by an array of vegetables and choice of crisp potato pancakes, a baked potato, or Swiss Rösti potatoes (shredded potato mixed with onion, bacon, eggs, and spices, fried in a pancake, and garnished with grated parmesan). If you'd like more than one of the above selections, the waiters generally comply. The finale: homemade apple or peach strudel, served warm (topped with vanilla ice cream if you so desire). Tea or coffee is included. The wine list offers wines by the glass and a large selection of beers, 19 varieties of schnapps, and exotic cocktails.

After dinner, if you can still move, check out the adjoining gift shop's selection of cuckoo clocks, crystal, beer steins, music boxes, cowbells, and Hummel figures. There's also a bar/lounge and a separate downstairs restaurant called the Rathskellar (details below).

Ginza

1000 E. Sahara Ave., near State St., between Paradise Rd. and Maryland Pkwy. ☎ **702/732-3080.** Reservations for large parties only. Main courses $12.55–$17.50. AE, MC, V. Tues–Sun 5pm–1am. JAPANESE.

For almost two decades, this charming little restaurant has attracted a devoted clientele of local Japanese and Japanese food aficionados. There's a sushi bar in the front room, and the main dining area has shoji screen–covered windows, tables sheltered by shingled eaves, rice paper–style lighting fixtures, and cream walls adorned with Japanese fans, paintings, and prints. Four spacious, red leather booths are the sole concession to Las Vegas style.

You might begin with a shared appetizer of tempura shrimp and vegetables. Entrees—such as beef, chicken, or salmon sprinkled with sesame seeds in a thick teriyaki sauce—come with soup (miso or egg flower), salad, and green tea. Sushi is a highlight, and there are about 30 à la carte selections to choose from. Be sure to try an appetizer or entree portion of Ginza's unique Vegas rolls—salmon, tuna, yellowtail, and avocado rolled with seaweed in sesame-studded rice and quickly deep-fried so the sesame seeds form a crunchy crust. It's served with lemon soy sauce. Also delicious are seaweed-wrapped California rolls. The fish is extremely fresh, and everything here is made from scratch. A bottle of sake is recommended. For dessert there's lemon sherbet or ginger and green tea ice creams.

Hard Rock Cafe

4475 Paradise Rd., at Harmon Ave. ☎ **702/733-8400.** Reservations not accepted. Main courses $8.95–$13.95; burgers & sandwiches $5.50–7.95. AE, DC, MC, V. Sun–Thurs 11am–11:30pm, Fri–Sat 11am–midnight. AMERICAN.

The Hard Rock was created by Peter Morton so that people would "have a place to go where they could experience the fun of rock 'n' roll, past and present, while enjoying a great meal." And that pretty much describes it. The Las Vegas branch is fronted by an 88-foot guitar and a sidewalk of the stars honoring rock legends. Its interior, in the Hard Rock tradition, is aclutter with rock memorabilia—Roy Orbinson's Harley Davidson, a signed Rolling Stones guitar, Elvis Presley gold records, an outrageous Elton John costume, and so on. Also in the Hard Rock tradition: It's a place where the average Joe and Jane can come and gape at stars, and, amazingly, stars frequently show up to be gaped at. Sheryl Crow, Michael Keaton, the Ramones, Pat Benatar, and Eddie Van Halen are just a few who've made the scene here.

The menu offers some good salads, such as a crisp tortilla piled high with greens, cheddar cheese, black beans, guacamole, and sliced grilled chicken. A burger and fries here are as good as they get. And entree choices include fajitas and Texas ribs in watermelon barbecue sauce. Wash it down with anything from a Heineken to a thick chocolate shake. Or skip the latter and indulge in a hot fudge sundae for dessert. An inexpensive children's menu is a plus for families. Don't be frightened by the line outside—it's usually not for the restaurant but the on-premises Hard Rock merchandise store. The Hard Rock Hotel and Casino is next door (see chapter 5).

Ⓢ Hippo & the Wild Bunch

4503 Paradise Rd., at Harmon Ave., just across from the Hard Rock Hotel. ☎ **702/731-5446.** Main courses $5.95–$13.95; children's menu $1.75–$2.95. AC, CB, DC, DISC, MC, V. Sun–Thurs 11am–3am, Fri–Sat 11am–5am. AMERICAN.

Georges La Forge, owner of the cozily romantic Pamplemousse (see description above), surprised everyone when he opened this wildly whimsical restaurant in 1995. Its kooky-cluttery interior includes cartoon-like animal sculptures (such as a hippo in a treehouse), a tangle of vines strung overhead, and walls painted with bright jungle foliage. There are balloons tied to many chairs, and often a balloon artist is on the scene creating twisty animals and hats for guests. There are usually several exuberant parties going on (some of them children's parties), and the chaotic ambience is exacerbated by loud rock music, a waitstaff on roller skates, a bustling exhibition kitchen, and TV monitors over the bar airing sporting events. Tuesday to Sunday from 8pm to 3am, a DJ plays music for dancing.

Hippo's "party-on" atmosphere notwithstanding, the food is superb. Come at lunch to enjoy it without all the hoopla; at dinner, weather permitting, you might sit out on the quieter, tree-bordered patio. Noteworthy items on La Forge's eclectic menu include delicious potstickers with chili oil/soy dipping sauce, a classic salad niçoise, pizzas, and spicy Southwestern ravioli in a red pepper sauce topped with diced vegetables. Burgers here are as good as burgers get, char-grilled and served on fresh-baked buns (ask for garlic mashed potatoes instead of fries). There's a dynamite tiramisu for dessert, and beverages, including a full bar, range from fresh-squeezed juices to coffee specialties.

Ⓢ Romano's Macaroni Grill

2400 W. Sahara Ave., two blocks west of I-15 (on your right, directly across from Palace Station, if you're coming from the Strip). ☎ **702/248-9500** for priority seating. Main courses $4.95–$9.25 at lunch, $6.50–$16.95 at dinner (most under $12). AE, CB, DC, DISC, MC, V. Sun–Thurs 11am–10pm, Fri–Sat 11am–11pm. NORTHERN ITALIAN.

The Macaroni Grill is a stellar exception to the general mediocrity of chain restaurants. The first thing you'll notice is its cheerful interior, with arched stone walls, shuttered windows, colorful murals of Venice, and lights festively strung from rafters overhead. This warmly welcoming ambience is enhanced by the glow from an oak-burning pizza oven tended by white-toqued chefs; strolling opera singers (there's recorded Italian music at other times); and aesthetic displays of foodstuffs, chianti, flowers, and desserts.

But the big surprise is the food. Everything is made from the freshest ingredients, and the quality of cuisine would be notable at twice the price. Thin-crusted pizzas (order one topped with pancetta, ricotta, gruyère, smoked mozzarella, and sun-dried tomatoes) are scrumptious, as are pastas such as farfalle (bowties) tossed with grilled chicken, pancetta, and red and green onions in asiago cream sauce. Equally good: an entrée of sautéed chicken with mushrooms, artichoke hearts, capers, and pancetta in lemon butter, served with spaghettini. There are fresh-baked breads—foccacia and ciabatta (a crusty country loaf) for sopping up sauces or dipping in extra virgin olive oil. And desserts—especially an apple custard torte with hazelnut crust and caramel topping—keep to the same lofty standard. Macaroni Grill has a full bar, premium wines are sold by the glass, and a children's menu offers an entree and beverage for just $3.25.

Z Tejas Grill

3824 Paradise Road, between Twain Ave. and Corporate Dr. ☎ **702/732-1660.** Reservations recommended. Main courses $7.25–$ll.95 lunch, $9.75–$16.95 dinner. AE, CB, DC, DISC, MC, V. Daily 11am–5pm lunch, 5–11pm dinner. TEX-MEX WITH CAJUN AND COASTAL INFLUENCES.

This Austin, Texas–based restaurant's rather odd name came about because its original chef, a Frenchman, kept referring to it as "zee" Tejas Grill. I'm partial to its sleek split-level knotty-pine interior, with oak shutters separating dining areas, pine beams overhead, muted turquoise and peach walls hung with large abstract paintings, and cactus-motif central chandelier. During the day sunshine streams in through large windows (especially on the plant-filled enclosed patio); at night, soft lighting and candlelit tables make this a good choice for romantic dinners.

A unique, and very tasty, appetizer here is the Navajo roll—crisp-fried Mexican cheeses, seasoned fresh lump crabmeat, and vegetables wrapped in herb bread and topped with fried spinach and cornmeal crumbs. Follow it up with spicy grilled Jamaican jerk chicken, nuanced with lime and served with peanut sauce and rum-spiked coconut-banana ketchup; it comes with two side dishes—perhaps roasted-garlic/skin-on mashed potatoes and mixed vegetables. Swig down a few of the Grill's excellent made-from-scratch margaritas with your meal, but do leave room for some graham cracker-crusted praline cheesecake smothered with pecans. During Happy Hour (4 to 7pm weekdays), stop by for half priced appetizers and 50¢ off on drinks.

INEXPENSIVE

Chili's Grill & Bar

2590 S. Maryland Pkwy., between Sahara and Karen aves., in the Sahara Town Square Shopping Center. ☎ **702/733-6462.** Main courses mostly $4.99–$10.29. AE, CB, DC, DISC, MC, V. Mon–Thurs 11am–10pm, Fri–Sat 11am–11pm, Sun 11:30am–10pm. Free parking. SOUTHWESTERN.

Chili's is a national chain, based in Texas, offering superior "bowls of red" and other southwestern specialties. This branch is a sunny, brick-floored restaurant with many plants flourishing in the light streaming in through numerous windows. Seating is in comfortable upholstered booths, ceramic-tiled tables are situated beneath hanging lamps made from old copper chili pots, and walls are adorned with framed posters and photographs of chili cook-offs. This is a great choice for family dining.

Chili is, of course, a specialty, available with or without beans. Equally popular are the fabulous half-pound burgers, made from fresh-ground beef and served with home-style fries and various toppings (I like cheese and chili). Or order up a sizzling platter of steak or chicken fajitas. Lighter items include a grilled chicken Caesar salad or a plate of steamed vegetables. Similarly, desserts run the gamut from a brownie topped with ice cream, hot fudge, chopped walnuts, and whipped cream to low-fat frozen yogurt. A children's menu, listed on a place mat with games and puzzles, offers full meals for $2.79, including "bottomless fountain drinks."

The Rathskellar

3003 Paradise Rd., between Riviera Blvd. and Convention Center Dr. ☎ **702/734-6888.** Reservations recommended. Burgers and sandwiches $4.25–$7.50, main courses $8.75–$11.95. AE, CB, DC, DISC, MC, V. Sun–Thurs 5–10pm, Fri–Sat 5–11pm. GERMAN/AMERICAN.

The Rathskellar is a rollicking downstairs adjunct to the Alpine Village Inn (see above)—a cozy beer hall, with red-and-white checkered tablecloths and a floor strewn with peanut shells (there are bowls of peanuts on every table). A pianist and singer entertain nightly, and everyone sings along. Choices here include a sauerbraten sandwich on pumpernickel rye served with German potato salad; a hot open-faced turkey sandwich served with mashed potatoes, cranberry sauce, and gravy (salad bar included); barbecued pork ribs with baked beans; half-pound burgers; and beer-battered deep-fried buffalo wings with french fries. For dessert, there's apple or peach strudel à la mode. An extensive children's menu makes this a popular choice for family dining.

5 East Las Vegas/Flamingo Road

VERY EXPENSIVE

✪ The Tillerman

2245 E. Flamingo Rd., at Channel 10 Dr. (just west of Eastern Ave.). ☎ **702/731-4036.** Reservations not accepted. Main courses $15.95–$36.95. AE, CB, DC, DISC, MC, V. Nightly 5–11pm, bar/lounge until midnight. STEAK/SEAFOOD.

Ask any local for a list of favorite restaurants, and you can be sure the Tillerman in east Las Vegas will be on it. Its verdant, plant-filled interior is under a lofty beamed cathedral ceiling with retractable skylights. Candlelit dining areas offer seating amid a grove of ficus trees, and the woodsy ambience is furthered by exquisite oak paneling and tree-trunk pillars. A circular stained-glass window provides a lovely focal point. There's additional seating on the mezzanine level, where diners enjoy treetop views. All the top Strip performers are regular Tillerman customers.

Your meal here begins with a relish tray and a basket of delicious oven-fresh breads. Also complimentary is a Lazy Susan salad bar served at your table with a choice of homemade dressings, including a memorable chunky blue cheese. Portions are immense, so appetizers are really not necessary, but then again, they're too good to pass up. Especially notable: ultrafresh, plump red médaillons of yellowfin tuna blackened and served almost rare in spicy mustard sauce. Meat entrees include prime center-cut New York strip steak, fork-tender filet mignon, and a center-cut veal chop. And there are at least a dozen fresh seafood specials each night. On a recent visit I had a piece of snowy white halibut, charcoal-broiled and brushed with pecan pesto. Entrees come with a white and wild rice mixture tossed with slivered almonds and chives and fresh vegetables. Homemade desserts—such as Bavarian cream with strawberries and bananas—change nightly. The wine list highlights California selections.

In case you want to see the world.

At American Express, we're here to make your journey a smooth one. So we have over 1,700 travel service locations in over 120 countries ready to help. What else would you expect from the world's largest travel agency?

do more

AMERICAN EXPRESS

Travel

http://www.americanexpress.com/travel

In case you want to be welcomed there.

We're here to see that you're always welcomed at establishments everywhere. That's why millions of people carry the American Express® Card – for peace of mind, confidence, and security, around the world or just around the corner.

do more

Cards

In case you're running low.

We're here to help with more than 118,000 Express Cash locations around the world. In order to enroll, just call American Express before you start your vacation.

do more

Express Cash

And just in case.

We're here with American Express® Travelers Cheques and Cheques *for Two*.® They're the safest way to carry money on your vacation and the surest way to get a refund, practically anywhere, anytime.

Another way we help you...

do more

Travelers Cheques

Note: Since the Tillerman doesn't take reservations, arrive early to avoid waiting, or else plan a pre-dinner cocktail in the cozy, oak-paneled lounge with a working fireplace.

MODERATE

✪ Fog City Diner

325 Hughes Center Drive, off Flamingo Rd. at Howard Hughes Pkwy. (it's between Koval Lane and Paradise Rd.) ☎ **702/737-0200.** Reservations recommended. Main courses $6.50–$13.95. CB, DC, DISC, MC, V. Sun–Thurs 11:30am–11pm, Fri–Sat 11:30am–midnight. AMERICAN.

Its palm-fringed exterior agleam with neon and chrome, this renowned San Francisco transplant beckons diners with the commanding phrase "Get In Here." I, for one, am happy to comply. Fog City's sleek post-deco/*Orient Express* interior—with retro murals, pristine white-tile flooring, glossy mahogany paneling, and alabaster lighting fixtures—is just gorgeous. You can slip into a leather-upholstered booth or dine more casually at the backlit onyx oyster bar facing the open kitchen.

The menu changes seasonally. Your best option here is to graze on a variety of small dishes, such as succulent crisp-fried Dungeness crabcakes with ancho chile succotash (a crunchy mix of sautéed sugar snap peas, corn, black-eyed peas, and red pepper); grilled poblano peppers stuffed with four cheeses and served with chunky avocado salsa; and tangy stir-fried pork and julienned vegetables wrapped in delicate burritos. Farm-raised oysters also merit consideration, and you might want to order a warm, crusty loaf of garlic/leek/basil bread. Many wines are available by the glass. For dessert, the moist chocolate chile tart in orange rind sauce, topped with a scoop of Häagen-Dazs coffee ice cream, is ambrosial.

Papamios

Sam's Town, 5111 Boulder Hway., at Flamingo Rd. ☎ **702/454-8041.** Reservations recommended. Main courses $9.95–$12.95; pizzas $6.95–$7.95. Weekend brunch $12.95. AE, CB, DC, DISC, MC, V. Sun–Thurs 5–10pm, Fri–Sat 5–11pm; Sat–Sun brunch 9am–3pm. ITALIAN.

Make dinner or brunch here an occasion to visit Sam's Town, and, if possible, snag a table on the festive veranda overlooking verdant Mystic Falls Park, the enclosed atrium with fern gullies, babbling brooks, and gushing waterfalls. You don't have to worry about the weather; in this vast climate-controlled park, it's always 70°. The veranda is a great venue for viewing nightly laser shows. And Papamios' interior is also appealing—casually elegant, with dining areas defined by Corinthian-colonnaded archways, checker-clothed tables lit by oil lamps, and strings of colored lights suspended overhead.

An appetizer of roasted mushrooms and fried polenta topped with buffalo mozzarella makes a great beginning. Entrees, served with salad, include shrimp scampi on a bed of angel hair pasta; veal marsala with spinach and tiger-striped mushroom ravioli; and linguini tossed with shrimp, mussels, and lobster in lemon/champagne Alfredo sauce with fresh tomato garnish. Tiramisu is the house specialty dessert. More than a dozen wines are offered by the glass.

Weekend brunches here are also lovely. They feature bountiful buffets (with shrimp and crab, salads, fruits, and breakfast pastries), a glass of champagne, and a choice of entrees ranging from grilled baby lamb chops with pineapple relish to huevos rancheros.

Ricardo's

2380 Tropicana Ave., at Eastern Ave. (northwest corner). ☎ **702/798-4515.** Reservations recommended. Main courses $7.50–$12.95; lunch buffet $6.95; children's plates $2.95–$3.50, including milk or soft drink with complimentary refills. AE, CB, DC, DISC, MC, V. Mon–Thurs 11am–10pm, Fri–Sat 11am–11pm, Sun 11am–10pm. MEXICAN.

This hacienda-style restaurant is a great favorite with locals. It has several stucco-walled dining rooms separated by arched doorways—all of them lovely, with candlelit oak tables and booths upholstered in Aztec prints. One room is a plant-filled greenhouse, another a garden room under a lofty pine-beamed ceiling. Yet a third dining area has a ceramic-tiled fireplace (ablaze in winter) and a dark wood coffered ceiling. Strolling Mexican musicians entertain at night.

Start off with an appetizer of deep-fried battered chicken wings served with melted cheddar (ask for jalapeños if you like your cheese sauce hotter). Nachos smothered with cheese and guacamole are also very good here. For an entree, you can't go wrong with chicken, beef, or pork fajitas served sizzling on a hot skillet atop sautéed onions, mushrooms, and peppers; they come with rice and beans, tortillas, a selection of salsas, guacamole, and tomato wedges with cilantro. All the usual taco/enchilada/tamale combinations are also listed. A delicious dessert is helado Las Vegas—ice cream rolled in corn flakes and cinnamon, deep-fried, and served with honey and whipped cream. Be sure to order a pitcher of Ricardo's great margaritas. The same menu is available all day, but a buffet is offered at lunch. The kids' menu—on a place mat with games and puzzles—features both Mexican and American fare.

INEXPENSIVE

Einstein Bros. Bagels

4626 S. Maryland Pkwy., between Harmon and Tropicana Aves. in the University Gardens Shopping Center. ☎ **702/795-7800.** All items under $6. MC, V. Mon–Sat 6am–8pm (till 6pm in summer), Sun 7am–5pm. BAGEL SANDWICHES.

Personally, I don't like digging into an enormous buffet first thing in the morning, and continental breakfast in a hotel is usually a rip-off. A welcome alternative is a fresh-baked bagel, of which there are 15 varieties here—everything from onion to wild blueberry. Cream cheeses also come in many flavors, my favorites being sun-dried tomato, vegetable, and jalapeño. Einstein's is a pleasant place for the morning meal, with both indoor seating and outdoor tables cooled by misters. Service is friendly, and four special blend coffees are available each day.

❂ Mediterranean Café and Market

4147 S. Maryland Pkwy., at Flamingo Rd., in the Tiffany Square strip mall. ☎ **702/731-6030.** No reservations. Main courses $3.99–$8.49 (all sandwiches under $5). AE, MC, DISC, V. Daily 8am–10pm. MEDITERRANEAN.

I was thrilled to find this totally authentic mom-and-pop Middle Eastern restaurant in Las Vegas, where high-quality ethnic eateries are scarce. When the weather's cool, it's pleasant to sit out front at umbrella tables. Inside, tables are covered with fruit-motif plastic cloths, walls adorned with Mediterranean landscapes (paintings and photographs) and Persian miniatures; a plastic grape arbor girds the room; and shelves are cluttered with inlaid ivory boxes, hookahs, and brassware. Background music is Greek, Turkish, and Arabic.

Everything here is homemade and delicious. You might order up a gyro (slivers of rotisseried beef and lamb enfolded into a pita with lettuce and tomato). Other good choices are a phyllo pie layered with spinach and feta cheese, served with hummus; skewers of grilled chicken and vegetable kabab with lavash bread and hummus; and a combination platter of hummus, tabouli, stuffed grape leaves, and felafel. All entrees come with pita bread and salad. I also like to get a side order of bourrani (creamy yogurt dip mixed with steamed spinach, sautéed garlic, and slivered almonds). Finish up with baklava and rich Turkish coffee. Wine and beer are available. You can also come by in the morning for Middle Eastern breakfasts. A Mediterranean market adjoins.

6 Downtown

VERY EXPENSIVE

Andre's

401 S. 6th St., at Lewis Avenue, a few blocks south of Fremont St. ☎ **702/385-5016.** Reservations recommended. Main courses $19.75–$33. AE, CB, DC, MC, V. Nightly from 6pm; closing hours vary. FRENCH/CONTINENTAL.

Owner-chef Andre Rochat has created a rustic country-French setting in a converted 1930s house in Downtown Las Vegas. Low ceilings are crossed with rough-hewn beams, and wainscoted stucco walls (embedded with straw) are hung with provincial pottery and copperware. Soft lighting emanates from candles and sconces. In addition to a catacomb of cozy interior rooms, there's a lovely, ivy-walled garden patio under the shade of a mulberry tree. This is a major celebrity haunt where you're likely to see Strip headliners. I was there one night when Tom Hanks, Steven Spielberg, and James Spader joined some pals for a bachelor party.

The menu changes seasonally. On a recent visit, appetizers included jumbo sea scallops rolled in a crunchy macadamia nut crust with citrus beurre blanc and red beet coulis. And among the entrees, a fan of pink, juicy slices of sautéed duck came with a confit of port wine and onions. A medley of vegetables—perhaps pommes lyonnaise, asparagus, broccoli hollandaise, and baby carrots—accompanies each entree, and sorbets are served between courses. For dessert, I love Andre's classic fruit tarts—flaky butter crusts layered with Grand Marnier custard and topped with fresh, plump berries. An extensive wine list (more than 900 labels) is international in scope and includes many rare vintages; consult the sommelier.

INEXPENSIVE

Binion's Horseshoe Coffee Shop

Binion's Horseshoe, 128 E. Fremont St., at Casino Center Blvd. ☎ **702/385-7111.** Main courses $4.25–$14.95 (most under $8). AE, CB, DC, DISC, MC, V. Daily 24 hours. AMERICAN.

Down a flight of steps from the casino floor, this is no humble hotel coffee shop. It's heralded by a gorgeous stained-glass dome and entered via doors embellished with antique beveled-glass panels. The interior is equally impressive, with a magnificent pressed-copper ceiling, rich oak paneling, walls hung with original oil paintings you'll wish you owned, and displays of antiques, turn-of-the-century magazine covers, and black-and-white photographs of the Old West. Notice, too, an exhibit of vintage playing cards that depict real kings and queens (e.g. Henry VIII and Anne Boleyn).

The menu lists all the traditional Las Vegas coffee shop items: sandwiches, burgers, Southern-fried chicken, steak and seafood entrees, along with breakfast fare. And you can't beat Binion's specials: two eggs with an immense slab of grilled ham, home fries, toast, and tea or coffee ($2.99 from 6am to 2pm); a 10-ounce New York steak dinner with baked potato, salad, and roll and butter ($3.99 from 10pm to 5:45am); a 7-ounce New York steak with eggs, home fries, and toast ($2.99 from 10pm to 5:45am); and 10-ounce prime rib dinner, including soup or salad, potato, and vegetables ($5.25 from 5 to 9:45pm); $6.25 for a 16-ounce T-bone steak instead of prime rib. All bar drinks are available, and there's peanut butter cream pie for dessert.

Carson Street Café

Golden Nugget, 129 E. Fremont St. between 1st St. and Casino Center Blvd. ☎ **702/ 382-1600.** Main courses mostly $5.95–$14.95. AE, CB, DC, DISC, MC, V. Daily 24 hours. AMERICAN.

Dining Downtown

Andre's **6**
Binion's Horshoe
  Coffee Shop **3**
Center Stage **1**
Golden Nugget
  Buffet **2**
Lady Luck
  Buffet **5**
Sam Boyd's
  Fremont
  Buffet **4**
Showboat
  Captain's
  Buffet **7**

Las Vegas has many delightful 24-hour hotel restaurants. The Golden Nugget's is reminiscent of an elegant street cafe on the Champs-Elysées . . . albeit one overlooking a gorgeous hotel lobby instead of a Paris street. Its jewel-toned interior—under a white-fringed green awning, with murals of park scenes and topiary, white latticing, and seating amid potted orange trees and planters of greenery—couldn't be lovelier.

And the food is notably excellent. A wide-ranging menu offers terrific salads (such as Oriental chicken), overstuffed deli sandwiches, burgers, Mexican fare (chicken burritos, fajita sandwiches), numerous breakfast items, and entrees running the gamut from filet mignon to country fried steak with mashed potatoes and vegetables. From 4 to 11pm, a 10-ounce prime rib dinner (with baked potato and a vegetable) is $9.95. And from 11pm to 7am an 8-ounce grilled ham steak with eggs, hash browns and toast costs $3.95. There's a full bar. Desserts options include fresh-baked eclairs, strawberry shortcake, and hot fudge or butterscotch sundaes.

Center Stage
Jackie Gaughan's Plaza Hotel Casino, 1 Main St., at Fremont St. ☎ **702/386-2110.** Reservations essential. Main courses $5.95–$16 (many under $10). AE, DISC, MC, V. Nightly 5–11pm. STEAK AND SEAFOOD.

The aptly named Center Stage offers a dramatic vantage point—the best in town— for viewing the Fremont Street Experience. The restaurant occupies a second-story glass dome, with a windowed wall directly facing Fremont Street. Seating is in semi-circular booths, all of which provide good-to-excellent views of downtown's nightly laser-light show, the music for which is piped into the restaurant. This is both a comfortable and attractive dining room, done up in aesthetically pleasing shades of green with planters of lush faux foliage.

It's a thrilling place to be. What's less than thrilling, though the menu is extremely low priced, is the lackluster performance in the kitchen. Best bet is to stick to the most basic menu items. Order the prime rib au jus, served with onion soup or salad (take the salad), warm sourdough bread and butter, a vegetable, and baked potato, rice, or fettuccine Alfredo (take the potato). It's just $7.95, and you get to see the show. Be sure to make reservations and arrive early to snag one of the best seats.

7 Buffets & Sunday Brunches

Las Vegas is famous for its lavish low-priced buffets. These abundant all-you-can-eat meals—devised by casino hotels to lure guests to the gaming tables—range from lackluster steam-table provender to lovingly prepared and exquisitely presented banquets with free-flowing champagne. Similarly, the settings for buffet meals run the gamut from fluorescent-lit rooms that look like bingo parlors to plush, softly illumined precincts. There are dozens of hotel buffets in town; the most noteworthy are described below.

Note: Buffet meals are extremely popular, and reservations are usually not taken. Arrive early (before opening) or late to avoid a long line, especially on weekends.

ON OR NEAR THE STRIP

VERY EXPENSIVE

✪ Bally's Sterling Sunday Brunch

3645 Las Vegas Blvd. S. ☎ **702/739-4111.** Reservations recommended. Brunch is $49.95. Sunday only 9:30am–2:30pm.

This brunch is served in the clubby elegant precincts of Bally's Steakhouse. Flower arrangements and ice sculptures grace lavish buffet spreads tended by white-hatted chefs. There's a waffle and omelet station, a sushi and sashimi bar, a carving station, and a brimming dessert table. You might choose smoked fish with bagels and cream cheese or help yourself from a mound of fresh shrimp. Entrees vary weekly. On my last visit the possibilities included rolled chicken stuffed with pistachios and porcini mushrooms, beef tenderloin, steak Diane, seared salmon with beet butter sauce and fried leeks, roast duckling with black currant and blueberry sauce, and penne Florentine with pine nuts and smoked chicken in vodka sauce. Of course, there are deli and breakfast meats, vegetables and scrumptious salads, cheeses, raw bar offerings, seasonal fruits and berries, and side dishes such as stuffed potatoes with caviar and sour cream. Champagne flows freely.

EXPENSIVE

✪ Tropicana Sunday Brunch Buffet

3801 Las Vegas Blvd. S. ☎ **702/739-2376.** $20.95 for adults, $12.95 for children 10 and under. Sunday only 9:30am–2pm.

This elaborate spread is served in the elegant El Gaucho Steak House (see description under hotel listing in chapter 5). Tables are elegantly appointed, and food displays are embellished with an ice sculpture and a cascade of fresh fruit. Try and get a seat by the wall of windows that overlooks a flamingo pond in the pool area. On my last visit, this impressive feast was comprised of sushi, ceviche, raw oysters, cold shrimp, smoked seafood (trout, salmon, whitefish, and sable), caviar, a carving station proffering at least five items (perhaps turkey, roast beef, rack of lamb, salmon

Florentine, and roast pork), a waffle and omelet station, a full complement of breakfast meats and potato dishes, cheeses and cold cuts, an extensive salad bar, steak and tuna tartare, fresh vegetables, pasta dishes, numerous entrees (stuffed Maine lobster, filet mignon in burgundy sauce, roast chicken breast stuffed with fruit, red snapper in dill butter sauce, and roast pork with mustard sauce, among others), unlimited champagne, and dozens of desserts (including bananas Foster).

MODERATE

✪ Bally's Big Kitchen Buffet

3645 Las Vegas Blvd. S., ☎ **702/739-4111.** Brunch $8.95; dinner $12.95. Brunch daily 7:30am–2:30pm; dinner daily 4–10pm.

This gorgeous spread is served in a carpeted and crystal-chandeliered dining room with comfortably upholstered armchair seating. Everything is extremely fresh and of the highest quality. There's always a prime rib and turkey carving station, a bountiful salad bar, a good choice of fruits and vegetables, entrees (perhaps seafood casserole in a creamy dill sauce, baked red snapper, pork chops sautéed in Cajun spices, barbecued chicken, and broiled steak in peppercorn sauce), pastas, rice and potato dishes, cold cuts, and a vast array of fresh-baked desserts. The brunch buffet includes breakfast fare and all-you-can-eat shrimp, while the dinner buffet adds Chinese selections.

✪ Caesars Palace Palatium Buffet

3570 Las Vegas Blvd. S. ☎ **702/731-7110.** Breakfast $7.45; lunch $9.30; dinner $13.95; Sat brunch $13.35; Sun brunch $14.95 adults, $10.95 children 7 to 12, under 6 free (includes unlimited champagne). Breakfast Mon–Fri 7:30–11:30am; lunch Mon–Fri 11:30am–3:30pm; dinner daily 4:30–10pm; brunch Sat–Sun 8:30am–2:30pm.

Named for the 2nd-century meeting place of Rome's academy of chefs, this elegant dining room is adorned with murals of ancient Rome and fronted by an imposing colonnaded pediment. Selections at lunch and dinner include elaborate salad bars, carving stations for roast meats and poultry, a wide array of entrees, fresh-baked breads, desserts, and much, much more. The evening meal includes a cold seafood station. Especially lavish are weekend brunches with omelet stations (in addition to egg dishes), breakfast meats, fresh-squeezed juices, potatoes prepared in various ways, pastas, rice casseroles, carved meats, cold shrimp, smoked salmon, and a waffle and ice-cream sundae bar in addition to two dessert islands spotlighting cakes and pastries. That's not the half of it.

The MGM Grand Oz Buffet

3799 Las Vegas Blvd. S. ☎ **702/891-7777.** Breakfast $6.75; lunch $7.75; dinner $10.25; reduced prices for children under 10, free for children under 4. Breakfast daily 7–11am; lunch daily 11am–4pm; dinner daily 4–10pm.

This buffet is served in an enchanted garden amid planters of flowers, topiaries, and murals of Oz. This cheerful room has poppy-motif carpeting, white chairs with butterfly backs, leaf chandeliers, and food display tables under big scalloped umbrellas. Breakfast buffets include all the expected fare plus eggs Benedict, biscuits with creamed gravy, and a tempting assortment of fresh-baked pastries. Lunch and dinner feature a large display of fresh fruits and crudités, cooked vegetables, carving stations (roast sirloin or prime rib with creamed horseradish sauce plus roast turkey or ham), a baked potato bar, a tortilla/fajita bar, and six or seven entrees (which might include beef teriyaki, seafood Newburg, Chinese pepper steak, Yankee pot roast, beef Stroganoff, fajitas, chicken stuffed with almonds and apples, and tortellini Alfredo). For dessert, there's a nice assortment of fresh-baked cakes, pies, and pastries (the chef's specialty is lemon lush) plus an ice cream/frozen yogurt make-your-own-sundae bar.

Also available: low-fat, sugar-free desserts! And at all meals you get a full pot of coffee on your table. *Note:* At press time, there was talk of remodeling and possibly going to more of a food court format with a variety of stations.

The Mirage Buffet

3400 Las Vegas Blvd. S. ☎ **702/791-7111.** Breakfast $7.50; lunch $8.95; dinner $12.95; Sun brunch $13.95; reduced prices for children ages 4 to 10, children under 4 free. Breakfast Mon–Sat 7–10:45am; lunch Mon–Sat 11am–2:45pm; dinner Mon–Sat 3–9:30pm; Sun brunch 8am–9:30pm.

The Mirage offers lavish spreads in a lovely garden-themed setting with palm trees, a plant-filled stone fountain, and seating under verdigris eaves and domes embellished with flowers. All meals except breakfast feature a carving station (fresh roast turkey and honey-baked ham at lunch; prime rib is added at brunch and dinner). A typical Mirage buffet meal proffers a choice of about a dozen hot entrees, always including a fresh catch of the day and a pasta dish; other selections might range from roast chicken stuffed with wild rice to braised Korean short ribs of beef. The chefs are creative with salads, offering about 25 at each meal—choices such as Thai beef, seafood, niçoise, tabbouleh, Chinese chicken, Créole rice, and tortellini. At brunch champagne flows freely and a scrumptious array of smoked fish is added to the board, along with such items as fruit-filled crêpes and blintzes. And every meal features a spectacular dessert table (the bread pudding in bourbon sauce is noteworthy). For healthful eating there are many light items to choose from, including sugar- and fat-free puddings. And on Sundays a nonalcoholic sparkling cider is a possible champagne alternative.

INEXPENSIVE

The Circus Circus Buffet

2880 Las Vegas Blvd. S. ☎ **702/734-0410.** Breakfast $2.99; lunch $3.99; dinner $4.99. Breakfast daily 6–11:30am; lunch daily noon–4pm; dinner daily 4:30–11pm.

This buffet is housed in a large, cheerful room decorated with whimsical circus-themed paintings and pink-and-white canvas tenting. There are 45 items at each meal, and though the food is nothing extraordinary, plates are oversized to hold plenty. At dinner, for instance, there's a carving station (roast beef and ham), along with numerous entrees (fried fish, fried chicken, lasagne, egg rolls, sweet-and-sour pork, barbecued beef and chicken, and Salisbury steak on a recent visit). You'll also find a big salad bar, rice and potato dishes, vegetables, and desserts, plus a make-your-own-sundae station and beverages. Four serving lines keep things moving along quickly. At breakfast, fresh-squeezed orange juice is a plus, not to mention oven-fresh biscuits, cheese blintzes, pancakes, and waffles.

$ Excalibur's Round Table Buffet

3850 Las Vegas Blvd. S. ☎ **702/597-7777.** Breakfast $3.99; lunch $4.99; dinner $5.99. Breakfast daily 7–11am; lunch daily 11am–4pm; dinner daily 4–10pm.

Like all facilities here, the buffet room is a medieval setting, with crossed swords and paintings of knights in armor adorning castle-like faux stone walls and vast wrought-iron candelabra chandeliers overhead. The fare served isn't fancy, but it's freshly made, abundant, and inexpensive. Breakfast features eggs Benedict, along with all the expected morning meal components. Lunch and dinner offer a number of hot and cold entrees (fried chicken, fried fish, stuffed cabbage, stuffed shells, and barbecued baby back ribs on a recent visit), along with dozens of salads, soup, rice and potato dishes, vegetables, fresh fruits, desserts, beverages, and a make-your-own sundae bar. At dinner there's a roast beef and turkey carving station. The plates are large, so you don't have to make as many trips to the buffet tables.

The Flamingo Hilton Paradise Garden Buffet

3555 Las Vegas Blvd. S. ☎ **702/733-7311.** Breakfast $5.95; lunch $6.95; dinner $8.95 (includes 2 glasses of wine). Breakfast daily 6am–noon; lunch daily noon–2:30pm; dinner daily 4:30–10pm.

The buffet here occupies a vast room, with floor-to-ceiling windows overlooking a verdant tropical landscape of cascading waterfalls and a pond filled with ducks, swans, and flamingos. The interior—one of the most pleasant in Las Vegas—is equally lush, though its palm trees and tropical foliage are faux. At dinner, tables are laden with numerous daily-changing entrees—perhaps chicken piccata, pork teriyaki, baked cod in cream sauce, lasagne, barbecued ribs, pot roast, and seafood stew. And these are supplemented by a carving station (roast beef plus turkey or honey-baked ham) and an extensive international food station (which changes monthly) presenting French, Chinese, Mexican, German, or Italian specialties. A large salad bar, fresh fruits, pastas, vegetables, potato dishes, and a vast dessert display round out the offerings. Lunch is similar, featuring a mix of international cuisines as well as a stir-fry station and a soup/salad/pasta bar. At breakfast, you'll find all the expected fare, including a made-to-order omelet station, waffles, eggs Benedict, blintzes, and fresh-baked breads and breakfast pastries (including croissants and doughnuts).

Harrah's Galley Buffet

3475 Las Vegas Blvd. S. ☎ **702/369-5000.** Breakfast $4.99; lunch $5.99; dinner $7.99. Breakfast daily 7–11am; lunch daily 11am–4pm; dinner daily 4–11pm (taxes not included).

The buffet at Harrah's is served in a very pleasant riverboat-themed room with murals of Mississippi paddle wheelers and vintage signs from shipping companies on the wall. A lavish food display under a stained-glass skylight features a full panoply of hot entrees (perhaps braised beef burgundy, teriyaki chicken, stuffed grape leaves, baked cod, pastas, barbecued chicken, and buffalo wings), an array of fresh vegetables and potato dishes, an Asian food station, a fresh fruit and salad bar, and a make-your-own sundae station in addition to a variety of homemade desserts. There's an omelet station at breakfast and a roast beef carving station at dinner.

Note: Harrah's is currently in the throes of a massive $150 million renovation, including a change of theme from Mississippi riverboat to Mardi Gras. Plans call for a Fresh Market Square Buffet room that will feature international foods and interactive cooking stations.

The Luxor Buffet

3900 Las Vegas Blvd. S. ☎ **702/262-4000.** Breakfast $3.95; lunch $4.95; dinner $6.95. Breakfast daily 7–11am; lunch daily 11am–4pm; dinner daily 4–11pm.

Note: At press time, the Luxor's buffet room was about to undergo a total renovation, and no description of the new room was available. Food offerings, I'm told, will remain the same.

There's an omelet station at breakfast, while other meals feature teppanyaki and carving stations (roast beef with creamed horseradish sauce, turkey or prime rib, and ham). Additional offerings include a vast array of salads and fresh fruit, cold cuts, entrees (such as linguine, stuffed shells, lemon chicken, broiled sea bass in cream sauce, bratwurst, Swiss steak, and stir-fry vegetables), and a make-your-own-sundae bar.

Monte Carlo Buffet

3770 Las Vegas Blvd. S. ☎ **702/730-7777.** Breakfast $5.49; lunch $6.59; dinner $8.49. Breakfast daily 7–11am; lunch daily 11am–4pm; dinner daily 4–10pm.

A "courtyard" under a painted sky, the Monte Carlo's buffet room has a Moroccan market theme, with murals of Arab scenes, Moorish archways, Oriental carpets, and walls hung with photographs of, and artifacts from, Morocco. Dinner includes a carving station (for ribeye or roast beef, ham, and turkey), a rotisserie (for chicken and pork loin or London broil), a Chinese food station, a choice of at least five entrees (perhaps seared pork chops with brown sauce, mixed sausages, baked swordfish teriyaki, veal goulash, and buttered fettuccine noodles), soup, a taco/fajita bar, a baked potato bar, numerous salads and side dishes, and more than a dozen desserts plus frozen yogurt and ice cream machines. Lunches are similar. At breakfast, the expected fare is supplemented by an omelet station, and choices include crêpes, blintzes, corned beef hash, eggs Benedict, waffles, and french toast. Fresh-baked New York-style bagels are a plus.

✪ The Rio's Carnival World Buffet

3700 W. Flamingo Rd. ☎ **702/252-7777**. Breakfast $3.99; lunch $5.99; dinner $7.99; brunch $7.99 (champagne is $1 per glass). Breakfast Mon–Fri 7–10:30am; lunch Mon–Fri 11am–3pm; dinner daily 3:30–10pm; brunch Sat–Sun 7am–3:30pm.

The buffet here is located in a festively decorated room with variegated wide sequined ribbons looped overhead and seating amid planters of lush faux tropical blooms. Chairs and booths are upholstered in bright hues—green, purple, red, orange, and turquoise. This is an excellent buffet with cheerfully decorative food booths set up like stations in an upscale food court. A barbecued chicken and ribs station offers side dishes of baked beans and mashed potatoes. Other stations proffer stir-fry (chicken, beef, pork, and vegetables), Mexican taco fixings and accompaniments, Chinese fare, a Japanese sushi and teppanyaki grill, a Brazilian mixed grill, Italian pasta and antipasto, and fish and chips. There's even a diner setup for hot dogs, burgers, fries, and milk shakes. All this is in addition to the usual offerings of most Las Vegas buffets: entrees running the gamut from baked cod in herbed cream sauce to stuffed pork loin with apple dressing and pan gravy, a prime rib carving station, a vast salad bar, soups, fresh fruits, and, at breakfast and brunch, an omelet station. A stunning array of oven-fresh cakes, pies, and pastries (including sugar-free and low-fat desserts) are arranged in a palm-fringed circular display area, and there's also a make-your-own sundae bar. A full cash bar is another Rio plus. Everything is fresh and beautifully prepared and presented.

The Sahara Oasis Buffet

2535 Las Vegas Blvd. S. ☎ **702/737-2111**. Breakfast $3.49; brunch $3.49; dinner $5.49. Breakfast daily 6–11am; brunch daily 11:30am–3:30pm; dinner daily 4–10pm.

This buffet is a vast spread served in an attractive room with a wall of windows overlooking the pool and brass palm trees shading the food display tables. It's not fancy fare, but it is abundant, fresh, and tasty. A typical dinner buffet, for instance; will feature a ham, turkey, and baron of beef carving station, dozens of salads, about eight hot entrees (usually including one or two ethnic dishes each night such as tacos and burritos, Chinese stir-fry, or bratwurst and sauerkraut), vegetables, rice, mashed potatoes, a big dessert display of oven-fresh pies and cakes, and beverages.

Note: All of this may change with the renovation now in progress.

Stardust Warehouse Buffet

3000 Las Vegas Blvd. S. ☎ **702/732-6111**. Breakfast $4.95; lunch $5.95; dinner $7.95; brunch $6.95. Breakfast Mon–Sat 7–10:30am; lunch Mon–Sat 10:30am–3pm; dinner daily 4–10pm; Sunday brunch 7am–3:30pm.

This buffet features, as the name suggests, a raftered warehouse decor, with big restaurant cans of olive oil and chili, sacks of flour, crates of apples, and other provender on display. Tables are covered in laminated burlap potato sacking. It's a pleasant setting for very good buffet meals, featuring a carving station (roast beef, ham, and turkey), a wide variety of salads and hot and cold entrees, fresh fruit, and many fresh-baked breads, cakes, and pastries. You can also pump your own frozen yogurt.

Stratosphere Buffet

2000 Las Vegas Blvd. S. ☎ **702/380-7711.** Breakfast $5.99; lunch $7.99; dinner $9.99. Breakfast daily 7am–11am; lunch daily 11am–4pm; dinner Sun–Thursday 4–10pm, Fri–Sat 4–11pm.

In a cheerful World's Fair–themed buffet room—with a hot air–balloon motif adorning murals, columns, and carpeting—the Stratosphere sets out fresh-looking fare and plenty of it. Breakfast features 11 kinds of eggs (with all the expected accompaniments), plus Southwestern items (e.g., breakfast burritos), bagels and lox, and some international fare. There are carving stations (roast beef, ham, turkey, and rotisserie chicken at lunch; prime rib and turkey at dinner); fresh fruit, salads, and veggies, including a tempting display of crudités; stations for Mexican, Chinese, and kosher-style fare; daily changing international stations (perhaps Jamaican, Creole or Italian); and a station for picnic food such as fried chicken and hot dogs. Hot entrees might include baked chicken, barbecued ribs, and fried catfish, along with numerous side dishes such as dilled red potatoes, candied yams, and wild rice. And fresh-baked cakes and pies are supplemented by a make-your-own-sundae frozen-yogurt bar and a flambé dessert station turning out bananas Foster and cherries jubilee.

Treasure Island Buffet

3300 Las Vegas Blvd. S. ☎ **702/894-7111.** Breakfast $5.39; lunch $6.99; dinner $8.99; brunch $8.99. Breakfast Mon–Sat 7–10:45am; lunch Mon–Sat 11am–3:45pm; dinner daily 4–10:30pm; Sun brunch 7:30am–3:30pm.

The buffet is served in two internationally themed rooms. The American room—under a central rough-hewn beamed canopy hung with the flags of the 13 colonies—re-creates New Orleans during the era of Jean Lafitte. And the Italian room, modeled after a Tuscan villa overlooking a bustling piazza, has strings of festival lights overhead and food displays under a striped awning. Both rooms are filled with authentic antiques and artifacts typical of their locales and time periods. And both also serve identical fare, including extensive American breakfasts. Dinners offer a wide range of entrees (perhaps halibut in caper cream sauce, beef burgundy, seafood quiche, honey-garlic wings, herb-roasted chicken, and meatloaf) as well as a trio of pastas, a carving station (prime rib, turkey, and a third item such as salmon), a Chinese food station, peel-and-eat shrimp, a salad bar, potato and rice side dishes, cheeses and cold cuts, fresh fruits and vegetables, breads, and a large choice of desserts. Lunch is similar, and Sunday brunch includes unlimited champagne.

Tropicana Island Buffet

3801 Las Vegas Blvd. S. ☎ **702/739-2800.** Breakfast $6.95; lunch $6.95; dinner $9.95; brunch $9.95. Breakfast Mon–Fri 7:30–11:30am; lunch Mon–Fri 11:30am–2:30pm; dinner daily 5–10pm; brunch Sat–Sun 7:30am–10pm.

This buffet is served in a large and delightful dining room lushly planted with tropical flowers and foliage. There are coral-reef aquariums at the entrance, and the appealing interior keeps to the island theme. Big semicircular booths backed by mirrored walls are separated by bead curtains, and, on the lower level, floor-to-ceiling windows overlook the Trop's stunning palm-fringed pool. Dinners here feature an extensive salad bar, peel-and-eat-shrimp, a carving station for roast turkey and roast beef with creamed horseradish (along with a third meat—perhaps leg of lamb), vegetables, potato and rice dishes, and about five entrees (chicken enchiladas, spicy blackened redfish, barbecued ribs, Cajun pork chops, and linguine Alfredo on a recent visit). An array of luscious fresh-baked desserts always looks especially tempting. A full complement of breakfast fare is available each morning, lunch is a lighter version of the above-described, and weekend brunches include unlimited champagne.

CONVENTION CENTER AREA
MODERATE

✪ Las Vegas Hilton Buffet of Champions

3000 Paradise Rd. ☎ **702/732-5111.** Breakfast $5.99; lunch $7.99; dinner $12.99; brunch $9.99 (includes unlimited champagne). Breakfast Mon–Fri 7–10am; lunch Mon–Fri 11am–2:30pm; dinner daily 5–10pm; brunch Sat–Sunday 8am–2:30pm.

This buffet is served in a beautiful garden-like dining room with pristine white trellises, big planters of flowers, and magnificent white wrought-iron chandeliers and sconces. As the name implies, the room—located near the casino entrance to the race and sports SuperBook—is sports themed. Cream walls are adorned with attractive murals and photographs of hockey, football, boxing, and horse racing, and there are bookshelves stocked with sporting literature. All in all, it's one of the loveliest buffet rooms in town. And the fare is fresh and delicious. At lunch and dinner, the tempting array includes a roast beef and turkey carving station; hot entrees such as crabcakes, roast chicken, and pot roast, along with Chinese dishes; gorgeous salads and fresh fruits; many fresh vegetables; and a good selection of homemade desserts plus an ice cream/frozen yogurt sundae station. Dinner additionally features all-you-can-eat crab and shrimp.

EAST LAS VEGAS/FLAMINGO ROAD
INEXPENSIVE

✪ Sam's Town, The Great Buffet

5111 Boulder Hwy. ☎ **702/456-7777.** Breakfast $3.99; lunch $5.99; dinner $7.99 (Fri seafood buffet $11.99); brunch $6.99; all buffets half price for children 6 and under. Breakfast Mon–Sat 8–11am; lunch Mon–Sat 11am–3pm; dinner Sun–Thur 4–9pm (Fri 4–10pm); Sun brunch 8am–3pm.

Friendly service and good food have made Sam's Town's buffets extremely popular. About 70% of their clientele consists of local folks, not tourists. The buffet room is as homey as your living room, with fruit-motif carpeting, gaslight-style brass chandeliers, and planters of foliage creating intimate dining niches. Cheerful yellow walls, set off by glossy white wainscoting, are hung framed botanical prints.

Dinners feature carving stations (roast beef, turkey, and, usually, ham), about five additional hot entrees (perhaps Southern-style fried chicken, baked canneloni, roast pork with apple stuffing, penne pasta with ham and peas, and Cajun red snapper), a Chinese stir-fry station, a burger grill, and a wide array of side dishes and fresh fruits and vegetables. For dessert, numerous pies and cakes are supplemented by frozen yogurt with homemade fudge, homemade candies, caramel apples, and fruit cobbler. Tuesday nights Cajun seafood entrees are featured. But best of all are the Friday seafood buffets, offering paella, deep-fried oysters, crawfish étouffée, Cajun red snapper, steamed Dungeness crab with drawn butter, shrimp scampi with pasta, raw oysters, peel-and-eat shrimp, and much more. Lunches are similar to dinners; breakfast fare includes French toast, waffles, pastries, and an omelet station; and Sunday champagne brunches offers extensive breakfast and lunch fare, including blintzes, Mexican breakfast tortes, a carving station, Southern and Cajun specialties, and unlimited champagne.

DOWNTOWN
MODERATE

✪ The Golden Nugget Buffet
129 E. Fremont St. ☎ 702/385-7111. Breakfast $5.75; lunch $7.50; dinner $10.25; brunch $10.25. Breakfast Mon–Sat 7–10:30am; lunch Mon–Sat 10:30am–3pm; dinner Mon–Sat 4–10pm; Sun brunch 8am–10pm.

This buffet has often been voted No. 1 in Las Vegas. Not only is the food fresh and delicious, but it's served in an opulent dining room with marble-topped serving tables amid planters of greenery and potted palms. Mirrored columns, beveled mirrors, etched glass, and brass add sparkle to the room, and swagged draperies provide a note of elegance. Most of the seating is in plush booths. Lunch and dinner feature carving stations (turkey, roast beef, ham) plus five or six entrees (perhaps Calcutta chicken in a curry fruit sauce, sliced leg of lamb, whitefish in salsa, seafood scampi, beer-battered cod, and linguine alla carbonara). The buffet tables are also laden with an extensive salad bar (about 50 items), fresh fruit, and marvelous desserts including Zelma Wynn's (Steve's mother) famous bread pudding. Every night fresh seafood is featured. Most lavish is the all-day Sunday champagne brunch, which adds such dishes as eggs Benedict, blintzes, pancakes, creamed herring, and smoked fish with bagels and cream cheese. *Note:* This stunning buffet room is also the setting for a $2.99 late-night meal of steak eggs with home fries and biscuits with gravy; it's served 11pm to 4am.

INEXPENSIVE

The Lady Luck Banquet Buffet
206 N. 3rd St. ☎ 702/477-3000. Breakfast $2.99; lunch $3.99; dinner $6.99. Breakfast daily 6–10:30am; lunch daily 10:30am–2pm; dinner daily 4–10pm.

This buffet is served in a pretty garden-themed room with trellised dividers separating comfortable leather booths and leaf-design chandeliers overhead. Dinner includes all-you-can-eat prime rib, plus a variety of hot entrees (perhaps baked lasagne, homemade meat loaf, barbecued ribs, grilled mahimahi, and fried chicken). Frequently, there are Chinese, Polynesian, and Italian specialties as well. Offerings additionally include an extensive salad bar, a make-your-own-sundae bar, an array of fresh-baked pies and cakes, and beverages.

✪ Sam Boyd's Fremont Paradise Buffet
200 E. Fremont St. ☎ 702/385-3232. Breakfast $4.95; lunch $5.95; dinner $8.95 ($13.95 for Seafood Fantasy); brunch $7.95. Breakfast Mon–Sat 7–10:30am; lunch Mon–Sat 11am–3pm; dinner Mon, Wed, Thur 4–10pm (Sat until 11pm); Seafood Fantasy Sun and Tues 4–10pm (Fri until 11pm); Sun brunch 7am–3pm.

This buffet is served in an attractive, tropically themed room. Diners sit in spacious booths amid lush jungle foliage—birds of paradise, palms, and bright tropical blooms—and the buffet area is surrounded by a "waterfall" of Tivoli lighting under a reflective ceiling. Island music, enhanced by bird calls and the sound of splashing waterfalls, helps set the tone. Meals here are on the lavish side. A typical dinner features a carving station with three meats (perhaps baked ham, top round, and roast turkey) and six hot entrees (beef Stroganoff, barbecued Thai chicken, fettuccine Alfredo, eggplant parmigiana, salmon ovals with lemon butter, and shrimp fried rice on a recent visit). Fresh salads, soup, cold cuts, vegetables, rice and potato dishes, and desserts ranging from bakery-fresh pies and cakes to make-your-own sundae fixings round out the offerings.

Sunday, Tuesday, and Friday nights the buffet is renamed the Seafood Fantasy, and food tables, adorned with beautiful ice sculptures, are laden with lobster claws, crab legs, shrimp, raw oysters, smoked salmon, clams, and entrees such as steamed mussels, shrimp scampi, and scallops Provençale—all in addition to the usual meat carving stations and a few nonseafood entrees. It's great! And finally, the Fremont has a delightful champagne Sunday brunch served by "island girls" in colorful Polynesian garb. It includes not only unlimited champagne, but a full carving station, lox with bagels and cream cheese, an omelet station, and desserts.

Showboat Captain's Buffet

2800 Fremont St. ☎ **702/385-9123.** Lunch $4.95; dinner $6.45; steak & lobster buffet $7.95; Seafood Spectacular $7.95; brunch $5.95. Lunch Mon–Fri 10am–3:30pm; dinner daily 4:30–10pm (Wed is steak and lobster buffet, Fri is Seafood Spectacular); brunch Sat–Sun 8am–3pm.

This buffet occupies a cheerful New Orleans garden–themed room. Centered on a gazebo, it's decorated in raspberry and peach and adorned with lovely still lifes. There are stunning floral-motif chandeliers overhead; seating is in booths with trellised dividers or at umbrella tables. Lunch and dinner menus offer entrees such as chicken, broiled salmon, tortellini primavera, and charbroiled tenderloin. There's also a carving station serving up roast beef, turkey, and honey-glazed ham. In addition, you'll find an extensive salad bar, a vast selection of pastries, and a build-your-own ice-cream (or frozen-yogurt) sundae bar. Wednesday is all-you-can-eat New York strip steak night. A seafood buffet every Friday evening features stuffed crab, fried shrimp, bouillabaisse, crab legs, raw shrimp, and more. And weekend champagne brunch buffets include an omelet station, fruit-stuffed pancakes, and smoked fish with bagels and cream cheese. The Showboat initiated Las Vegas hotel buffets, and its buffets are still among the best in town.

7

What to See & Do
in Las Vegas

Las Vegas is unlike any other tourist mecca. Here the main attraction is gambling, and if you're staying at one of the casino megahotels, you have not only casino gaming, but accommodations, dining, sightseeing, sports facilities, and entertainment under one roof. The more lavish the hotel, the more Disneyesque its attractions—from the erupting volcano and white tiger habitat at the Mirage to Caesars' OMNIMAX™ movies and Magical Empire. Just strolling the Strip—especially at night when every hotel is spectacularly illuminated in multihued neon—is a mind-boggling experience. There's nothing like it anywhere else in the world.

But there's much more to a Las Vegas vacation than gaming action and headliner entertainment. There are many other points of interest here, ranging from the sublime (magnificent vistas like Red Rock Canyon and Valley of Fire) to the slightly ridiculous (the Liberace Museum). Nearby Hoover Dam is a major sightseeing attraction, and Lake Mead is one of several pristinely beautiful recreation areas. Nevada, and neighboring Arizona, offer stunning scenery, whether you venture just outside Las Vegas or all the way to the Grand Canyon. You can study ancient petroglyphs and learn about Native-American cultures dating back 12,000 years, visit ghost towns, raft the Colorado River, hike or ride horseback through canyons, even ski in winter. To my mind, the ideal Las Vegas vacation combines the glitz and glitter of casino hotels with explorations of the area's majestic canyons and desert wilderness. The latter are the perfect antidote to the former. In this chapter, all sightseeing options are described in detail. Check them out—along with "excursions" listed in chapter 11—and plan an itinerary that suits your interests.

Be sure to take a look at attractions listed for children, many of which may also interest adults.

SUGGESTED ITINERARIES

The itineraries outlined here are for adults. If you're traveling with kids, incorporate some of the suggestions "Especially for Kids" listed below. The activities mentioned briefly here are described more fully later in this chapter.

If You Have 1 Day

Go to the Mirage, get tickets for *Siegfried & Roy,* and spend as much time as you like gambling in the casino. While you're here, see the rain forest, tiger and dolphin habitats, and aquarium. Head next door to Caesars, entering via the Forum Shops People Mover. Peruse the shops and statuary, have lunch at Spago, and see an IMAX™ film. Then head in the other direction and catch the ship battle at Treasure Island. Consider spending some time at your hotel swimming pool during the day. Enjoy a leisurely preshow dinner at one of the many restaurants at the Mirage (details in chapters 5 and 6).

If You Have 2 Days

You may wish to procure show tickets for additional days at the outset. On the second day, drive out to Red Rock Canyon. The panoramic 13-mile Scenic Loop Drive is best seen early in the morning when there's little traffic. If you're so inclined, spend some time hiking here. Have lunch at nearby Bonnie Springs Ranch. After lunch enjoy a guided trail ride into the desert wilderness (see chapter 11 for details). Return to town and loll by the pool with a good book. Suggested evening show: Cirque du Soleil's *Mystère* at Treasure Island.

If You Have 3 Days

On the third day, plan a tour to Hoover Dam. Leave early in the morning. Return to Las Vegas after lunch via Valley of Fire State Park, stopping at the Lost City Museum in Overton en route (see chapter 11 for details). At night, if you still have energy, hit the casinos and/or catch another show—either a headliner favorite or *Country Fever* Downtown. This will also provide an opportunity to see the Fremont Street Experience. Another possibility: a romantic evening at the Palace Court piano bar at Caesars Palace (have dinner here first if you feel like splurging).

If You Have 4 Days or More

Instead of returning from your Hoover Dam trip the same day, stay overnight—or longer—at the charming Lake Mead Lodge. Take a dinner cruise on the *Desert Princess* and spend part of your fourth day enjoying Lake Mead's many recreational facilities before returning to town via Valley of Fire State Park.

As you plan any additional days, consider excursions to other nearby attractions such as Mount Charleston, Goodsprings, or the Grand Canyon. Inquire about interesting tours at your hotel sightseeing desk. Plan lunch or dinner around Caesars Magical Empire show. Or visit some additional hotels that are sightseeing attractions in their own right—most notably the Luxor, Treasure Island, and the MGM Grand.

1 Attractions in Las Vegas

✪ Caesars Magical Empire

Caesars Palace, 3570 Las Vegas Blvd. S. ☎ **800/445-4544** or 702/731-7333. Admission (including a three-course meal and wine, gratuities extra): $45–$50 with lunch, $65–$75 with dinner. Daily: lunch shows 1:30am–4:10pm, dinner shows 4:30–11:30pm. Children must be at least 10 years of age.

In 1996, Caesars unveiled a spellbinding new attraction: an elaborately themed 3-hour magical experience. It's great fun and well worth the price. You'll be welcomed in the Celestial Court and ushered into the Chamber of Destiny, where the floor gives way and you plummet "100 feet below the surface of the earth" to an ancient catacomb. A centurion guides you to a plush stone-walled dining chamber, dimly lit by candles and sconces. Each of these 10 grotto-like dining rooms accommodates only 24 guests, so the meal has an intimate ambience, like an elegant private party. Your host—during a delicious three-course feast marked by mysterious happenings—is a wizard who performs wondrous feats of magic while you dine. After a dramatic finale, visitors are guided through eerie passageways to the Sanctum Secorum, a vast enchanted realm (beware of bottomless pits) under a seven-story dome, with massive Egyptian columns and sculptures and prisms creating dazzling rainbow patterns on the floor. At your leisure, view Lumineria, a five-minute show combining smoke, dancing fire, and high-tech lighting effects; it takes place at frequent intervals. First head for the Secret Pagoda, a Chinese-themed circular room where a 13-minute magic show takes place, and the exotic Sultan's Palace, site of a 30-minute show. Be sure to visit the two lounges off the Sanctum as well. In the Spirit Bar, a 2,000-year-old spirit (a hologram) performs magic tricks. And the Grotto Bar (which nestles in a dragon's mouth cave) is the home of Isabella, an invisible pianist who plays any musical request (don't miss her!). Nearby are a pair of wisecracking skeletons named Habeas and Corpus. Both bars feature specialty drinks, and, for those suffering withdrawal symptoms in these few hours outside the casino, video poker.

Note: While you're at Caesars, check out the talking statues at the Forum Shops and catch an OMNIMAX™ movie.

Caesars OMNIMAX™ Theatre

Caesars Palace, 3570 Las Vegas Blvd. S. ☎ **800/634-6698** or 702/731-7901. Admission $7 adults; seniors, children 2–12, hotel guests, and military personnel $5. Shows on the hour between 2 and 10pm Sun–Thurs, additional shows at noon, 1, and 11pm Fri–Sat. You must purchase tickets at the box office (open daily 9am–11pm) on the day of the performance.

I saw my first OMNIMAX™ movie at Caesars when the hotel pioneered this exciting entertainment concept in the 1970s, and though I've seen dozens of them since, the thrill has never abated. If you've never seen one of these 3-D-like films, you're in for a treat. The OMNIMAX™ Theatre here is housed in a geodesic dome—a space-age environment with 368 seats that recline 27 degrees, affording a panoramic view of the curved 57-foot screen. The movies, projected via 70mm film (which is 10 times the frame size of ordinary 35mm film), offer an awesome visual display enhanced by a state-of-the-art sound system (89 speakers engulf the audience in sound). Depending on the film being shown, viewers might soar over the Rocky Mountains, plummet down steep waterfalls, ride the rapids, travel into outer space, or perch at the rim of an erupting volcano. Shows change frequently, but whatever you see will be stupendous.

An Evening in Vienna

Excalibur Hotel, 3850 Las Vegas Blvd. S. ☎ **702/597-7600**. Admission $7.95 adults, $5.95 for children under 12 and seniors (including tax). Mon–Thurs 2pm, Sat–Sun noon and 2pm. Dark Fri. Seating is on a first-come, first-served basis. Tickets can be purchased up to 3 days in advance at Excalibur ticket booths.

In its vast arena, Excalibur presents *An Evening in Vienna,* starring the world-famous Lipizzaner stallions. Developed in Moorish Spain from three superior equine breeds (Spanish Andalusian, Arabian, and the swift and sturdy Karst of the Adriatic coast), these regal white horses were trained in the elegant and graceful movements of dressage and haute école and shown in Vienna's magnificent riding halls. The Excalibur show is in that centuries-old tradition. Riders in the military uniforms of imperial Austria present their stallions in a dignified procession set to classical music, and put them through a variety of complex movements—leaps, kicks, battlefield maneuvers, and historic equestrian arts.

Fremont Street Experience

Fremont Street, between Main St. and Las Vegas Blvd. in Downtown Las Vegas.

For years, the Strip has been experiencing a phenomenal economic and building boom. Now, thanks to a $70 million revitalization project, some of the focus of

Attractions in Las Vegas

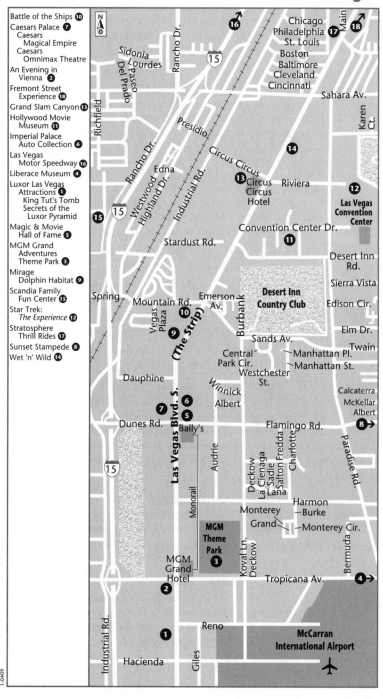

Battle of the Ships ⑩
Caesars Palace ⑦
  Caesars
    Magical Empire
  Caesars
    Omnimax Theatre
An Evening in
  Vienna ②
Fremont Street
  Experience ⑱
Grand Slam Canyon ⑬
Hollywood Movie
  Museum ⑪
Imperial Palace
  Auto Collection ⑥
Las Vegas
  Motor Speedway ⑯
Liberace Museum ④
Luxor Las Vegas
  Attractions ①
    King Tut's Tomb
    Secrets of the
      Luxor Pyramid ⑮
Magic & Movie
  Hall of Fame ⑤
MGM Grand
  Adventures
  Theme Park ③
Mirage
  Dolphin Habitat ⑨
Scandia Family
  Fun Center ⑮
Star Trek:
  The Experience ⑫
Stratosphere
  Thrill Rides ⑰
Sunset Stampede ⑧
Wet 'n' Wild ⑭

1-0409

Fun Fact
_____

Fremont Street was hub of Las Vegas for almost four decades before the first casino hotel, El Rancho, opened on the Strip in 1941.

_____

development in Las Vegas has shifted downtown. Glitter Gulch has been transformed into the Fremont Street Experience, a five-block open-air pedestrian mall under a 90-foot-high steel-mesh "celestial vault" designed to shelter a festive, lushly landscaped strip of outdoor cafes, vendor carts and colorful kiosks purveying food and merchandise, and 50,000 square feet of high-concept new indoor retail space. Much of this is yet to come. What is operative at this writing is *Sky Parade*—a dazzling high-tech light and laser show (the canopy is equipped with more than 2.1 million lights) enhanced by a concert hall–quality sound system, which takes place several times nightly. The latter also provides music in between shows. Not only does the canopy provide shade, it is cooled by a misting system in summer and warmed by radiant heaters in winter. Asphalt on the street has been replaced by a shimmering patterned streetscape lit by runway-type strobe lights. As the project develops, Fremont Street is meant to become an ongoing festival—the scene of live entertainment, holiday celebrations, and special events. Many of the 11 casino hotels that face the attraction are already adding and remodeling rooms, renovating their Fremont Street facades, and creating street cafes. A 1,400-space parking lot has been built at the eastern end of Fremont Street to accommodate visitors to the new attraction. *Note:* One of the best vantage points for viewing *Sky Parade* is the Center Stage restaurant at Jackie Gaughan's Plaza (see chapter 6 for details).

Hollywood Movie Museum

Debbie Reynolds Hotel, 305 Convention Center Dr. ☎ **702/7-DEBBIE.** Admission $7.95 adults, $5.95 children 3–12. Daily 11am–10pm, with tours every hour on the hour.

Debbie Reynolds has been buying up Hollywood memorabilia for decades. Her $30-million collection—comprising items from more than a half century of American movies—celebrates Hollywood's Golden Age. Changing exhibits showcase some 3,000 costumes—the famous white dress worn by Marilyn Monroe in *The Seven Year Itch,* Elizabeth Taylor's *Cleopatra* headdress, Vivien Leigh's hats from *Gone With the Wind,* Doris Day's mermaid outfit from *Glass Bottom Boat,* the sequined royal-blue swimsuit Esther Williams wore in *Deep in My Heart,* a pair of Judy Garland's ruby slippers from *The Wizard of Oz,* and the dancing shoes of Fred Astaire and Cyd Charisse, among them. Additionally, props, artifacts, and furnishings from classic films (she has a 36,000-square-foot warehouse filled with them) include the dagger used by Errol Flynn in *The Adventures of Don Juan,* Yul Brynner's bullwhip and throne from *The King and I,* Winchester rifles from *Annie Get Your Gun,* and the Ark of the Covenant from *The Ten Commandments.* Museum displays are enhanced by a 35-minute multimedia show presented in a high-tech 80-seat theater that re-creates the intimate ambience of a Hollywood screening room. Guests are greeted by Debbie (on screen), who narrates a nostalgic overview of Hollywood's classic and epic motion pictures. A 30-foot revolving stage, two 10-foot revolving platforms, and lighted dioramas on the side walls permit the dramatic display of film clips, sets, and costumes.

Imperial Palace Auto Collection

Imperial Palace Hotel, 3535 Las Vegas Blvd. S. ☎ **702/731-3311.** Admission $6.95 adults, $3 seniors and children under 12, free for children under 5 and AAA members. Daily 9:30am–11:30pm.

❓ Did You Know?

- Las Vegas—"sin city"—has more churches per capita than any other city in America.

- Las Vegas has been called the "Marriage Capital of America." No waiting period or blood test is required, and there are 43 chapels in town where quickie weddings are performed 24 hours a day.

- Illusionists Siegfried & Roy have sawed a woman in half more times than anyone else.

- Visitors on a trail ride once brought a horse into the crowded casino of the Thunderbird Hotel. They put a pair of dice between his lips at the craps table, and he threw a natural seven.

- In 1953, the Sands buried a time capsule on its grounds containing Sugar Ray Robinson's boxing gloves, Bing Crosby's pipe, and a wax impression of Jimmy Durante's nose, among other treasures.

This fascinating museum at the Imperial Palace hotel displays, on a rotating basis, some 800 antique, classic, and special-interest vehicles spanning more than 100 years of automotive history. It's one of the premier collections of its kind. Some 200 vehicles—enhanced by mannequins and period tableaux—are on exhibit at any given time. A 15,000-square-foot room houses the world's largest collection of Model J Duesenbergs (43 vehicles valued at $50 million!), including cars once owned by James Cagney, Max Baer, Doris Duke, Father Divine, and Tyrone Power, among others. The Duesenberg Room also features a cocktail lounge with 1880s Brunswick furnishings.

In President's Row, JFK's 1962 "bubbletop" Lincoln Continental, Lyndon Johnson's 1964 Cadillac, Eisenhower's 1952 Chrysler Imperial 20-foot-long parade car, Truman's 1950 Lincoln Cosmopolitan with gold-plated interior, FDR's unrestored 1936 V-16 Cadillac, and Herbert Hoover's 1929 Cadillac are on display. Yet another area showcases Adolf Hitler's armored, bulletproof, and mineproof 1936 Mercedes-Benz 770K, Emperor Hirohito's 1935 Packard, Czar Nicholas II's 1914 Rolls-Royce, former Mexican president Lazaro Cardenas's black 1939 V-12 Packard (armor-plated to resist 50-caliber machine gun bullets), and Argentinean strongman Juan Peron's 1939 straight-8 Packard.

Commercial vehicles of bygone days include antique buses, military transport, taxis (among them, the 1908 French model that appeared in the movie version of *My Fair Lady*), gasoline trucks, fire engines, delivery trucks and vans, dump trucks, and pickup trucks. Other highlights are Al Capone's 1930 V-16 Cadillac, Elvis Presley's powder blue 1976 Cadillac Eldorado, Liberace's pale-cream 1981 Zimmer (complete with candelabra), W. C. Field's black 1938 Cadillac V-16 touring sedan with built-in bar, Caruso's 1920 green and black Hudson, Howard Hughes's 1954 Chrysler (because of his phobia about germs, Hughes installed a special air-purification system that cost more than the car itself!), a 1947 Tucker (one of only 51 manufactured before the company went out of business), a 1977 Safarikar with an all-leather exterior and doors that can be extended to ward off attacking jungle animals, and motorcycles that belonged to Steve McQueen, Clark Gable, and Sammy Davis Jr. A gift shop carries a wide selection of automotive books, scale models, and memorabilia.

Las Vegas Motor Speedway

7000 Las Vegas Blvd. N., directly across from Nellis Air Force base (take I-15 north to Speedway exit 54). ☎ **702/644-4443** for ticket information.

This 107,000-seat facility, the first new superspeedway to be built in the southwest in over two decades, opened shortly after press time with a 500K Indy Racing League event. A $100 million state-of-the-art motorsports entertainment complex, it includes a 1.5-mile superspeedway, a 2.5-mile FIA-approved road course, paved and dirt short-track ovals, and a 4,000-foot drag strip. Also on the property are facilities for Go-Kart, Legends Car, Sand Drag, and Motocross competition. The new speedway, which will be accessible via shuttle buses to and from major casino hotels, will feature major Indy Racing League and Nascar events.

Liberace Museum

1775 E. Tropicana Ave., at Spencer St. ☎ **702/798-5595.** Admission $6.50 adults, $4.50 seniors over 60, $3.50 students, $2 children 6–12, free for children under 6. Mon–Sat 10am–5pm, Sun 1–5pm.

This is an only-in-Vegas phenomenon—an entire museum devoted to the career memorabilia of "Mr. Showmanship," Walter Valentino Liberace. Three exhibit areas house his spectacular cars (he owned more than 50 automobiles), antique and custom-made pianos, dazzling costumes and capes, glittering stage jewelry, a miniature-piano collection (during his lifetime fans gave him more than 3,000 of these), honorary degrees and awards, musical arrangements, and photographs. There's also a re-creation of his office (which contains an inlaid ormolu Louis XV desk originally owned by Czar Nicholas II of Russia) and an ornate bedroom suite. Visitors are greeted at a piano-shaped desk.

Among the fabulous pianos on display here is a 19th-century hand-painted concert grand piano that Chopin played at Versailles. Then there are the cars, including the glittering red, white, and blue bicentennial Rolls-Royce that Liberace drove onstage at New York's Radio City Music Hall in 1976 (he wore matching red-, white-, and blue-spangled hot pants and boots). Dozens of fur-trimmed, feathered, beaded, sequined, and bejeweled costumes include a Czar Nicholas uniform with 22-karat-gold braiding and a blue velvet cape styled after the coronation robes of King George V and covered with $60,000 worth of rare chinchilla! Among the jewelry on display is a candelabra ring with platinum candlesticks and diamond flames and a spectacular piano-shaped ring containing 260 diamonds with keys made of ivory and black jade (a gift from Barron Hilton). Other notable exhibits are his famed candelabras and a $50,000 50.6-pound rhinestone—the world's largest—presented to him by the grateful Austrian firm that supplied all his costume stones. There's a gift shop on the premises where you can buy anything from miniature crystal grand pianos to Liberace logo thimbles, along with performance videos, cassettes, and CDs. The museum is 2¹/₂ miles east of the Strip on your right.

☉ Magic and Movie Hall of Fame

O'Shea's Casino, 3555 Las Vegas Blvd. S., between Sands Avenue and Flamingo Road. ☎ **702/737-1343.** Admission $9.95 adults, $3 children under 12 accompanied by an adult. Tues–Sat 10am–6pm. Magic shows at 11:30am and I:30, 3, and 4:30pm.

This is the best value in town, offering hours of intriguing entertainment. Not only is the price of entry very reasonable, you can almost always get a $5 discount coupon out front or in the casino's food court. Admission includes a half-hour show in the Houdini Theatre (note performance hours above) featuring magician/ventriloquist Valentine Vox.

After the performance, visitors tour a vast museum that houses props and artifacts of famous magicians such as Houdini (bound with ropes and shackled in leg irons and handcuffs, Houdini once had himself lowered into the East River in a wood packing case that was nailed shut and weighed down with 200 pounds of lead; he freed himself in just 57 seconds!), levitation master Harry Kellar, Sevais Le Roy (who "cremated" a girl on stage), Thurston (his spike cabinet is on display), the Mephistophelian Dante (who popularized the phrases "hocus-pocus" and "abracadabra"), and Carter the Great (Houdini was his assistant as a teenager).

Exhibits are enhanced by dozens of video clips of actual performances. Modern-day practitioners are also included; a highlight is a behind-the-scenes video tour with illusionists Siegfried & Roy. Another section contains antique automata, mechanical devices, Gypsy fortune telling booths, vintage arcade games, Nickelodeons, and music boxes, some of them operable by visitors. You'll learn about the history of ventriloquism, which dates back to the 5th century B.C. and was used by ancient diviners to imitate the voices of the dead. Hundreds of antique and modern dummies are on display, and there's entertaining video footage of the greats—Edgar Bergen with Charlie McCarthy and Mortimer Snerd, Arthur Prince with Jim (Prince smoked a cigar while he did his dummy's voice), Valentine Vox (who you've seen in the show), Paul Winchell with Jerry Mahoney, and others. You can attempt ventriloquism yourself in a how-to booth equipped with a dummy and instructions. Movie costumes—such as a dress Liz Taylor wore in *Cleopatra* and Clark Gable's jacket from *Gone With the Wind*—are displayed in another area, along with tableaux of famous movie scenes. The tour winds up in a gift shop where a magician demonstrates many of the wares (magic tricks, juggling equipment, etc.) on sale, providing further entertainment.

Mirage Dolphin Habitat

Mirage Hotel, 3400 Las Vegas Blvd. S. ☎ **702/791-7111.** Admission $3, free for children under 10. Mon–Fri 11am–7pm, Sat–Sun and holidays 9am–7pm. Children under 12 must be accompanied by an adult.

This is no theme park exhibit. The Mirage's dolphin habitat was designed to provide a healthy and nurturing environment and to educate the public about marine mammals and their role in the ecosystem. Mirage owner Steve Wynn is a dedicated environmentalist whose hotel restaurants serve only dolphin-safe tuna (they do not serve Icelandic fish to protest that nation's whaling practices). No fur is sold in Wynn's hotel boutiques. Specialists worldwide were consulted in creating the habitat, which was designed to serve as a model of a quality secured environment. The pool is more than four times larger than government regulations require, and its 2.5 million gallons of man-made seawater are cycled and cleaned once every 2 hours. The habitat houses seven Atlantic bottle-nosed dolphins in a lush tropical setting. The facility offers visitors the opportunity to watch dolphins frolicking from above- and below-water viewing areas, and the 15-minute tour is entertaining and informative to adults and children alike. A highlight is a video of a resident dolphin (Duchess) giving birth (to Squirt) underwater. After the tour you can stay in the area and continue watching the dolphins.

While you're at the Mirage, visit the royal white tiger habitat and see the 53-foot, 20,000-gallon simulated coral reef aquarium behind the registration desk. The latter accommodates more than 1,000 fish and sea creatures—including sharks and rays—indigenous to the Caribbean, Hawaii, Tonga, Fiji, the Red Sea, the Marshall Islands, and Australia.

STAR TREK: *The Experience*
Las Vegas Hilton, 3000 Paradise Rd. ☎ **702-732-5111.** Admission will be about $10. Hours not yet available.

Trekkers take note: Opening in the spring of 1997, STAR TREK: *The Experience* promises to "boldly go where no entertainment experience has gone before." Visitors will become Starfleet crew members on an intergalactic journey that utilizes simulator rides, interactive videos, morphing and virtual-reality stations, holograms, and state-of-the-art computer games. Your voyage will begin in a "history-of-the-future" museum filled with authentic *Star Trek* costumes, weaponry, and props. From the Starfleet Gallery Room, you'll be "beamed up" to the Bridge of the Starship Enterprise and board a shuttlecraft for a simulated journey through the universe. Upon successful completion of your mission, you'll disembark at Deep Space Nine to play (there's a state-of-the-art video-game room), dine, shop—and encounter aliens—in the 24th century. A Cardassian-style restaurant will serve futuristically named foods, such as Glop-on-a-Stick, and, in the lounge, you'll order food and drinks from machines equipped with voice-recognition capabilities.

Stratosphere Thrill Rides
Stratosphere, 2000 Las Vegas Blvd. S. ☎ **702/380-7777.** Admission for either ride is $5, plus $5 to ascend the tower (if you dine in the buffet room or Top of the World, there's no charge to go up to the tower). Sun–Thurs 10am–midnight, Fri–Sat 10am–2am. Minimum height requirement for both rides is 48 inches.

Atop the 1,149-foot Stratosphere Tower are two marvelous thrill rides. The **Let It Ride High Roller** (the world's highest roller-coaster) was recently revamped to go at even faster speeds as it zooms around a hilly track that is seemingly suspended in mid-air. Even more fun, I think, is the **Big Shot,** a breathtaking free-fall ride that thrusts you 160 feet in the air along a 228-foot spire at the top of the tower, then plummets back down again. Sitting in an open car, you seem to be dangling in space over Las Vegas. Loved it!

Sunset Stampede
Sam's Town, 5111 Boulder Hway., at Flamingo Rd. ☎ **702/456-7777.** Free admission. Daily shows at 2, 6, 8, and 10pm.

This 10-minute laser-light and water spectacular takes place four times daily in the lush and lovely 25,000-square foot Mystic Falls Park. I prefer the evening shows, when the lighting effects are more thrilling. The show begins with jets of steam over the park's waterfall, which is bathed in purple light. Soon a mist envelops the entire garden. An animatronic wolf howls at the top of the mountain as the show begins. Water shoots up in a lofty geyser, enhanced by high-tech lighting effects and laser wildlife creatures racing across the "great plains." The musical backdrop is dramatic and enchanting. To signal the end of the show, the wolf howls once again. If you don't have a car, free bus transport is available to and from the Strip; call for details.

LUXOR ATTRACTIONS
Both of these attractions are located in the **Luxor Las Vegas,** 3900 Las Vegas Blvd. S. ☎ **702/262-4000.**

King Tut's Tomb and Museum
Admission $4. Sun–Thurs 9am–11pm, Fri–Sat 9am–11:30pm.

This full-scale reproduction of King Tutankhamen's Tomb includes the antechamber, annex, burial chamber, and treasury housing replicas (all handcrafted in Egypt by artisans using historically correct gold leaf and linens, pigments, tools, and ancient

The Battle of the Ships

Every 90 minutes between 4 and 11:30pm, a live sea battle between the pirate ship *Hispaniola* and the British frigate HMS *Britannia* takes place on Buccaneer Bay in front of the Treasure Island hotel. Arrive at least half an hour early to get a good viewing spot. The *Hispaniola* is docked by the village banks to unload a cache of ill-gotten goods. As seagulls chatter and waves crash against the shore, a rowboat manned by two pirates hovers into view. An ominous-sounding version of "Rule Britannia" heralds the approach of the HMS *Britannia* stealing around Skull Point. A British officer orders the pirates to lay down their arms and receive a marine boarding party "in the name of His Royal Britannic Majesty, King of England, and all that he surveys." "The only thing we'll receive from you is your stores, valuables, and whatever rum ye might have on board, you son of a footman's goat," responds the pirate captain brazenly. The verbal battle soon escalates to cannon and musket fire. Amid thrilling pyrotechnics, huge masts snap and plunge into the sea and sailors are catapulted into the air. The British captain warns, "Unless you scum want a real taste of His Majesty's naval artillery, I suggest you lower your colors and prepare to be boarded." "Never! To Hades with their rotten hearts," is the pirate rejoinder. The Brits send a broadside into the pirates' powder warehouse, which ignites in magnificent flames and fireworks. But just as the pirates seem to be defeated, the buccaneer captain does an Errol Flynn swing across the ship from bow to stern, grabs a smoldering ember, and fires a final cannonball at the *Britannia*, hitting it dead center. The *Britannia* sways and slowly sinks, as its sailors plunge overboard, but the proud captain defiantly goes down with his ship. This is Las Vegas. The pirates always win!

methods) of the glittering inventory discovered by archaeologists Howard Carter and Lord Carnarvon in the Valley of Kings at Luxor in 1922. All items have been meticulously positioned according to Carter's records. On display are gilded-wood guardian statues, chariots, funerary beds, alabaster vases, ceramic wine jars, baskets, faience vessels and bead collars, hunting gear, lamps, jewelry, shrines, and mother-of-pearl inlay boxes. Notable artifacts include Tutankhamen's golden throne and sarcophagus (the outer coffin, of solid gold, weighed more than a ton), an ornate canopic gold chest that contained his internal organs, preserved foods to ensure that his spirit would not go hungry in the next world, hundreds of servant statues (to do his bidding in the afterlife), and a model of a royal boat to transport his soul to its next life. Two miniature coffins in the treasury are believed to contain the mummies of two of the king's premature babies. On the west wall is a depiction of 12 baboon deities representing the hours of the night through which the sun and the king must travel before achieving rebirth at dawn. King Tutankhamen ascended the throne in the 14th century B.C. at the age of 9 and died about 10 years later of unknown causes. A 20-minute audio tour (available in English, French, Spanish, and Japanese) is preceded by a 4-minute introductory film.

Secrets of the Luxor Pyramid

Admission "In Search of the Obelisk" $5, "Luxor Live" $4, "The Theater of Time" $5. A combined ticket for all three episodes is $13. "Search" Sun–Thurs 9am–11pm, Fri–Sat 9am–11:30pm; "Live" and "Time" Sun–Thurs 10am–11pm, Fri–Sat 10am–11:30pm.

This attraction-floor entertainment comprises a three-part adventure that takes about 90 minutes to complete.

For "In Search of the Obelisk," motion-simulator technology is used to create an action adventure involving a chase sequence inside a pyramid. In a rapidly plummeting elevator (the cable has broken!) you'll descend to an ancient temple 2 miles beneath the Luxor pyramid. Against the orders of militaristic government agent Colonel Claggert, you'll accompany Mac MacPherson and Carina Wolinski (the good guys) in their search for a mysterious crystal obelisk containing the secrets of the universe. In a thrill ride through the temple's maze, you'll experience an explosive battle with evil forces, rescue Carina from the clutches of Dr. Osiris (sinister cult leader of the Enlightened Society for Global Transformation; it is believed he sabotaged the elevator), and narrowly escape death before returning to the surface.

In the "Luxor Live" show, you become part of the audience for a live broadcast that begins as a tabloid TV talk show. The topic is the mysterious happenings below the pyramid. Claggert and MacPherson are guests. Remote cameras take us to Egypt (where Wolinski is covering a total solar eclipse) for a 3-D vision. Suddenly the studio set collapses, and the host reveals himself as the High Priest of Paradise before disintegrating into light.

In "The Theater of Time," voyagers (that's us) visit the future via a cosmic time machine that incorporates IMAX™ film projected on a seven-story screen. The fate of the world is in jeopardy as the sinister Dr. Osiris uses the crystal obelisk's power to hijack us (along with Mac and Carina) into his bleak vision of the future aboard his time machine. He forces Carina to activate the obelisk for his own evil purposes. Our mission: to save Carina, reclaim the obelisk, and favorably alter the course of history.

2 Attractions in Nearby Henderson

About 6 miles from the Strip in the town of Henderson are four factories in fairly close proximity to one another. All offer free tours to the public. It's best to see them on a weekday when they're fully operative. To get to Henderson, drive east on Tropicana Avenue, make a right on Mountain Vista, then go 2 miles to Sunset Way; turn left into Green Valley Business Park. You will soon see Ethel M Chocolates, a good place to begin. Use the map in this section to find your way to the other three facilities.

Cranberry World West

1301 American Pacific Dr., Henderson. ☎ **702/566-7160.** Free admission. Daily 9am–5pm.

At this Ocean Spray juice processing and distribution plant, the message is that cranberries are more than a Thanksgiving side dish. Visitors view a 7-minute film about cranberry history, harvesting, and the manufacturing processes. Ocean Spray, you'll learn, is also the leading grapefruit grower in the country. The film is followed by a self-guided tour with interactive exhibits, a look at the plant from a view station, and a visit to the juice bar and test kitchen for a free sampling of 10 Ocean Spray juice drinks, cranberry-studded baked goods, and other products from the company's gourmet line (cranberry mustard, salsa, and others). The tour winds up in the gift shop where you can purchase Ocean Spray products.

Ethel M Chocolates

2 Cactus Garden Dr., just off Mountain Vista and Sunset Way in the Green Valley Business Park. ☎ **702/433-2500,** for recorded information, or 702/458-8864. Free admission. Daily 8:30am–7pm. Closed Christmas.

Just 6 miles from the Strip is the Ethel M Chocolate Factory and Cactus Garden, a tourist attraction that draws about 2,000 visitors a day. Ethel Mars began making fine

Henderson Attractions

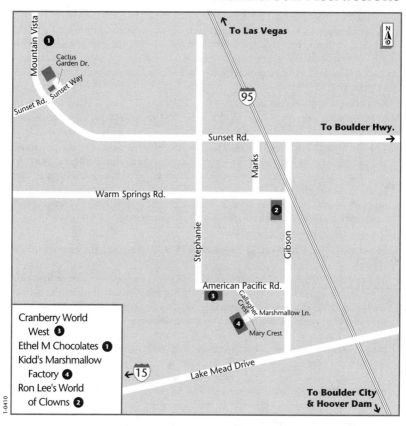

Mountain Vista

① Cactus Garden Dr.

Sunset Rd. Sunset Way

↑ To Las Vegas

95

N

Sunset Rd.

To Boulder Hwy. →

Marks

Warm Springs Rd.

Stephanie

②

Gibson

American Pacific Rd.

③

Gallagher Crest

Marshmallow Ln.

④

Mary Crest

Cranberry World
  West ③
Ethel M Chocolates ①
Kidd's Marshmallow
  Factory ④
Ron Lee's World
  of Clowns ②

← 15

Lake Mead Drive

To Boulder City
& Hoover Dam ↓

1-0410

chocolates in a little candy kitchen around the turn of the century and her small enterprise evolved to produce not only dozens of varieties of superb boxed chocolates but some of the world's most famous candies—M&Ms, Milky Way, 3 Musketeers, Snickers, and Mars bars.

On a self-guided tour of the plant, you'll see the candy-making process from a glass-enclosed viewing aisle. All of the equipment is marked to aid visitor comprehension. "Kitchen" procedures include the cooking of buttery cream fillings in immense copper kettles, the hand-sorting of nuts, grinding of fresh peanut butter, and fudge making. In one production-line process, little creamy centers are bathed in chocolate and decorated with Ethel M's trademark swirls. On another line, chocolate is deposited into molds, vibrated to eliminate air bubbles, cooled, filled (with nuts, creams, and/or liqueurs), and hand boxed. There are actually employees whose job involves the "arduous" task of tasting for quality control. Depending on what's being made the day you visit, you may observe all or little of the above; however, you will see it all in informative video presentations shown along the aisle. The tour winds up in an attractive gift shop where you can sample a free piece of chocolate candy (my favorite is almond butter krisp) and hand-dipped ice cream; here, you can also purchase chocolates and have them shipped anywhere in the United States.

Also on the premises is a 2.5-acre garden displaying 350 species of rare and exotic cacti with signs provided for self-guided tours. It's best appreciated in spring when the cacti are in full bloom. Behind the garden, also with a self-guided tour, is Ethel M's "Living Machine"—a natural waste water–treatment and recycling plant that consists of aerated tanks, ecological fluid beds, a constructed wetlands, reed beds, and a storage pond.

Kidd's Marshmallow Factory

1180 Marshmallow Lane, Henderson. ☎ **800/234-2383** or 702/564-3878. Free admission. Mon–Fri 9am–4:30pm, Sat–Sun 9:30am–4:30pm.

This factory has a delicious aroma. Here you can observe the marshmallow manufacturing process via large windows—corn starch being rolled smooth on a conveyer belt, then cut into marshmallow shapes which are bounced in a drum, bagged, and boxed into cartons. Signs along the way explain the process. The tour ends in a gift shop where you'll receive free samples and can purchase marshmallow products and logo items. Kidd & Company was founded in Chicago in the 1880s.

Ron Lee's World of Clowns

330 Carousel Parkway, Henderson. ☎ **800/829-3928** or 702/434-3920. Free admission. Daily 8am–5:30pm.

In this 30,000-square-foot factory, manufacturer Ron Lee creates collector figurines of Hobo Joe and other clowns, as well as Disney and Warner Brothers characters. Visitors can tour the factory, and, via large windows, observe workers making models and rubber molds, soldering parts together, deburring, painting, finishing, and shipping. The procedures are explained on videotapes overhead. Also on the premises are a carousel, a museum of Ringling Bros. costumes and props, a display of about 600 hand-painted eggs depicting famous clowns, a large gift shop, and displays of clown sculptures and mechanical miniature carousels and Ferris wheels. The Carousel Cafe on the premises offers gourmet coffees, sandwiches, and fresh-baked desserts. There's seating inside and on a terrace cooled by misters.

3　Especially for Kids

Las Vegas used to be an adults-only kind of town. These days, it's actively pursuing the family travel trade and offering dozens of child-oriented activities. Personally, I have very mixed feelings about Las Vegas as a family destination. This is a city where every third taxicab is topped by a large picture placard advertising the "Topless Girls of Glitter Gulch." Similarly sexy images are everywhere. I wonder, too, about the advisability of exposing young children to the lure of gambling.

You should also be aware, if you bring your children to Las Vegas, that most of the attractions for them are quite costly. Kids can easily spend $30 an hour (and more) at video-game arcades and carnival midways; theme parks and motion-simulator rides are overpriced. My feeling is, it would be better—and maybe even cheaper—to hire someone to care for them during your trip. That said, I will add that children love all the flash and excitement. Here's a rundown of the current kid-pleasers both in town and further afield.

Circus Circus (see p. 71) has ongoing circus acts throughout the day, a vast video game and pinball arcade, and dozens of carnival games on its mezzanine level. Behind the hotel is Grand Slam Canyon, detailed below. **Excalibur** (see p. 62) also offers video and carnival games, plus thrill cinemas and free shows (jugglers, puppets, etc.). At **Caesars Palace,** both the Magical Empire (for kids 12 and older only, see p. 133) and OMNIMAX™ movies (see p. 134) are a thrill for everyone in the family; a video-game arcade adjoins the OMNIMAX™ Theater. Animated talking statues in the **Forum Shops** are also a kick. The ship battle in front of **Treasure Island** (see box on p. 141) is sure to please, as will the erupting volcano (see p. 58) and the dolphin habitat at the **Mirage;** while you're here, see the tigers and the sharks. Ditto the attractions at the **Luxor Las Vegas** (see p. 66).

Kids will enjoy **The Magic and Movie Hall of Fame** (see p. 138), but they'll want to leave before you do.

Of moderate interest to youngsters are the quartet of **factory tours in Henderson** (see p. 142), especially Ethel M Chocolates and Kidd's Marshmallow Factory where free samples sweeten the learning experience.

Appropriate shows for kids include *King Arthur's Tournament* at Excalibur (see p. 186), *Siegfried & Roy* at the Mirage (see p. 187), *Lance Burton* at the Monte Carlo (see p. 186), *Starlight Express* at the Hilton (see p. 189), *EFX* at the MGM Grand (see p. 183), and Cirque du Soleil's *Mystère* at Treasure Island (see p. 183). As a general rule, early shows are less racy than late-night shows.

Beyond the city limits (see chapter 11 for details on all of these) is **Bonnie Springs Ranch/Old Nevada,** with trail and stagecoach rides, a petting zoo, old-fashioned melodramas, stunt shootouts, a Nevada-themed wax museum, crafts demonstrations, and more. **Lake Mead** has great recreational facilities for family vacations. Finally, organized tours (see p. 147) to the Grand Canyon and other interesting sights in southern Nevada and neighboring states can be fun family activities. Check your hotel sightseeing desk.

Specifically kid-pleasing attractions are described below.

Grand Slam Canyon Theme Park

2889 Las Vegas Blvd. S., behind Circus Circus Hotel. ☎ **702/734-3939.** Admission is free, but there's a charge for each ride. An unlimited ride ticket is available. Park hours vary; call ahead.

This indoor amusement park enclosed in a glittering pink-glass dome offers a unique asset in a city where temperatures often soar above 100°F; it's air-conditioned! Themed around the Grand Canyon, its interior suggests southwestern terrain with mountains, sandstone cliffs, and waterfalls. You can have a lot of fun here. Highlights include Canyon Blaster (a really good double-loop, double-corkscrew roller coaster with dark tunnels), Rim Runner (a water flume with a 60-foot free-fall splashdown), Hot Shots Laser Tag (a futuristic battle game played with laser guns in a dark cavelike chamber equipped with smoke generators and eerie sound effects), and a triplex IMAX™ theater. About half a dozen rides, a face-painting booth, a sandbox, nets for climbing, and a ball crawl are geared to little kids. Strolling entertainers (jugglers, clowns, mimes, and magicians) roam the park throughout the day. A miniature *Jurassic Park*-themed area houses animatronic dinosaurs. And there are many carnival midway games in addition to a Sega video-game arcade. Several snack bars and a moderately priced Mexican restaurant are on the premises.

MGM Grand Adventures

Behind the MGM Grand Hotel, 3799 Las Vegas Blvd. S. ☎ **702/891-7777.** Admission $17 adults, $10 children up to 42" (or age 12), free for children under 4. (*Note:* Rates may vary seasonally.) Daily (hours vary seasonally). Children under 10 must be accompanied by an adult.

This 33-acre facility is divided into geographically themed areas, including a New York street, an Asian village, and Olde England. New attractions are still being added at this writing. Current highlights include: Lightning Bolt—a roller-coaster careening through outer space (kind of a mini Space Mountain); Deep Earth Exploration—a motion-simulator journey into the earth's core, complete with rock slides, menacing creatures on a crystallized lake, and an erupting volcano; Backlot River Tour—your

> **❓ Did You Know?**
>
> - In January, a Las Vegas visitor can ski the snowy slopes of Mount Charleston and water-ski on Lake Mead in the same day.
> - Former President Ronald Reagan performed at the Last Frontier in 1954. Those who saw him said he was a pretty good song and dance man.
> - Edgar Bergen sometimes sat at casino gaming tables making his bets and wise-acre commentary via dummy Charlie McCarthy.
> - Marlene Dietrich and Louis Armstrong shared the Riviera stage in 1962 and showed the audience how to do the twist, the dance craze of the decade.
> - Bandleader Xavier Cugat and Spanish bombshell singer Charo were the first couple to exchange vows at Caesars Palace, two days after its 1966 opening.
> - During a heat wave in the summer of 1953, the Sands moved a roulette table into the swimming pool so gamblers could play in comfort.

canopied boat, which sails past simulated movie sets and production areas, is threatened by swamp creatures, explosions, and bad weather; Over the Edge—a log flume; Grand Canyon Rapids—a simulated white-water-rafting experience; and Parisian Taxis—bumper cars.

Rides are complemented by shows. Plan your show schedule when you enter, and be sure to catch "Dueling Pirates," a humorous stunt show (hero saves fair maiden amid much tumbling, dancing, comedy, acrobatics, dueling, Errol Flynn rope swings, pratfalls, and pyrotechnics) in the 950-seat outdoor Pirate's Cove Theatre. The "Three Stooges" create hilarious havoc in Dr. Frankenbean's lab in a live show at the Magic Screen Theatre. And there's also a Chinese acrobat show.

Costumed characters (Betty Boop, Popeye, Olive Oyl, Brutus, and King LJ—with his lion family) wander the park. There are 11 retail shops, two wedding chapels, and numerous food and beverage outlets, most of which offer open-air seating. Best of the lot is the Kenny Rogers Roasters, an attractive pine-paneled cafeteria specializing in chicken spit-roasted over a hardwood fire.

Scandia Family Fun Center

2900 Sirius Ave., at Rancho Dr. between Sahara Ave. and Spring Mountain Rd. offramps. ☎ **702/364-0070.** Admission free, but there's a fee for each game or activity. Super Saver Pass $10.95 (includes 1 round of miniature golf, two rides, and 5 game tokens); Unlimited Wristband Package $14.95 (includes unlimited bumper boat and car rides, unlimited miniature golf, and 10 tokens for batting cages or arcade games). Sept–early June: Sun–Thurs 10am–11pm, Fri–Sat until midnight; mid-June–August: Sun–Thurs 10am–midnight, Fri–Sat until 1am.

This family amusement center just a few blocks off the Strip offers three 18-hole miniature golf courses ($5.50 per game, children under 6 free), a state-of-the-art video arcade with 225 machines, miniature car racing and bumper boats ($3.95 per ride, small children ride free with an adult), and automated softball- and baseball-pitching machines for batting practice ($1.25 for 25 pitches). A snack bar is on the premises.

Wet 'n' Wild

2601 Las Vegas Blvd. S., just south of Sahara Ave. ☎ **702/878-7811.** Admission $21.95 adults, half-price seniors over 55, $15.95 children under 10, free for children under 3. Daily early May–Sept 30, 10am–6 or 8pm (sometimes later). Season and hours vary somewhat from year to year, so call ahead.

When temperatures soar, head for this 26-acre water park right in the heart of the Strip and cool off while jumping waves, careening down steep flumes, and running rapids. Among the highlights: Royal Flush, a thrill ride that washes you down a precipitous chute into a saucer-like bowl at 45 mph, then flushes you into a bottomless pool; Surf Lagoon, a 500,000-gallon wave pool; Banzai Banzai, a roller-coaster-like water ride (aboard a plastic sled, you race down a 45-degree-angled 150-foot chute and skip porpoiselike across a 120-foot pool); Der Stuka, the world's fastest and highest water chute; Raging Rapids, a simulated white-water rafting adventure on a 500-foot-long river; Lazy River, a leisurely float trip; Blue Niagara, a dizzying descent inside intertwined looping tubes from a height of six stories; Willy Willy (a hydra-hurricane that propels riders on inner tubes around a 90-foot-diameter pool at 10 miles per hour); Bomb Bay (enter a bomblike casing 76 feet in the air for a speedy vertical flight straight down to a pool target); and the Black Hole (an exhilaratingly rapid space-themed flume descent in the dark enhanced by a bombardment of colorful fiber-optic star fields and spinning galaxy patterns en route to splashdown). There are additional flumes, a challenging children's water playground, and a sunbathing area with a cascading waterfall, as well as video and arcade games. Food concessions are located throughout the park, and you can purchase swimwear and accessories at the Beach Trends Shop.

4 Organized Tours

Just about every hotel in town has a sightseeing desk offering a seemingly infinite number of tours in and around Las Vegas. You're sure to find a tour company that will take you where you want to go.

Gray Line (☎ 702/384-1234) offers a rather comprehensive roster, including:

- 8¹/₂-hour city tours, including visits to Ethel M Chocolates and Cranberry World, the view from the Stratosphere Tower, and the Fremont Street Experience.
- Full-day excursions to Laughlin, Nevada, an up-and-coming mini-Las Vegas 100 miles south with casino hotels on the banks of the Colorado River.
- Half- and full-day excursions to Hoover Dam and Lake Mead (see Chapter 11 for details).
- A full-day excursion to Red Rock Canyon and Mt. Charleston.
- An 8-hour excursion to the Valley of Fire that includes lunch at a Lake Mead resort and a drive by Wayne Newton's Ranch.
- A full-day river-rafting tour on the Colorado River from the base of Hoover Dam through majestic Black Canyon.
- A morning or afternoon air tour (and you thought they only had buses) of Grand Canyon.
- A 10-hour Grand Canyon excursion that includes "flightseeing" and river rafting on the Colorado.
- An overnight trip to Grand Canyon.

Call for details or inquire at your hotel sightseeing desk, where you'll also find free magazines with coupons for discounts on these tours.

GRAND CANYON TOURS   Generally, tourists visiting Las Vegas don't drive 300 miles to Arizona to see the Grand Canyon, but there are dozens of sightseeing tours departing from the city daily. In addition to the Gray Line tours described above, the major operator, Scenic Airlines (☎ 800/634-6801 or 702/638-3200), runs deluxe, full-day guided air-ground tours for $189 per person ($149 for children 2 to 11); the price includes a bus excursion through the national park, a flight over the canyon, lunch, and a screening of the IMAX™ movie *Grand Canyon—the Hidden Secrets*. All Scenic tours include "flightseeing." The company also offers both full-day and overnight tours with hiking. And though all Scenic tours include hotel pickup and drop-off, if you take the Premium Deluxe Tour ($229 for adults, $179 for children) you'll be transported by limo.

Scenic also offers tours to other points of interest and national parks, including Yellowstone and Grand Teton. Ask for details when you call.

INDIVIDUALIZED TOURS   A totally different type of tour is offered by Char Cruze of Creative Adventures (☎ 702/361-5565). Char, a charming fourth-generation Las Vegan (she was at the opening of the Flamingo), spent her childhood riding horseback through the mesquite and cottonwoods of the Mojave Desert, discovering magical places you'd never find on your own or on a commercial tour. Char is a lecturer and storyteller as well as a tour guide. She has extensively studied southern Nevada's geology and desert wildlife, its regional history and Native American cultures. Her personalized tours—enhanced by fascinating stories about everything from miners to mobsters—visit haunted mines, sacred Paiute grounds, ghost towns, canyons, and ancient petroglyphs. Depending on your itinerary, the cost is about $100 a day if you use your own car (more, depending on the number of people, if rental transportation is required). It's a good idea to make arrangements with her prior to leaving home.

5 Playing Golf

There are dozens of local courses, including very challenging ones—the Sheraton Desert Inn Country Club and the Mirage Golf Club. Both have hosted many PGA tournaments. Beginner and intermediate golfers might prefer the other courses listed.

Angel Park Golf Club
100 S. Rampart Blvd., between Charleston Blvd. and Westcliff St. ☎ **702/254-4653.**

This 36-hole par-70/71 public course, was designed by Arnold Palmer. In addition to the 18-hole Palm and Mountain Courses, Angel Park offers a night-it Cloud 9 course (12 holes for daylight play, 9 at night), where each hole is patterned after a famous par-3. **Yardage:** Palm Course 6,438 championship, 5,721 regular, 4,565 ladies; Mountain Course 6,783 championship, 6,272 regular, 5,143 ladies. **Facilities:** pro shop, nightlit driving range, 18-hole putting course, restaurant, snack bar, cocktail bar, beverage cart.

Black Mountain Golf & Country Club
500 Greenway Rd., in nearby Henderson. ☎ **702/565-7933.**

This 18-hole, par-72 semi-private course requires reservations 4 days in advance. **Yardage:** 6,541 championship, 6,223 regular, 5,478 ladies. **Facilities:** pro shop, putting green, driving range, restaurant, snack bar, and cocktail lounge.

Craig Ranch Golf Club
628 W. Craig Rd., Losee Rd. and Martin Luther King Blvd. ☎ **702/642-9700.**

This is an 18-hole, par-70 public course. **Yardage:** 6,001 regular, 5,221 ladies. **Facilities:** driving range, pro shop, PGA teaching pro, putting green, and snack bar.

Desert Inn Golf Club
3145 Las Vegas Blvd. S. ☎ **702/733-4290.**

The Desert Inn course gets the nod from champions. It's an 18-hole, par-72 resort course. **Yardage:** 7,066 championship, 6,270 regular, 5,719 ladies. **Facilities:** driving range, putting green, pro shop, and restaurant. You can reserve 90 days in advance for Sunday through Thursday, 2 days in advance for Friday and Saturday. This is the most famous and demanding course in Las Vegas. *Golf Digest* calls it one of America's top resort courses. The driving range is open to Desert Inn and Caesars guests only; anyone can play the course, but nonguests pay a higher fee.

Desert Rose Golf Club

5483 Clubhouse Dr., three blocks west of Nellis Blvd., off Sahara Ave. ☎ **702/431-4653.**

This is an 18-hole, par-71 public course. **Yardage:** 6,511 championship, 6,135 regular, 5,458 ladies. **Facilities:** driving range, putting and chipping greens, PGA teaching pro, pro shop, restaurant, and cocktail lounge.

Las Vegas Hilton Country Club

1911 Desert Inn Rd., between Maryland Pkwy. and Eastern Ave. ☎ **702/796-0016.**

This is an 18-hole, par-72 public course. **Yardage:** 6,815 championship, 6,418 regular, 5,741 ladies. **Facilities:** pro shop, golf school, driving range, restaurant, and cocktail lounge. Hilton guests enjoy preferred tee times and rates.

6 Staying Active

Bring your sports gear to Las Vegas. The city and surrounding areas offer plenty of opportunities for active sports. In addition to many highly rated golf courses (described above), just about every hotel has a large swimming pool and health club, and tennis courts abound. All types of water sports are offered at Lake Mead National Recreation Area, there's rafting on the Colorado, horseback riding at Mount Charleston and Bonnie Springs, great hiking in the canyons, and much, much more. Do plan to get out of those smoke-filled casinos and into the fresh air once in a while. It's good for your health and your finances.

Note: When choosing a hotel, check out its recreational facilities, all listed in chapter 5.

Bicycling   Escape the City Streets (☎ **702/596-2953**) rents 21-speed mountain bikes and offers free delivery to all downtown and Strip hotels. Rates are $26 for the first day, $20 for a half day or consecutive days, $90 for a full week. You must show a major credit card (American Express, MasterCard, or VISA). Inquire about bike trips to Red Rock Canyon and other good biking areas.

Bowling   The Showboat Hotel & Casino, 2800 E. Fremont St. (☎ **702/ 385-9153**), is famous for housing the largest bowling center in North America— 106 lanes—and for being the oldest stop on the Professional Bowlers Tour. A major renovation a few years back made its premises bright and spiffy. Open 24 hours.

Bungee Jumping   At A.J. Hackett Bungy, 810 Circus Circus Dr. between Las Vegas Blvd. S. and Industrial Rd. (☎ **702/385-4321**), an elevator in the shape of a rocket takes you to the top of a 175-foot tower—the base for an exhilarating plunge toward a large swimming pool below. The price is $49 for your first jump ($79 with a T-shirt and videotape), $29 for the second and third jumps; the fourth is free. Students and military with ID should inquire about discounts. If you're under 18, you must be accompanied by a parent. Owner A.J. Hackett, who claims to have been the first commercial developer of bungee jumping (in New Zealand), has overseen more than 500,000 jumps without an accident. Call for hours.

Fishing   One doesn't usually think of fishing in the desert, but there are lakes and large ponds. Closest to Las Vegas are the ponds in **Floyd R. Lamb State Park,** 9200 Tule Springs Rd. (☎ **702/486-5413**). The park is about 15 miles from the Strip. To get there take I-15 to U.S. 95 north, get off at the Durango exit and follow the signs. You can fish here for catfish, trout, bluegill, sunfish, and large-mouth bass. You will need your own gear, bait, and tackle, as well as a Nevada fishing license, which is available at any sporting goods store (check the Las Vegas yellow pages). There's also fishing at Lake Mead (see listing in chapter 11 for details).

Health Clubs   Almost every hotel in Las Vegas has an on-premises health club. The facilities, of course, vary enormously. Descriptions are given of each club in hotel facilities listings in chapter 5.

But none offers the amazing range of facilities you'll find at the **Las Vegas Sporting House,** 3025 Industrial Rd., right behind the Stardust Hotel (☎ **702/ 733-8999**). Opened in 1978, this 65,000-square-foot club is ultraluxurious. UNLV teams and many athletes and Strip headliners (including Siegfried and Roy) work out here. Facilities include: 10 racquetball/handball courts, two squash courts, two outdoor tennis courts (lit for night play), a full gymnasium for basketball and volleyball, an outdoor pool and sunbathing area, a 25-meter indoor pool for lap swimming, indoor and outdoor jogging tracks, treadmills, Lifecycles, Virtual Reality bikes, stair machines, and free weights. In addition, there are full lines of Cybex, Universal, and Paramount machines, along with some Nautilus equipment; sauna, steam, and Jacuzzi; a pro shop; men's and women's skin care and hair salons; massage; free babysitting service while you work out; restaurant, bar, and lounge. Aerobics classes are given at frequent intervals throughout the day, and you can try "spinning"—a new workout technique that burns 800 calories in 40 minutes!. Cost for a single visit is $15 to $20 (depending on the club's arrangement with your hotel); reduced weekly rates are available. Open daily 24 hours.

Horseback Riding   The **Mt. Charleston Riding Stables** (☎ **800/955-1314** or 702/872-5408), under the auspices of the Mount Charleston Resort, offer glorious scenic trail rides to the edge of the wilderness. They depart from stables on Kyle Canyon Road. Since the schedule varies, it's best to call in advance for details. Cost is $45 for two hours, $60 for three. The stables also offer sleigh rides in winter and hayrides in summer. Riding stables at **Bonnie Springs Ranch** (☎ **702/875-4191**) also offer guided trail rides daily. Rates are $18 per hour.

Hiking   Except in summer, when the temperature can reach 120° in the shade, the Las Vegas area is great for hiking. The best hiking season is November through March. Great locales include the incredibly scenic Red Rock Canyon, Valley of Fire State Park, and Mount Charleston (see individual headings in chapter 11 for details).

Jet-Skiing   **Las Vegas Adventure Tours (LVAT)** (☎ **800/553-5452** or 702/ 564-5452) offers jet-ski rides on Lake Mead. Call LVAT, too, about horseback riding, hot-air ballooning, Grand Canyon flightseeing, and all-terrain-vehicle desert tours.

Racquetball   There are courts in several locations around town. The **Las Vegas Athletic Club East,** 1070 E. Sahara Ave., at Maryland Pkwy. (☎ **702/733-1919**), has seven courts open 24 hours a day, 7 days a week. Rates are $10 per person, per day; $25 per week. Call to reserve a court.

The **Las Vegas Athletic Club West,** 3315 Spring Mountain Rd., between I-15 and Valley View Blvd. (☎ **702/362-3720**), has eight courts open weekdays 5am to 11pm; weekends 8am to 8pm. Rates are $10 per person, per visit; $25 per week.

The **Las Vegas Sporting House,** 3025 Industrial Rd., right behind the Stardust Hotel (☎ **702/733-8999**), has 10 racquetball/handball courts open 24 hours a day, 7 days a week. Rates are $15 per visit if you're staying at a local hotel.

The **University of Nevada, Las Vegas (UNLV),** 4505 Maryland Pkwy., just off Swenson St. (☎ **702/895-3150**), has eight racquetball courts open weekdays 6am

---

Desert Hiking Tips

Hiking in the desert is exceptionally rewarding, but it can be dangerous. Some safety tips:

1. Do not hike alone.

2. Carry plenty of water and drink it often. Don't assume spring waters are safe to drink. A gallon of water per person, per day is recommended for hikers.

3. Be alert for signs of heat exhaustion (headache, nausea, dizziness, fatigue, and cool, damp, pale, or red skin).

4. Gauge your fitness accurately. Desert hiking may involve rough or steep terrain. Don't take on more than you can handle.

5. Check weather forecasts before starting out. Thunderstorms can turn into raging flash floods, which are extremely hazardous to hikers.

6. Dress properly. Wear sturdy walking shoes for rock scrambling, long pants (to protect yourself from rocks and cacti), a hat, sunscreen, and sunglasses.

7. Carry a small first-aid kit.

8. Be careful when climbing on sandstone, which can be surprisingly soft and crumbly.

9. Don't feed or play with animals, such as wild burros in Red Rock Canyon.

10. Be alert for snakes and insects. Though they're rarely encountered, you'll want to look into a crevice before putting your hand into it.

11. Visit park or other information offices before you start out and acquaint yourself with rules and regulations and any possible hazards. It's also a good idea to tell them where you are going, when you will return, how many are in your party, and so on. Some park offices offer hiker-registration programs.

12. Follow the hiker's rule of thumb: "Take only photographs, and leave only footprints."

---

to 9:45pm, Saturdays 8am to 5:30pm, Sundays 10am to 5:30pm. Hours may vary somewhat each semester. Rates are $2 per person, per hour. Call before you go to find out if a court is available. You must pick up a guest pass in the Physical Education Building.

River Rafting   Black Canyon Inc. (☎ **800/696-RAFT** or 702/293-3776) offers daily raft trips on the Colorado River from February 1 through the end of November. As an authorized concessionaire, Black Canyon can get into otherwise restricted areas at the base of the dam. Trips include 3 hours of scenic rafting and lunch. You'll see waterfalls gush from majestic canyon walls, pass tranquil coves, spy bighorn sheep on sheer cliffs, and spot blue herons, cormorants, and falcons. Knowledgeable guides provide a lot of fascinating area history and geology. Each raft is piloted by an experienced navigator. Rates, including Las Vegas hotel pickup an return, are $74.95 per person, $64.95 if you drive to and from the expedition depot.

Rock Climbing   Red Rock Canyon, just 19 miles west of Las Vegas, is one of the world's most popular rock-climbing areas. In addition to awe-inspiring natural beauty, it offers everything from bouldering to big walls. If you'd like to join the bighorn sheep, Red Rock has more than 1,000 routes to inaugurate beginners and challenge accomplished climbers. Experienced climbers can contact the Visitor Center (☎ 702/363-1921) for information.

If you're interested in learning or improving your skills, an excellent rock-climbing school and guide service called **Sky's the Limit** (☎ 800/733-7597 or 702/363-4533) offers programs for beginning, intermediate, and advanced climbers. No experience is needed. The school is accredited by the American Mountain Guides Association.

Tennis   Tennis buffs should choose one of the many hotels in town that have tennis courts.

Bally's (☎ 702/739-4598) has eight night-lit hard courts. Fees per hour range from $10 to $15 for guests, $15 to $20 for nonguests. Facilities include a pro shop. Hours vary seasonally. Reservations are advised.

The **Flamingo Hilton** (☎ 702/733-3444) has four outdoor hard courts (all lit for night play), and a pro shop. They are open to the public Monday to Friday from 7am to 8pm, Saturday and Sunday from 7am to 6pm. Rates are $20 per hour for nonguests, $12 for guests. Lessons are available. Reservations are required.

The **Riviera** (☎ 702/734-5110) has two outdoor hard courts (both lit for night play) that are open to the public, subject to availability; hotel guests have priority. They are open 24 hours. There is no charge for guests; nonguests pay $10 per hour. Reservations are required.

The **Desert Inn** (☎ 702/733-4557) has five outdoor hard courts (all lit for night play) and a pro shop. They are open to the public. Hours are daybreak to 10pm. Rates are $10 per person for a daily pass (you book for an hour but can stay longer if no one is waiting); they are free for guests. Reservations are necessary.

In addition to hotels, the **University of Nevada, Las Vegas (UNLV),** Harmon Ave. just east of Swenson St. (☎ 702/895-0844) has a dozen courts (all lit for night play) that are open weekdays from 6am to 9:45pm, on weekends from 8am to 9pm. Rates are $5 per person, per day on weekdays; $10 weekends. You should call before going to find out if a court is available.

7 Spectator Sports

Las Vegas isn't known for its sports teams. Except for minor league baseball and hockey, the only consistent spectator sports are those at UNLV. The new Las Vegas Motor Speedway (described in detail earlier in this chapter) is a major new venue for car racing and should draw major events to Las Vegas.

But since the city has several top-notch sporting arenas, there are important annual events that take place in Las Vegas, details for which can be found in the "Las Vegas Calendar of Events" in chapter 2. The **PBA Invitational Bowling Tournament** is held in the Showboat's massive bowling center each January. The **PGA Tour Las Vegas Senior Classic** is held each April in nearby Summerlin, and **Las Vegas Invitational** in Las Vegas each October. The **National Finals Rodeo** is held in UNLV's Thomas and Mack Center each December. From time to time, you'll find NBA exhibition games, professional ice skating tournaments, or gymnastics exhibitions. Then there are the only-in-Vegas spectaculars, such as Evel Knievel's ill-fated attempt to jump the fountains in front of Caesars.

Finally, Las Vegas is well known as a major location for boxing matches. These are held in several Strip hotels, most often at Caesars or the MGM Grand, but sometimes at the Mirage or Aladdin. Tickets are hard to come by and quite expensive.

BASEBALL

The **Las Vegas Stars,** a AAA baseball team, play from April through August at the 10,000-seat **Cashman Field Center,** 850 Las Vegas Blvd. N. (☎ 702/386-7200 for tickets and information). Tickets are priced at $4 to $7.

Major Sports Venues in Hotels

The **Aladdin's** 7,000-seat **Theatre for the Performing Arts,** 3667 Las Vegas Blvd. S. (☎ **800/637-8133** or 702/736-0240) is occasionally used for professional boxing matches.

Caesars Palace (☎ **800/634-6698** or 702/731-7110) has a long tradition of sporting events, from Evel Knievel's attempted motorcycle jump over its fountains in 1967 to Grand Prix auto races. Mary Lou Retton has tumbled in gymnastic events at Caesars, and Olympians Brian Boitano and Katarina Witt have taken to the ice, as has Wayne Gretzky (he led the L.A. Kings to victory over the New York Rangers in a preseason exhibition game). And well over 100 world-championship boxing contests have taken place here since the hotel opened. In the spirit of ancient Rome, Caesars awards riches and honors to the "gladiators" who compete in its arenas.

The **MGM Grand's Garden Events Arena** (☎ **800/929-1111** or 702/891-7777) is a major venue for sporting events: professional boxing matches, rodeos, tennis, ice-skating shows, World Figure Skating Championships, and more.

The Mirage (☎ **800/627-6667** or 702/791-7111) also features occasional championship boxing matches.

BASKETBALL

The Thomas and Mack Center, also on the UNLV campus at Tropicana Ave. and Swenson St. (☎ **702/895-3900**), is an 18,500-seat facility used for a variety of sporting events. It is home to the **UNLV's Runnin' Rebels**, who play 16 to 20 games during a November-to-March season. Other events here include major boxing tournaments, NBA exhibition games, and rodeos. For information and to charge tickets, call the stadium number or Ticketmaster (☎ **702/474-4000**).

FOOTBALL

The Sam Boyd Stadium at the University of Nevada, Las Vegas (UNLV), Boulder Hwy. and Russell Rd. (☎ **702/895-3900**), is a 32,000-seat outdoor stadium. The **UNLV Rebels** play about six football games here each year between September and November. And the stadium is also used for motorsports and supercross events, truck and tractor pulls, high school football games, and the Las Vegas Bowl in December. For information and to charge tickets, call the above number or Ticketmaster (☎ **702/474-4000**).

HOCKEY

Las Vegas Thunder (International Hockey League) plays about 40 games at UNLV's Thomas and Mack Center (Tropicana Ave. and Swenson St.) between October and early April (call **702/798-PUCK** for information).

8 About Casino Gambling

Most people don't come to Las Vegas simply to visit the Liberace Museum. The Las Vegas economy depends upon gambling, and even the hotels here conceive of themselves basically as casinos with rooms. Visitors range from cautious types who play nickel slots for an hour and fret about losing a few dollars to flamboyant high rollers risking hundreds—if not thousands—of dollars on a roll of the dice, a blackjack hand, or a spin of the roulette wheel. These diverse gamblers have just one thing in common: secretly, every one of them expects to win. It's this elusive dream that keeps people coming back, trying out elaborate systems, reading books on how to beat the odds, betting excitedly when a craps table gets hot, and dropping spare change into slot machines.

Of course, there is no system that really beats the odds. And if there were, the casinos would be on it faster than a New York minute. The best system is to decide how much you're willing to risk, learn the rules of any game you're playing, and, if you have the fortitude, walk away with moderate winnings. Many good players hold out for a 50% profit. Keep in mind that it's extremely easy to get carried away trying to recoup losses. I've personally seen tragic cases of average folks losing large sums, and, desperate to win them back, making larger and larger bets until they've gambled away cars, homes, and savings.

The first part of this chapter tells you the basics of betting. Knowing how to play the games not only improves your odds but makes playing more enjoyable. In addition to the instructions below, you'll find dozens of books on how to gamble at all casino hotel gift shops, and many casinos offer free gaming lessons on the premises. The second part of this chapter describes all the major casinos in town.

1 The Games

BACCARAT

The ancient game of baccarat—or *chemin de fer*—is played with eight decks of cards. Firm rules apply, and there is no skill involved other than deciding whether to bet on the bank or the player.

Baccarat Rules

Player's Hand

Having

0-1-2-3-4-5	Must draw a third card.
6-7	*Must stand.*
8-9	Natural. Banker cannot draw.

Banker's Hand

Having	**Draws** When giving Player 3rd card of:	**Does Not Draw** When giving Player 3rd card of:
3	1-2-3-4-5-6-7-9-10	8
4	2-3-4-5-6-7	1-8-9-10
5	4-5-6-7	1-2-3-8-9-10
6	6-7	1-2-3-4-5-8-9-10
7	*Must stand.*	
8-9	Natural. Player cannot draw.	

If the player takes no third card, the banker must stand on 6. No one draws against a natural 8 or 9.

Any beginner can play, but check the betting minimum before you sit down. The cards are shuffled by the croupier and then placed in a box that is called the "shoe."

Players may wager on "bank" or "player" at any time. Two cards are dealt from the shoe and given to the player who has the largest wager against the bank, and two cards are dealt to the croupier acting as banker. If the rule calls for a third card (see rules on chart shown here), the player or banker, or both, must take the third card. In the event of a tie, the hand is dealt over.

The object of the game is to come as close as possible to the number 9. To score the hands, the cards of each hand are totaled and the *last digit* is used. All cards have face value. For example: 10 plus 5 equals 15 (score is 5); 10 plus 4 plus 9 equals 23 (score is 3); 4 plus 3 plus 3 equals 10 (score is 0); and 4 plus 3 plus 2 equals 9 (score is 9). The closest hand to 9 wins.

Each player has a chance to deal the cards. The shoe passes to the player on the right each time the bank loses. If the player wishes, he or she may pass the shoe at any time.

Note: When you bet on the bank and the bank wins, you are charged a 5% commission. This must be paid at the start of a new game or when you leave the table.

BIG SIX

Big Six provides pleasant recreation and involves no study or effort. The wheel has 56 positions on it, 54 of them marked by bills from $1 to $20 denominations. The other two spots are jokers, and each pays 40 to 1 if the wheel stops in that position.

All other stops pay at face value. Those marked with $20 bills pay 20 to 1; the $5 bills pay 5 to 1; and so forth.

BLACKJACK

The dealer starts the game by dealing each player two cards. In some casinos they're dealt to the player faceup, in others facedown, but the dealer always gets one card up and one card down. Everybody plays against the dealer. The object is to get a total that is higher than that of the dealer without exceeding 21. All face cards count as 10; all other number cards except aces count as their number value. An ace may be counted as 1 or 11, whichever you choose it to be.

Starting at his or her left, the dealer gives additional cards to the players who wish to draw (be "hit") or none to a player who wishes to "stand" or "hold." If your count is nearer to 21 than the dealer's, you win. If it's under the dealer's, you lose. Ties are a push and nobody wins. After all the players are satisfied with their counts, the dealer exposes his or her facedown card. If his two cards total 16 or less, the dealer must "hit" (draw an additional card) until reaching 17 or over. If the dealer's total goes over 21, he or she must pay all the players whose hands have not gone "bust." It is important to note here that the blackjack dealer has no choice as to whether he or she should stay or draw. A dealer's decisions are predetermined and known to all the players at the table.

HOW TO PLAY   Here are eight "rules" for blackjack.

1. Place the amount of chips that you want to bet on the betting space on your table.

2. Look at the first two cards the dealer starts you with. If your hand adds up to the total you prefer, place your cards *under your bet money,* indicating that you don't wish any additional cards. If you elect to draw an additional card, you tell the dealer to "hit" you by making a sweeping motion with your cards, or point to your open hand (watch your fellow players).

3. If your count goes over 21, you go "bust" and lose—even if the dealer also goes "bust" afterward. Unless hands are dealt faceup, *you then turn your hand faceup on the table.*

4. If you make 21 in your first two cards (any picture card or 10 with an ace), you've got blackjack. *You expose your winning hand immediately,* and you collect $1\frac{1}{2}$ times your bet—unless the dealer has blackjack, too, in which case it's a push and nobody wins.

5. If you find a "pair" in your first two cards (say, two 8s or two aces) you may "split" the pair into two hands and treat each card as the first card dealt in two separate hands. *Turn the pair faceup on the table,* place the original bet on one of these cards, then place an equal amount on the other card. *Split aces are limited to a one-card draw on each.*

6. You may double your original bet and make a one-card draw after receiving your initial two cards. *Turn your hand faceup* and you'll receive one more card facedown.

7. Anytime the dealer deals himself or herself an ace for the "up" card, you may insure your hand against the possibility that the hole card is a 10 or face card, which would give him or her an automatic blackjack. To insure, you place an amount up to one-half of your bet on the "insurance" line. If the dealer does have a blackjack, you do not lose, even though he or she has your hand beat, and you keep your bet and your insurance money. If the dealer does not have a blackjack, he or she takes your insurance money and play continues in the normal fashion.

8. *Remember:* The dealer *must* stand on 17 or more and *must* hit a hand of 16 or less.

PROFESSIONAL TIPS   Advice of the experts in playing blackjack is as follows.

1. *Do not* ask for an extra card if you have a count of 17, 18, 19, 20, or 21 in your cards, no matter what the dealer has showing in his or her "up" card.

2. *Do not* ask for an extra card when you have 12, 13, 14, 15, 16, or more . . . if the dealer has a 2, 3, 4, 5, or 6 showing in his or her "up" card.

3. *Do ask* for an extra card or more when you have a count of 12 through 16 in your hand...if the dealer's "up" card is a 7, 8, 9, 10, or ace.

There's a lot more to blackjack-playing strategy than the above, of course. So consider this merely as the bare bones of the game.

A final tip: Avoid insurance bets; they're sucker bait!

CRAPS

The most exciting casino action is always at the craps tables. Betting is frenetic, play fast-paced, and groups quickly bond yelling and screaming in response to the action.

The Table   The craps table is divided into marked areas (Pass, Come, Field, Big 6, Big 8, and so on), where you place your chips to bet. The following are a few simple directions.

Pass Line   A "Pass Line" bet pays even money. If the first roll of the dice adds up to 7 or 11, you win your bet; if the first roll adds up to 2, 3, or 12, you lose your bet. If any other number comes up, it's your "point." If you roll your point again, you win, but if a 7 comes up again before your point is rolled, you lose.

Don't Pass Line   Betting on the "Don't Pass" is the opposite of betting on the Pass Line. This time, you lose if a 7 or an 11 is thrown on the first roll, and you win if a 2 or a 3 is thrown on the first roll.

If the first roll is 12, however, it's a push (standoff), and nobody wins. If none of these numbers is thrown and you have a point instead, in order to win, a 7 will have to be thrown before the point comes up again. A "Don't Pass" bet also pays even money.

Come   Betting on "Come" is the same as betting on the Pass Line, but you must bet *after* the first roll or on any following roll. Again, you'll win on 7 or 11 and lose on 2, 3, or 12. Any other number is your point, and you win if your point comes up again before a 7.

Don't Come   This is the opposite of a "Come" bet. Again, you wait until after the first roll to bet. A 7 or an 11 means you lose; a 2 or a 3 means you win; 12 is a push, and nobody wins. You win if 7 comes up before the point. (The point, you'll recall, was the first number rolled if it was none of the above.)

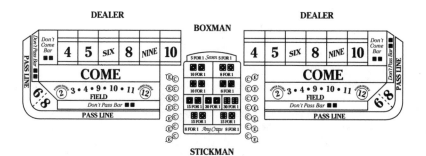

Field   This is a bet for one roll only. The "Field" consists of seven numbers: 2, 3, 4, 9, 10, 11, and 12. If any of these numbers is thrown on the next roll, you win even money, except on 2 and 12, which pay to 2 to 1 (at some casinos 3 to 1).

Big 6 and 8   A "Big 6 and 8" bet pays even money. You win if either a 6 or an 8 is rolled before a 7.

Any 7   An "Any 7" bet pays the winner five for one. If a 7 is thrown on the first roll after you bet, you win.

"Hard Way" Bets   In the middle of a craps table are pictures of several possible dice combinations together with the odds the casino will pay you if you bet and win on any of those combinations being thrown. For example, if 8 is thrown by having a 4 appear on each die, and you bet on it, the bank will pay 10 for 1; if 4 is thrown by having a 2 appear on each die, and you bet on it, the bank will pay 8 for 1; if 3 is thrown, the bank pays 15 for 1. You win at the odds quoted if the *exact* combination of numbers you bet on comes up. But you lose either if a 7 is rolled or if the number you bet on was rolled any way other than the "Hard Way" shown on the table. In-the-know gamblers tend to avoid "Hard Way" bets as an easy way to lose their money. And note that the odds quoted are *not* 3 to 1, 4 to 1, or 8 to 1; here the key word is *for*—that is, 3 for 1 or 8 for 1.

Any Craps   Here you're lucky if the dice "crap out"—if they show 2, 3, or 12 on the first roll after you bet. If this happens, the bank pays for 8 for 1. Any other number is a loser.

Place Bets   You can make a "Place Bet" on any of the following numbers: 4, 5, 6, 8, 9, and 10. You're betting that the number you choose will be thrown before a 7 is thrown. If you win, the payoff is as follows: 4 or 10 pays at the rate of 9 to 5; 5 or 9 pays at the rate of 7 to 5; 6 or 8 pays at the rate of 7 to 6. "Place Bets" can be removed at any time before a roll.

Some Probabilities   Because each die has six sides numbered from 1 to 6—and craps is played with a pair of dice—the probability of throwing certain numbers has been studied carefully. Professionals have employed complex mathematical formulas in searching for the answers. And computers have data-processed curves of probability.

Suffice it to say that 7 (a crucial number in craps) will be thrown more frequently than any other number over the long run, for there are six possible combinations that make 7 when you break down the 1 to 6 possibilities on each separate die. As to the total possible number of combinations on the dice, there are 36.

Comparing the 36 possible combinations, numbers—or point combinations—run as follows:

> *2 and 12* may be thrown in *1 way only.*
> *3 and 11* may be thrown in *2 ways.*
> *4 and 10* may be thrown in *3 ways.*
> *5 and 9* may be thrown in *4 ways.*
> *6 and 8* may be thrown in *5 ways.*
> *7* may be thrown in *6 ways.*

So 7 has an advantage over all other combinations, which, over the long run, is in favor of the casino. You can't beat the law of averages. Players, however, often have winning streaks—a proven fact in ESP studies—and that's when the experts advise that it's wise to increase the size of bets. But when a losing streak sets in, stop playing!

	PRICE PER WAY	PRICE PER GAME
$50,000.00 LIMIT TO AGGREGATE PLAYERS EACH GAME		
MARK NUMBER OF SPOTS OR WAYS PLAYED	NO. OF GAMES	TOTAL PRICE

WINNING TICKETS MUST BE COLLECTED IMMEDIATELY AFTER EACH KENO GAME IS CALLED.

1	2	3	4	5	6	7	8	9	10
11	12	13	14	15	16	17	18	19	20
21	22	23	24	25	26	27	28	29	30
31	32	33	34	35	36	37	38	39	40

WE PAY ON MACHINE ISSUED TICKETS - TICKETS WITH ERRORS NOT CORRECTED BEFORE START OF GAME WILL BE ACCEPTED AS ISSUED.

41	42	43	44	45	46	47	48	49	50
51	52	53	54	55	56	57	58	59	60
61	62	63	64	65	66	67	68	69	70
71	72	73	74	75	76	77	78	79	80

WE ARE NOT RESPONSIBLE FOR KENO RUNNERS TICKETS NOT VALIDATED BEFORE START OF NEXT GAME.

KENO

This is one of the oldest games of chance. Originating in China, the game can be traced back to a time before Christ, when it operated as a national lottery. Legend has it that funds acquired from the game were used to finance construction of the Great Wall of China.

Keno was first introduced into the United States in the 1800s by Chinese railroad construction workers. Easy to play, and offering a chance to sit down and converse between bets, it is one of the most popular games in town—despite the fact that *the house percentage is greater than that of any other casino game!*

To play, you must first obtain a keno form, available at the counter in the keno lounge and in most Las Vegas coffee shops. In the latter, you'll usually find blank keno forms and thick black crayons on your table. Fill yours out, and a miniskirted keno runner will come and collect it. After the game is over, she'll return with your winning or losing ticket. If you've won, it's customary to offer a tip, depending on your winnings.

Looking at your keno ticket and the keno board, you'll see that it is divided horizontally into two rectangles. The upper half (in China the yin area) contains the numbers 1 through 40, the lower (yang) half contains the numbers 41 through 80. You can win a maximum of $50,000—even more on progressive games—though it's highly unlikely (the probability is less than a hundredth of a percent). Mark up to 15 out of the 80 numbers; bets range from about 70¢ on up. A one-number mark is known as a one-spot, a two-number selection is a two-spot, and so on. After you have selected the number of spots you wish to play, write the price of the ticket in the right hand corner where indicated. The more you bet, the more you can win if your numbers come up. Before the game starts, you have to give the completed form to a keno runner—or hand it in at the keno lounge desk—and pay for your bet. You'll get back a duplicate form with the number of the game you're playing on it. Then the game begins. As numbers appear on the keno board, compare them to the numbers you've marked on your ticket. After 20 numbers have appeared on the board, if you've won, turn in your ticket immediately for a payoff—before the next game begins. Otherwise, you will forfeit your winnings, a frustrating experience to say the least.

On a straight ticket that is marked with one or two spots, all of your numbers must appear on the board for you to win anything. With a few exceptions, if you mark from 3 to 7 spots, 3 numbers must appear on the board for you to win anything. Similarly, if you mark 8 to 12 spots, usually at least 5 numbers must come up for you to win the minimum amount. And if you mark 13 to 15 spots, usually at least 6 numbers must come up for a winning ticket. To win the maximum amount ($50,000), which requires that all of your numbers come up, you must select at least 8 spots. The more numbers on the board matching the numbers on your ticket, the more you win. If you want to keep playing the same numbers over and over, you can replay a ticket by handing in your duplicate to the keno runner; you don't have to keep rewriting it.

In addition to the straight bets described above, you can split your ticket, betting various amounts on two or more groups of numbers. To do so, circle the groups. The amount you bet is then divided by the number of groups. You could, if you so desired, play as many as 40 two-spots on a single ticket. Another possibility is to play three groups of four numbers each as eight spots (any two of the three groups of four numbers can be considered an eight spot). It does get a little complex, since combination betting options are almost infinite. Helpful casino personnel in the keno lounge can help you with combination betting.

POKER

Poker is *the* game of the Old West. There's at least one sequence in every western where the hero faces off against the villain over a poker hand. In Las Vegas poker is a tradition, although it isn't played at every casino.

There are lots of variations on the basic game, but one of the most popular is Hold 'Em. Five cards are dealt face up in the center of the table and two are dealt to each player. The player uses the best five of seven, and the best hand wins. The house dealer takes care of the shuffling and the dealing and moves a marker around the table to alternate the start of the deal. The house rakes 1% to 10% (it depends on the casino) from each pot. Most casinos include the usual seven-card stud and a few have hi-lo split.

If you don't know how to play poker, don't attempt to learn at a table. Find a casino that teaches it in free gaming lessons.

Pai gow poker (a variation on poker) has become increasingly popular. The game is played with a traditional deck plus one joker. The joker is a wild card that can be used as an ace or to complete a straight, a flush, a straight flush, or a royal flush. Each player is dealt seven cards to arrange into two hands—a two-card hand and a five-card hand. As in standard poker, the highest two-card hand is two aces, and the highest five-card hand is a royal flush. The five-card hand *must* be higher than the two-card hand (if the two-card hand is a pair of sixes, for example, the five-card hand must be a pair of sevens or better). Any player's hand that is set incorrectly is an automatic lose. The object of the game is for both of the player's hands to rank higher than both of the banker's hands. Should one hand rank exactly the same as the banker's hand, this is a tie (called a "copy"), *and the banker wins all tie hands.* If the player wins one hand but loses the other, this is a "push," and no money changes hands. The house dealer or any player may be the banker. The bank is offered to each player, and each player may accept or pass. Winning hands are paid even money, less a 5% commission.

ROULETTE

Roulette is an extremely easy game to play, and it's really quite colorful and exciting to watch. The wheel spins, and the little ball bounces around, finally dropping into one of the slots, numbered 1 to 36, plus 0 and 00. You can bet on a single number, a combination of numbers, or red or black, odd or even. If you're lucky, you can win as much as 35 to 1 (see the table). The method of placing single-number bets, column bets, and others is fairly obvious. The dealer will be happy to show you how to "straddle" two or more numbers and make many other interesting betting combinations. Each player is given different-colored chips so that it's easy to follow the numbers you're on.

A number of typical bets are indicated by means of letters on the roulette layout depicted here. The winning odds for each of these sample bets are listed. These bets can be made on any corresponding combinations of numbers.

Roulette Chart Key	Odds	Type of Bet
		Straight Bets
A	35 to 1	*Straight-up:* All numbers, plus 0 and 00.
B	2 to 1	*Column Bet:* Pays off on any number in that horizontal column.
C	2 to 1	*First Dozen:* Pays off on any number 1 through 12. Same for second and third dozen.
D	Even Money	
		Combination Bets
E	17 to 1	*Split:* Pays off on 11 or 12.
F	11 to 1	Pays off on 28, 29, or 30.
G	8 to 1	*Corner:* Pays off on 17, 18, 20, or 21.
H	6 to 1	Pays off on 0, 00, 1, 2, or 3.
I	5 to 1	Pays off on 22, 23, 24, 25, 26, or 27.

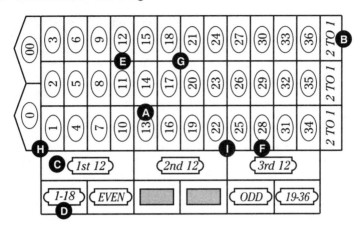

SLOT CLUBS

If you play slots or video poker, it definitely pays to join a slot club. These so-called clubs are designed to attract and keep customers in a given casino by providing incentives—meals, shows, discounts on rooms, gifts, tournament invitations, discounts at hotel shops, VIP treatment, and (more and more) cash rebates. Of course, your rewards are greater if you play just in one casino, but your mobility is limited.

When you join a slot club (inquire at the casino desk), you're given something that looks like a credit card which you must insert into an ATM-like device whenever you play. (Don't forget to retrieve your card when you leave the machine, as I always do—though that may work in your favor if someone comes along and plays the machine without removing it.) The device tracks your play and computes bonus points.

Which slot club should you join? Actually, you should join one at any casino where you play, since even the act of joining usually entitles you to some benefits. It's convenient to concentrate play where you're staying; if you play a great deal, a casino hotel's slot-club benefits may be a factor in your accommodations choice. One way to judge a slot club is by the quality of service when you enroll. Personnel should politely answer all your questions (for instance, is nickel play included, or is there a time limit for earning required points) and be able to tell you exactly how many points you need for various bonuses.

To maximize your slot-club profits and choose the club that's best for you is a complex business. If you want to get into it in depth, order a copy of Jeffrey Compton's *The Las Vegas Advisor Guide to Slot Clubs* ($9.95 plus shipping), which examines just about every facet of the situation (☎ **800/244-2224**). Compton gives high ratings to the clubs at Caesars Palace, the Desert Inn, the Mirage, Treasure Island, the Flamingo Hilton, the Rio, the Sahara, Sam's Town, the Four Queens, the Golden Nugget, and Lady Luck.

SPORTS BOOKS

Most of the larger hotels in Las Vegas have sports book operations—they look a lot like commodities-futures trading boards. In some, almost as large as theaters, you can sit comfortably and watch ball games, fights, and, at some casinos, horse races on huge TV screens. To add to your enjoyment, there's usually a deli/bar nearby that serves sandwiches, hot dogs, soft drinks, and beer. As a matter of fact, some of the best sandwiches in Las Vegas are served next to the sports books. Sports books take bets on virtually every sport.

2 The Casinos

Each casino has its own personality and special features. Generally, the more upscale the hotel, the more upscale the casino crowd, the swankiest precinct being the Desert Inn. Downtown casinos, with the exception of the plush Golden Nugget, tend to be more informal than Strip casinos. The following is a rundown of each, including exact gaming facilities:

BALLY'S LAS VEGAS   Bally's casino is one of the most cheerful on the Strip—a large (it's the size of a football field), brightly lit facility with lots of colorful signage. There's a Most Valuable Player Slot Club, offering members cash rebates, room discounts, free meals and show tickets, and invitations to special events, among other perks. The casino hosts frequent slot tournaments, and free gaming lessons are offered. Gaming facilities include a keno lounge, a state-of-the-art race and sports book, blackjack tables, craps, roulette, baccarat, minibaccarat, Caribbean stud (Bally's innovated this now popular Las Vegas game), pai gow, a Big Six wheel, Let-It-Ride tables, and 1,565 slot/video poker machines (with more to come). There are also blackjack tables and slot/video poker machines in Bally's Avenue Shoppes.

BARBARY COAST   The Barbary Coast has a cheerful 1890s-style casino ornately decorated with $2 million worth of gorgeous stained-glass skylights and signs, as well as immense crystal-dangling globe chandeliers over the gaming tables. It's worth stopping in just to take a look around when you're in the central "four corners" area of the Strip. The casino has a free Fun Club for slot players; participants earn points toward cash and prizes. Gaming facilities include a race and sports book, keno, blackjack tables, craps, roulette, minibaccarat, Let-It-Ride, pai gow poker, and 525 slot/video poker machines.

BINION'S HORSESHOE   The Horseshoe's famed 50,000-square-foot casino, a mecca for high rollers, claims the highest betting limits in Las Vegas on all games (probably in the entire world, according to a spokesperson). It offers single-deck blackjack and $2 minimums, 10-times odds on craps, and high progressive jackpots. I especially like the older part of the casino here, which—with its flocked wallpaper, gorgeous lighting fixtures, and gold-tasseled burgundy velvet drapes—looks like a turn-of-the-century Old West bordello. Gaming facilities include a keno lounge, race and sports book, a 500-seat bingo parlor, blackjack, craps, roulette, baccarat, minibaccarat, pai gow poker, Let-It-Ride, Caribbean stud, Big Six, and 1,639 slot and video poker machines. Binion's is located downtown at 128 E. Fremont St. between Casino Center Boulevard and First Street.

   While you're visiting Binion's casino, be sure to see the display of $1 million (comprised of 100 $10,000 bills) encased in a gold horseshoe-shaped vault. If you'd like a photograph of yourself with all that moolah, you can get one taken free from 4pm to midnight daily.

CAESARS PALACE   Caesars has two interconnecting deluxe gaming rooms—the high-end **Forum Casino** (with the action under crystal-fringed black domes) and the slightly more casual **Olympic Casino.** A notable facility in the latter is the state-of-the-art Race and Sports Book, with huge electronic display boards and giant video

The World's Series—Las Vegas Style

Binion's Horseshoe is internationally known as the home of the World Series of Poker. It was "Nick the Greek" Dondolos who first approached Benny Binion in 1949 with the idea for a high-stakes poker marathon between top players. Binion agreed, with the stipulation that the game be open to public viewing. The competition, between Dondolos and the legendary Johnny Moss, lasted five months with breaks only for sleep. Moss ultimately won about $2 million. As Dondolos lost his last pot, he rose from his chair, bowed politely, and said, "Mr. Moss, I have to let you go."

In 1970, Binion decided to re-create the battle of poker giants, which evolved into the annual World Series of Poker. Johnny Moss won the first year, and went on to snag the championship again in 1971 and 1974. Thomas "Amarillo Slim" Preston won the event in 1972 and popularized it on the talk-show circuit. Last year, there were more than 4,000 entrants from 22 countries, and total winnings were in excess of $11 million (more than $93 million in prize money has been distributed since the tournament began). A Poker Hall of Fame wall in the casino honors great players (running the gamut from Edmond Hugh, who created the rules, to Wild Bill Hickok).

screens. (Caesars pioneered computer-generated wagering data that can be communicated in less than half a second and sophisticated satellite equipment that can pick up virtually any broadcast sporting event in the world.) The domed VIP slot arena of the Forum Casino (minimum bet is $5, but you can wager up to $1,500 on a single pull!) is a plush, crystal-chandeliered precinct with seating in roomy adjustable chairs. Slot players can accumulate bonus points toward cash back, gifts, gratis show tickets, meals, and rooms by joining the Emperors Club. Club membership also lets you in on grand-prize drawings, tournaments, and parties. Most upscale of Caesars' gaming rooms is the intimate European-style casino adjoining the **Palace Court** restaurant. Total facilities in all three casinos contain craps tables, blackjack, roulette, baccarat, minibaccarat, Let-It-Ride, Caribbean stud, pai gow poker, two Big Six wheels, more than 2,000 slot/video poker machines, and a keno lounge.

CALIFORNIA HOTEL/CASINO The California caters to a largely Hawaiian clientele, hence, dealers in its attractive marble and crystal-chandeliered casino wear colorful aloha shirts. This friendly facility actually provides sofas and armchairs in the casino area—an unheard-of luxury in this town. Players can join the Cal Slot Club and amass points toward gifts and cash prizes or participate in daily slot tournaments. Gaming facilities include a keno lounge, sports book, blackjack tables, craps, roulette, minibaccarat, pai gow poker, Let-It-Ride, Caribbean stud, and over 1,000 slot and video poker machines.

CIRCUS CIRCUS This vast property has three full-size casinos that, combined, comprise one of the largest gaming operations in Nevada (more than 100,000 square feet). The main casino is the one entered via the front door off the Strip. And there are additional gaming facilities in the Circus Circus Main Tower and Skyrise buildings. The Ringmaster Players Club offers slot/video poker and table players the opportunity to earn points redeemable for cash, discounted rooms and meals, and other benefits. Circus Bucks progressive slot machines here build from a jackpot base of $500,000, which players can win on a $2 pull. Gaming facilities include a

10,000-square-foot race and sports book with 30 video monitors ranging from 13 to 52 inches, 40-seat and 89-seat keno lounges, poker tables, blackjack, craps, roulette, a Big Six wheel, Let-It-Ride, pai gow poker, dice, Caribbean stud poker, and 2,400 slot and video poker machines.

DESERT INN   This is one of my favorite Las Vegas casinos—a low-key setting typical of the hotel's country-club elegance. And it is being revamped at this writing as the hotel strives to achieve an even more refined, upscale profile. Crystal chandeliers here replace the usual neon glitz, and gaming tables are comfortably spaced. The ambience is reminiscent of intimate European gaming houses. Since there are fewer slot machines here than at most major casinos, there's less noise in ringing bells and clinking coins. Most table games have a $5 minimum. Facilities include a race and sports book, poker, blackjack, Spanish 21 (like blackjack, but there are no 10s in the deck), craps, pai gow, pai gow poker, Let-It-Ride, Caribbean stud, minibaccarat, baccarat, roulette, and 500 slot/video poker machines. A sophisticated casino lounge is a plus.

EL CORTEZ   This friendly Downtown casino features frequent big-prize drawings (up to $50,000) based on your Social Security number. It's also popular for low limits (10¢ roulette and 25¢ craps). Gaming facilities include a race and sports book, keno, blackjack, craps, roulette, minibaccarat, and 1,500 slot/video poker machines.

EXCALIBUR   As you might expect, the Excalibur casino is replete with suits of armor, stained-glass panels, knights, dragons, and velvet and satin heraldic banners, with gaming action taking place beneath vast iron and gold chandeliers fit for a medieval castle fortress. A popular feature here is Circus Bucks—a progressive slot machine that builds from a jackpot base of $500,000; players can win on a $3 pull. Excalibur's 100,000-plus square feet of gaming facilities also include a race and sports book, a keno lounge, a poker room, blackjack, minibaccarat, Caribbean stud, Let-It-Ride, casino war (like the game you played as a kid), craps, roulette, pai gow poker, Big Six, and 2,630 slot/video poker machines. A nonsmoking area is a plus.

FITZGERALDS   At this 47,000-square-foot Irish-themed casino, guests are greeted by Mr. O'Lucky (a costumed leprechaun who roams the casino), and they can rub pieces of the actual Blarney stone from County Cork for good luck. Blackjack, craps, and keno tournaments are frequent events here. Slot machines that paid back over 100% the previous week are marked with a Mr. Lucky sign. The Fitzgerald Card offers slot players gifts, meals, and other perks for accumulated points. Several slot machines have cars as prizes, fun books provide two-for-one gaming coupons, and there are $1 minimum blackjack tables. Facilities include a sports book, a keno lounge, blackjack, craps, Let-It-Ride, roulette, Spanish 21 (see the Desert Inn above), "21" Superbucks, Caribbean stud, and 1,100 slot and video poker machines.

FLAMINGO HILTON   The Flamingo's 70,000-square-foot, Caribbean-themed casino, brilliantly lit by pink and orange neon lights that mirror its landmark facade, has "faux" skylights overhead through which chinks of painted sky are visible. Actual daylight streams in as well from windows and glass doorways on the Strip.

Impressions

Stilled forever is the click of the roulette wheel, the rattle of dice, and the swish of cards.
                                              —Short-sighted editorial in the *Nevada State Journal*
                                                                            after gambling was outlawed in 1910

There are slots here offering Cadillacs and Continentals as jackpots. Players Club slot bettors qualify for free meals, shows, rooms, and other play-based incentives. Free gaming lessons are offered weekdays. Gaming facilities include a keno lounge, a state-of-the-art race and sports book, poker room, Caribbean stud, blackjack, Let-It-Ride, "double down" poker, craps, roulette, minibaccarat, pai gow poker, *sic bo,* Big Six, and 2,100 slot/video poker machines.

FOUR QUEENS   The Four Queens' casino is pleasant and cheerful looking, with Mardi Gras-motif carpeting, light beige slot machines, and gaming tables under turn-of-the-century-style globe chandeliers. The facility boasts the world's largest slot machine (more than 9 feet high and almost 20 feet long; six people can play it at one time!) and the world's largest blackjack table (it seats 12 players). The Reel Winners Club offers slot players bonus points toward cash rebates. Slot, blackjack, and craps tournaments are frequent events, and there are major poker tournaments every January and September. The casino also offers exciting multiple-action blackjack (it's like playing three hands at once with separate wagers on each). Gaming facilities include a keno lounge, sports book, blackjack, craps, roulette, pai gow poker, Caribbean stud, Let-It-Ride, and 1,081 slot/video poker machines.

GOLDEN NUGGET   This luxurious Downtown resort has a gorgeous casino reminiscent of the opulent gaming houses of Europe. Tables are located beneath stained-glass panels, and neon glitz is replaced by tivoli lighting. Slot players can earn bonus points toward complimentary rooms, meals, shows, and gifts by joining the 24 Karat Club. Gaming facilities include an attractive and comfortable keno lounge, a race and sports book, blackjack ($1 minimum bet), craps, roulette, baccarat, pai gow, pai gow poker, red dog, Big Six, and 1,136 slot/video poker machines.

HARD ROCK HOTEL AND CASINO   The Hard Rock's cheerful 30,000-square-foot circular casino, where you can place your bets to a high-energy beat, is a big favorite with the under-35 crowd. Note the chandelier at the entrance made from 32 gold saxophones. Roulette tables are piano-shaped, slot machines have guitar-neck handles, win-a-Harley slots are equipped with motorcycle seats for players, and Elton John's bejeweled piano overlooks another bank of slots. Most original, however, is a bank of slots that make gambling an act of charity; environmentally committed owner Peter Morton (the Hard Rock's motto is "Save the Planet") donates profits from specified slots to organizations dedicated to saving the rain forests. A Back Stage Pass allows patrons to rack up discounts on meals, lodging, and gift shop items while playing slots and table games. The race and sports book here provides comfortable seating in leather-upholstered reclining armchairs. Gaming facilities (with selected nonsmoking tables) include blackjack, roulette, craps, Caribbean stud, minibaccarat, Let-It-Ride, pai gow poker, and 802 slot/video poker machines.

HARRAH'S   At this writing, Harrah's riverboat-motif casino is undergoing a $150-million renovation and expansion to 95,300 square feet. Its new theme will be "Mardi Gras/Carnaval." Harrah's is the scene of numerous year-round slot and keno tournaments offering big prizes.

A special feature is the zany balloon-festooned Party Pit (in action daily from noon to 4pm), where rock music is played, dealers sing and dance, and players get prizes and party favors. If you win a slot jackpot at Harrah's, entertainers (women dressed as riverboat belles, men as gamblers or Huck Finn) come by, play the song "Celebration," take your picture with a Polaroid camera, and present you with a medal and a package of "lucky dust." Slot and table game players can earn bonus points toward

Impressions

*I am, after all, the best hold 'em player alive. I'm forced to play this tournament, you
understand, to demonstrate this fact.*

—Casino owner Bob Stupak on why he entered
Binion's Horseshoe World Series of Poker

complimentary rooms, meals, and show tickets by acquiring a Harrah's Gold Card
in the casino. Facilities include a sports book, keno lounge, poker room, blackjack,
craps, roulette, minibaccarat, pai gow poker, red dog, casino war (in the Party Pit),
Let-It-Ride, Big Six, and 2,220 slot and video poker machines. There are nonsmoking
areas, and free gaming lessons are offered weekdays.

IMPERIAL PALACE   The 75,000-square-foot casino here reflects the hotel's
pagoda-roofed Asian exterior with a dragon-motif ceiling and giant wind-chime
chandeliers. Visitors can get free Scratch Slotto cards for prizes up to $5,000 in cash
(cards and free passes to the auto collection are distributed on the sidewalk out front).
A gaming school offers lessons in craps and blackjack, and slots tournaments take
place daily. The Imperial Palace boasts a 230-seat race and sports book, attractively
decorated with oil murals of sporting events; the room is tiered like a grandstand, and
every seat has its own color monitor. Other gaming facilities include a keno lounge,
blackjack, craps, roulette, minibaccarat, pai gow poker, Caribbean stud, Big Six, and
2,000 slot/video poker machines.

JACKIE GAUGHAN'S PLAZA HOTEL/CASINO   The Plaza has a lively and
attractive crystal-chandeliered casino where gaming facilities include a keno lounge
(featuring double keno), race and sports book, blackjack, craps, roulette, baccarat,
Caribbean stud, pai gow poker, poker, pan, Let-It-Ride, and 1,572 slot/video poker
machines. Cautious bettors will appreciate the $1 blackjack tables and penny slots
here.

LADY LUCK   I like to gamble at the Lady Luck casino, a friendly Downtown
facility. Dazzling neon signs, marquee lights, and balloons attached to slot machines
make for a festive setting. The Mad Money Slot Club offers scrip, cash, meals,
accommodations, and prizes as incentives. Liberal game rules are attractive to gamblers. You can play "fast action hold 'em" here—a combination of 21, poker, and pai
gow poker. Other gaming facilities include a keno lounge, blackjack, craps, roulette,
minibaccarat, pai gow poker, and 800 slot/video poker machines.

LAS VEGAS HILTON   Austrian crystal chandeliers make the Hilton's 67,000-
square-foot casino one of the city's most elegant. Especially plush are the vast 6,900-
square-foot baccarat room—with gorgeous crystal chandeliers, silk-covered walls, and
velvet-upholstered furnishings—and the VIP slot area where personnel are attired in
tuxedos. Both areas offer gracious service to players. Because so many conventioneers stay here, the crowd is more changeable than at most casinos. The Hilton's Race
and Sports SuperBook is, at 30,500 square feet, the world's largest race and sports
book facility. It, too, is a luxurious precinct equipped with the most advanced
audio, video, and computer technology available, including 46 TV monitors, some
as large as 15 feet across. In fact, its video wall is second in size only to NASA's. By
joining Club Magic, a slot club, you can amass bonus points toward cash prizes, gifts,
and complimentary rooms, meals, and show tickets. In addition to the above, gaming facilities include a keno lounge, blackjack, craps, roulette, baccarat, pai gow, pai
gow poker, Caribbean stud, Big Six, and 1,130 slot/video poker machines.

Note: When STAR TREK: *The Experience* opens shortly at the Hilton, its gateway will be the futuristic new 22,000-square-foot Spacequest Casino. Overhead, "space windows," will offer a constantly changing vista of planets, stars, and space ships; the casino's ceiling will appear to separate to make way for a projectile launch; and stars will glitter brightly in the night sky.

LUXOR LAS VEGAS   This massive 100,000-square-foot casino—with red ceiling, carpeting, and gaming tables—evokes ancient Egypt with reproductions of artifacts and hieroglyphics found in the tombs and temples of Luxor and Karnak. Larger-than-life gold statues represent tomb guardians. In a variation on a horse race game, Egyptian boats race around a pyramid. And King Tut heads and sphinxes adorn slot areas. There's a nonsmoking slot area. The Gold Chamber Club offers rewards of cash, merchandise, meals, and special services to slot and table players. And sports action unfolds on 17 large-screen TVs and 128 personalized monitors in Luxor's race and sports book. Additional gaming facilities include a keno lounge, blackjack, craps, roulette, poker, baccarat, minibaccarat, pai gow, Big Six, Caribbean stud, and 2,500 slot/video poker machines.

MGM GRAND   The world's largest casino (171,500 square feet—that's bigger than Yankee Stadium!) is divided into four themed areas: Emerald City includes a seven-story replica of the wizard's castle, a yellow-brick road, a 63-color rainbow, and a cast of robotic Oz characters. Hollywood is glitzy, with red and yellow marquee lights; it features a high-roller slot area with machines that operate on coins valued at $100 and $500! The sports casino houses a big poker room, a state-of-the-art race and sports book, and the Turf Club Lounge. And the French Riviera–themed Monte Carlo casino has a luxurious marble-columned and gold-draped private high-end gaming area. Carousels of progressive slots unique to the MGM Grand include Majestic Lions high-frequency $1 slot machines that pay out more than $1 million daily and Lion's Share $1 slots capable of jackpots exceeding $1 million each at any time. And since Chrysler is a resort sponsor, there are several win-a-car slots. The MGM Grand Director's Club offers guests prizes ranging from complimentaries and gifts to cash rebates. Additional gaming facilities include a keno lounge, blackjack, craps, roulette, baccarat, minibaccarat, pai gow, pai gow poker, Caribbean stud, Let-It-Ride, Casino War, Big Six, and 3,500 slot/video poker machines.

MAXIM   This friendly, but dimly lit, 25,000-square-foot casino presents plaques to big slot winners. Its slot machines offer a red Grand Cherokee Laredo Jeep as a prize. Pick up a fun book here for a free $1,000 slot pull. Gaming facilities include a keno lounge, sports book, blackjack, craps, roulette, Caribbean stud, Let-It-Ride, pai gow poker, and 848 slot/video poker machines.

THE MIRAGE   Entered via a tropical rain forest, this 95,400-square-foot casino is designed to resemble a Polynesian village with gaming areas under separate roofs to create a more intimate ambience. Facilities include a separate poker room and a plush European-style *salon privé* for high rollers at baccarat, blackjack, and roulette; an elegant dining room serves catered meals to gamblers there. Slot players can join the Club Mirage and work toward bonus points for cash rebates, special room rates, complimentary meals and/or show tickets, and other benefits. The elaborate race and sports book offers theater stereo sound and a movie theater-size screen. Other gaming facilities here: a keno lounge, over 75 blackjack tables, craps, roulette, baccarat, minibaccarat, pai gow, pai gow poker, Big Six, and more than 2,250 slot and video poker machines. It's one of the most pleasant, and popular, casinos in town.

MONTE CARLO   With 90,000 square feet of gaming space designed to suggest the Monaco's opulent Place du Casino, this facility is replete with fanciful arches, crystal-chandeliered domes (there's much more crystal than neon here), and fleur-de-lis carpeting on gleaming marble floors. Particularly posh is the high-end slot area, under a magnificent stained-glass ceiling. There's a large and comfortable race and sports book area, with its own cocktail lounge. And you can win a BMW sports car at a bank of 25¢ "Rich and Famous" slots. The Club Monte Carlo offers slot players cash rebates, merchandise, rooms, and meals for accumulated points. Other gaming facilities include a keno lounge, bingo room, poker room, blackjack, craps, roulette, baccarat, minibaccarat, Let-It-Ride, Caribbean stud, pai gow, pai gow poker, Big Six, and 2,200 slot and video poker machines.

THE RIO   This Brazilian-themed resort's 85,000-square-foot casino is aglitter with neon and marquee lights. Rio Rita—a Carmen Miranda look-alike in a towering fruit-covered hat—presides over the casino from a thatched hut filled with colorful stuffed parrots. She greets visitors, congratulates winners, announces contests and promotions, and runs frequent slot, craps, and blackjack tournaments. In an area called Jackpot Jungle, slot machines amid lush foliage and live palms are equipped with TV monitors that present old movies and in-house information while you play. And in the high-end slot area ($5 to $100 a pull), guests enjoy a private lounge and gratis champagne. There are nonsmoking slot and gaming table areas. Facilities include a keno lounge, race and sports book, blackjack, craps, roulette, baccarat, minibaccarat, pai gow, Caribbean stud, survival dice, Let-It-Ride, Big Six, and 2,200 slot and video poker machines.

THE RIVIERA   The Riviera's 100,000-square-foot casino—one of the largest in the world—is also one of the most attractive on the Strip. A wall of windows lets daylight stream in (most unusual), and the gaming tables are situated beneath gleaming brass arches lit by recessed pink neon tubing. The casino's Slot and Gold (seniors) clubs allow slot players to earn bonus points toward free meals, rooms, and show tickets. The race and sports book here offers individual monitors at each of its 250 seats, and this is one of the few places in town where you can play the ancient Chinese game of *sic bo* (a fast-paced dice game resembling craps). Additional facilities include a large keno parlor, blackjack, craps, roulette, baccarat, pai gow poker, Caribbean stud, Let-It-Ride, Big Six, and more than 1,200 slot/video poker machines.

THE SAHARA   In keeping with the hotel's desert theme, this 56,275-square-foot casino is watched over by statues of turbaned soldiers with scimitars at the ready. Not to worry, though; the dealers are friendly. (Actually, the casino's appearance may change when the Sahara completes a massive Moroccan-motif renovation, currently in progress.) The Sahara runs frequent slot tournaments and other events, and its slot club, Club Sahara, offers cash rebates and other perks. Gaming facilities include a race and sports book, keno lounge, blackjack, craps, roulette, poker, Let-It-Ride, pai gow poker, Caribbean stud, a Big Six wheel, and more than 1,000 slot/video poker machines. *Note:* This is the only Strip casino that offers pan, a card game.

SAM BOYD'S FREMONT HOTEL & CASINO   This 32,000-square-foot casino offers a relaxed atmosphere and low gambling limits ($2 blackjack, 25¢ roulette). Just

Impressions

If you aim to leave Las Vegas with a small fortune, go there with a large one.
                                                        —Anonymous American saying

50¢ could win you a Cadillac or Ford Mustang here, plus a progressive cash jackpot. Casino guests can accumulate bonus points redeemable toward cash by joining the Five Star Slot Club, and take part in frequent slot and keno tournaments. Gaming facilities include two keno lounges, a race and sports book, blackjack, craps, roulette, Caribbean stud, Let-It-Ride, pai gow poker, and 1,100 slot/video poker machines.

SAM'S TOWN   In its three immense floors (153,083 square feet!) of gaming action, Sam Town's maintains the friendly, just-folks ambience that characterizes the entire property. The casino is adorned with Old West paraphernalia (horseshoes, Winchester rifles, holsters, and saddlebags) and country music plays nonstop. Sam's Town claims its friendliness extends to looser slots. The casino gives away a house (with a car and $10,000 in cash) every three months and offers 10-times odds on craps and single-deck blackjack. Join the Sam's Town Slot Club to earn points towards rooms, meals, and cash rebates. Free gaming lessons are offered weekdays from 11am to 4pm, poker lessons at other times. Gaming facilities include a race and sports book with more than 60 monitors, 2 keno lounges, a 590-seat bingo parlor, blackjack, craps, roulette, poker, pai gow poker, Caribbean stud, and 2,800 slot/video poker machines (including a nonsmoking slot area).

SHOWBOAT   The Showboat's casino, recently renovated, has a Mardi Gras/Bourbon Street theme. Gorgeous flower murals and trellised arches laced with flowery vines embellish the Showboat's enormous 24-hour bingo parlor—a facility also noted for high payouts. Slot players can join a club to accumulate bonus points toward free meals, rooms, gifts, and cash prizes. And if you're traveling with kids ages two to seven, you can leave them at an in-house babysitting facility free for 3 hours while you gamble. Older kids can be dropped at the Showboat's 106-lane bowling center. In addition to bingo, gaming facilities include a keno lounge, race and sports book, blackjack (including single deck "21"), craps, roulette, Let-It-Ride, pai gow, Caribbean stud, and over 1,000 slot and video poker machines.

THE STARDUST   Always mobbed, this popular casino features 90,000 square feet of lively gaming action, including a 250-seat race and sports book with a sophisticated satellite system and more than 50 TV monitors airing sporting events and horse racing results around the clock. Adjacent to it is a sports handicapper's library offering comprehensive statistical information on current sporting events. Stardust Slot Club members win cash rebates, with credit piling up even on nickel machines; free rooms, shows, meals, and invitations to special events are also possible bonuses. Other gaming facilities: a large, well-lit keno lounge, a poker room, an elegant baccarat lounge, blackjack, craps, roulette, minibaccarat, pai gow poker, Caribbean stud, Let-It-Ride, Big Six, and over 2,000 slot and video poker machines. If you're a novice, avail yourself of gratis gaming lessons.

THE STRATOSPHERE   The Stratosphere's 100,000-square-foot gaming center, under a painted sky, is comprised of three themed areas: The Pavilion of the World features murals and bas reliefs of international landmarks; the festive Pavilion of Fun is themed around a turn-of-the-century circus; and the Pavilion of Imagination celebrates the history of art, flight, space travel, inventions, and so on. Be sure to see the whimsical Rotunda lined with enlarged travel postcards that are fun to read.

There's a test area for new slot games, a Harley slot area with motorcycle-seat stools, and a high-roller slot room ($5 minimum bet) where chairs move up and down and can vibrate to give you a back massage while you play. The Stratosphere Players Club sponsors frequent tournaments, and its members can earn points towards gifts, VIP perks, discounted room rates, meals, and cash rebates. Other facilities include a keno lounge, a sports book, bingo, blackjack, craps, roulette, poker, minibaccarat, pai gow, pai gow poker, Caribbean stud, Let-It-Ride, Big Six, and 2,494 slot and video poker machines.

TREASURE ISLAND   Treasure Island's huge casino is one of the most elegant in Las Vegas. It is, however, highly themed. Niches—amid the rough-hewn oak beams of a woven-rattan ceiling—contain treasure chests overflowing with pirate loot, and the carpeting is also littered with buccaneer booty. Especially luxurious are a high-limit baccarat/blackjack area (where players enjoy a buffet of hot hors d'oeuvres) and a high-limit slot area. Slot club members can earn meals, services, show tickets, and cash rebates. There are nonsmoking gaming tables in each pit. A race and sports book boasts state-of-the-art electronic information boards and TV monitors at every seat as well as numerous large-screen monitors. Other facilities include a keno lounge, over 50 blackjack tables, craps, roulette, poker, minibaccarat, pai gow, pai gow poker, Caribbean stud, Let-It-Ride, Big Six, and over 2,000 slot and video poker machines.

TROPICANA   The Trop casino is simply gorgeous, with gaming tables situated beneath a massive stained-glass archway and art nouveau lighting fixtures. In summer it offers something totally unique—swim-up blackjack tables located in the hotel's stunning 5-acre tropical garden and pool area. Slot and table game players can earn bonus points toward rooms, shows, and meals by obtaining an Island Winners Club card in the casino. A luxurious high-end slot area has machines that take up to $100 on a single pull. Numerous tournaments take place here, and free gaming lessons are offered weekdays. Facilities include a sports book, keno lounge, poker room, blackjack, craps, roulette, baccarat, pai gow poker, Let-It-Ride, Caribbean stud, minibaccarat, pai gow, and 1600 slot and video poker machines.

WESTWARD HO HOTEL & CASINO   This small but centrally located strip casino hosts many slot tournaments, and slot players who obtain Preferred Customer cards can amass credits toward complimentary rooms, meals, and shows, among other benefits. Gaming facilities include blackjack, craps, roulette, Big Six, and 1,000 slot/video poker machines.

9

Las Vegas Shopping

Unless you're looking for souvenir decks of cards, styrofoam dice, and miniature slot machines, Las Vegas is not exactly a shopping mecca. It does, however, have several noteworthy malls that can amply supply the basics. And many hotels also offer comprehensive, and sometimes highly themed, shopping arcades, most notably Caesars Palace (details below).

1 The Malls

Boulevard Mall

3528 S. Maryland Pkwy., between Twain Ave. and Desert Inn Rd. ☎ **702/ 732-8949.** Mon–Fri 10am–9pm, Sat 10am–8pm, Sun 11am–5pm.

The Boulevard's 144-plus stores and restaurants are arranged in arcade fashion on a single floor occupying 1.2 million square feet. Geared to the average consumer (not the carriage trade), it has anchors like Sears, JCPenney, Woolworth, Macy's, Dillard's, and Marshalls. Other notables include The Disney Store, The Nature Company, a 23,000-square-foot Good Guys (electronics), The Gap, Gap Kids, The Limited, Victoria's Secret, Colorado (for outdoor clothing and gear), Howard & Phil's Western Wear, and African & World Imports. There's a wide variety of shops offering moderately priced shoes and clothing for the entire family, books and gifts, jewelry, and home furnishings, plus over a dozen fast-food eateries. In short, you can find just about anything you need here. There's free valet parking.

Fashion Show Mall

3200 Las Vegas Blvd. S., at the corner of Spring Mountain Rd. ☎ **702/ 369-8382.** Mon–Fri 10am–9pm, Sat 10am–7pm, Sun noon–6pm.

This luxurious and centrally located mall—one of the city's largest—opened in 1981 to great hoopla. Designers Adolfo, Geoffrey Beene, Bill Blass, Bob Mackie, and Pauline Trigere were all on hand to display their fashion interpretations of the "Las Vegas look."

The mall comprises more than 130 shops, restaurants, and services. It is anchored by Neiman-Marcus, Saks Fifth Avenue, Macy's, Robinsons-May, and Dillard's. Other notable tenants: Abercrombie & Fitch, The Disney Store, The Walt Disney Gallery, The Discovery Channel Store, Lillie Rubin (upscale women's clothing), The Gap, Benetton, Uomo, Banana Republic, Victoria's Secret, Caché, Williams-Sonoma Grand Cuisine, The Body Shop, Mondi (upscale women's clothing), Waldenbooks, Louis Vuitton, and Sharper Image. There are several card and book shops, a wide selection of apparel stores for the whole family (including large sizes and petites), nine jewelers, 21 shoe stores, and gift and specialty shops. There are dozens of eating places (see chapter 6 for specifics). Valet parking is available, and you can even arrange to have your car hand washed while you shop.

Galleria at Sunset

1300 W. Sunset Rd., at Stephanie St. just off I-515 in nearby Henderson. ☎ **702/434-0202.** Mon–Sat 10am–9pm, Sun 11am–6pm.

This upscale 1 million-square-foot shopping center, nine miles southeast of downtown Las Vegas, opened in 1996, with performing Disney characters on hand to welcome shoppers and a nighttime display of fireworks. The mall has a southwestern motif, evidenced in the use of terra-cotta stone, interior landscaping, cascading fountains, and skylights; eight 20-foot hand-carved pillars flank the main entrance. Anchored by four department stores—Dillard's, JCPenney, Mervyn's California, and Robinsons-May—the Galleria's 110 emporia include branches of The Disney Store, The Gap/Gap Kids/Baby Gap, The Limited and The Limited Too, Eddie Bauer, Miller's Outpost, Ann Taylor, bebe, Caché, Compagnie International, Lane Bryant, Lerner New York, Victoria's Secret, The Body Shop, B. Dalton, and Sam Goody. In addition to shoes and clothing for the entire family, you'll find electronics, eyewear, gifts, books, home furnishings, jewelry, and luggage here. Dining facilities include an extensive food court and two restaurants.

The Meadows

4300 Meadows Lane, at the intersection of Valley View and U.S. 95. ☎ **702/878-4849.** Mon–Fri from 10am to 9pm, Sat and Sun until 6pm.

Another immense mall, the Meadows comprises 144 shops, services, and eateries, anchored by four department stores—Macy's, Dillard's, Sears, and JCPenney. In addition, there are 15 shoe stores, a full array of apparel for the entire family (including maternity wear, petites, and large sizes), an extensive food court, and shops purveying toys, books, CDs and tapes, luggage, gifts, jewelry, home furnishings (The Bombay Company, among others), accessories, and so on. Fountains and trees enhance the Meadows' ultramodern, high-ceilinged interior, and a 1995 renovation added comfortable conversation/seating areas and made the mall lighter and brighter. It is divided into five courts, one centered on a turn-of-the-century carousel (a plus for kids). A natural history-themed court has a "desert fossil" floor, and an entertainment court is the setting for occasional live musical and dramatic performances. You can rent strollers at the Customer Service Center.

2 Factory Outlets

Las Vegas has two big factory outlets just a few miles past the southern end of the Strip. If you don't have a car, you can take a no. 301 CAT bus from anywhere on the Strip and change at Vacation Village to a no. 303.

Belz Factory Outlet World

7400 Las Vegas Blvd. S., at Warm Springs Rd. ☎ **702/896-5599.** Mon–Sat 10am–9pm, Sun 10am–6pm.

Belz houses 137 air-conditioned outlets, including a few dozen clothing stores and shoe stores. It offers an immense range of merchandise at savings up to 75% off retail prices. Among other emporia, you'll find Adolfo II, Casual Corner, Levi's, Nike, Dress Barn, Oshkosh B'Gosh, Leggs/Hanes/Bali, Esprit, Aileen, Bugle Boy, Carters,

Reebok, Spiegel, Guess Classics, Oneida, Springmaid, We're Entertainment (Disney and Warner Bros.), Bose (electronics), Danskin, Van Heusen, Burlington, Royal Doulton, Lennox (china), Waterford (crystal), and Geoffrey Beene here. And since this is Las Vegas, laser shows are presented every hour on the hour. At this writing, 65 new stores are about to open.

Factory Stores of America

9155 Las Vegas Blvd., at Serene St. ☎ **702/897-9090.** Mon–Sat 10am–8pm, Sun 10am–6pm.

A 30-acre open-air mall with Spanish-style architecture, this is the only outlet center in the country with a casino bar/lounge on its premises. Its 51 stores include Corning/Revere, Izod, Mikasa, American Tourister, Van Heusen, B.U.M. Equipment, Spiegel, London Fog, VF (sportswear), Book Warehouse, Geoffrey Beene, and Adolfo II. Come here for clothing, housewares, shoes, china, and much, much more.

3 Hotel Shopping Arcades

Just about every Las Vegas hotel offers some shopping opportunities. The following have the most extensive arcades. *Note:* The Forum Shops at Caesars—as much a sightseeing attraction as a shopping arcade—are in the must-see category.

BALLY'S Bally's Avenue Shoppes number around 20 emporia offering pro-team sports apparel, toys, clothing (men's, women's, and children's), logo items, gourmet chocolates, liquor, jewelry, nuts and dried fruit, flowers, handbags, and T-shirts. In addition, there are several gift shops, three restaurants, art galleries, and a poolwear shop. There are blackjack tables and slot and video poker machines right in the mall, as well as a race and sports book. You can dispatch the kids to a video arcade here while you shop.

CAESARS PALACE Since 1978, Caesars has had an impressive arcade of shops called the Appian Way. Highlighted by an immense white Carrara-marble replica of Michelangelo's *David* standing more than 18 feet high, its shops include the aptly named Galerie Michelangelo (original and limited-edition artworks), jewelers (including branches of Ciro and Cartier), a logo merchandise shop, and several shops for upscale men's and women's clothing. All in all, a respectable grouping of hotel shops, and an expansion is in the works.

But in the hotel's tradition of constantly surpassing itself, in 1992 Caesars inaugurated the fabulous Forum Shops—an independently operated 250,000-square-foot Rodeo-Drive-meets-the-Roman-Empire affair complete with a 48-foot triumphal arch entranceway, a painted Mediterranean sky that changes as the day progresses from rosy-tinted dawn to twinkling evening stars, acres of marble, lofty scagliola Corinthian columns with gold capitals, and a welcoming Goddess of Fortune under a central dome. Its architecture and sculpture span a period from 300 B.C. to A.D. 1700. Storefront facades—some topped with statues of Roman senators—resemble a classical Italian streetscape, with archways, piazzas, ornate fountains, and a barrel-vaulted ceiling. The "center of town" is the magnificent domed Fountain of the Gods, where Jupiter rules from his mountaintop surrounded by Pegasus, Mars, Venus, Neptune, and Diana. And at the Festival Fountain, seemingly immovable "marble" animatronic statues of Bacchus (slightly in his cups), a lyre-playing Apollo, Plutus, and Venus come to life for a seven-minute revel with dancing waters and high-tech laser-light effects. The shows take place every hour on the hour.

More than 70 prestigious emporia here include Louis Vuitton, Plaza Escada, Bernini, Christian Dior, A/X Armani Exchange, bebe, Caché, Gucci, Ann Taylor, and Gianni Versace, along with many other clothing, shoe, and accessory shops.

Other notables include: a Warner Brothers Studio Store (a sign at the exit reads THATIUS FINITUS FOLKUS), The Disney Store, Kids Kastle (beautiful children's clothing and toys), Rose of Sharon (classy styles for large-size women), Sports Logo (buy a basketball signed by Michael Jordan for $695!), Field of Dreams (more autographed sports memorabilia), Museum Company (reproductions ranging from 16th-century hand-painted Turkish boxes to ancient Egyptian scarab necklaces), West of Santa Fe (western wear and Native American jewelry and crafts), Antiquities (neon Shell gas signs, 1950s malt machines, Americana; sometimes "Elvis" is on hand), Endangered Species Store (ecology-themed merchandise), Brookstone (one-of-a-kind items from garden tools to sports paraphernalia), and Victoria's Secret. There's much more—including jewelry shops and art galleries.

And at this writing, a 283,000-square-foot expansion, including 37 stores and two new restaurants, is nearing completion. New residents will include FAO Schwartz, Fendi, Polo, NikeTown, a Virgin Records megastore, and Wolfgang Puck's Asian Cafe. The centerpiece of the new area will be a Roman Great Hall of heroic proportions, featuring a dramatic high-tech interactive attraction called "Atlantis."

While you shop, send the kids downstairs for spine-tingling Motion-Simulator Cinema Rides in 3-D. Four 5-minute shows simulate a flight into outer space to destroy a runaway nuclear missile, a submarine race through the ancient ruins of Atlantis, a bicycle ride through a haunted graveyard, and a roller-coaster adventure. (Price is $6 for one film, $8 for a double feature. Children must be at least 42 inches high.)

Dining choices range from a pastrami on rye at the Stage Deli, to a thick, juicy steak at The Palm, to Wolfgang Puck's sublime Spago creations. Several Forum Shops restaurants are described in chapter 6.

The shops are open Sunday to Thursday from 10am to 11pm, Friday and Saturday 10am to midnight. An automated walkway transports people from the Strip to the shopping complex. Heralded by a marble temple housing four golden horses and a charioteer, it is flanked by flaming torchiers and fronted by a waterfall cascading over a bas-relief of the god Neptune—you can't miss it! Often a gladiator with sword and shield is there to greet you at the other end. Valet parking is available.

CIRCUS CIRCUS   About 15 on-premises shops offer a wide selection of gifts and sundries, logo items, toys and games, jewelry, liquor, resort apparel for the entire family, T-shirts, homemade fudge/candy/soft ice cream, and, fittingly, clown dolls and puppets. At Amazing Pictures you can have your photo taken as a pinup girl, muscle man, or whatever else your fantasy dictates. There are additional shops in Grand Slam Canyon, the hotel's amusement park.

EXCALIBUR   The shops of "The Realm," for the most part reflect the hotel's medieval theme. Dragon's Lair, for example, features items ranging from pewter swords and shields to full suits of armor, and Merlin's Mystic Shop carries crystals, luck charms, and gargoyles. Other shops carry more conventional wares—gifts, candy, jewelry, women's clothing, and Excalibur logo items. A child pleaser is Kids of the Kingdom, which displays licensed character merchandise from Disney, Looney Tunes, Garfield, and Snoopy. Wild Bill's carries western wear and Native American jewelry and crafts. And at Fantasy Faire you can have your photo taken in Renaissance attire.

FLAMINGO HILTON   The Crystal Court shopping promenade here accommodates men's and women's clothing/accessories stores, gift shops, and a variety of other emporia selling jewelry, beachwear, southwestern crafts, fresh-baked goods, logo items, children's gifts, toys, and games.

A Las Vegas Specialty Store

Gambler's Book Shop, 630 S. 11th St., just off Charleston Blvd. ☎ **800/ 522-1777** or 702/382-7555.

Here you can buy a book on any system ever devised to beat casino odds. Owner Edna Luckman carries more than 4,000 gambling-related titles, including many out-of-print books, computer software, and videotapes. She describes her store as a place where "gamblers, writers, researchers, statisticians, and computer specialists can meet and exchange information." On request, knowledgeable clerks provide on-the-spot expert advice on handicapping the ponies and other aspects of sports betting. The store's motto is "knowledge is protection."

Open: Mon–Sat 9am–5pm.

HARRAH'S   Harrah's offers a 6,000-square-foot New Orleans–style shopping complex called Jackson Square. Shops include Maison Rose for women's fashions (some items for men and children, too), Louisiana Limited (an old-fashioned general store for Louisiana/Las Vegas gifts), Holiday Jazz (liquor, snacks); and Cajun Spice (New Orleans gourmet items). Inside the hotel are a gift shop, logo shop, a florist, a jewelry shop, and a store featuring casual clothing for the whole family. Some of this may change when the current renovation is completed.

LUXOR HOTEL/CASINO   This hotel's unique retail outlets together comprise a kind of Egyptian bazaar. Especially noteworthy is The Source, on the lower level, where you'll find museum-quality Egyptian antiquities such as an alabaster portrait of Ptolemy V (205 B.C.) for $3,000 or a bronze Isis statue (664–525 B.C.) for $10,000. More affordable are beautiful Egyptian jewelry (both straight reproductions and Egypt-inspired designs), gift items (mother-of-pearl inlay boxes and tables, paintings, pottery, scarabs, and amulets), and books about ancient Egypt. An extensive selection of Egyptian-themed art, jewelry, apparel featuring King Tut and Nefertiti, pottery, musical instruments, and logo items can be found at the Scarab Shop, the Park Avenue Shop, and the rock-walled Innerspace (the latter also offers oils and incense, crystals, and New Age music). A more typical hotel gift/newspaper/magazine shop is Sobek's Sundries.

THE MGM GRAND   The hotel's Star Lane Shops include more than a dozen upscale emporia lining the corridors en route from the monorail entrance. The Knot Shop carries designer ties by Calvin Klein, Gianni Versace, and others. El Portal features luggage and handbags—Coach, Dior, Fendi, Polo Ralph Lauren, and other exclusive lines. Grand 50's carries *Route 66* jackets, Elvis T-shirts, photos of James Dean, and other mementos of the 1950s. MGM Grand Sports sells signed athletic uniforms, baseballs autographed by Michael Jordan, and the like; it is the scene of occasional appearances by sports stars such as Floyd Patterson and Stan Musial. You can choose an oyster and have its pearl set in jewelry at The Pearl Factory. Other Star Lane Shops specialize in movie memorabilia, Betty Boop–themed merchandise, *EFX* wares, children's clothing, decorative magnets, MGM Grand logo items and Las Vegas souvenirs, seashells and coral, candy, and sunglasses. Refreshments are available at a Häagen-Dazs ice cream counter and Yummy's Coffees and Desserts. In other parts of the hotel, retail shops include a *Wizard of Oz*–themed gift shop, Front Page (for newspapers, books, magazines, and sundries), a spa shop selling everything from beachwear to top-of-the-line European skin care products, a liquor store, a candy store, Kenneth J. Lane jewelry, and Marshall Rousso (men's and women's clothing). In addition, theme park emporia sell Hollywood memorabilia, cameras and photographic supplies, MGM Grand and theme park logo products, toys, fine china and crystal, animation cels, collectibles (limited-edition dolls, plates, figurines), Hollywood-themed clothing and accessories, and western wear. At Arts and Crafts you can watch artisans working in leather, glass, wood, pottery, and other materials, and at Photoplay Gallery, you can have your picture taken as *Time* magazine's man or woman of the year.

MONTE CARLO   An arcade of retail shops here includes Bon Vivant (resort wear for the whole family, dresswear for men), Crown Jewels (jewelry, leather bags, crystal, Fabergé eggs, gift items), a florist, logo shop, jeweler, food market, dessert store, and Lance Burton magic paraphernalia shop.

THE RIVIERA   The Riviera has a fairly extensive shopping arcade comprising art galleries, jewelers, a creative photographer, and shops specializing in women's shoes and handbags, clothing for the entire family, furs, gifts, logo items, toys, phones and electronic gadgets, and chocolates.

SAM'S TOWN   Though Sam's Town does not contain a notably significant shopping arcade, it does house the huge Western Emporium (almost department-store size) selling western clothing for men and women, boots (an enormous selection), jeans, belts, silver and turquoise jewelry, Stetson hats, Native American crafts, gift items, and old-fashioned candy. You can have your picture taken here in period western costume. Open daily at 9am; closing hours vary.

STRATOSPHERE   Shopping is no afterthought here. The internationally themed second floor Tower Shops promenade, which will soon house 40 stores, is entered off an escalator from the casino. Some shops are in "Paris," along the Rue Lafayette and Avenue de l'Opéra (there are replicas of the Eiffel Tower and Arc de Triomphe in this section). Others occupy Hong Kong and New York City streetscapes. Already-extant emporia include: The Money Company (money-motif items from T-shirts to golf balls), a T-shirt store, a magic shop, Key West (body lotions et al.), Victoria's Secret, a magnet shop, Norma Kaplan (for glitzy/sexy women's footwear), an electronics boutique, a logo shop, and several gift shops. There are branches of Jitters (a coffee house) and Häagen-Dazs, and stores are supplemented by cart vendors.

TREASURE ISLAND   Treasure Island's shopping promenade—doubling as a portrait gallery of famed buccaneers (Blackbeard, Jean Lafitte, Calico Jack, Barbarosa)—has wooden ship figureheads and battling pirates suspended from its ceiling. Emporia here include the Treasure Island Store (your basic hotel gift/sundry shop, also offering much pirate-themed merchandise, plus a section devoted to Calvin Klein clothing), Loot 'n' Booty (stocked with exotic wares from India, Morocco, and other ports, as well as ship models and ships in bottles), Candy Reef (an old-fashioned candy store with beaded-silk Victorian lighting fixtures overhead), Captain Kid's (children's clothing, logo items, and toys), and Damsels in Dis'Dress (women's sportswear and accessories). The Mutiny Bay Shop, in the video-game arcade, carries logo items and stuffed animals. In the casino are the Buccaneer Bay Shoppe (logo merchandise) and the Treasure Chest (a jewelry store; spend those winnings right on the spot). And the Crow's Nest, en route to the Mirage monorail, carries Cirque du Soleil logo items. Cirque du Soleil and Mystère logo wares are also sold in a shop near the ticket office.

10 Las Vegas After Dark

No city in the world offers more excitement after dark than Las Vegas. In addition to casino gambling (see chapter 8), you have your choice of dozens of shows ranging from lavish production spectaculars to superstar entertainment.

On my last visit, the following big-name entertainers were performing at showrooms around town: Paul Anka, Barbara Mandrell, José Feliciano, Wynonna, Johnny Mathis, Nancy Wilson, Ramsey Lewis, The Righteous Brothers, The Beach Boys, Chuck Berry, Buddy Hackett, and Penn & Teller.

There were—and are—more than a dozen elaborate production shows in town, including magic/illusion shows, all featuring high-tech lighting and laser effects, sexy showgirls in feathered and sequined costumes, and great choreography. These shows cost a lot of money to produce, so they have long runs. I've described every show now running in Las Vegas in detail, and though most will still be on when you read this book, some will no doubt have closed. Things change.

Casino lounge shows, which are either free or charge a one-drink minimum, also offer first-rate entertainment. Many of the headliners you see on major stages started out as lounge acts. You could have a great time just going from lounge to lounge without spending very much money. You'll find lounge shows described in hotel listings in chapter 5.

Admission to shows runs a wide gamut, from about $18.95 for *An Evening at La Cage* (a female impersonator show at the Riviera) to $80 and more for top headliners or *Siegfried & Roy*. Prices usually include two drinks or, in rare instances, dinner.

To find out who will be performing during your stay, you can call the various hotels featuring headliner entertainment, using toll-free numbers. Or call the **Las Vegas Convention and Visitors Authority** (☎ 702/892-0711) and ask them to send you a free copy of *Showguide*.

Every hotel entertainment option is described below with information on ticket prices, what is included in the price (drinks, dinner, taxes, and/or gratuities), showroom policies (as to preassigned or maître d' seating and smoking), and how to make reservations. Whenever possible, reserve in advance, especially on weekends and holidays. If the showroom has maître d' seating (as opposed to assigned seats), you may want to tip him to upgrade your seat. A tip of $15 to $20 per couple will usually do the trick at a major show, less at a small showroom. An alternative to tipping the maître d' is to wait until the captain shows you to your seat. Perhaps it will be adequate, in which case you've saved some money. If not, you can offer the captain a tip for a better seat. If you do plan to tip, have the money ready; maître d's and captains tend to get annoyed if you fumble around for it. They have other people to seat. You can also tip with casino chips (from the hotel casino where the show is taking place only) in lieu of cash. Whatever you tip, the proper etiquette is to do it rather subtly—a kind of palm-to-palm action. There's really no reason for this, since everyone knows what's going on, but being blatant is in poor taste. Arrive early at maître d' shows to get the best choice of seats.

If you buy tickets for an assigned-seat show in person, you can look over a seating chart. Avoid sitting right up by the stage if possible, especially for big production shows. Dance numbers are better viewed from the middle of the theater. With headliners, you might like to sit up close.

Note: All of these caveats and instructions aside, most casino-hotel showrooms offer good visibility from just about every seat in the house.

Best Bets: the incomparable *Siegfried & Roy* at the Mirage and the Cirque du Soleil's enchanting *Mystère* at Treasure Island. Best value for the money: *Country Fever* at the Golden Nugget, *Danny Gans: The Man of Many Voices* at the Stratosphere, and Kenny Kerr's *Boylesque* at Debbie Reynolds.

In addition to the below listed, consider the Fremont Street Experience and Sunset Stampede at Sam's Town, both described in chapter 7.

1 What's Playing Where

The following section will describe, by name, each of the major production shows currently playing in Las Vegas. This section lists each major hotel and the production show(s) playing there in the event you want to catch a show in a particular location.

- Aladdin Hotel, *Country Tonite* (country music review)
- Bally's, ✪ *Jubilee* (Las Vegas–style review)
- Debbie Reynolds Hotel, ✪ *Boylesque* (female impersonators) and the ✪ *Debbie Reynolds Show* (Las Vegas–style review featuring Debbie)
- Excalibur, *An Evening in Vienna* (show featuring the Lippizaner Stallions described in chapter 7) and *King Arthur's Tournament* (medieval themed review)
- Flamingo Hilton, *Forever Plaid* (off-Broadway review featuring '60s music) and *The Great Radio City Spectacular* (Las Vegas–style review featuring the Radio City Music Hall Rockettes)
- Golden Nugget, ✪ *Country Fever* (country music review)
- Harrah's, *Spellbound* (magic review)
- Holiday Inn Boardwalk, ✪ *Teeze* (sexy Las Vegas–style review)
- Imperial Palace, *Legends in Concert* (musical impersonators)
- Jackie Gaughan's Plaza, *Xposed* (sexy Las Vegas–style review)
- Las Vegas Hilton, *Starlight Express* (Andrew Lloyd Webber's Broadway show)
- MGM Grand, ✪ *EFX* (special-effects review featuring David Cassidy)
- The Mirage, ✪ *Siegfried & Roy* (magical extravaganza)
- Monte Carlo, ✪ *Lance Burton: Master Magician* (magic show and review)
- Rio Suite Hotel, *Copacabana Dinner Show* (Latin-themed review)
- Riviera Hotel, *An Evening at La Cage* (female impersonators), *Bottoms Up* (Las Vegas–style review), *Crazy Girls* (sexy Las Vegas–style review), and *Splash II* (aquatic review)

- Stardust, *Enter the Night* (Las Vegas-style review)
- Stratosphere Tower, ✪ *American Superstars* (an impression-filled production show)
- Treasure Island, ✪ Cirque du Soleil's *Mystère* (unique circus performance)
- Tropicana, *Folies Bergère* (Las Vegas–style review)

2 The Major Production Shows

This category covers production shows major and minor, including country music shows, magic shows, female impersonator shows, and racy revues like Teeze and Xposed.

✪ American Superstars

Stratosphere, 2000 Las Vegas Blvd. S. ☎ **800/99-TOWER** or 702/380-7777.

This high-energy, 70-minute show takes place in the hotel's Image Cabaret, an a ttractive nightclub. A talented cast of singers—backed up by a band and a quartet of scantily clad dancers—does very good impressions (singing, not lip-synching) of Gloria Estefan, Michael Jackson, Charlie Daniels, Madonna, and the Four Tops. After the show, the performers mingle with the crowd.

- **Showroom Policies:** Smoking permitted; seating is first come first serve.
- **Price:** Admission is free; there's a two-drink minimum (average drink $2.50).
- **Show Times:** Fri–Wed at 8 and 10pm. Dark Thurs.
- **Reservations:** Not accepted.

Bottoms Up

Riviera Hotel, 2901 Las Vegas Blvd. S. ☎ **800/634-6753** or 702/734-9301.

Bottoms Up, billed as a "laughter-noon delight," combines vaudeville, burlesque, and musical comedy into a lively hour-long revue. Shows are presented on the second level of the Mardi Gras Plaza.

- **Showroom Policies:** Nonsmoking with maître d' seating.
- **Price:** $9.95 (drinks, tax, and gratuity extra).
- **Show Times:** Fri–Wed at 2 and 4pm. Dark Thurs.
- **Reservations:** Tickets can be purchased at the box office only, in advance if you wish.

✪ Boylesque

Debbie Reynolds Hotel, 305 Convention Center Dr. ☎ **800/633-1777** or 702/7-DEBBIE.

A sophisticated female-impersonator revue starring "hostess" Kenny Kerr, *Boylesque* has been playing somewhere in Las Vegas since 1970. This is Kenny's best show yet: He's looking great, his repartee is sparkling, and his vast array of costumes is simply stunning. An evening with Kenny is marvelously outrageous and over-the-top, with lots of double-entendre jokes and even a bit of beefcake. A talented cast, backed up by a dance troupe, does take-offs (mostly lip-synching, but Kenny really sings) on Marilyn Monroe, Dolly Parton, Janet Jackson, Diana Ross, Barbra Streisand, Liza Minnelli, and others—even Pocahontas. But most impressive is the lively improvisational patter of Kerr himself, who fields questions, some of them very personal, with humor and panache and creates an intimate rapport with his audience.

- **Showroom Policies:** Nonsmoking with maître d' seating.
- **Price:** $24.95 (includes tax, one drink, and gratuity).
- **Show Times:** Mon–Fri 10:30pm, Sat 9pm (9pm Mon–Sat when Debbie Reynolds is out of town).
- **Reservations:** You can reserve by phone up to 3 days in advance.

✪ Cirque du Soleil's Mystère

Treasure Island, 3300 Las Vegas Blvd. S. ☎ **800/392-1999** or 702/894-7723.

The superbly talented international Cirque du Soleil troupe stages *Mystère*, its most ambitious production to date, in Treasure Island's state-of-the-art 1,541-seat theater-in-the-round. Under a lofty ceiling laced with catwalks and painted to suggest a parchment world map, the huge stage includes a circus ring, a 28-foot revolving turntable, and sail-like screens used to project mists of kaleidoscopic color and form. A cast of 70 artists—acrobats, clowns, actors, comedians, stilt-walkers, ventriloquists, singers, dancers, and musicians—perform with the grace of a ballet company and the precision of Olympic athletes. This surreal postmodern circus, combining high-tech special effects, seemingly superhuman ability, and commedia dell'arte whimsy, is like nothing you've ever seen before. The curved silver rods of a juggling act become figures in a dance, acrobats scamper up and down poles with the agility of chimps, Japanese Taiko drummers rap out primal rhythms, iridescent-plumed trapeze artists on bungee cords soar like birds, and opaque white Apollonian "human statues" bathed in chartreuse light perform feats of strength and balance in mesmerizing slow motion. Throughout the show, the audience is caught up in a dazzling mystical dream world. The music is haunting, the choreography and conception brilliantly creative, the lighting exquisite, costumes and sets ethereal. Cirque du Soleil is flawless.

- **Showroom Policies:** Nonsmoking with preassigned seating.
- **Price:** $59.95 adults, $29.95 for children under 11 (drinks and tax extra).
- **Show Times:** Wed–Sun at 7:30 and 10:30pm. Dark Mon–Tues.
- **Reservations:** You can reserve by phone via credit card up to 90 days in advance (do reserve early since it often sells out).

Copacabana Dinner Show

Rio Suite Hotel & Casino, 3700 W. Flamingo Rd. ☎ **800/PLAY-RIO** or 702/252-7777.

The Rio's deluxe Copacabana Showroom—a state-of-the-art theater-in-the-round with tiered seating at individual tables—is the setting for the *Copacabana Dinner Show*. Exotic, upbeat, and pulsating with Latin rhythms, it stars a Carmen Miranda–like Rio Rita in a parade of elaborate tropical costumes. As you dine, a Latin band plays music for dancing, and gorgeous scenery of Brazil is projected onto two 96-foot video walls. Acts include a Latin dance exhibition and lavish song and dance numbers. Food presentation, under the auspices of the zany Chef Rico, is a big part of the show. Chefs ascend from a recessed central stage, and as a cadre of waiters serves dinner, sexy dancers with carrot, corn, tomato, eggplant, and radish hats and lettuce-leaf fans are tossed into a vast salad bowl. At the end of the show, the audience—led by a cast member—congas out of the showroom and into the casino.

- **Showroom Policies:** Nonsmoking with preassigned seating.
- **Price:** $39.95 (includes dinner; tax, gratuity; cocktails extra).
- **Show Times:** Tues–Sat at 6 and 8:30pm. Dark Sun–Mon.
- **Reservations:** You can reserve by credit card up to 30 days in advance.

✪ Country Fever

Golden Nugget, 129 E. Fremont St. ☎ **800/777-4658** or 702/386-8100.

A few years back, the Golden Nugget redecorated its showroom walls with a display of western paraphernalia, neon cacti, steer heads, and cowboy boots. It's the setting for *Country Fever*—the best foot-stompin', hand-clappin' country music show in town—featuring a cast of tremendously talented singers and dancers, including bare-buttocked showgirls in fringed country thongs and cowboy boots (This *is* Las Vegas!). They're backed up by an outstanding nine-piece band called The Posse. The cast also includes a gospel choir and a first-rate stand-up comic, Kirby St. Romaine. Special kudos to the exuberant star of the show, T.J. Weaver. Since light fare is served, arrive at least an hour early, so you're through with it when the show begins.

- **Showroom Policies:** Nonsmoking with maître d' seating.
- **Price:** $22.50 (including a drink and a basket of taco chips with two dipping sauces and chicken tenders; tax and gratuity extra).
- **Show Times:** Sat–Thurs at 7:15 and 10:15pm. Dark Fri.
- **Reservations:** You can reserve as far in advance as you like.

Country Tonite
Aladdin Hotel, 3667 Las Vegas Blvd. S. ☎ **800/637-8133** or 702/736-0240.

The Aladdin presents *Country Tonite,* a lively revue with plenty of singin', fiddlin', guitar strummin', and foot-stompin' western dances. Highlights include Karen Brownlee's rendition of the legendary Patsy Kline's "Sweet Dreams," a lasso- and gun-twirling exhibition, cloggers, a "Devil Went Down to Georgia" fiddling contest, and the antics of ventriloquist Sammy King and his Mexican parrot dummy. The show ends in a patriotic finale, with American flags flanking the stage and the cast performing "America the Beautiful," "All Gave Some, Some Gave All," "God Bless the USA," "Stand Up," and "We Shall Be Free."

- **Showroom Policies:** Nonsmoking with maître d' seating.
- **Price:** $17.95 adults, $11.95 for children under 12 (tax and drinks extra). With buffet adults pay $21.95, children $14.95.
- **Show Times:** Wed–Mon at 7:15 and 10pm. Dark Tues.
- **Reservations:** You can reserve up to 2 weeks in advance by phone.

Crazy Girls
Riviera Hotel, 2901 Las Vegas Blvd. S. ☎ **800/634-6753** or 702/734-9301.

Crazy Girls, presented in an intimate theater, is probably the raciest revue on the Strip. It features sexy showgirls with perfect bodies in erotic song and dance numbers enhanced by innovative lighting effects. Think of *Penthouse* poses come to life.

- **Showroom Policies:** Nonsmoking with maître d' seating.
- **Price:** $16.95 (includes two drinks; tax and gratuity extra).
- **Show Times:** Tues–Sun at 8:30 and 10:30pm, with an extra midnight show Sat. Dark Mon.
- **Reservations:** Tickets can be purchased at the box office only, in advance if you wish.

✪ Debbie Reynolds Show
Debbie Reynolds Hotel, 305 Convention Center Dr. ☎ **800/633-1777** or 702/7-DEBBIE.

The very talented and boundlessly energetic Debbie Reynolds projects a warmth and relaxed stage presence seen only in the most seasoned of pros. And her beautiful 500-seat, state-of-the-art Star Theatre (son Todd Fisher designed it) is filled to bursting with devoted fans at every performance. Debbie, as cute and exuberant as ever, sings shows clips from her famous movies (like *Singin' in the Rain* and *The Tender Trap*), does impressions (her repertoire includes Katharine Hepburn, Bette Davis, Mae West, Zsa Zsa Gabor, Dolly Parton, Edith Bunker, and Barbra Streisand), cracks jokes, tells stories about her Hollywood heyday, and mingles with the audience. She is ably assisted by the Uptown Country Singers who perform popular country music songs and sing and dance with Debbie. The show ends with a tribute to the big-band era. After each performance Debbie meets fans in the showroom to sign autographs and pose for pictures.

- **Showroom Policies:** Nonsmoking with maître d' seating.
- **Price:** $34.95 (includes tax, two drinks, and gratuity).

- **Show Times:** Mon–Fri at 7:30pm. Dark Sat–Sun.
- **Reservations:** You can reserve by phone up to 3 days in advance.

✪ EFX

MGM Grand, 3799 Las Vegas Blvd. S. ☎ **800/929-1111** or 702/891-7777.

Not surprisingly, this megahotel houses several entertainment facilities. Most notably, the 1,700-seat Grand Theatre, which presents *EFX*, a "multi-media megamusical" extravaganza starring David Cassidy (of *Partridge Family* fame) and a cast of 70 singers, dancers, acrobats, stunt people, and aerial artists. As the majestic *EFX* Master, Cassidy takes us on a surrealistic high-tech journey through time and space to "worlds beyond imagination." He enters the vast stage soaring through clouds to introduce the masters of the four forces that govern *EFX:* Magic, Laughter, Spirit, and Time. In the persona of Merlin (backed by an elaborate stage set of a castle in an enchanted forest, complete with a mountain waterfall), he teaches young King Arthur about the magic of the natural world and engages in a deadly wizard's duel of magical powers with the sorceress Morgana. He next presents an intergalactic circus of wonders starring alien performers (two-headed women, peacocks of Pluto, and other strange creatures) who arrive onstage in a rainbow-hued spaceship. Next, Cassidy appears as Houdini (many of whose famous illusions are re-created) at a seance led by Houdini's wife on the anniversary of his death. Finally, as H.G. Wells, he takes us on a mesmerizing 3-D journey through time—from the primitive world to the future. The $40-million-plus production utilizes state-of-the-art scenery, lighting (there's enough electrical power here to power 1,440 homes!) and sound systems, mind-boggling special effects, phantasmagorical costumes, lasers, pyrotechnics, vibrating seats, and magnificent 3-D movie footage—not to mention animatronic fire-breathing dragons.

- **Showroom Policies:** Nonsmoking with preassigned seating.
- **Price:** $70 (including one drink, tax, and gratuity).
- **Show Times:** Fri–Sat and Mon–Wed at 7:30 and 10:30pm, Sun at 7:30pm. Dark Thurs.
- **Reservations:** You can reserve by phone any time in advance.

✪ Enter the Night

The Stardust, 3000 Las Vegas Blvd. S. ☎ **800/824-6033** or 702/732-6111.

The Stardust Theatre has traditionally offered top-flight entertainment (Siegfried & Roy were here for years), and its current show is one of the very best in town. *Enter the Night* is a sophisticated version of the classic Las Vegas spectacular—a multimedia production extraordinaire with awe-inspiring laser/lighting and other special

---

⊕ Family-Friendly Shows

Appropriate shows for kids, all described in this chapter, include the following:

- King Arthur's Tournament at Excalibur *(see p. 186)*
- Siegfried & Roy at the Mirage *(see p. 187)*
- Burton at the Monte Carlo *(see p. 186)*
- Starlight Express at the Hilton *(see p. 189)*
- EFX at the MGM Grand *(see p. 183)*
- Cirque du Soleil's *Mystère* at Treasure Island *(see p. 181)*

As a general rule, early shows are less racy than late-night shows.

effects (including rain, fire and a waterfall on stage), stunning sets and costumes, gorgeous showgirls (and guys), enchanting dance numbers, and great music that runs the gamut from original songs to Fats Waller tunes. Performers include world-champion ice-skaters and Argentinean gaucho dancers; especially impressive is an beautifully choreographed number in which six performers dance with laser lights. This show never flags but moves from height to height, concluding with a massive Busby Berkley–style finale.

- **Showroom Policies:** Nonsmoking with preassigned seating.
- **Price:** Most seats $29.85, booths $33.15 to $55 (includes two drinks, tax and gratuity).
- **Show Times:** Tues, Wed, Thurs, Sat at 7:30 and 10:30pm, Sun–Mon at 8pm only. Dark Fri.
- **Reservations:** You can reserve up to a month in advance by phone.

An Evening at La Cage

Riviera Hotel & Casino, 2901 Las Vegas Blvd. S. ☎ **800/634-6753** or 702/734-9301.

The racy revue, *An Evening at La Cage,* is based on the premise that "boys will be girls," with transvestite performers doing lip-synch impersonations of Diana Ross, Cher, Bette Midler, Dionne Warwick, Liza Minnelli, and others. There's also a first-rate Michael Jackson impersonator in the show; having a female impersonator portray a male performer brings new meaning to the concept of androgyny. Frank Marino is "mistress of ceremonies" in the persona of comedienne Joan Rivers. There's lots of hilarious spicy schtick in this show, which is presented in a small theater on the third-floor Mardi Gras Plaza.

- **Showroom Policies:** Nonsmoking with maître d' seating.
- **Price:** $18.95 (includes two drinks; tax and gratuity extra).
- **Show Times:** Wed–Mon at 7:30 and 9:30pm, with an extra show at 11:15pm Wed and Sat. Dark Tues.
- **Reservations:** Tickets can be purchased at the box office only, in advance if you wish.

Folies Bergère

Tropicana, 3801 Las Vegas Blvd. S. ☎ **800/468-9494** or 702/739-2411.

The Trop's famous *Folies Bergère* is the longest-running production show in town and one of the few remaining dinner shows. It's the quintessential Las Vegas extravaganza with a French accent—an enchanting mix of innovative scenery, lively music, bare-breasted showgirls in lavish feathered/rhinestoned/sequined costumes, and fast-paced choreography. Scene I is set in a turn-of-the-century Parisian music hall. Scene II salutes American music—gospel, blues, movie melodies, and the big-band and swing eras—culminating in a medley of oldies from the '50s through the '90s. A highlight is a kaleidoscope dance number (they do it with mirrors). Scene III once more celebrates the belle époque, leading up to a colorful can-can finale. Acts are punctu-ated by acrobatic numbers and comedy routines. *Note:* If you'd like to take a back-stage tour of the Folies set, they are scheduled Sunday through Thursday at 12:30, 1:30, and 2:30pm. Tickets cost $2; call the above phone number for details.

- **Showroom Policies:** Nonsmoking with maître d' seating.
- **Price:** $23.95 (includes two drinks; tax and gratuity extra). You can have dinner at the 7:30pm show (admission is based on your entree price ($30.95–$33.95; tax and gratuity extra).
- **Show Times:** Sun–Fri at 7:30 and 10:30pm. Dark Sat and sometimes Fri.
- **Reservations:** You can charge tickets in advance via credit card.

Fun Fact

The main character in Paul Verhoven's *Showgirls* gets a job in the production show of The Stardust.

Forever Plaid

Flamingo Hilton, 3555 Las Vegas Blvd. S. ☎ 702/733-3333.

The Flamingo Hilton presents the off-Broadway hit *Forever Plaid* in its Bugsy's Celebrity Theatre. The plot line is bizarre, to say the least. The Plaids, an early 1960s harmony quartet on the order of The Four Freshmen, are killed on their way to their first big gig (at the Airport Hilton) when their car is broadsided by a busload of parochial-school girls en route to see the Beatles' U.S. television debut on "The Ed Sullivan Show." After 30 years, they've mysteriously returned to Earth (it has to do with the power of harmony and expanding holes in the ozone layer) to finally perform the show they never got to do in life. This totally weird context is just an excuse for a zany musical stroll down memory lane consisting of 29 oldies—songs like "Rags to Riches," "Sixteen Tons," "Love is a Many-Splendored Thing," "Three Coins in the Fountain," and "No, Not Much." If you're sentimental about that era, you'll love it.

- **Showroom Policies:** Nonsmoking with maître d' seating.
- **Price:** $19.95 (drinks and tax extra).
- **Show Times:** Tues–Sun 7:30 and 10:30pm.
- **Reservations:** Tickets can be reserved a week in advance.

The Great Radio City Spectacular

Flamingo Hilton, 3555 Las Vegas Blvd. S. ☎ 702/733-3333.

The *Great Radio City Spectacular* begins with early movie footage of New York's Radio City Music Hall, a prelude to the synchronized shapely leg-kicking appearance of the world's most famous chorus line—the Rockettes. Highlights include a tribute to Fred Astaire, whose movies all debuted at Radio City; a Busby Berkley–esque Strauss waltz number with large white feather fans; a stunningly costumed and imaginatively choreographed dance to Ravel's *Bolero;* the charming "Parade of the Wooden Soldiers" from the Radio City Christmas show; and a "Stairway to the Stars" grand finale. Co-starring with the Rockettes are a series of guest hosts (originally Susan Anton, at this writing Maurice Hines, but that will change) who perform between dance numbers. Also featured are illusionists Tim Kole and Jenny Lynn; comic juggler Nino Frediani; and "Stacy Moore & His Mess of Mutts," a comic dog troupe (Moore's highly trained canines are all abandoned animals he rescued from shelters and dog pounds). The dinner show menu features a choice of coq au vin, steak, roast prime rib, or poached salmon.

- **Showroom Policies:** Nonsmoking with maître d' seating.
- **Price:** Dinner show based on main-course price ($45.50–$53.54, including tax and gratuity; cocktail show $38.20 (includes two drinks, tax, and gratuity).
- **Show Times:** Nightly dinner show at 7:45pm, cocktail show at 10:30pm.
- **Reservations:** You can reserve by phone 2 weeks in advance.

✪ Jubilee

Bally's, 3645 Las Vegas Blvd. S. ☎ 800/237-7469 or 702/739-4567.

The 1,000-seat showroom—with its vast stage, excellent design (not a bad seat in the house), and state-of-the-art technical equipment—presents a classic Las Vegas spectacular called *Jubilee.* It features dazzling sets and lighting effects and a magnificently costumed cast (many outfits were designed by Bob Mackie) of close to 100 singers and dancers. There are beautiful topless showgirls in sequins and feathers and hunky guys in studded-leather thongs. The show ranges from nostalgia numbers—honoring the songs and stars of yesteryear (a tribute to Elvis comprises the most up-to-date music)—to lavish production extravaganzas built around such themes as Samson and Delilah (culminating in the fiery destruction of the temple), the sinking of the *Titanic* (involving 5,000 gallons of water cascading through the set), and a World War I air battle. Interspersed with these are specialty acts (comics, acrobats, et al.). And the finale—a tribute to Fred Astaire and Ginger Rogers, Cole Porter, Jerome Kern, and George Gershwin—culminates in a parade of showgirls modeled after the Ziegfeld Follies.

- **Showroom Policies:** Nonsmoking with preassigned seating.
- **Price:** $46 (tax included, drinks extra).
- **Show Times:** Sun–Mon at 8pm, Tues–Thurs and Sat at 8 and 11pm. Dark Fri.
- **Reservations:** You can reserve up to 6 weeks in advance.

King Arthur's Tournament
Excalibur, 3850 Las Vegas Blvd. S. ☎ **702/597-7600.**

Excalibur's primary entertainment offering is in keeping with its medieval theme. *King Arthur's Tournament* is a colorful tale of gallant knights and fair ladies—of romance, magic, medieval games, and pageantry—enlivened by pyrotechnics, fiber optics, and fancy lighting effects. Bursts of fireworks herald the presence of Merlin the magician in his star-spangled blue robe, and lasers add flash and drama to sword fights and jousting contests. The story is about the battle between the evil black knight and the heroic white knight for the princess's hand in marriage. Each section of the arena is given a knight to cheer, and the audience is encouraged to hoot, holler, and pound on the tables (kids adore it). Knightly battles are complemented by lively dances, equestrian acrobatics, tumblers, jugglers, and stunt riders. And the show culminates, of course, in the victory of the white knight and his marriage to King Arthur's fair daughter in a magnificent court wedding. Dinner, served during the show by "serfs" and "wenches," is a robust affair eaten in lusty medieval style without utensils. It includes a pot of creamy chicken soup, Cornish game hen, stuffed baked potato, vegetable, biscuits, apple tart, and beverage.

- **Showroom Policies:** Nonsmoking with preassigned seating.
- **Price:** $29.95 (including dinner, beverage, tax, and gratuity).
- **Show Times:** "Knightly" at 6 and 8:30pm.
- **Reservations:** You can reserve up to 6 days in advance by phone.

✪ Lance Burton: Master Magician
Monte Carlo, 3770 Las Vegas Blvd. S. ☎ **800/311-8999** or 702/730-7000.

A luxurious $27-million theater—with gold-fringed velvet curtains, ornate beveled mirrors, and crystal chandeliers and sconces, not to mention state-of-the-art sound and lighting systems—is the magnificent setting for Lance Burton, one of the nation's most acclaimed magicians. Many Las Vegas illusionists are pale copies of Siegfried & Roy. Backed up by a talented troupe of sexy showgirls and brilliant comic juggler Michael Goudeau, Burton—who looks a little like Elvis and sounds a lot like Jack Nicholson—eschews the trend towards wild animals onstage. Instead, he brings high-tech panache to classic sleight of hand and Houdini-esque escapes, changing candles into doves, doves into silk scarves; performing miraculous feats of levitation; turning a berserk ballerina into a duck; mysteriously disappearing and reappearing; even dueling with death. Little kids in the audience get to go up on stage, where, enchanted by Burton's magic, they're charming and adorable. The show concludes—after a palatial midnight-at-the-masked-ball sequence, complete with harlequins and ladies of the court in Marie Antoinette hairdos and gowns—when Burton drives a car off the stage into midair.

- **Showroom Policies:** Nonsmoking with preassigned seating.
- **Price:** $34.95 (includes tax, drinks extra).
- **Show Times:** Tues–Sat at 7:30 and 10:30pm. Dark Sun–Mon.
- **Reservations:** Tickets can be purchased 60 days in advance.

Legends in Concert
Imperial Palace, 3535 Las Vegas Blvd. S. ☎ **702/794-3261.**

An extravaganza called *Legends in Concert* has been playing at the 800-seat Imperial Theatre since May 1983. It has appeared on Broadway and, in 1991, toured the Russian cities of Moscow and St. Petersburg. Performers impersonate superstar entertainers with actual singing (no lip-synching), paying tribute to Michael Jackson, Whitney Houston, Liberace, Marilyn Monroe, the Blues Brothers, Buddy Holly, Neil Diamond, Paul McCartney, Cher, Madonna, Tom Jones, Elton John, Dolly Parton, and Barbra Streisand, among others. The roster of stars impersonated changes weekly, so you may not see all of the above, but I can guarantee an Elvis sighting nightly. The show utilizes dazzling high-tech lighting and laser effects, and singers are backed by a live onstage orchestra. Photographic blowups of the stars being imitated flank the stage.

- **Showroom Policies:** Nonsmoking, with maître d' seating.
- **Price:** $29.50 (includes two drinks or one Polynesian cocktail such as a mai tai or zombie; tax and gratuity extra).
- **Show Times:** Mon–Sat at 7:30 and 10:30pm. Dark Sun.
- **Reservations:** You can make reservations by phone up to a month in advance.

Luxor Production Show
Luxor Las Vegas, 3900 Las Vegas Blvd. S. ☎ **702/262-4900.**

✪ Siegfried & Roy
The Mirage, 3400 Las Vegas Blvd. S. ☎ **800/627-6667** or 702/792-7777.

The most spectacular hotel on the Strip also has the ultimate entertainment package featuring illusionists par excellence *Siegfried & Roy*. Not to mince praise, I'd as soon go to India and not visit the Taj Mahal as miss S&R in Las Vegas. For more than 2 decades, the Las Vegas show starring this dynamic duo has been the top show in town, playing to sellout audiences twice a night. Leave it to Steve Wynn to give them carte blanche (and $25 million) to build the 1,500-seat Siegfried & Roy Theatre to their own specifications. Producer Ken Feld contributed another $30 million to the new spectacle—making it the most expensive theatrical attraction ever staged. Singer Michael Jackson wrote and produced a song just for the show! The luxurious and very comfortable theater—designed so that no seat is more than 100 feet from the edge of the stage—features the world's most advanced computerized lighting and audio

Impressions

By creating a series of enchanted moments, we hope our audience will recall the time in their lives when they felt that anything was possible.

—Siegfried & Roy

system. And the cast includes a company of 60 dancers and 2 dozen wild animals. Among the latter are the rare royal white tigers that have become an S&R trademark; they freely roam the stage during the show. These sorcerers supreme make elephants disappear, transform beautiful women into tigers, ride horses sideways and backwards, impale themselves on swords, are captured by aliens, levitate, set the stage on fire, and leap through flaming hoops. Enchanting dreamlike dance numbers feature demons, gossamer-winged fairies, and armies of human and mechanized soldiers in gold and silver armor battling a fire-breathing dragon. The laser and lighting effects, costumes, scenery, and choreography are unparalleled. Don't miss this awe-inspiring world of wonders.

- **Showroom Policies:** Nonsmoking with preassigned seating.
- **Price:** $83.85 (includes 2 drinks, souvenir brochure, tax, and gratuity).
- **Show Times:** Performances are Fri–Tues at 7:30 and 11pm, except during occasional dark periods.
- **Reservations:** Tickets can be purchased 3 days in advance.

Spellbound
Harrah's, 3475 Las Vegas Blvd. S. ☎ **800/392-9002** or 702/369-5111.

Harrah's fast-paced and very entertaining magical extravaganza, *Spellbound,* is enlivened by a pulsating rock- music score, a troupe of talented dancers in sexy costumes, and futuristic laser and lighting effects. The stars of the show—magician Mark Kalin and his beautiful assistant Jinger—combine great charm with thrilling artistry. Mark puts Jinger into a box and runs flaming swords through her (when he opens it, she is gone), transforms her into a slinky black panther (and himself into a tiger), lets her climb through his body, impales her on the point of a sword, and levitates her (passing a flaming hoop over her supine form). Joining Kalin and Jinger is the astounding Human Design—a superb trio, two of them Olympic athletes—whose slow-motion act, creating the illusion of ever-changing statues, is an amazing display of strength, controlled synchronized movement, and acrobatic skill. The show also features a comedian and exotic jungle animals.

- **Showroom Policies:** Nonsmoking with preassigned seating.
- **Price:** $29.65 (includes one drink, tax, and gratuity).
- **Show Times:** Mon–Sat at 7:30 and 10pm. Dark Sun.
- **Reservations:** You can charge tickets up to 30 days in advance via credit card.

Splash II
Riviera Hotel, 2901 Las Vegas Blvd. S. ☎ **800/634-6753** or 702/734-9301.

The Riviera presents four big shows nightly, making it a Strip leader in entertainment offerings. Most lavish is *Splash II*—a lively revue that has been playing to sellout audiences in the Versailles Theatre since 1985. As the name implies, the show is an aquacade extravaganza with an onstage, 20,000-gallon tank surrounded by dancing fountains and waterfalls. A uniquely thrilling number features four stunt motorcyclists racing inside a 16-foot sphere. There are gorgeous showgirls, mermaids, seahorses, and starfish, as well as divers, water ballet, comedy, magic, the world's fastest juggler, an exotic bird show, and an ice-skating duo, all of which lead up to a spectacular finale—a musical excursion to the lost city of Atlantis. The show is enhanced by state-of-the-art lighting and laser technology.

- **Showroom Policies:** Nonsmoking with preassigned seating.
- **Price:** $31.75–$53.75, the latter for best seats in the house (includes tax; drinks and gratuity extra).

- **Show Times:** Nightly at 7:30 and 10:30pm (10:30pm show is topless).
- **Reservations:** You can reserve by phone up to a month in advance.

Starlight Express

Las Vegas Hilton, 3000 Paradise Rd. ☎ **800/222-5361** or 702/732-5755.

In 1993 the Hilton transformed its famed showroom into a gorgeous 1,500-seat oval theater to house Andrew Lloyd Webber's musical extravaganza on roller skates, *Starlight Express*. It's a dazzling high-energy, high-tech production, with futuristic sets and costumes, state-of-the-art sound and lighting effects, pyrotechnics, lasers, and a pulsating score that incorporates rock, country, jazz, and rap music. The fantasy of a nine-year-old boy playing with his model trains, *Starlight Express* is a love story, a sports story featuring a series of exciting train races enhanced by movie footage, and an inspirational tale of the triumph of the human spirit. Key characters include Rusty, a shy, well-intentioned steam engine who fears modern technology has passed him by; the Elvis-like Greaseball, a sleek diesel engine; Electra, a high-tech electric engine with an androgynous rock-star persona; and Rusty's dad, Poppa, a wise old steam engine. Needless to say, this modern version of "the little engine that could" is a great show choice for kids.

- **Showroom Policies:** Nonsmoking with preassigned seating.
- **Price:** $19.50–$45 (tax and drinks extra); $19.50 for children under 12.
- **Show Times:** Tues, Thurs, Sat, Sun at 7:30 and 10:30pm; Mon and Wed at 7:30pm. Dark Fri.
- **Reservations:** You can reserve by phone up to 3 months in advance.

✪ Teeze

Holiday Inn Boardwalk, 3750 Las Vegas Blvd. S. ☎ **702/735-2400.**

Okay, call me a snob, but when I took a seat in the Lighthouse Lounge at this Holiday Inn to see a racy revue, my expectations were low. The good news is that my expectations were disappointed; Teeze was terrific. Things got off to a sizzling start (with a soupçon of S&M) as the show's talented Ska Dancers performed their first number to a pulsating primitive beat. Next came the Walker family (Greg, Bill, and Kathy), a mellow vocal group who, at first glance looked like relatives of the Osmonds, an illusion enhanced by their singing the pretty C&W ditty, "I Swear." The Walkers went on to amaze and delight the audience with their vast range of talent—for singing, comedy, and a dozen or more brilliant impressions of everyone from George Burns and Gracie Allen to Sonny and Cher. A high-energy score and fresh, original choreography enlivened all the dance numbers. A highlight was a sexy version of "Take Me Out to the Ballgame" with suggestive uses for the bat.

- **Showroom Policies:** Early show nonsmoking, late show smoking; seating is first come, first served.
- **Price:** $19.95 (drinks and tax extra).
- **Show Times:** Wed–Mon at 7:15 and 10:30pm. Dark Tues.
- **Reservations:** You can make reservations by phone up to a 7 days in advance.

Xposed

Jackie Gaughan's Plaza, 1 Main St. ☎ **800/634-6575** or 702/386-2444.

The racily titled *Xposed*—billed as a "fast-paced, steamy, adults-only revue . . . "—begins with a rather weird number featuring its cast of dancers attired in black cloaks suggesting figures of Death. Those capes soon come off and the cast of dancers is revealed . . . topless, bottomless, and surprisingly androgynous with small breasts and very short hair. In the typical wacky format of Las Vegas' most racy revues—which vary untrammeled sexuality and nuances of S&M with acts that could be performed before an audience of Mormons—other numbers include a cutesy version of the song "Triplets" and a magician/juggler who performs to the *William Tell Overture*. Vocalist Robin Lewis sings "When a Man Loves a Woman" (with about as much soul as Michael Bolton) and does a tribute to country singer Patsy Cline.

- **Showroom Policies:** Smoking permitted, maître d' seating.
- **Price:** $19.95 (includes one drink from the bar).
- **Show Times:** Sat–Thurs at 8 and 10pm. Dark Fri.
- **Reservations:** You can reserve up to a week in advance by phone.

3 Headliner Showrooms

Aladdin Theatre for the Performing Arts

Aladdin Hotel, 3667 Las Vegas Blvd. S. ☎ **800/637-8133** or 702/736-0419.

The 7,000-seat **Theatre for the Performing Arts**—a major Las Vegas entertainment venue—hosts headliner concerts has featured such acts as Kenny Rogers, Pearl Jam, the Allman Brothers, Yanni, Alan Jackson, the Scorpions, Sawyer Brown, Luther Vandross, Tears for Fears, and Meatloaf. These alternate with Broadway shows (with touring-company casts) such as *Phantom of the Opera, Nutcracker on Ice, Dreamgirls,* and *Cats* and professional boxing and wrestling matches. There are several bars in the theater.

- **Showroom Policies:** Nonsmoking with preassigned seating.
- **Price:** $13–$100, depending on the event (tax included; drinks extra).
- **Show Times:** Vary with the performer or show.
- **Reservations:** Policy varies with the performer, theatrical production, or event. Most shows can be reserved via Ticketmaster (☎ **702/474-4000** or your local outlet) or the Aladdin Theatre box office as soon as they are announced.

Bally's Celebrity Room

Bally's, 3645 Las Vegas Blvd. S. ☎ **800/237-7469** or 702/739-4567.

Superstar headliners play the 1,400-seat Celebrity Room. Dean Martin inaugurated the facility. Today, frequent performers include Barbara Mandrell, Engelbert Humperdinck, Bernadette Peters, Liza Minnelli, Jeff Foxworthy, Hall and Oates, Steve and Eydie Gorme, George Carlin, Andrew Dice Clay, Paul Anka, Anne Murray, Louie Anderson, and Penn & Teller.

- **Showroom Policies:** Nonsmoking and preassigned seating.
- **Price:** $25–$45, depending on the performer (tax included, drinks extra).
- **Show Times:** There are one or two shows a night at varying times (this also depends on the performer).
- **Reservations:** You can reserve up to 6 weeks in advance.

Caesars Circus Maximus Showroom

Caesars Palace, 3570 Las Vegas Blvd. S. **800/445-4544** or 702/731-7333.

From its opening in 1966, Caesars' 1,200-seat Circus Maximus Showroom has presented superstar entertainment—everyone from Judy Garland to Frank Sinatra. Many current headliners started out here as opening acts for established performers, among them Richard Pryor for singer Bobbie Gentry, Jay Leno for Tom Jones, and the Pointer Sisters for Paul Anka. The current lineup of luminaries includes Julio Iglesias, David Copperfield, Howie Mandel, Clint Black, Jerry Seinfeld, Natalie Cole, Diana Ross, Chicago, The Moody Blues, Wynonna, and Johnny Mathis. The luxurious showroom keeps to the Roman theme. Illuminated shields along the wall are replicas of those used by the legions of Caesar, and plush royal purple booths are patterned

---

Headliner Stadiums

Two arenas are worth a special mention since they often feature major entertainers. **Sam Boyd Stadium,** the outdoor stadium at the University of Nevada, Las Vegas (UNLV), has been host to such major acts as Paul McCartney, U2, the Eagles, and Metallica. **Thomas & Mack Center,** the university's indoor arena, has a more comprehensive concert schedule, including such names as Van Halen, Michael Bolton, and Celine Dion, as well as shows like *Disney on Ice* and Ringling Bros. Circus. Both are located on the **UNLV campus** at Boulder Highway and Russell Road (☎ **702/895-3900**). Ticketmaster (☎ **702/474-4000**) handles ticketing for both arenas.

---

after Roman chariots.

- **Showroom Policies:** Nonsmoking with preassigned seating.
- **Price:** $45–$75, depending on the performer (including tax, drinks optional).
- **Show Times:** One or two shows nightly; times depend on performer.
- **Reservations:** You can reserve any time in advance (as soon as a show is confirmed) via credit card.

Desert Inn Crystal Room
3145 Las Vegas Blvd S. ☎ **800/634-6906** or 702/733-4444.

The Desert Inn has a long history of superstar entertainment. Frank Sinatra's Las Vegas debut took place in the hotel's Painted Desert Room in 1951, and other early performers included Maurice Chevalier, No'l Coward, Buster Keaton, and Marlene Dietrich. Jimmy Durante once broke the piano board on a new spinet and yelled to the audience, "Mr. Hughes, it was broke when I got it!" And on one memorable night the entire Rat Pack (Dean Martin, Frank Sinatra, Joey Bishop, Sammy Davis, Jr., and Peter Lawford) invaded the stage when Eddie Fisher was performing! Today this historic showroom has been renamed the Crystal Room. Currently among its current major headliners are Smokey Robinson, The Temptations, The Golden Boys (Frankie Avalon, Fabian, and Bobby Rydell), Dennis Miller, Neil Sedaka, and Rita Rudner.

- **Showroom Policies:** Nonsmoking with maître d' seating.
- **Price:** $35–$50, depending on the performer (including two drinks; tax and gratuity extra).
- **Show Times:** Days vary; shows are usually at 9pm.
- **Reservations:** You can reserve up to 3 engagements in advance.

Hard Rock Hotel's The Joint
Hard Rock Hotel, 4455 Paradise Rd. ☎ **800/693-7625** or 702/693-5000.

When the Hard Rock Hotel opened in 1995, The Eagles were the first act to play its 1,400-seat state-of-the-art, live concert venue, The Joint. Other performers during the hotel's opening festivities were Melissa Etheridge (with Al Green), B.B. King, Iggy Pop, Duran Duran, and Sheryl Crow. Since then the facility has presented Bob Dylan, Ziggy Marley, Hootie & the Blowfish, the Black Crowes, Donna Summer, Stephen Stills, Jimmy Cliff, Tears for Fears, Johnny Cash, Lyle Lovett, and James Brown.

- **Showroom Policies:** Smoking permitted; seating preassigned or general, depending on the performer.
- **Price:** $20 to $100, depending on the performer (drinks and tax extra).

Impressions

If I stand still while I'm singing, I'm a dead man. I might as well go back to driving a truck.

—Legendary Las Vegas headliner Elvis Presley

- **Show Times:** 8:30pm (nights of performance vary).
- **Reservations:** You can reserve up to 30 days in advance.

Las Vegas Hilton: Fabulous Fridays

3000 Paradise Rd. ☎ **800/222-5361** or 702/732-5755.

Before it became the venue for Andrew Lloyd Webber's *Starlight Express,* the Hilton showroom presented superstar headliners for more than two decades. Barbra Streisand was the first in 1969, Gladys Knight the last in 1993, and in between Elvis played 837 sold-out shows over a 10-year period. On Fridays, when *Starlight Express* is dark, the Hilton has begun presenting headliners once again. Among those who've appeared so far are Creedence Clearwater, political comedian Bill Maher, Nancy Wilson (on a double bill with Ramsey Lewis), Lou Rawls, The Monkees, Johnny Cash & The June Carter Family, Al Jarreau, K.C. & The Sunshine Band, and Peaches and Herb.

- **Showroom Policies:** Nonsmoking with preassigned seating.
- **Price:** $29 to $59, depending on the performer (drinks and tax extra).
- **Show Times:** Usually 9pm.
- **Reservations:** You can reserve up to 60 days in advance.

MGM Grand Garden Events Arena

MGM Grand, 3799 Las Vegas Blvd. S. ☎ **800/929-1111** or 702/891-7777.

The 15,222-seat MGM Grand Garden Events Arena is a major venue for sporting events. It also hosts big-name concerts. Barbra Streisand returned to the stage here after an absence of 25 years on New Year's Eve 1993. Others who have played the Arena include Neil Diamond, Sting, Jimmy Buffett, Luther Vandross, Janet Jackson, The Rolling Stones, Bette Midler, Billy Joel, Elton John, and Whitney Houston. Grand Garden Events tickets are generally also available through Ticketmaster (☎ **702/474-4000**).

- **Showroom Policies:** Nonsmoking with preassigned seating.
- **Price:** Varies with event or performer.
- **Show Times:** Vary with event or performer.
- **Reservations:** Advance-reservations policy varies with event or performer.

MGM Grand Hollywood Theatre

MGM Grand, 3799 Las Vegas Blvd. S. ☎ **800/929-1111** or 702/891-7777.

The 650-seat Hollywood Theatre hosts headliners such as Wayne Newton, Tom Jones, the Righteous Brothers, Jeff Foxworthy, Dennis Miller, Rita Rudner, and Randy Travis. It has also featured occasional live telecasts of "The Tonight Show" with Jay Leno.

- **Showroom Policies:** Nonsmoking with preassigned seating.
- **Price:** Usually $44–$55, varies with performer (tax and drinks extra).
- **Show Times:** Vary with performer; there's usually a show at 9pm.
- **Reservations:** Tickets can be ordered anytime in advance as soon as they become available.

Sahara Hotel Showroom
2535 Las Vegas Blvd. S. ☎ **702/737-2878.**

Since the Sahara was just completing a major renovation at press time, few details were available about its showroom. It will present headliner performers. Call for details or check local show listings when you're in town.

✪ Stratosphere: Danny Gans: The Man of Many Voices
2000 Las Vegas Blvd. S. ☎ **800/99-TOWER** or 702/380-7777.

The Stratosphere's 650-seat Broadway Showroom, a headliner venue, has currently booked *Danny Gans: The Man of Many Voices* for an indefinite run. If he's still on when you visit, don't miss him. Gans, who has starred on Broadway, is an impressionist extraordinaire. Natalie Cole, who heard him perform her father's famous song, "Unforgettable," exclaimed "No one has ever done a better impression of my dad." His show is also unforgettable. In addition to startlingly realistic impressions of dozens of singers (everyone from Sinatra to Springsteen), he does movie scenes (such as Fonda and Hepburn in *On Golden Pond),* Bill Clinton, weird duets (Michael Bolton and Dr. Ruth or Stevie Wonder singing to Shirley MacLaine "I Just Called to Say I Was You"), and, of course, a first-rate Elvis. A mind-boggling highlight is Gans' rendition of "The Twelve Days of Christmas" in 12 different voices, which necessitates rapidly switching back and forth from such diverse impressions as Paul Lynde, Clint Eastwood, Peter Falk, and Woody Allen, among others. This show gets a standing ovation every night.

- **Showroom Policies:** Nonsmoking with maître d' seating.
- **Price:** $29.50 (including tax, drinks extra).
- **Show Times:** Thurs–Mon at 9pm. Dark Tues–Wed.
- **Reservations:** Tickets can be ordered up to 30 days in advance.

4 Comedy Clubs

Catch a Rising Star
MGM Grand, 3799 Las Vegas Blvd. S. ☎ **800/929-1111** or 702/891-7777.

Like The Improv, Catch a Rising Star presents nationally known talent from the comedy circuit. Three comedians perform each night.

- **Showroom Policies:** Nonsmoking with maître d' seating.
- **Price:** $12.50 (tax and drinks extra).
- **Show Times:** Nightly at 8 and 10:30pm.
- **Reservations:** You can charge tickets up to 30 days in advance via credit card.

Comedy Club
Riviera Hotel, 2901 Las Vegas Blvd. S. ☎ **800/634-6753** or 702/734-9301.

The Riviera's comedy club, on the second floor of the Mardi Gras Plaza, showcases four comedians nightly. Once a month, usually on the last weekend, the club hosts a late-night XXXTREME Comedy Showcase for shock and X-rated comedians. Other special events include the *All Gay Comedy Revue* and R-rated hypnotist Frank

Impressions

I've built my own world here. Wayne's world.
—Las Vegas superstar Wayne Newton talking about his
52-acre estate, Casa de Shenandoah, 5 miles out of town

Santos.

- **Showroom Policies:** Nonsmoking with maître d' seating.
- **Price:** $14.95 (includes two drinks; tax and gratuity extra).
- **Show Times:** Nightly at 8 and 10pm, with an extra show Fri and Sat at 11:45pm.
- **Reservations:** Tickets can be purchased at the box office only, in advance if you wish.

Comedy Max
Maxim, 160 E. Flamingo Rd. ☎ **800/634-6987** or 702/731-4423.

The Maxim's very attractive nightclub features three comics nightly, and every seat is good.

- **Showroom Policies:** Nonsmoking, maître d' seating.
- **Price:** $16.25 (includes two drinks, tax, and gratuity). For $19.95 you can enjoy a buffet dinner as well.
- **Show Times:** Nightly at 7, 9, and 10:30pm.
- **Reservations:** You can reserve up to a week in advance by phone.

Comedy Stop
Tropicana, 3801 Las Vegas Blvd. S. ☎ **800/468-9494** or 702/739-2411.

Similar to clubs described above, the Comedy Stop here features three nationally known comedy headliners nightly.

- **Showroom Policies:** Smoking permitted with maître d' seating.
- **Price:** $14.30 (includes two drinks; tax and gratuity extra).
- **Show Times:** Nightly at 8 and 10:30pm.
- **Reservations:** You can charge tickets in advance via credit card.

The Improv
Harrah's, 3475 Las Vegas Blvd. S. ☎ **800/392-9002** or 702/369-5111.

This offshoot of Budd Friedman's famed comedy club (the first one opened in 1963 in New York City), presents about four comedians per show in a 400-seat showroom. These are talented performers—the top comics on the circuit who you're likely to see on Leno and Letterman. You can be sure of an entertaining evening.

- **Showroom Policies:** Nonsmoking with preassigned seating.
- **Price:** $14.95 (tax and drinks extra).
- **Show Times:** Tues–Sun at 8 and 10:30pm. Dark Mon.
- **Reservations:** You can charge tickets up to 30 days in advance via credit card.

✪ The Unknown Comic
Holiday Inn Boardwalk, 3750 Las Vegas Blvd. S. ☎ **702/735-2400.**

The Unknown Comic is Murray Langston, so called because he performs a large part of his act with a bag over his head. Come early to see pre-show video clips of his numerous TV appearances on everything from *The Tonight Show* to *Oprah*. Langston is zany (some might say insane) and very manic, a king of one-liners such as "What's the most successful pick-up line in the South?" "Nice tooth." He also does a bit of ventriloquism with a little bag face called Sad Sack for a dummy. It's weird, but fun.

- **Showroom Policies:** Smoking permitted; seating is first come, first served.
- **Price:** $5.95 (drinks and tax extra).
- **Show Times:** Tues–Sun at 9pm. Dark Mon.
- **Reservations:** You can make reservations by phone up to 7 days in advance.

Note: Monday through Saturday, G. David Howard, another stand-up comic, performs after Murray Langston. Showroom policies and reservations information are the same. Price is $5.50 Shows take place Mon 9pm, Tues 10:30pm. Wed–Sat 11:55pm. Dark Sun.

5 Piano Bars

In addition to the below listed, consider the ultraelegant **Palace Court Terrace Lounge,** adjoining the Palace Court restaurant at Caesars (see chapter 6). This romantic piano bar has a stained-glass skylight that retracts for a view of open star-lit sky. Off the lounge is an intimate crystal-chandeliered European-style casino for high-stakes players only. **Gatsby's** at the MGM Grand (see chapter 6) also has a sophisticated and stunning adjoining piano bar.

Alexis Park Resort: Pisces Bistro
375 E. Harmon Ave. ☎ **702/796-3300.**

The very upscale Alexis Park offers live entertainment in a beautiful room under a 30-foot domed ceiling; planters of greenery cascade from tiered balconies. When the weather permits, it's lovely to sit at umbrella tables on a terra-cotta patio overlook-ing the pool. Live music is featured Tuesday through Saturday nights from 8pm till about midnight; a versatile pianist and vocalist perform everything from show tunes to oldies to Top 40. Light fare is available. No cover or minimum.

The Carriage House: Kiefer's
105 E. Harmon Ave. ☎ **702/739-8000.**

This rooftop restaurant has a plushly furnished adjoining piano bar/lounge. Win-dowed walls offer great views of the Las Vegas neon skyline, making this a roman-tic setting for cocktails and hors d'oeuvres. There's piano music Thursday through Saturday from 7 to 11pm to midnight. No cover or minimum.

Club Monaco
1487 E. Flamingo Rd., between Maryland Pkwy. and Tamarus St. (on your right as you come from the Strip; look for the LA-Z-Boy Furniture Gallery). ☎ **702/737-6212.**

This low-key, sophisticated piano bar—its walls lined with oil paintings of icons such as Elvis, Bogart, James Dean, and Marilyn Monroe (not to mention Rodney Dangerfield, finally getting respect)—is a romantic setting for cocktails and classic piano-bar entertainment. There's a small dance floor. Friday and Saturday a talented vocalist is on hand as well. Club Monaco is far from a meat market, but it is a relaxed atmosphere in which to meet people. The crowd is over 30. A menu offers salads, burgers, steak sandwiches, pastas, and gourmet appetizers such as oysters Rockefeller and escargot-stuffed mushrooms. Open 24 hours. No cover or minimum.

6 Gay Bars

Angles
4633 Paradise Rd., at Naples St. ☎ **702/791-0100.**

This 24-hour gay bar, though among the most upscale in Las Vegas, is a casual neigh-borhood hangout compared to gay bars in other cities. The clientele is mostly local—about 85% men (including drag queens) in their mid-20s to early 30s. Wednesday nights there's a drag show in the front room, while the back room hosts Gothic Night. Weekends, male and female strippers perform from midnight till about 4 or

5pm. There's a dance floor (the music's pretty loud), a small outdoor courtyard, and a game room with pool tables, darts, and pinball machines. No cover or minimum.

The Buffalo
4640 Paradise Rd. ☎ **702/733-8355.**

Close to both Angles and Gipsy, this is a leather/Levis bar popular with motorcycle clubs. It features beer busts (all the beer you can drink for $5) Friday nights from 9pm to midnight.

Gipsy
4605 Paradise Rd., at Naples St. ☎ **702/731-1919.**

Just next door to Angles, Gipsy is more of a dance club, with more of a gay/straight, male/female mix (men still predominate). The music isn't quite as blaring, and the bar adjoining the dance floor is separated from it by a glass wall, making audible conversation an option. Personally, I prefer Gipsy to Angle's, but their proximity makes it easy to see for yourself. There's always good dance music. Monday there are Latin female-impersonator shows, Tuesday is Variety Night featuring amateur strip shows and dance revues, and Thursday there are lip-synching contests for cash prizes. There's a $4 cover nightly except Wednesday and Sunday; no minimum. Open daily 10pm to 6pm.

7 Other Bars

In addition to the below-listed, consider hanging out at **Country Star,** the **Hard Rock Cafe,** and **Planet Hollywood,** all described in chapter 6.

Debbie Reynolds Hotel: Jazz & Jokes with Debbie Reynolds and Friends
305 Convention Center Dr. ☎ **702/737-0711.**

Every Friday and Saturday night from 10pm to 2am, this informal "show" takes place in the comfortable Celebrity Café. Basically, it's an intimate after-hours place where Strip entertainers, who are usually too keyed up to go home immediately after their shows, can hang out and unwind with Debbie. And being entertainers, they love to take the mike and belt out a few numbers. Among those who have already dropped by are Tony Bennett, blues singer Bobby Jones, Keely Smith, and comedian Steve Rossi. At its best this is great impromptu entertainment with a chance to stargaze at close quarters. There is a $5 cover, plus a 2-drink minimum.

Holy Cow
2432 Las Vegas Blvd. S., at Sahara Ave. ☎ **702/732-COWS.**

The Holstein is holy at this enormous 24-hour microbrewery, pub, and casino. It's extensively cow themed, from paintings of cows dancing with pigs to cow-motif lighting fixtures. You can take a free tour of the upstairs brewery and/or taste the four hand-crafted microbrews (pale ale, wheat beer, brown ale, and a monthly changing brewmaster's special) it produces. The Cow is a friendly place (cigar friendly, too), with six TV monitors over the main bar airing sporting events. There's plenty of casino action (more than 80 slot/video poker/keno machines; ask for a token for a free slot machine spin), and a better-than-average-pub-fare menu highlights bratwurst platters with sauerkraut and red potato salad. Breakfast is also served around the clock.

8 Dance Clubs

The Beach
365 S. Convention Center Dr., at Paradise Rd. ☎ **702/731-9298.**

This is an immense two-story club. The staff sings, performs skits, shoots customers with water pistols, and dances on the bars. Speaking of bars, there are five downstairs alone, surrounding a large dance floor. There's also a patio with umbrella tables. Upstairs is a sports bar with a unique feature; you can place bets on the games you're watching (there are over 100 TV monitors in the club, including seven giant screens), a hip, female-friendly alternative to casino sports books. Also upstairs are pool tables, foosball, pinball, basketball machines, and slot/video-poker machines. The Beach opened in 1995 with a Buster Poindexter concert, and it's still the scene of frequent big-name concerts (Steppenwolf, Edgar Winter, Electric Light Orchestra, 38. Special, Christopher Cross, Vince Neil, Cheap Trick, Kansas, The Romantics). Other nights, there are local bands or a DJ. There seems to be a special theme for every night of the week. The crowd, about half local, ranges in age from early 20s through 40s; it can vary depending on what conventions are in town (during Comdex, Bill Gates was dancing on the bar). Light fare is available throughout the evening, including full breakfasts from 2 to 7am. Open 24 hours. No cover (except during special events) or minimum. There's free valet parking, and, if you've driven here and become intoxicated, they'll drive you back home at no charge.

Bobby McGee's

1030 E. Flamingo Rd., at Cambridge St. ☎ **702/733-0388.**

Bobby McGee's is a place to party—the kind of hang-loose club where dance contests, trivia games, putting contests, and the like are frequent events. The restaurant waitstaff is attired in costumes ranging from Davy Crockett to Alice in Wonderland. A DJ is on hand nightly playing top-40 tunes, country, rock, and oldies, and sporting events are aired on eight TV monitors and one big screen over the bar. The crowd is mainstream, ages 21 through about 40, typified by the businesspeople who drop by after work to partake of Bobby McGee's free—and extensive—internationally themed happy-hour buffets. A full menu—steak, seafood, pastas, and lighter fare—is served through 1am. Open Sunday through Thursday till 2am, Friday and Saturday till 4am. No cover or minimum.

Cleopatra's Barge Nightclub

Caesars Palace, 3570 Las Vegas Blvd. S. ☎ **702/731-7110.**

Live bands play Top 40 dance tunes aboard Cleopatra's Barge, a replica of the majestic ships that sailed the Nile in ancient Egypt. This waterborne dance club is also afloat on "the Nile," complete with oars, ostrich-feather fans, statues of ancient pharaohs, and furled sails. You board via gangplanks, and hydraulic mechanisms rock the barge gently. There's seating on the main barge and on the dock. Nubian-inspired cocktail waitresses in diaphanous togas bring drinks. In the early days of this facility, Caesars found it necessary to construct a dockside fence to keep awestruck sightseers from falling into the river. No cover; there's a 2-drink minimum Friday and Saturday only. Open Tuesday to Sunday 10pm to 4am.

Club Rio

Rio Suite Hotel, 3700 W. Flamingo Rd. ☎ **800/634-6787** or 702/597-5970.

One of the hottest spots in town for young sophisticates (the crowd ranges from about ages 25 to 40, with more of the former than the latter) is Club Rio, a chic after-hours venue that occupies the luxurious Copacabana Showroom after the dinner show. It couldn't be more plush, with comfy tiered booths lit by table lamps girding a large dance floor and tuxedoed bartenders adding panache to the scene. Especially upscale is the velvet-roped VIP section where the bar minimum is $100 to $300. A DJ plays top-40 tunes and other high-energy sounds from 11pm to 3am nightly (sometimes later), and there's frequent live entertainment as well (including big names like Blondie, Kool & the Gang, Eddie Money, Jodie Watley, Montel Jordan, and David Lee Roth). Wednesday is disco night, featuring '70s sounds. The

Rio has state-of-the-art sound and lighting systems, and guests view music videos (and themselves) on two immense video walls. There's a $10 cover charge (for men only), no drink minimum. Cover may be higher (and include women) for headliner concerts.

Drink

200 E. Harmon Ave., at Koval Lane ☎ **702/796-5519.**

Decidedly more sophisticated than the ultra-casual Beach, but not quite as serious as Club Rio, the 17,000-square-foot Drink is hip and happening, the scene of occasional cigar-smokers' dinners (the club is cigar friendly and maintains a humidor). It draws a good-looking, upscale professional crowd in the 20-to-40 age range, with occasional visiting celebs; Jay Leno, Matthew Perry, Dennis Rodman, and Charles Barkley are among those who've partied here. There's a labyrinth of variously decorated rooms, all candlelit, ranging from the cozy cigar room—also the VIP lounge—to a cave-walled Tribal Room with rope swings, a totem pole, and barstools fashioned from steel drums. A 3,600-square-foot outdoor courtyard—the main dance area with a 16-foot video wall—is the scene of concerts and foam nights (when the dance floor is covered with foam to neck level). Drink hosts about two live concerts a month. Thursday nights a retro disco band is on hand; other times, a DJ plays a mix of techno, dance, and classic rock, everything but rap and country. You can enjoy a vast variety of drinks here, including 50 international and microbrewery beers, single-malt scotches, and 30 different kinds of premium vodkas (the latter served in a psychedelically decorated room). A moderately priced menu is available. Drink was created by Michael Morton (brother of Hard Rock's Peter). Open Monday to Thursday till 3am, Friday and Saturday till 5am. Closed Sunday. Cover is $5 to $10 ($15 to $25 when major artists are performing); women are admitted free Tuesday nights. There's no minimum. Self parking is free, valet parking $3.

Monte Carlo Pub & Brewery

Monte Carlo Resort, 3770 Las Vegas Blvd. S. ☎ **702/730-7777.**

After 9pm nightly, this immense warehouse-like pub and working microbrewery (see details in chapter 6) turns from a casual restaurant into a rollicking, high-energy dance club that is very popular with Gen-X-to-thirtysomething locals. Rock videos blare forth from a large screen and 40 TV monitors around the room, while, onstage, dueling pianos provide music and audience-participation entertainment. The Pub is cigar friendly and maintains a humidor. There's a full bar, and, of course, the house microbrews are featured; you can also order pizza. There's no cover or minimum. Open until 1am Sunday to Thursday, till 3am Friday and Saturday.

Sam's Town Western Dance Hall

Sam's Town, 5111 Boulder Hwy. ☎ **702/456-7777.**

Attracting a large local crowd, Sam's Town houses a rustic dance hall, its weathered barnwood walls hung with steer horns, neon beer signs, wagon wheels, and other things Western. You can dance here to music provided by live country bands Monday through Saturday from 9am to 3pm. Come by from 7:30 to 9pm for free lessons in line dancing and West Coast swing. Sunday is karaoke night, with a DJ on hand from 9pm. There's no cover or minimum.

Side Trips from Las Vegas

Anyone who has seen the cascades of neon and outsized hotels along the Strip would agree that the Las Vegas way is to do things on a grand scale. What most visitors to Las Vegas don't realize is that the sense of being somewhere extraordinary only shifts gears at the city limits; seeing the stark grandeur of the surrounding desert is an unforgettable experience in its own right. Also within easy reach are some of the country's most imposing man-made and natural wonders, such as the Hoover Dam and Red Rock Canyon; ghost towns, and other places where you can experience the flavor of the Old West; and innumerable opportunities for outdoor recreation—from white-water rafting, to precipitous downhill skiing, to desert hiking—all in a landscape like none other.

The following excursions will take you from 20 to 60 miles out of town. Every one of them offers a memorable travel experience.

1 Goodsprings—A Ghost Town

35 miles SW of Las Vegas

The shadowy phenomenon of ghost towns—once-flourishing areas that were later deserted and abandoned—has always been an intriguing and romantic image. Many of these towns began with one lone traveler who serendipitously stumbled upon mineral-rich rocks while out on another pursuit—perhaps tracking game or strayed livestock. He would mark off his area, stuff his pockets and knapsacks with specimens, and rush off to register his claim. Soon adventurers, drifters, and raggedy prospectors would flock to the area, set up meager lodgings, break out picks and shovels, and get to work. If the yield was promising, word would spread quickly, and entrepreneurs would arrive with provisions. A main street would develop around a general-merchandise store, followed by other shops and the inevitable mining-camp saloons, gambling houses, and red-light district. Eventually a real town would emerge.

But then the mines would begin drying up. Little by little, businesses would fold, and the population would dwindle. Vandalism, wind, and fire would ravage the remaining structures, leaving only ghost-inhabited remnants of what had been. And so the town died. Nevada has at least 40 such towns, of which Goodsprings is the closest to Las Vegas.

Founded in the 1860s, and named for Joseph Good, a prospector, Goodsprings flourished as a silver and lead mining town around the turn of the century. During World War I, the Goodsprings Hotel was advertised in New York newspapers as "the finest in the West," and people from Las Vegas flocked here to shop, gamble, and see shows. The thriving metropolis had a population of 2,000, nine bars, several restaurants, a theater, churches, homes, and businesses. A narrow-gauge railroad carried ore from the surrounding mines to the Union Pacific tracks at nearby Jean. As the biggest town in Nevada, Goodsprings was a regular stop for Barnum & Bailey.

Shortly thereafter, mining days ended, and the town began its decline. It has had only one brief brush with fame since. On January 16, 1942, Goodsprings made headlines because it was the closest town to Potosi Mountain, where a plane lost in a storm crashed with movie star Carole Lombard on board. Her husband, Clark Gable, stayed briefly at the Goodsprings Hotel while awaiting further news. By 1967, Goodsprings's population had shrunk to 62. The hotel had burned to the ground, and one of its last remaining businesses, a general store, was torn down. Today it is an authentic ghost town—an eerie relic of Nevada's boom-and-bust mining era. All that remains of the once-thriving town is the rotting machinery of mining companies, discarded wrecks of old, abandoned cars—and the still-extant Pioneer Saloon.

ESSENTIALS

By car, follow I-15 south out of Las Vegas and turn onto Nev. 161 west at the Jean-Goodsprings turnoff. The first thing you'll pass—about a half mile before you get to the town itself—is a cemetery.

WHAT TO SEE & DO

Stop at the cemetery and poke around a bit. It's a down-at-the-heels sort of place where perpetual care has not been a big thing. A couple of markers are wood, weathered almost to the point of illegibility. Most of the standard headstones are in a segment of the yard that has been fenced off by a low rail. All of these stones belong to the Fayle family, who were prominent Goodsprings citizens in the town's heyday. Surprisingly, there are some recent graves of desert-rat bikers here. In the area near the cemetery, you can search for Native American arrowheads, spearheads, and other artifacts.

The heart of Goodsprings is the **Pioneer Saloon** (☎ 702/874-9362), which from its dusty, run-down exterior does not look operative. It has, however, been a going concern since 1913. The only complete decorative-metal building left standing anywhere in the United States, the saloon has pressed-tin walls (interior and exterior) and ceiling. If you're nostalgic about old-time western saloons, you'll love the Pioneer. It's heated by a potbellied stove in winter and cooled by a swamp cooler in summer. Many of its fixtures and furnishings (even the curtains) are original to the saloon. Bartenders at the century-old cherry and mahogany bar regale customers with anecdotes about Goodsprings's past. A copy of the 1916 *Goodsprings Gazette* that carries an advertisement for the saloon is displayed on one wall; while you're looking at the walls, note the bullet holes—legacy of a long-ago gunfight over a poker game. In addition to authentic ambience, the Pioneer offers such diverse entertainments as a pool table, dart board, jukebox, and poker machines. Personally, I found it thrilling to play pool in a ghost town. The Pioneer is open daily from 10am to midnight.

These days, Goodsprings may be making something of a comeback. Two big casino hotels, the **Gold Strike** and **Nevada Landing,** have been erected nearby, and the population is now up to about 130.

Excursions from Las Vegas

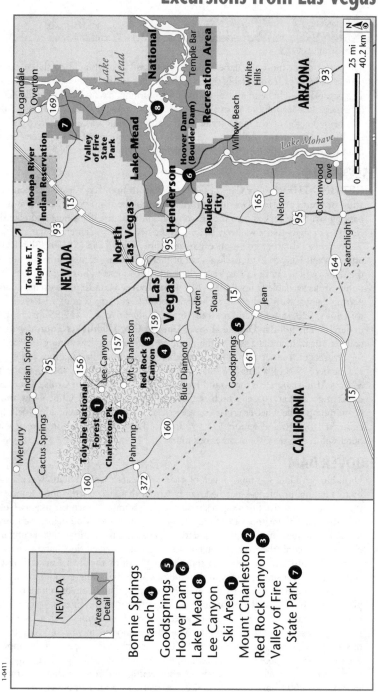

Bonnie Springs Ranch ④
Goodsprings ⑤
Hoover Dam ⑥
Lake Mead ⑧
Lee Canyon
Ski Area ①
Mount Charleston ②
Red Rock Canyon ③
Valley of Fire
State Park ⑦

1-0411

2 Hoover Dam & Lake Mead

30 miles SE of Las Vegas

This is one of the most popular excursions from Las Vegas, visited by 2,000 to 3,000 people daily. Wear comfortable shoes; the dam tour involves quite a bit of walking. The best plan would be to tour the dam in the morning, have lunch in Boulder City, take the Lake Mead dinner cruise, and stay a night or two at Lake Mead Lodge (details below) enjoying the area's scenic beauty and recreation facilities. Drive back to Las Vegas through the Valley of Fire, which is about 60 magnificently scenic miles from Lake Mead (purchase gas before your start!).

ESSENTIALS

GETTING THERE   By Car   Take U.S. 93 south from Las Vegas (it's a continuation of Fremont Street Downtown). As you near the dam, you'll see a five-story parking structure tucked into the canyon wall on your left. Park here and take the elevators or stairs to the walkway leading to the new Visitor Center.

If you would rather go on an **organized tour, Gray Line** (☎ 702/384-1234) offers several Hoover Dam packages, all of them including admission and a tour of the dam. When you're in Las Vegas, look for discount coupons in numerous free publications available at hotels. The 6¹/₂ hour **Hoover Dam Express** excursion, departing daily at 8am and noon, includes a stop at Cranberry World; price is $22.95 for adults, $20.45 for children 10 to 16 and seniors over 62, $17.95 for children under 10. The full-day **Deluxe Hoover Dam & City Highlights Tour,** departing daily at 10am, includes a stop at the Heritage Museum to view mining and ranching artifacts of frontier days, a buffet lunch at the Railroad Pass Casino, and a visit to Cranberry World; adults $28.60, children 10 to 16 and seniors $26.10, under 10 $23.60. Most elaborate is the **Grand Hoover Dam & Lake Mead Cruise Tour,** also departing daily at 10am, which includes a visit to Ethel M Chocolates and a 45-minute paddle wheeler cruise on Lake Mead with a light lunch; adults $36.60, children 10 to 16 and seniors $34.10, under 10 $31.60. You can inquire at your hotel sightseeing desk about other bus tours.

HOOVER DAM

Until Hoover Dam was built, much of the southwestern United States was plagued by two natural problems—parched, sandy terrain that lacked irrigation for most of the year and extensive flooding in spring and early summer when the mighty Colorado River, fed by melting snow from its source in the Rocky Mountains, overflowed its banks and destroyed crops, lives, and property. On the positive side, raging unchecked over eons, the river's turbulent, rushing waters carved the Grand Canyon.

In 1928, prodded by the seven states through which the river runs during the course of its 1,400-mile journey to the Gulf of California, Congress authorized construction of a dam at Boulder Canyon (later moved to Black Canyon) under the auspices of the Bureau of Reclamation, U.S. Department of the Interior—the agency that still operates it today. The Senate's declaration of intention was that "A mighty river, now a source of destruction, is to be curbed and put to work in the interests of society." Construction began in 1931. Because of its vast scope, and the unprecedented problems posed in its realization, the project generated significant advances in many areas of machinery production, engineering, and construction. An army of more than 5,200 laborers was assembled, and work proceeded 24 hours a day. Completed in 1936, 2 years ahead of schedule, the dam stopped the annual floods and conserved water for irrigation, industrial, and domestic use. Equally important, it

Lake Mead & Vicinity

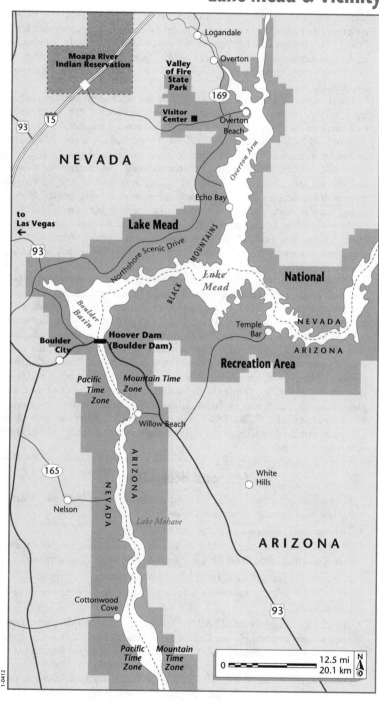

became one of the world's major electrical generating plants, providing low-cost, pollution-free hydroelectric power to a score of surrounding communities. Hoover Dam's $165-million cost has been repaid with interest by the sale of inexpensive power to a number of California cities and the states of Arizona and Nevada. The dam is a government project that paid for itself—a feat almost as awe-inspiring as its engineering.

The dam itself is a massive curved wall, 660 feet thick at the bottom and tapering to 45 feet where the road crosses it at the top. It towers 726.4 feet above bedrock (about the height of a 60-story skyscraper) and acts as a plug between the canyon walls to hold back up to 9.2 trillion gallons of water in Lake Mead—the reservoir created by its construction. Four concrete intake towers on the lake side drop the water down about 600 feet to drive turbines and create power, after which the water spills out into the river and continues south. All the architecture is on a grand scale, with beautiful art deco elements unusual in an engineering project. Note, for instance, the monumental 30-foot bronze sculpture, *Winged Figures of the Republic,* flanking a 142-foot flagpole at the Nevada entrance. According to its creator, Oskar Hansen, the sculpture symbolizes "the immutable calm of intellectual resolution, and the enormous power of trained physical strength, equally enthroned in placid triumph of scientific achievement."

The dam has become a major sightseeing attraction along with Lake Mead—America's largest man-made reservoir and a major Nevada recreation area.

Seven miles northwest of the dam on U.S. 93, you'll pass through **Boulder City,** which was built to house managerial and construction workers. Sweltering summer heat (many days it is 125°F) ruled out a campsite by the dam, whereas the higher elevation of Boulder City offered lower temperatures. The city emerged within a single year, turning a desert waste into a community of 6,000 with tree-shaded lawns, homes, churches, parks, restaurants, hotels, and schools. By 1934 it was Nevada's 3rd-largest town. Today, it continues to thrive with a population of 13,500; you might plan on having lunch here at **Totos,** a reasonably priced Mexican restaurant at 806 Buchanan Blvd. (☎ **702/293-1744**); it's in the Von's shopping center. About 300 yards past Boulder City, at the top of a slight incline, Lake Mead comes into view.

Fast Facts: Hoover Dam

- The amount of concrete used in the construction of the dam could pave a standard highway from San Francisco to New York.
- The minimum wage paid on the project was $4 a day.
- Ninety-six men died while building, excavating, blasting, and scaling mountains during construction, and on-the-job injuries totaled about 1,500 a month.
- In summer, the canyon rocks are so hot you could literally fry an egg on them.
- Lake Mead contains enough water to cover the entire state of Pennsylvania to a 1-foot depth.
- The dam was originally called Boulder Dam because of its first-designated canyon site, then renamed Hoover Dam in 1930 to honor Herbert Hoover's years of work making the project a reality. Unofficially it was renamed Boulder Dam by FDR who did not wish to honor Hoover; it finally regained the name Hoover Dam under Truman, who, in 1947, asked the 80th Congress to find out just what the "dam" name really was. Both names are still in popular usage.

Impressions

Everybody knows Las Vegas is the best town by a dam site.
—Masthead slogan of the *Las Vegas Review Journal*

TOURING THE DAM

The **Hoover Dam Visitor Center,** a vast three-level circular concrete structure with a rooftop overlook, opened in 1995. You'll enter the Reception Lobby, where you can buy tickets, peruse informational exhibits, photographs, and memorabilia, and view three 12-minute video presentations in a rotating theater (respectively, about the importance of water to life, the events leading up to the construction of Hoover Dam, and the construction itself as well as the many benefits it confers). Additional exhibition galleries are in the works at this writing. Those on the Plaza Level will house interactive displays on the environment, habitation and development of the Southwest, the people who built the dam, and related topics. Yet another floor up, galleries on the Overlook Level demonstrate, via sculpted bronze panels, the benefits of Hoover Dam and Lake Mead to the states of Arizona, Nevada, and California. The Overlook Level additionally provides an unobstructed view of Lake Mead, the dam, the power plant, the Colorado River, and Black Canyon. You can visit an exhibit center across the street where a 10-minute presentation in a small theater focuses on a topographical map of the 1,400-mile Colorado River and the 14 dams and diversions along it. This building also houses a turbine and generator model and an information desk. A gift shop and food concession are under construction in the parking structure.

Thirty-minute tours of the dam depart from the Reception Lobby every few minutes daily, except Christmas. The Visitor Center opens at 8:30am, and the first tour departs soon after. The last tour leaves at 5:30pm, and the center closes at 6:30pm. Admission is $5 for adults, $2.50 for senior citizens and children 10 to 16, free for children under 10. More extensive—and expensive—hard-hat tours, offered every half hour between 9:30am and 4pm—can be arranged by calling in advance (☎ **702/ 294-3522**).

The tour begins with a 520-foot elevator descent into the dam's interior, where an access tunnel leads to the Nevada wing of the power plant. The power plant consists of two similar wings, each 650 feet long, on either side of the river. From the visitor's balcony of the Nevada wing, you'll see eight huge hydroelectric generators (nine from the Arizona wing). These generators are driven by individual turbines located 40 feet below the floor. Water is delivered from the reservoir to the turbines (through canyon walls) via massive 30-foot-diameter pipes called penstocks. You'll learn about the manufacture of these generating units, each of which produces sufficient electrical energy to supply the domestic needs of a city of 95,000 people. Units lighted at the top are in operation. After visiting the generating room below, you'll go outside to see a tunnel through the 600-foot canyon wall that provides access to vehicles entering the power-plant area. However, heavy equipment is lowered by a cableway that has a capacity of 150 tons! Looking up, you can see the control room for the cable operation. During construction, entire railroad cars loaded with materials were lowered into the canyon via this cableway. The drumlike tanks on the deck above are electrical transformers.

With the aid of a diagram, your guide will explain construction procedures of the four tunnels that were drilled and blasted through solid rock and used to divert the river around the damsite. These diversion tunnels averaged 4,000 feet in length and

56 feet in diameter. When construction work advanced beyond the point where it was no longer necessary to divert water around the damsite, the tunnels were permanently sealed off. You'll also learn about the four intake towers which control the supply of water drawn from Lake Mead for the power plant turbines, and the spillways which, one on each side of the lake, control its maximum depth and ensure that no flood will ever overflow the dam. Finally, visitors stand in one of the diversion tunnels and view one of the largest steel water pipes ever made (its interior could accommodate two lanes of automobile traffic).

LAKE MEAD NATIONAL RECREATION AREA

Under the auspices of the National Park Service, the 1.5-million-acre Lake Mead National Recreation Area was created in 1936 around Lake Mead (the reservoir lake resulted from the construction of Hoover Dam) and later Lake Mohave to the south (formed with the construction of Davis Dam). Before the lakes emerged, this desert region was brutally hot, dry, and rugged—unfit for human habitation. Today it is one of the nation's most popular playgrounds, attracting about 9 million visitors annually. The two lakes comprise 290.7 square miles. At an elevation of 1,221.4 feet, Lake Mead itself extends some 110 miles upstream toward the Grand Canyon. Its 550-mile shoreline, backed by spectacular cliff and canyon scenery, forms a perfect setting for a wide variety of water sports and desert hiking.

VISITOR INFORMATION   The **Alan Bible Visitor Center,** 4 miles northeast of Boulder City on U.S. 93 at Nev. 166 (☎ **702/293-8990**) can provide information on all area activities and services. You can pick up trail maps and brochures here, view informative films, and find out about scenic drives, accommodations, ranger-guided hikes, naturalist programs and lectures, birdwatching, canoeing, camping, lakeside RV parks, and picnic facilities. The center also sells books and videotapes about the area. It's open daily 8:30am to 4:30pm. For information on accommodations, boat rentals, and fishing also, call **Seven Crown Resorts** (☎ **800/752-9669**).

OUTDOOR ACTIVITIES

Hiking   The best season for hiking is November through March (too hot the rest of the year). Some ranger-guided hikes are offered via the Alan Bible Visitor Center, which also stocks detailed trail maps. Three trails—ranging in length from three-quarters of a mile to 6 miles—originate at the Visitor Center. The 6-mile trail goes past remains of the railroad built for the dam project. Be sure to take all necessary desert-hiking precautions (see details in chapter 7).

Camping   Lake Mead's shoreline is dotted with campsites, all of them equipped with running water, picnic tables, and grills. Available on a first-come, first-served basis, they are administered by the **National Park Service** (☎ **702/293-8990**). There's a charge of $8 per night at each campsite.

Boating and Fishing   A store at **Lake Mead Resort & Marina** under the auspices of Seven Crown Resorts (☎ **800/752-9669** or 702/293-3484), rents fishing boats, ski boats, personal watercraft, and patio boats. It also carries groceries, clothing, marine supplies, sporting goods, water-skiing gear, fishing equipment, and bait and tackle. You can get a fishing license here ($51 a year or $12 for one day, $4 for each consecutive day; $9 a year for children 12 to 15, under 12 free). The staff is knowledgeable and can apprise you of good fishing spots. Largemouth bass, striped bass, channel catfish, crappie, and bluegill are found in Lake Mead, rainbow trout, largemouth bass, and striped bass in Lake Mohave. You can also arrange here to rent a fully equipped houseboat at **Echo Bay,** 40 miles north.

Other convenient Lake Mead marinas offering similar rentals and equipment are **Las Vegas Bay** (☎ 702/565-9111), which is even closer to Las Vegas, **Callville Bay** (☎ 702/565-8958), which is the least crowded of the five on the Nevada Shore.

Scuba Diving   October to April, there's good visibility, lessened in summer months when algae flourishes. A list of good dive locations, authorized instructors, and nearby dive shops is available at Alan Bible Visitor Center. There's an underwater designated diving area near Lake Mead Marina.

Rafting   Rafting trips on the Colorado River are offered February 1 through November 30 by **Black Canyon, Inc.,** 1297 Nevada Hwy. in Boulder City (☎ 800/696-7238 or 702/293-3776). Twelve-mile trips begin at the base of Hoover Dam. You'll see canyon waterfalls and wildlife (bighorn sheep, wild burros, chuckwalla lizards, mallards, grebe, and the occasional golden eagle) and stop at a quiet cove for a picnic lunch. There are stunning rock formations en route, and the area is rich in history—southern Paiute rock shelters and 1920s river-gauging stations and cableways. Guides are quite knowledgeable about local lore. Prices (including lunch): $64.95 for adults, $35 for children ages 5 to 12, under 5 free. Bus transportation back to Las Vegas is available. Even if you don't go rafting, stop by Black Canyon, Inc.'s Boulder City headquarters to see exhibits about the area and a film on Hoover Dam. Their office also functions as an information center and tour operator for a wide array of area activities (Grand Canyon flights, jetskiing, skydiving, and more).

Canoeing   The Alan Bible Visitor Center can provide a list of outfitters who rent canoes for trips on the Colorado River. There's one catch, however: A canoeing permit ($5 for one; $10 for 2 to 5 canoes) is required in advance from the Bureau of Reclamation. Call **702/293-8204** Monday through Thursday for information.

Lake Cruises   A delightful way to enjoy Lake Mead is on a cruise aboard the *Desert Princess* (☎ 702/293-6180), a Mississippi-style paddle wheeler. Cruises depart year-round from a terminal near Lake Mead Lodge (see below) and a dock right at Hoover Dam (inquire at the Visitor Center). It's a relaxing, scenic trip (enjoyed from an open promenade deck or one of two fully enclosed, climate-controlled decks) through Black Canyon and past colorful rock formations known as the "Arizona Paint Pots" en route to Hoover Dam, which is lit at night. Options include buffet breakfast cruises ($21 adults; $10 children under 12), narrated midday cruises (light lunch fare available; $14.50 adults; $6 children), cocktail/dinner cruises ($29 adults, $15 children), and sunset dinner/dance cruises with live music ($43 adults, children not allowed). Add $1 to all rates if you depart from Hoover Dam. Dinner cruises include a meal of salad, hot garlic bread, entree, fresh vegetable, rice pilaf or roasted potatoes, dessert, and tea or coffee; it's served in a pleasant, windowed, air-conditioned dining room. There's a full bar on board. Call for departure times.

WHERE TO STAY

Lake Mead Lodge

322 Lakeshore Rd., Boulder City, NV 89005. ☎ **800/752-9669** or 702/293-2074. 45 rms. A/C TV. Early Mar–late Nov $50–$65, the rest of the year $35–$50. Extra person $6. Children under 5 stay free in parents' room. DISC, MC. V.

If you aren't properly outfitted for camping at Lake Mead (see above), it's heavenly to spend a few nights relaxing at this tranquil lakeside resort, enjoying the area's numerous recreational activities. It's an easy drive from Hoover Dam. The rooms, housed in terra-cotta-roofed cream-brick buildings, are comfortable and attractive with wood-paneled ceilings and walls of white-painted brick or rough-hewn pine. All offer full baths and cable TVs. A lovely pool glitters in its lakeside setting, surrounded by mountains and beautifully landscaped grounds planted with pines, palm trees, and flowering oleander bushes. Weathered-wood roped dock posts add a nautical look to the resort. You might want to relax with a good book in one of the gazebos on the property. About a half mile down the road is the marina, where you can while away a few hours over cocktails on a lakeside patio. The marina is headquarters for boating, fishing, and water sports; it also houses a large shop (see details above under "Boating and Fishing"). And Boulder Beach, also an easy walk from the lodge, has waterfront picnic tables and barbecue grills.

Dining/Entertainment: There's a nautically themed restaurant called **Tale of the Whale** (☎ 702/293-3484) at the marina, its rough-hewn pine interior embellished with harpoons, figureheads, ship lanterns, ropes, pulleys, and steering wheels. Open from 7am to 9pm Sunday to Thursday, till 10pm Friday and Saturday, it serves hearty breakfasts; sandwiches, salads, and burgers at lunch; and steak-and-seafood dinners, all at moderate prices. Sometimes there's live music Friday and Saturday nights.

3 Valley of Fire State Park

60 miles NE of Las Vegas

Most people visualize the desert as a vast expanse of undulating sands punctuated by the occasional cactus or palm-fringed oasis. The desert of America's southwest bears little relation to this Lawrence of Arabia image. Stretching for hundreds of miles around Las Vegas in every direction is a seemingly lifeless tundra of vivid reddish earth, shaped by time, climate, and subterranean upheavals into majestic canyons, cliffs, and ridges.

The 36,000-acre Valley of Fire State Park, typifying the mountainous red Mojave Desert, derives its name from the brilliant sandstone formations that were created 150 million years ago by a great shifting of sand and continue to be shaped by the geologic processes of wind and water erosion.

Although it's hard to imagine in the sweltering Nevada heat, for billions of years these rocks were under hundreds of feet of ocean. This ocean floor began to rise some 200 million years ago, and the waters became more shallow. Eventually the sea made a complete retreat, leaving a muddy terrain traversed by ever-diminishing streams. A great sandy desert covered much of the southwestern part of the American continent until about 140 million years ago. Over eons, winds, massive fault action, and water erosion sculpted fantastic formations of sand and limestone. Oxidation of iron in the sands and mud—and the effect of groundwater leaching the oxidized iron—turned the rocks the many hues of red, pink, russet, lavender, and white that can be seen today. Logs of ancient forests washed down from far away highlands and became petrified fossils which can be seen along two interpretive trails.

Human beings occupied the region—a wetter and cooler one—as far back as 4,000 years ago. They didn't live in the Valley of Fire, but during the Gypsum period (2000 B.C. to 300 B.C.), men hunted bighorn sheep (a source of food, clothing, blankets, and hut coverings) here with a notched stick called an atlatl that is depicted in the park's petroglyphs. Women and children caught rabbits, tortoises, and other small game. In the next phase, from 300 B.C. to A.D. 700, the climate became warmer and dryer. Bows and arrows replaced the atlatl and the hunters and gatherers discovered farming. The Anasazi people began cultivating corn, squash, and beans, and communities began replacing small nomadic family groups. These ancient people wove watertight baskets, mats, hunting nets, and clothing. Around A.D. 300 they learned how to make sun-dried ceramic pottery. Other tribes, notably the Paiutes, migrated to the area. By A.D. 1150 they had become the dominant group. Unlike the Anasazis, they were still nomadic and used the Valley of Fire region seasonally. These were the inhabitants white settlers found when they entered the area in the early- to mid-1800s. The newcomers diverted river and spring waters to irrigate their farmlands, destroying the nature-based Paiute way of life. About 300 descendants of those Paiute tribespeople still live on the Moapa Indian Reservation (about 20 miles northwest) that was established along the Muddy River in 1872.

ESSENTIALS

GETTING THERE   By Car   From Las Vegas take I-15 north to Exit 75 (Valley of Fire turnoff). However, the more scenic route is to take I-15 north, then travel Lake Mead Blvd. east to North Shore Rd. (Nev. 167), and proceed north to the Valley of Fire exit. The first route takes about an hour, the second 1 1/2 hours.

Numerous **sightseeing tours** go to Valley of Fire. **Gray Line** (☎ **702/384-1234**), has a 7-hour tour from Las Vegas, including lunch, that costs $29.95 for adults, $24.50 for children 17 and under. Inquire at your hotel tour desk.

Valley of Fire can also be visited in conjunction with Lake Mead. **From Lake Mead Lodge,** take Nev. 166 (Lakeshore Scenic Dr.) north, make a right turn on Nev. 167 (North Shore Scenic Dr.), turn left on Nev. 169 (Moapa Valley Blvd.) west—a spectacularly scenic drive—and follow the signs. Valley of Fire is about 65 miles from Hoover Dam.

WHAT TO SEE & DO

There are no food concessions or gas stations in the park; however, you can obtain meals or gas on Nev. 167 or in nearby **Overton** (15 miles northwest on Nev. 169). Overton is a fertile valley town replete with trees, agricultural crops, horses, and herds of cattle—quite a change in scenery.

At the southern edge of town is the **Lost City Museum,** 721 S. Moapa Valley Blvd. (☎ **702/397-2193**), commemorating an ancient Anasazi village that was discovered in the region in 1924. Its population reached one of the highest levels of Native American culture in the United States. Artifacts dating back 12,000 years are on display, as are clay jars, dried corn and beans, arrowheads, seashell necklaces, and willow baskets of the ancient Pueblo culture that inhabited this region between A.D. 300 and 1150. Other exhibits document the Mormon farmers who settled the valley in the 1860s. A large collection of local rocks—petrified wood, fern fossils, iron pyrites, green copper, and red iron oxide—along with manganese blown bottles turned purple by the ultraviolet rays of the sun are also displayed here. The museum is surrounded by reconstructed wattle-and-daub pueblos. Admission $2, free for children under 18. The museum is open daily from 8:30am to 4:30pm. Closed Thanksgiving, Christmas, and New Year's Day.

Information headquarters for Valley of Fire is the **Visitor Center** on Nev. 169, 6 miles west of North Shore Rd. (☎ **702/397-2088**). It's open 7 days a week from 8:30am to 4:30pm. Exhibits on the premises explain the origin and geologic history of the park's colorful sandstone formations, describe the ancient peoples who carved their rock art on canyon walls, and identify the plants and wildlife you're likely to see. Postcards, books, slides, and films are on sale here, and you can pick up hiking maps and brochures. Rangers can answer your park-related questions.

There are hiking trails, shaded picnic sites, and two campgrounds in the park. Most sites are equipped with tables, grills, water, and rest rooms. An $11 per night camping fee is charged for use of the campground; if you're not camping, it costs $4 to enter the park.

Some of the notable formations in the park have been named for the shapes they vaguely resemble—a duck, an elephant, seven sisters, domes, beehives, and so on. Mouse's Tank is a natural basin that collects rainwater, so named for a fugitive Paiute called Mouse who hid there in the late 1890s. And Native American petroglyphs etched into the rock walls and boulders—some dating as far back as 3,000 years ago—can be observed on self-guided trails. Petroglyphs at Atlatl Rock and Petroglyph Canyon are both easily accessible. Always awe-inspiring, the park is especially beautiful in early spring when the desert blooms with wildflowers—mallow, desert marigold, and indigo bush—in dramatic contrast to the predominant earth tones. Other desert life forms include bighorn sheep, ground squirrels, bats, kit foxes, jackrabbits, gila monsters, rattlesnakes, and lizards. And numerous birds—cactus and rock wrens, ravens, finches, and sage sparrows, as well as migrant species—are best observed in the early morning or late afternoon. In summer, when temperatures are usually over 100°, you may have to settle for driving through the park in an air-conditioned car.

4 Mount Charleston & Lee Canyon Ski Area

Mount Charleston: 40 miles NW of Las Vegas; Lee Canyon: 47 miles NW of Las Vegas

In summertime, the mountains that encircle Toiyabe National Forest are as much as 30° to 40° cooler than the sweltering desert city. These mountains, once an island in an ancient sea, are today a cool oasis in the desert. The highest peak towers 11,918 feet above sea level. It's a beautiful drive. Nev. 157 winds up for about 21 miles through gorgeous canyon scenery, and, as you ascend, desert vegetation—cactus, yucca, creosote bush, and Joshua trees—gives way to stands of juniper, dense ponderosa forest, aspen firs, and bristlecone pine. The highway ends at the lovely **Mount Charleston Resort.** You can plan a day around lunch here, with activities like hiking, camping, bird watching, and horseback riding. In winter, there are sleigh rides, and you can ski at nearby **Lee Canyon.** In summer, there are hayrides, scenic chairlift rides in the ski area, barbecues, and a music festival.

It's a twilight-zone feeling to come from hot and air-conditioned Las Vegas to this sometimes snowy region where you can sit in front of a blazing fire sipping hot buttered rum. Both the Mount Charleston Resort and the Mount Charleston Hotel serve as information centers for area activities. In addition to the below-listed attractions, see "Staying Active" in chapter 7.

ESSENTIALS

GETTING THERE   By Car   Take I-15 north and stay in the Reno Lane to U.S. 95 north. Make a left on Nev. 157.

During ski season you can catch a **bus** to the Lee Canyon Ski Area. Departure points vary each year. For details, call **702/878-5465.** There is no bus transportation to Mount Charleston.

WHAT TO SEE & DO

Under the auspices of the Mount Charleston Resort are the **Mt. Charleston Riding Stables** (☎ **800/955-1314** or 702/872-5408), offering marvelously scenic trail rides to the edge of the wilderness. These depart from stables on Kyle Canyon Road. Since the schedule varies, it's best to call in advance for details. Weather permitting, the stables also offer horse-drawn sleigh rides Thanksgiving Day through March ($8 for adults, $4 for children 10 and under) and hayrides Memorial Day through Labor Day ($5 for adults, $3 for children).

Forty pine-sheltered and secluded picnic groves are equipped with barbecue grills.

There are numerous **hiking trails,** ranging from short panoramic walks to waterfalls near the restaurant/lounge to more difficult hikes farther afield. A popular 5-mile trail beginning at Lee Canyon Highway takes you through a canyon of aspen and into forested areas of ponderosa, white fir, and bristlecone pine. There are picnic areas and campsites along some trails. For information on camping and hiking trails, contact the **U.S. Forest Service,** 2881 S. Valley View Blvd., Suite 16, Las Vegas, NV 89102 (☎ **702/873-8800**). For camping information and reservations, you can also call **800/280-CAMP.** Both the Mount Charleston Resort and the Mount Charleston Hotel can provide trail maps.

The **Las Vegas Ski and Snowboard Resort,** at the end of Nev. 156 (☎ **702/385-2-SKI**), has a base elevation of 8,510 feet which, along with an extensive snow-making system, provides an almost ideal climate and snow cover for skiing Thanksgiving Day through Easter Day. Facilities include a lodge, a complete ski school, an extensive ski-rental shop, a snowboard park, a coffee shop, and a lounge with blazing fireplace and sundeck. Three double chair lifts carry skiers over 40 acres of well-maintained slopes (in summer, you can ride them for scenic views Friday through Sunday). And summer weekends, the resort is the scene of a country/bluegrass and rock music festival.

WHERE TO STAY

The Mount Charleston Inn Hotel & Restaurant

2 Kyle Canyon Rd. (on Nev. 157). ☎ **702/872-5500.** 60 rms. 3 suites. A/C TV TEL. Single or double Sun–Thurs $49–$62, Fri–Sat $69–$89; $155 suite. Extra person $5. Children under 12 stay free in parents' room. Inquire about ski packages. AE, CB, DC, DISC, MC, V.

Nestled in the mountains, this three-story property offers lodgings in a rustic log and stone building. Its lobby, with massive stone fireplaces, mounted deer heads, and a lofty beamed pine ceiling, resembles a ski lodge. The accommodations aren't fancy, but they're attractively decorated in earth tones and forest green; cathedral ceilings and balconies make third-floor rooms especially desirable. And nicest of all are the suites with convertible sofas in the living rooms, larger balconies, and wood-burning stone fireplaces. Facilities include a Jacuzzi and sauna in a windowed room, a small video-game arcade, and a gift shop. Room service is available from 8am to 9pm.

Dining/Entertainment: The hotel's hexagonal **Canyon Dining Room** has a lot of rustic charm, with two working fireplaces, windows all around overlooking beautiful mountain scenery, and heavy wrought-iron chandeliers suspended from a cathedral pine ceiling. At night it's romantically candlelit. All meals are available here including full and continental breakfasts. Lunch fare includes moderately priced burgers, sandwiches, fajitas, pizzas, and salads (everything's under $9). And dinner entrees ($8.95 to $19.95) offer a choice of lighter fare (pizzas and pasta dishes) along with a steak-and-seafood menu. Like the restaurant, the simpatico Cliffhanger Lounge—scene of live music Friday through Sunday nights (Monday, football games are aired in-season)—has a full window wall and a working fireplace.

☺ Mount Charleston Resort

End of Nev. 157. ☎ **800/955-1314** or 702/872-5408. 24 cabins. Sun–Thurs standard cabin (for one or two) $105, deluxe (for up to four) $135; Fri–Sat standard cabin $160, deluxe $200. Extra person $10. Rates include full or continental breakfast. AE, CB, DC, DISC, MC, V.

These charmingly rustic pine log cabins, built right into the mountainside to insure stunning scenic views, are a delight. Beautifully decorated with southwestern and Native American artifacts (Paiute drums and decorative blankets, sheepskin rugs, steer horns), they have peaked ceilings beamed with rough-hewn logs, oak parquet floors, and lots of windows. Knotty-pine furnishings are complemented by oversized king beds and attractively upholstered armchairs and sofas, each room has a working gas fireplace and a whirlpool tub big enough for two, and in-room amenities include fan chandeliers and coffeemakers (coffee, tea, and cocoa are provided). A big plus: each cabin has a furnished mountain-view terrace which provides an ideal setting for the gratis continental breakfast (fresh-baked croissants, muffins, coffee, grapefruit, and juice) delivered to your room with the morning paper each day. Or you can opt for a full American or Mexican breakfast (also gratis) in the resort's restaurant (see details below). In addition to breakfast, a fresh fruit basket is delivered to your cabin every afternoon, and warm chocolate-chip cookies arrive about 7pm. This serene getaway is the perfect antidote to Las Vegas glitz and glitter, and, for couples, it would be hard to come by a more romantic setting.

WHERE TO DINE

Mount Charleston Resort

End of Nev. 157. ☎ **800/955-1314** or 702/872-5408. Reservations recommended. Breakfast main courses $4.50–$9.75; lunch main courses $3–$9.75; dinner main courses $13.50–$19.50. AE, CB, DC, DISC, MC, V. Sun–Thurs 8am–9pm, Fri–Sat until 10pm; the bar/lounge is open 24 hours. AMERICAN/CONTINENTAL.

This warmly inviting mountain chalet centers on a vast hooded fireplace stacked high with massive ponderosa pine and cedar logs. Wagon-wheel chandeliers are suspended from a lofty beamed ceiling, and large windows provide magnificent vistas. Mid-May to the end of October, you can sit at umbrella tables on a patio nestled in the wooded mountains, and you'd be hard pressed to find a more exquisitely peaceful setting. The lounge isn't fancy; it's a casual, kick-back kind of place. At night, however, it is romantically candlelit, and there's dancing to live music weekends and holidays. At lunch weekends and holidays, a Bavarian oompah-pah band called the Dummkopfs entertains.

The restaurant serves all meals, beginning with hearty country breakfasts (available through 5pm) such as eggs with wild-game sausages, hash browns, homemade biscuits, and gravy. Mexican breakfasts (eggs wrapped in tortillas with chili and cheddar) are another tempting option. At lunch there are sandwiches, salads, and full entrees ranging from Dijon-honey-glazed broiled salmon with rice pilaf and vegetable to broiled pork chops served with applesauce, vegetable, and fries. Dinner entrees include wild-game specialties such as marinated elk steak topped with snow crabmeat, asparagus, and sauce béarnaise. Other choices include steaks, pasta dishes, and seafood. Everything is fresh and cooked on the premises, including homemade breads and desserts. At night the bar here is quite popular. Come by after dinner for a hot buttered rum or Mount Charleston coffee—a Jamaican blend spiked with brandy and Scotch liqueur, topped with homemade vanilla ice cream and a dollop of real whipped cream.

5 Red Rock Canyon

19 miles W of Las Vegas

Less than 20 miles from Las Vegas, Red Rock Canyon is worlds away experientially— a magnificent unspoiled vista which, in its timeless beauty, is the perfect balm for your casino-aded soul. You can simply drive the panoramic 13-mile **Scenic Drive** (open daily 7am till dusk) or explore in depth. There are many interesting sights and trailheads along the drive itself. The wider **National Conservation Area** offers hiking trails and internationally acclaimed rock-climbing opportunities (especially notable is the 7,068-foot Mt. Wilson, the highest sandstone peak among the bluffs). There are picnic areas along the drive and also in nearby **Spring Mountain Ranch State Park** 5 miles south. Since Bonnie Springs Ranch (see the next section) is just a few miles away, it makes a great base for exploring Red Rock Canyon.

ESSENTIALS

GETTING THERE   By Car   You simply drive west on Charleston Blvd., which becomes Nev. 159. Look for the Visitor Center on your right.

You can also go on an **organized tour. Gray Line** (☎ 702/384-1234), among other companies, runs bus tours to Red Rock Canyon. Inquire at your hotel tour desk.

Finally, you can go **by bike.** Not very far out of town (at Rainbow Blvd.), Charleston Blvd. is flanked by a bike path that continues for about 11 miles to the Visitor Center/Scenic Drive. The path is hilly but not difficult if you're in reasonable shape. However, exploring Red Rock Canyon by bike should be attempted only by exceptionally fit and experienced bikers. For bike-rental information, see chapter 7.

Just off Nev. 159, you'll see the **Red Rock Canyon Visitor Center** (☎ 702/363-1921), where you can pick up information on trails and view history exhibits on the canyon. The center is open daily from 8:30am to 4:30pm. Red Rock Canyon can be combined with a visit to Bonnie Springs Ranch.

ABOUT RED ROCK CANYON

The geological history of these ancient stones goes back some 600 million years. Over eons, the forces of nature have formed Red Rock's sandstone monoliths into arches, natural bridges, and massive sculptures painted in a stunning palate of gray-white limestone and dolomite, black mineral deposits, and oxidized minerals in earth-toned sienna hues ranging from pink to crimson and burgundy. Orange and green lichens add further contrast, as do spring-fed areas of lush foliage. And formations like Calico Hill are brilliantly white where groundwaters have leached out oxidized iron. Cliffs cut by deep canyons tower 2,000 feet above the valley floor.

During most of its history, Red Rock Canyon was below a warm shallow sea. Massive fault action and volcanic eruptions caused this seabed to begin rising some 225 million years ago. As the waters receded, sea creatures died and the calcium in their bodies combined with sea minerals to form limestone cliffs studded with ancient fossils. Some 45 million years later, the region was buried beneath thousands of feet of windblown sand. The landscape was as arid as the Sahara. As time progressed, iron oxide and calcium carbonate infiltrated the sand, consolidating it into cross-bedded rock. Shallow streams began carving the Red Rock landscape, and logs that washed down from ancient highland forests fossilized, their molecules gradually replaced by quartz and other minerals. These petrified stone logs, which the Paiute Indians believed were weapons of the wolf god, Shinarav, can be viewed in the Chinle Formation at the base of the Red Rock Cliffs. About 100 million years ago, massive fault action began dramatically shifting the rock landscape here, forming spectacular limestone and sandstone cliffs and rugged canyons punctuated by waterfalls, shallow streams, and serene oasis pools. Especially notable is the Keystone Thrust Fault, dating back about 65 million years when two of the earth's crustal plates collided, forcing older limestone and dolomite plates from the ancient seas over younger red and white sandstones. Over the years, water and wind have been ever creative sculptors, continuing to redefine this strikingly beautiful landscape.

Red Rock's valley is home to more than 45 species of mammals, about 100 species of birds, 30 reptiles and amphibians, and an abundance of plant life. Ascending the slopes from the valley, you'll see cactus and creosote bushes, aromatic purple sage, yellow-flowering blackbrush, yucca and Joshua trees, and, at higher elevations, clusters of forest-green piñon, juniper, and ponderosa pines. In spring, the desert blooms with fiery red globe mallow, magenta monkeyflowers, pink-blossomed redbud trees, pristine white forget-me-nots, golden desert marigolds, and lavender phacelia. Among the animal denizens of the canyon are bighorn sheep, antelope ground squirrels, mule deer, kangaroo rats, lizards, California jackrabbits and desert cottontails, gray and kit foxes, tortoises, coyotes, bobcats, rattlesnakes, reclusive gila monsters, even mountain lions. Burros and wild horses are not indigenous but descended from animals that were set free by, or escaped from, miners in the 1800s. And commonly observed birds include eagles and hawks, roadrunners, turkey vultures, loggerhead shrike, cactus wrens, quail, mourning doves, broad-tailed hummingbirds, woodpeckers, horned larks, western bluebirds, American robins, northern mockingbirds, yellow warblers, and sage sparrows.

Archaeological studies of Red Rock—which turned up pottery fragments, remains of limestone roasting pits, stone tools, pictographs (rock drawings), and petroglyphs (rock etchings), along with other ancient artifacts—show that humans have been in this region since about 3000 B.C. (some experts say as far back as 10,000 B.C.). You can still see remains of early inhabitants on hiking expeditions in the park. The Anasazi (also known as the "Basketmaker" people and "the Ancient Ones") lived here from the 1st century A.D. Originally hunter-gatherers, they learned to farm maize, squash, and beans and began forming communities. From pit houses, they progressed to elaborate structures of up to 100 rooms and became known as the Pueblo Indians. They departed from the area (no one knows why) about A.D. 1150, and the Paiutes—who were still essentially hunter-gatherer nomads—became the dominant group. Until the mid-1800s, the Paiutes lived here in perfect harmony with nature—a harmony destroyed when white settlers arrived and began felling the pine forests for timber, introducing grazing livestock that destroyed food and medicinal plant sources, and decimating the Native American population with European diseases to which they had no immunity. By the 1880s, the Paiutes were forced onto reservations, their culture and way of life in shambles.

In the latter part of the 19th century, Red Rock was a mining site and later a sandstone quarry that provided materials for many buildings in Los Angeles, San Francisco, and early Las Vegas. By the end of World War II, as Las Vegas developed, many people became aware of the importance of preserving the canyon. In 1967 the Secretary of the Interior designated 62,000 acres as Red Rock Canyon Recreation Lands under the auspices of the Bureau of Land Management, and later legislation banned all development except hiking trails and limited recreational facilities. In 1990, Red Rock Canyon became a National Conservation Area, further elevating its protected status; its current acreage is 197,000.

Today Red Rock Canyon affords visitors the opportunity to experience nature's grandeur and serenity—to leave the stresses of daily life behind and get in touch with greater realities.

WHAT TO SEE & DO

First, you'll want to stop off at the Visitor Center. There you can view exhibits, enhanced by an audio tour, that tell the history of the canyon and depict its plant and animal life. You'll also see a fascinating video here about Nevada's thousands of wild horses and burros, protected by an Act of Congress since 1971. At the Center, you can obtain trail maps, brochures, permits for hiking and backpacking, and other information about the canyon. Call ahead to find out about ranger-guided tours as well as informative guided hikes offered by groups like the Sierra Club and the Audubon Society. Hiking trails range from a 0.7-mile loop stroll to a waterfall (its flow varying seasonally) at Lost Creek to much longer and more strenuous treks involving rock

A Close Encounter with Area 51

When scientists recently revealed the discovery of life on Mars, Nevada residents were not surprised. For years, people here have been spotting UFOs along a deserted, 98-mile stretch of State Highway 375. Debunkers maintain that the strange lights and oddly shaped craft observed along 375 are simply military aircraft from a nearby top-secret Air Force base. Some believe the craft are from the base—a base where the Air Force rebuilds and flies crashed alien spacecraft! As many people now know, this is the so-called "Area 51," featured in *Sixty Minutes, The X-Files,* and the movie *Independence Day.* Whatever the real story, this stretch of highway was renamed "The Extraterrestrial Highway" in 1996. If you'd like to explore it, take I-15, to U.S. 93, to the ET Highway, returning via U.S. 6 and U.S. 95. You can do the trip in a day from Las Vegas. Even if you don't meet up with any aliens, you'll enjoy the stark desert scenery. Stop in the town of **Rachel,** where the oddly named Little A'Le'Inn is headquarters for UFO watchers; it offers information, dining, groceries, gas, and lodging. You might also want to detour 28 miles east at the junction of ET Highway and U.S. 6 to see the **Lunar Crater,** a volcanic field, 100 miles square, that was used in the late 1960s to train astronauts for the Apollo moon mission. On the return trip via U.S. 6 and 95, if you have an extra day or two, visit old mining and ghost towns like Tonapah, Goldfield, and Rhyolite. For more information call the Nevada Commission on Tourism (☎ **800/NEVADA-8**), and ask them to send you their "Pioneer Territory" brochure and a list of ET Highway services (gas stations, lodgings, chambers of commerce, restaurants, and more). On the Internet, check out **http://www.ufomind.com** and **http://www. ufo-hyway.com.**

scrambling. A popular 2-mile round-trip hike leads to Pine Creek Canyon and the creekside ruins of a historic homesite surrounded by ponderosa pine trees. On trails along Calico Hills and the escarpment, look for "Indian marbles," a local name for small rounded sandstone rocks that have eroded off larger sandstone formations. And, if you're traveling with children, ask about the free *Junior Ranger Discovery Book* filled with fun family activities. Books and videotapes are on sale here, including a guidebook identifying more than 100 top-rated climbing sites. After you tour the canyon, drive over to Bonnie Springs Ranch (details in the next section) for lunch or dinner. See chapter 7 for further details on biking and climbing.

6 Bonnie Springs Ranch/Old Nevada

About 24 miles W of Las Vegas, 5 miles past Red Rock Canyon

Bonnie Springs Ranch/Old Nevada is a kind of Wild West theme park with accommodations and a charmingly rustic restaurant. If you're traveling with kids, a day or overnight trip to Bonnie Springs is recommended, but there's much for adults, too. It could even be a romantic getaway, offering horseback riding, gorgeous mountain vistas, proximity to Red Rock Canyon, and temperatures 5 to 10 degrees cooler than on the Strip.

ESSENTIALS

GETTING THERE   If you are traveling **by car,** a trip to Bonnie Springs Ranch can be combined easily with a day trip to Red Rock Canyon; it is about 5 miles. But you can also stay overnight.

For those without transportation, there are **Desert Action Jeep Tour** to and from Las Vegas. Call 702/796-9355 for details.

For additional information, you can call **Bonnie Springs Ranch/Old Nevada** at **702/875-4191.**

WHAT TO SEE & DO AT BONNIE SPRINGS RANCH

Old Nevada attractions are detailed below. However, even if you just come out here for lunch, you can enjoy several things free of charge. A **small zoo** on the premises is home to dozens of animals—burros, mouflon sheep, buffalo, steer, raccoons, ferrets, ducks, red squirrels, coyotes, coatis, an Arctic fox (donated by singer Wayne Newton), bobcats, guinea pigs, and rabbits. There are always baby animals, and llamas, potbelly pigs, deer, and miniature goats roam free and can be petted and fed.

There's also an **aviary** housing peacocks (including a rare white peacock), Polish chickens, peachface and blackmask lovebirds, finches, parakeets, ravens, ducks, pheasants, and geese.

Riding stables offer guided trail rides into the mountain area on a continuous basis throughout the day (from 9am to 3:15pm spring through fall, until 5:45pm in summer). Children must be at least 6 years old to participate. Cost is $18 per hour.

And scenic 20-minute **stagecoach rides** offered weekends and holidays cost $5 for adults, $3 for children under 12.

WHAT TO SEE & DO IN OLD NEVADA

Old Nevada (☎ 702/875-4191) is a microcosm of a mid-1800s western Nevada town, its main street lined with weathered-wood buildings fronted by covered verandas. It has a rustic turn-of-the-century **saloon** complete with red flocked wallpaper and wagon-wheel chandeliers overhead. Country music is played in the saloon during the day, except when **stage melodramas** take place (at frequent intervals between 11:30am and 5pm). In response to cue cards held up by the players, the audience boos and hisses the mustache-twirling villain, sobs in sympathy with the distressed heroine, laughs, cheers, and applauds. It's quite silly, but lots of fun; kids adore it. Drinks and snacks can be purchased at the bar.

Following each melodrama a **western drama** is presented outside the saloon, involving a bank robbery, a shootout, and the trial of the bad guy. A judge, prosecuting attorney, and defense attorney are chosen from the audience, the remainder of whom act as jury. The action always culminates in a hanging. We're not talking Neil Simon or anything, but the dialogue is quite funny.

Throughout the area, cowboys continually interact with visiting kids. There are also ongoing **stunt shootouts** in this wild frontier town, and some rather unsavory characters languish in the town jail.

A **wax museum** displays tableaux with replicas of John C. Frémont and Kit Carson (who actually stopped at this site in the 1840s), an animated Abraham Lincoln reading the proclamation that made Nevada a state, early trailblazers and mountain men, Brigham Young, 19th-century Paiute chief Old Winnemucca, and early Nevada madam Julia Bulette, among others. A 9-minute film on Nevada history is shown in the wax museum throughout the day.

In the **Old Nevada Photograph Shoppe** you can have a tintype picture taken in 1890s Wild West costume with a 120-year-old camera. There are replicas of a turn-of-the-century church and stamp mill; the latter, which has original 1902 machinery, was used for crushing rocks to separate gold and silver from the earth. Movies (one about nearby Red Rock Canyon, one a silent film) are shown in the **Old Movie House** throughout the day from 10:30am to 5pm. You can test your skills in a **shooting gallery,** peek into an old-fashioned **dentist/barbershop** (and surprise a man in his bath), see a **Bootleg Hill still,** and tour the remains of the **old Comstock lode silver mine.** The **Trading Post,** a museum and gift shop, displays a variety of 19th-century items (a switchboard, a craps table and slot machine, cash registers, radios, Victrolas, typewriters, a printing press, shotguns, and the remains of a New Mexico drugstore with many old-fashioned remedies). Other Old Nevada shops sell hand-blown glass, old-fashioned candy, Native American items (rugs, moccasins, silver and turquoise jewelry, baskets), and things Western. Eateries in Old Nevada are discussed below. There's plenty of parking; weekends and holidays, a free shuttle train takes visitors from the parking lot to the entrance.

Admission to Old Nevada is $6.50 for adults, $5.50 for seniors 62 and over, $4 for children ages 5 to 11, and free for children under 5. The park is open daily from 10:30am to 5pm November through April, and until 6pm the rest of the year.

WHERE TO STAY & DINE

Bonnie Springs Motel

Nev. 159. ☎ **702/875-4400.** 50 rms, including 13 suites and 5 fantasy rms. A/C TV TEL. Standard double $55–$65 Sun–Thurs, $65–$75 Fri–Sat; fantasy suite $110 Sun–Thurs, $125 Fri–Sat; family suite $85 Sun–Thurs, $95 Fri–Sat. An optional breakfast trail ride for motel guests is $18 per person; it departs at 9am every morning. Staying at the motel also entitles you to discounted tickets for Old Nevada. AE, MC, V.

The motel, housed in two-story weathered-wood buildings, is, like Old Nevada, evocative of a 19th-century western town. Even standard rooms offer scenic mountain views and are delightfully decorated with pine-plank-motif carpets, floral-print calico drapes and bedspreads, and handcrafted pine furnishings. Some rooms are equipped with electric fireplaces, and all feature inviting individual touches—perhaps an antique oak mirror stand with a ceramic bowl and jug, Indian rugs, a Mexican serape artfully draped on a branch, lamps with ruffled calico shades, or Victorian-style lighting fixture/fans overhead. All rooms have full baths, in-room coffee makers, and patios overlooking the mountains. There are beautiful family suites with fully equipped kitchens, bedrooms, living rooms (with convertible sofas), and dressing areas; these are equipped with two phones and two TVs. Fantasy rooms are romantic settings with sumptuous Jacuzzi tubs and mirrors over the bed. For instance, a Gay '90s room, decorated in mauve tones, is furnished with velvet-upholstered period chairs. It has a quaint bathtub on brass feet (in addition to an oversized faux-marble Jacuzzi), a lovely porcelain sink with hand-painted floral motifs, and a pink and black lace canopy over the bed. Other fantasy rooms are Chinese, Native American, Old West, and Spanish themed.

Dining: The **Bonnie Springs Ranch Restaurant** is cozily rustic, with rough-hewn pine walls, a beamed ceiling, and glossy cedar-slab tables. A wall of windows overlooks a serene pond with ducks and swans, and an aluminum-hooded wood-burning fireplace is ablaze in winter. Menus, printed on whiskey bottles, offer hearty breakfasts such as a chili-and-cheese omelet with ranch potatoes and homemade biscuits or thick slabs of Texas toast. Sandwiches, salads, burgers, and barbecued beef are featured at lunch, and dinner entrees include barbecued chicken and pork ribs, steaks, and seafood. Prices are moderate.

IN OLD NEVADA

The **Miner's Restaurant,** another rustic western setting, is right in town and has unfinished pine-plank floors, a beamed ceiling, and ruffled curtains. Inexpensive snack fare (sandwiches, burgers, pizza, hot dogs) is served, along with fresh-baked desserts. There are tables out on the porch. In summer, you can also get beer and soft drinks in a similarly old-fashioned **Beer Parlor.**

12 Utah's Dixie: The Southwest Corner

by Don & Barbara Laine

Small towns and big rocks—that's what you'll find in Utah's south-west corner, known as "Utah's Dixie" for its climate as well as its Civil War–era cotton growing. Those days are long gone, but the stiflingly hot summers and delightfully mild winters remain, making this region a terrific winter playground. Snow-weary Salt Lake City residents come here every year, seeking an escape from frigid temperatures and the cold-and-flu season. There's no need to ever put away the golf clubs or swimsuits in this neighborhood.

There's lots to see and do in this colorful corner of Utah. You can step back more than a hundred years in history at Brigham Young's winter home at St. George, the region's largest town, or go back in time a thousand years at Anasazi Indian Village State Park. Our favorite stops are outdoors: the rugged red rock cliffs at Snow Canyon State Park; the ruddy sands of Coral Pink Sand Dunes State Park; the panoramic views from atop Boulder Mountain.

Utah's Dixie isn't only a warm-weather destination, though. Its extremes of elevation can often mean that you can lounge around the pool in the morning and build a snowman that same afternoon. From the scorching desert at St. George, it's only 74 miles—and 7,500 feet up—to the cool mountain forest at Cedar Breaks National Monument. Home to a variety of scenic and recreation areas (you'll even find a ski resort here), a surprising number of historic attractions, and some excellent performing arts events (such as the Utah Shakespearean Festival), this region also serves as the gateway to most of Utah's spectacular national parks—probably the main reason you're here.

Despite the number of attractions in and around Utah's Dixie, don't expect much in terms of amenities. Many of the lodging and dining establishments here are somewhat basic—perfectly adequate, but not overly exciting. Keep in mind that distances are long— "nearby" can mean 100 miles away—and services may be far apart. But this is a starkly beautiful part of the American West—still very much like it was more than 100 years ago, and well worth a visit.

1 Getting Outside in Utah's Dixie

This is Utah's playground, a year-round mecca for hikers, mountain-bikers, golfers, boaters, anglers, and anybody else who just wants to get outdoors. Among the top spots for experiencing nature at its best are Boulder Mountain, with its alpine forests and pristine lakes and streams; Cedar Breaks National Monument, a high-mountain oasis of towering pines and firs, and wild-flowers galore; and state parks such as Snow Canyon, Coral Pink Sand Dunes, and Quail Creek.

The best seasons for outdoor activities here are based on elevation: In St. George and other lowlands, spring and fall are best, the winter's okay, and the summer is awful, with temperatures soaring well over 100°. But not everyone says no to St. George in the summer: Its desert climate makes it the golfing capital of Utah. The Sunbrook is considered the state's best course, with a challenging layout and spectacular views of the White Hills, but you can stay a week in St. George and play a different course each day. On the other side of the seasonal coin, don't try to drive to Cedar Breaks until June at the earliest; the roads will be closed by snow.

Our favorite way to see this part of Utah is on foot. Hiking trails abound at Boulder Mountain and throughout the Dixie National Forest north of St. George. But several of the best trails are in state parks, particularly Snow Canyon State Park near St. George and Escalante State Park in Escalante.

Biking here generally means mountainbiking. This is true even for those who confine most of their riding to city streets, because you never know when you're going to discover that great little trail turning off into the red rock desert or through alpine meadows. Also, some of the roads—especially secondary roads—can be a bit rough, with only minimal shoulders; a sturdy mountainbike will survive better. The best mountainbiking is at Brian Head Ski Resort near Cedar Breaks National Monument. Both road and mountainbikes can take you to beautiful areas in and around Snow Canyon State Park near St. George.

For an area with so much desert, there's certainly a lot of boating here: Utahns have had to create reservoirs to provide the desert and its residents drinking and irrigation water. The best boating is at Quail Creek State Park near St. George, but those who would like a bit more solitude might prefer the relatively undeveloped Gunlock State Park nearby. The top fishing hole in these parts is at Quail Creek State Park, but there are also plenty of smaller lakes and hidden streams in the forests on Boulder Mountain, and in the Dixie National Forest north of St. George.

Off-road vehicles can simply be a means to get to an isolated fishing stream or hiking trail, or part of the adventure itself. The old mining and logging roads in the Dixie National Forest or at Boulder Mountain are great for four-wheel exploring. Among the best is the Hole-in-the-Rock Scenic Backway near Escalante, which leads to a particularly scenic view of Lake Powell. Visitors with their own dune buggies will want to challenge the shifting dunes at Coral Pink Sand Dunes State Park, just outside Kanab.

There's an abundance of wildlife in this part of the state. Sure, you'll see deer, squirrels, chipmunks, and other furry creatures at Boulder Mountain and Cedar Breaks National Monument, but there's also animal life in the desert, including our favorites: the luminescent scorpions at Coral Pink Sand Dunes State Park, and the Gila monster at Snow Canyon State Park. Boulder Mountain and Snow Canyon are home to numerous songbirds, and Escalante State Park has the best wetland bird habitat in southern Utah.

It may be hot down in the desert, but there's plenty of snow up on those mountaintops. Your best bet here for downhill skiing is Brian Head Ski Re-sort. Cross-country skiers and snowmobilers will want to head to nearby Cedar Breaks National Monument after the winter snows have closed the roads to cars.

The Southwest Corner

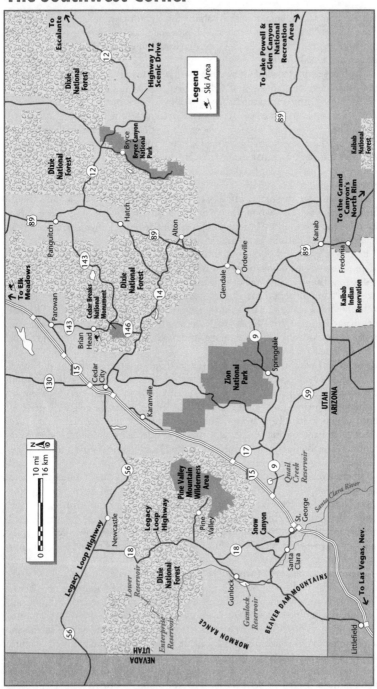

2 St. George, Gateway to Southern Utah's Natural Wonders

In the fall of 1861, Brigham Young sent 309 families to establish a cotton-growing community in the semi-arid Virgin River Valley; today, St. George has almost 40,000 inhabitants. Known as one of Utah's more conservative communities, life in St. George is still strongly influenced by the Mormon Church; it is also a winter home to many snowbirds and retirees, who love the hot, dry summers and mild winters. Despite the climate, this desert city appears quite green, with tree-lined streets and lovely grassy areas. There are eight golf courses, with more in the planning stages, and recreational and cultural facilities to suit every taste.

St. George is also the gateway to some of the most spectacular scenery in the West. Zion, Bryce, Grand Canyon, and Great Basin National Parks are within relatively easy driving distance, as are Cedar Breaks and Pipe Springs National Monuments and Snow Canyon, Gunlock, and Quail Creek State Parks. Depending on your itinerary, St. George may be your biggest stopping point en route to Lake Powell and Glen Canyon National Recreation Area, Capitol Reef National Park, and southeastern Utah's attractions.

ESSENTIALS
GETTING THERE

By Plane The closest major airport is **McCarran International Airport** in Las Vegas (☎ 702/261-5743). Most major airlines fly into McCarran, where you can rent a car and drive the 120 miles northeast on I-15 to St. George. The **St. George Shuttle** (☎ 801/628-8320) provides daily service to and from the Las Vegas airport.

Delta/Skywest Airlines (☎ 801/673-3451 or 800/453-9417) and **Pacific Air West Airlines** (☎ 801/674-0096 or 800/729-7229) fly into **St. George Airport** (☎ 801/628-0481), located on a bluff on the west side of the city.

For car rentals in St. George, see "Getting Around," below.

By Car St. George is on I-15, 120 miles northeast of Las Vegas and 305 miles south of Salt Lake City. Take exit 6 (Bluff Street) or 8 (St. George Boulevard) for St. George.

INFORMATION

The **St. George Area Chamber of Commerce** is in the historic Pioneer Courthouse at 97 E. St. George Blvd., St. George, UT 84770 (☎ 801/628-1658; fax 801/673-1587).

For information on the state and national parks in the area, as well as the Dixie National Forest and land administered by the Bureau of Land Management, call the numbers above or visit the **Interagency Offices and Visitor Center** at 345 E. Riverside Drive. Open seven days a week, the office has a variety of free brochures, plus maps, books, posters, and videos for sale. Rangers can answer questions and recommend trails, and supply backcountry permits. To get there, take exit 6 off I-15, and turn east. Or call the **Bureau of Land Management** at 801/628-4491 or the **United States Forest Service** at 801/652-3100.

You can also contact the **Dixie National Forest's Pine Valley Ranger District** office, 345 E. Riverside Dr., St. George, UT 84770 (☎ 801/652-3100); or the **BLM's Dixie Resource Area office,** 225 N. Bluff St., St. George, UT 84770 (☎ 801/673-4654).

GETTING AROUND

The street grid system is centered on the point where Tabernacle Street (running east–west) crosses Main Street (running north–south), with numbered streets increasing in each direction by hundreds. St. George Boulevard takes the place of 100 North, Bluff Street runs along a bluff at the western edge of the city, I-15 cuts through in a northeast direction (from exit 6 at the south end of Bluff Street to exit 8 at the east end of St. George Boulevard), and River Road lies at the eastern edge, becoming Red Cliffs Road north of St. George Boulevard. Other than that, the system stays true to the grid.

Car rental agencies with St. George offices include **ABC Rent-A-Car,** 219 W. St. George Blvd. (☎ 801/628-7355); **A-1 Car Rental,** 568 E. St. George Blvd. (☎ 801/673-8811); **Avis,** St. George Municipal Airport (☎ 801/673-3451 or 800/331-1212); **Budget Rent-A-Car,** 116 W. St. George Blvd. (☎ 801/673-6825 or 800/527-0700); **Dollar Rent-A-Car,** 1175 S. 150 East (☎ 801/628-6549); and **National Car Rental,** St. George Municipal Airport (☎ 801/673-5098 or 800/CAR-RENT).

For a taxi, call **Dixie Taxi Cab** (☎ 801/673-4068), or **Zion Limo** (☎ 801/628-9224).

There's free on-street parking in much of the city, and many of the streets are tree-lined and shady.

FAST FACTS: ST. GEORGE

One of the larger hospitals in this part of the state is **Dixie Regional Medical Center,** 544 S. 400 East (☎ 801/634-4000). The **post office** is located at 180 N. Main St. (☎ 801/673-3312). The regional **newspaper** is the *Daily Spectrum* (☎ 801/673-3511).

DISCOVERING MORMON HISTORY IN & AROUND ST. GEORGE

Because the Church of Jesus Christ of Latter-day Saints was the primary driving force in the settlement of St. George, it should come as no surprise that most of the sightseeing in town is church related. At the town's historic buildings, staffed by knowledgeable church members, you'll learn about all about the church as well as the specific site; expect a little sales pitch on the benefits of Christianity, and the Mormon faith in particular.

Brigham Young Winter Home Historical Site

67 W. 200 North. ☎ **801/673-2517.** Free guided tours. Memorial Day–Labor Day daily 8:30am–8:30pm; Labor Day–Memorial Day daily 9am–6pm. From I-15, take exit 8, head west on St. George Boulevard to Main Street, turn right (north) for one block, then left (west) onto 200 North.

Church leader Brigham Young was one of St. George's first snowbirds. He escaped the Salt Lake City cold during the last few winters of his life by coming south to this house. In addition to its obvious religious importance to the Church of Jesus Christ of Latter-day Saints, it's a handsome example of how the well-to-do of the late 19th century lived. Allow about a half hour for the guided tour.

Daughters of Utah Pioneer Museum

133 N. 100 East. ☎ **801/628-7274.** Free admission, donations accepted. Mon–Sat 10am–5pm. Closed last 2 weeks Dec. From I-15 take exit 8, head west on St. George Boulevard to 100 East and turn right (north).

This "Grandma's attic" contains an eclectic collection of items belonging to the pioneers who settled this area more than one hundred years ago. There's some furniture—including a bed used by Brigham Young—spinning wheels, an 1894 loom, guns, tools, musical instruments, and other relics from bygone days. Historic

St. George & Environs

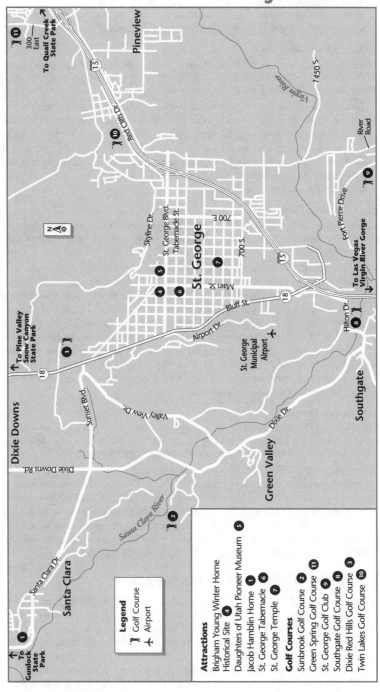

Legend
- ⅄ Golf Course
- ✈ Airport

Attractions
- Brigham Young Winter Home ❶
- Historical Site ❹
- Daughters of Utah Pioneer Museum ❺
- Jacob Hamblin Home ❶
- St. George Tabernacle ❻
- St. George Temple ❼

Golf Courses
- Sunbrook Golf Course ❷
- Green Spring Golf Course ⑪
- St. George Golf Club ❾
- Southgate Golf Course ❽
- Dixie Red Hills Golf Course ❸
- Twin Lakes Golf Course ❿

photos, mostly of pioneer families, are on display; you can purchase copies if you like. Guided tours are given by volunteers from the Daughters of Utah Pioneers.

✪ Jacob Hamblin Home

Main St., Santa Clara. ☎ 801/673-2161. Free guided tours. Memorial Day–Labor Day daily 8:30am–8pm; Labor Day–Memorial Day daily 9am–5pm. From St. George, go 3 miles west on U.S. 91 to the community of Santa Clara, then watch for sign.

This stone and pine house, built in the 1860s, is typical of pioneer homes throughout the West—and more of what you'd think of as a pioneer home than the refined houses of St. George—except for one aspect that is definitively Mormon: It has two identical bedrooms, one for each of Hamblin's wives. You'll also notice that the dining table is set in the typical Mormon fashion, with plates upside down and chairs facing away from the table to facilitate kneeling for before-meal prayers. The guided tour lasts about a half hour.

✪ St. George Tabernacle

Main and Tabernacle streets. ☎ 801/628-4072. Free guided tours. Daily 9am–6pm. From I-15 take exit 8, head west on St. George Boulevard to Main Street, turn left (south) for a block to the Tabernacle.

This is the most beautiful building in St. George. It's an excellent example of fine Old World craftsmanship, from the hand-quarried red stone walls to the intricate interior woodwork; craftsmen finished pine, which was all they had, to look like exotic hardwoods and even marble. Completed in 1876 after 13 years of work, the Tabernacle served as a house of worship and town meeting hall. During the 1880s, when a nearby silver strike brought many Catholics to the area, the Tabernacle was used for a Roman Catholic high mass led by a Roman Catholic priest, but with music from the liturgy sung by the local Mormon choir—in Latin. Today, the Tabernacle is a community center that presents free weekly concerts and other cultural events. The guided tour takes about a half hour.

St. George Temple

440 S. 300 East. ☎ 801/673-5181. Temple not open to the public; free guided tours of visitor center exhibits. Daily 9am–9pm. From I-15 take exit 8, head west on St. George Boulevard to 200 East, turn left and go about six blocks to the large parking lot on your left.

Completed in 1877, the St. George Temple was the first LDS temple in Utah, and remains the oldest still in use in the world today. The majestic white temple is not open to the general public, but you can walk among the beautiful gardens, and stop at the visitor center south of the Temple for a multimedia program on the beliefs of the Church of Jesus Christ of Latter-day Saints. At the conclusion of the tour/ program, which takes just under an hour, you'll be asked if you would like a member of the Church to call on you to discuss the church's beliefs further.

EXPLORING SNOW CANYON STATE PARK

✪ **Snow Canyon** is among Utah's most scenic state parks, offering great opportunities for photography, hiking, and horseback riding. You'll see rock cliffs and walls of Navajo sandstone in every shade of red imaginable, layered with white and black from ancient lava flows. Wander just a few feet from your campsite, and you're likely to discover ancient petroglyphs. Or hike the trails and discover shifting sand dunes, mysterious lava caves, colorful desert plants, and a variety of rock formations.

Because the summers here are hot—well over 100°F hot—the best time to visit is any other time. Winters are mild, but nights can be chilly. Spring and fall are probably the most popular, and therefore the busiest, times to visit. By the way, don't come looking for snow—Snow Canyon was named for the pioneers Lorenzo and Erastus Snow, who found it.

JUST THE FACTS

Be aware that rattlesnakes are common in this part of Utah, so watch where you put your hands and feet. If you do encounter a rattler, give it a wide berth.

Getting There   The park is located 11 miles northwest of St. George, off Utah 18.

Information, Fees & Regulations   For a copy of the park's full-color brochure, contact **Snow Canyon State Park Headquarters,** P.O. Box 140, Santa Clara, UT 84765-0140 (☎ 801/628-2255). Day-use fee is $3 per vehicle, or $1 per person on foot, bike, or motorcycle. Like most state parks, dogs are welcome, including on the trails, but must be leashed.

SPORTS & ACTIVITIES

Hiking   The best way to see Snow Canyon is on foot or horseback (see below). Several short trails make for easy full- or half-day hikes. The **Hidden Piñon Trail** is a 1½-mile round-trip self-guided nature trail that wanders among lava rocks, through several canyons, and onto rocky flatlands, offering panoramic views of the surrounding mountains. The trail begins across the highway from the campground; you can pick up a brochure at the park office/entrance station. The walk is fairly easy, but allow at least an hour, especially if you're planning to keep an eye out for Mormon tea, cliffrose, prickly pear cactus, and banana yucca.

An easy three-quarters-mile one-way trail leads to **Johnson Arch.** It begins just south of the campground, passes by the popular rock-climbing wall (see below), some low sand dunes, and then a small canyon with a view of Johnson Arch (named after pioneer wife Maude Johnson) high above.

Also popular is the **Lava Caves Trail,** a 1½-mile round-trip that starts just north of the campground. The caves are about a half mile along the trail, but watch carefully—it's easy to miss them. The caves were formed from liquid lava, and the large rooms have at times been occupied by Native American tribes. Another quarter mile past the caves is the West Canyon Overlook, with a breathtaking view into West Canyon.

Several longer and steeper trails lead to spectacular views of the canyons and distant vistas; check with park rangers.

Horseback Riding   Snow Canyon Stables, P.O. Box 577, Santa Clara, UT 84765 (☎ 801/628-6677), offers horseback rides of various lengths into some of the more inaccessible and beautiful parts of the park, year-round. Prices start at $15 for a 1-hour ride; an overnight camping trip, including dinner and breakfast, is $125.

Rock Climbing   Climbers love the tall wall of rock on the east side of the road just south of the campground, but it has become so popular that the park has issued a moratorium on bolting. Check with the park office for information.

Wildlife Watching   You're likely to see cottontail rabbits, ground squirrels, and songbirds; luckier visitors may also spot desert mule deer, bobcats, coyote, kit foxes, eagles, and owls. Although it's unlikely you'll see one, desert tortoises (a federally listed threatened species) and Gila monsters also live in the park. There are also some rattlesnakes, which you'll want to avoid.

CAMPING

The 36-site campground is one of the best in the state. One section has electric hookups, and sites there a bit close; those not needing electricity can set up camp in delightful little side canyons, surrounded by colorful red rocks and Utah juniper. The views are spectacular no matter where you choose to set up. There are hot showers, modern restrooms, and an RV sewage dump station. Campsites with electricity are $11 Sunday through Thursday, and $12 on Friday, Saturday, and holidays. Sites without electric hookups are $9 and $10, respectively. Reservations are recommended from February to May and September to November; call 800/322-3770. There's a $5 nonrefundable reservation fee.

MORE OUTDOOR ACTIVITIES IN THE ST. GEORGE AREA

In addition to what's available in Snow Canyon State Park, there's great hiking, biking, and fishing in the Dixie National Forest and on nearby lands administered by the Bureau of Land Management. For contact information, see "Information" under "Essentials," above.

Road Biking & Mountainbiking   For bike repairs and accessories, stop at **Bicycles Unlimited,** 90 S. 100 East (☎ 801/673-4492). You can get repairs or rentals at **Swen's Cyclery,** 1060 E. Tabernacle (☎ 801/673-0878), where mountainbike rental prices run from $5 per hour to $25 per day.

A popular road trip is the scenic **24-mile loop** from St. George through Santa Clara, Ivins, and Snow Canyon State Park. The trip is on paved roads with narrow shoulders but generally little traffic. Allow 2- to 3- hours. Head north out of St. George on Bluff Street (Utah 18), and follow it to its intersection with U.S. 91. Turn west (left) and go about 6 miles to the village of Santa Clara, where you can visit the Jacob Hamblin Home (see "Discovering Mormon History In & Around St. George," above). From Santa Clara, continue west about a mile before turning north (right); follow the signs to Ivins and the Tuacahn Amphitheater. At Ivins, turn east (right) onto the Snow Canyon Road, following signs for Snow Canyon State Park, where you can easily spend several hours or several days exploring the red rock formations, lava pools, and sand dunes. From the park, continue east to Utah 18, turn south (right), and pedal back into St. George.

Mountainbiking opportunities abound on land administered by the **U.S. Forest Service** (☎ 801/652-3100) and the **Bureau of Land Management** (☎ 801/628-4491); call for details.

Fishing   Quail Creek and Gunlock State Parks (see below) are the local fishing holes. For equipment, licenses, and tips on where they're biting, visit **Hurst Sports Center,** 160 N. 500 West (☎ 801/673-6141).

Golf   Utah's golf capital, St. George attracts golfers from around the country to more than a half-dozen public courses (and more on the way), known for their challenging designs, well-maintained fairways and greens, and spectacularly scenic settings. The best is the 18-hole, par-72 **Sunbrook Golf Course,** 2240 W. Sunbrook Dr. (☎ 801/634-5866), rated tops in the state for 1994–95 by *Golf Digest,* both for its design and spectacular scenery. Greens fees in the winter are $16 for 9 holes and $26 for 18 holes; in the summer they're $9 and $17, respectively. Also highly rated by *Golf Digest*—and considered by many to be the state's second-best course—is **Green Spring Golf Course,** 588 N. Green Spring Dr., Washington (☎ 801/673-7888), several miles northeast of St. George. Challenging Green Spring is an 18-hole, par-71 course, with winter greens fees of $14 for 9 holes and $24 for 18 holes ($10 and $16, respectively, in the summer).

Other 18-hole courses include the par-73 **St. George Golf Club,** 2190 S. 1400 East (☎ 801/634-5854); and the par-70 **Southgate Golf Course,** 1975 S. Tonaquint Dr. (☎ 801/628-0000). Green fees at both of these city-owned courses are $8 for 9 holes and $15 for 18 holes in the winter, and $7 for 9 holes and $9 for 18 holes in the summer. The Southgate also has a **Family Golf Center** (☎ 801/

674-7728), with an outdoor driving range and putting and chipping greens, plus state-of-the-art indoor facilities that include computerized golf swing analysis.

Nine-hole courses in St. George include the par-34 **Dixie Red Hills Golf Course,** 100 N. 700 West (☎ 801/634-5852), with winter green fees of $8 for 9 holes and $15 for 18 holes (and summer fees of $7 and $9, respectively); and the par-27 **Twin Lakes Golf Course,** 660 N. Twin Lakes Dr. (☎ 801/673-4441), with year-round fees of $4.50 for 9 holes.

Golfers can often save money by checking with local motels on various lodging/golf packages; see "Where to Stay," below.

Hiking Some of the best hiking in the area is at Snow Canyon State Park (see above). The Dixie National Forest to the north also offers vast opportunities, with some 200 miles of trails. Check with forest rangers on current trail conditions, and be sure to carry detailed maps on any long hikes, especially if you're venturing into the Pine Valley Wilderness Area. Stop in at the **Interagency Offices and Visitor Center** at 345 E. Riverside Drive for maps and details.

TWO STATE PARKS FOR WATER SPORTS ENTHUSIASTS

Year-round warm weather makes Utah's Dixie, home to several large reservoirs, a mecca for water sports enthusiasts. **Quail Creek State Park** (P.O. Box 1943, St. George, UT 84770-1943; ☎ 801/879-2378), 14 miles northeast of St. George off I-15 and Utah 9, has the warmest water in the state in the summer, making it extremely popular with boaters, water-skiers, wind surfers, scuba divers, and swimmers. The two boat ramps accommodate practically all types of watercraft; there are also docks and sandy beaches. Quail Creek Reservoir is considered one of the state's best fishing holes for largemouth bass; anglers also catch rainbow trout, blue gill, and crappie. Facilities include a fish-cleaning station, modern restrooms, a campground with 23 sites (but no showers or RV hookups), and a picnic area with barbecue grills. The park is open year-round; day-use costs are $3 per vehicle or $1 per individual on foot, bike, or motorcycle; camping is $7 Sunday to Thursday and $8 on Friday, Saturday, and holidays.

Gunlock State Park (P.O. Box 140, Santa Clara, UT 84765-0140; ☎ 801/628-2255), 15 miles northwest of St. George via U.S. 91, is also a great place to enjoy water sports year-round, in a less developed setting than Quail Creek. Activities at the 240-acre Gunlock Reservoir include boating (there's a boat ramp), water-skiing, swimming, and excellent fishing for bass and catfish. There's no day-use fee. The park offers free primitive camping, although with pit toilets and no security; you'll probably be happier camping (and paying) at Snow Canyon State Park (see above), about 20 miles away.

Neither Quail Creek nor Gunlock State Parks offer on-site boat rentals, but rentals are available from several dealers in St. George: **RV Rental Express,** 875 E. St. George Blvd. (☎ 801/680-7447), has 14-foot aluminum fishing boats with 10-horsepower outboard motors starting at about $50 per day, and ski boats from about $150 per day; both include trailers and life jackets. **Funtime Rentals,** 770 E. 700 South (☎ 801/628-6511), rents 2- and 3-passenger personal watercraft, including trailers and life jackets, for $100 to $135 per day. Fuel is extra.

SPECTATOR SPORTS

Team Sports The **Dixie College Rebels** are the ones to root for in St. George. The football, women's volleyball, men's and women's basketball, men's baseball, and women's softball teams at this two-year community college are often nationally ranked. You're not likely to have any trouble getting tickets to join the school's 3,000 students in the 5,000-seat Hansen Stadium or Burns Arena. Tickets cost from $3 to $7, and are available at the Athletic Department offices (☎ 801/652-7525).

Drag Racing   Drag racing fans head to **St. George Raceway Park** (☎ 801/635-2447) during its March through November season for two to three racing days per month. Special races take place on Memorial Day, Labor Day, and Thanksgiving. Admission is $8; kids under 12 get in free. To get to the raceway, take I-15 to exit 8 on the north side of St. George, head south on River Road for about 4 1/2 miles, then watch for signs to the track.

SHOPPING

You probably wouldn't travel across the country to shop in St. George; the stores are similar to what you'd find almost anywhere in Middle America. Some of the town's more interesting shops (and one of our favorite local restaurants—see "Where to Dine," below) are located at **Ancestor Square,** at the corner of St. George Boulevard and Main Street. Among the shops are **Cassidy's Casuals,** 2 W. St. George Blvd. (☎ 801/628-6665), specializing in all-cotton fashions; and **Artists' Gallery,** 5 W. St. George Blvd. (☎ 801/628-9293), showing the works of regional and local artists.

You'll find WalMart, ZCMI department store, and the standard mall fare at **Red Cliffs Mall,** 1770 E. Red Cliffs Dr. (☎ 801/673-0099). It's located on the east side of I-15, between exits 8 (St. George Boulevard) and 10 (Green Springs Drive), and is open Monday to Saturday 10am to 9pm, and Sunday noon to 5pm.

If you can't resist a bargain, head for **Zion Factory Stores,** 250 N. Red Cliffs Dr. (☎ 801/674-9800), where you'll find more than three dozen outlet shops, including Corning-Revere, London Fog, Book Warehouse, Toy Liquidators, Bass, Etienne Aigner, Carter's, J. Crew, Cape Isle Knitters, Clothestime, and Van Heusen. Located on the east side of I-15 just north of exit 8, the mall is open Monday to Saturday from 10am to 8pm, and Sunday 11am to 5pm.

Those in the market for alcoholic beverages will find them at the **Utah State Liquor Store,** 929 W. Sunset Blvd. (☎ 801/673-9454).

WHERE TO STAY

You'll find a good selection of lodgings in St. George, with a range of facilities and prices. Most are on St. George Boulevard and Bluff Street, within easy walking distance of restaurants and attractions. Summer is the slow season here—people tend to head to the mountains when the temperature hits 115°F—so prices are low-est then. High seasons are spring and fall, and it's almost impossible to find a room during the World Senior Games in mid- to late October. Golfers will want to ask about special golf packages offered by many hotels and motels in St. George.

In addition to the accommodations described below, you'll find branches of the following reliable chain motels: **Motel 6,** 205 N. 1000 East St. (exit 8 off I-15), St. George, UT 84770 (☎ 801/628-7979 or 505/891-6161), with rates for two of $35.99–$39.99; **Super 8 Motel,** 915 S. Bluff St., St. George, UT 84770 (☎ 801/628-4251 or 800/800/8000, fax 801/628-6534), charging $46.88–$49.88 for two people; and **Comfort Inn,** 999 E. Skyline Dr., St. George, UT 84770 (☎ 801/628-4271 or 800/221-2222), with rates for two of $48–$64.

Room tax adds about 9% to your lodging bill. Pets are not accepted unless otherwise noted.

Best Western Coral Hills

125 E. St. George Blvd., St. George, UT 84770. ☎ **801/673-4844** or 800/542-7733. Fax 801/673-5352. 98 rms, including 5 suites. A/C TV TEL. $49–$65 double. Rates include continental breakfast. AE, CB, DC, DISC, MC, V.

A bit more homey than your average Best Western, the Coral Hills has floral bedspreads and lace curtains, along with king- or queen-sized beds and polished-wood furnishings that include an armoire/dresser combo that hides the TV. Swimmers can choose between good-sized indoor and outdoor heated pools, both with whirlpools, plus a kiddie pool. There's also a game room with a pool table, an exercise room, and a putting green. If you're here to work, fax and photocopy services are available.

Dixie Palms Motel

185 E. St. George Blvd., St. George, UT 84770. ☎ **801/673-3531.** 15 rms. A/C TV TEL. $26–$30 double. MC, V.

Travelers on tight budgets should head to the Dixie Palms—basic lodging at bargain-basement rates. Located right in the center of town, within walking distance of several restaurants and attractions, this older, redbrick property doesn't have a swimming pool and some rooms have showers only, but rooms are clean and well-maintained, and the price is right.

Claridge Inn

1187 S. Bluff St., St. George, UT 84770. ☎ **801/673-7222** or 800/367-3790. Fax 801/634-0773. 50 rms. A/C TV TEL. Sun–Thurs $31–$33 double; Fri–Sat $43–$49 double; higher for special events. Rates include continental breakfast at a nearby restaurant. AE, DISC, MC, V.

This recently built motel is popular with families because of its outdoor heated pool and low rates. The rooms—most with two queen-sized beds—are well-kept but rather plain, with stucco walls and no artwork. All have a small dining table with two comfortable chairs. The Claridge Inn is entirely nonsmoking.

⑨ Econo Lodge

460 E. St. George Blvd., St. George, UT 84770. ☎ **801/673-4861** or 800/424-4777. 54 rms, including 4 suites. A/C TV TEL. Feb–early Sept $42–$72 double; early Sept–Jan $40–$68 double. AE, DISC, JCB, MC, V.

This attractive and well-kept Econo Lodge boasts a large, well-landscaped outdoor heated swimming pool, making the poolside rooms the best choice. Rooms come in a variety of sizes and bed choices, with standard motel furnishings. The four king suites, however, are extra special, with a king bed, wet bar with refrigerator, a couch, tables and chairs, and plenty of room—perfect for families. Also above average is the motel's one wheelchair-accessible room, with its very spacious and easy-to-use bath facilities. Pets are welcome.

Greene Gate Village Bed & Breakfast

76 W. Tabernacle St., St. George, UT 84770. ☎ **801/628-6999** or 800/350-6999. Fax 801/628-5068. 15 rms, 1 large family unit. A/C TV TEL. $50–$115 double. Rates include full breakfast. AE, DISC, MC, V.

One of the most delightful places to stay in southwest Utah, this bed-and-breakfast inn is actually nine separate buildings, all restored pioneer homes from the late 1800s, sitting in their own flower-filled little "village" in downtown St. George. There are lots of genuine antiques—mostly Victorian—plus modern "necessities" such as TVs; some rooms also have VCRs. Most rooms have shower/tub combos, but some have showers only. Breakfasts are full and generous, and Bentley's Fine Dining (see "Where to Dine," below) serves dinner Thursday, Friday, and Saturday evenings, by reservation only. There's a small outdoor heated pool and hot tub. Unlike at many

B&Bs, children, even babies, are welcome; pets generally are not. Tobacco use of any kind is prohibited inside.

Hilton Inn of St. George

1450 S. Hilton Dr., St. George, UT 84770. ☎ **801/628-0463** or 800/662-2525 in Utah. Fax 801/628-1501. 100 rms, including 2 suites. A/C TV TEL. $70–$105 double (rates are highest in spring and fall; lowest in the summer). AE, CB, DC, DISC, EU, JCB, MC, V.

One of the few full-service hotels in southwest Utah, this Hilton is everything you'd expect from such a respected chain. What makes the hotel particularly interesting is that all the rooms are different: Some have two sinks, some one; some are decorated with dark wood, others light; and a variety of color themes and wallpaper designs are used. All rooms are done in a subdued Southwest decor and have computer dataports and voice mail; some have desks. A full range of services are provided, and facilities include two large pools (one indoor, one out), a sundeck, three lighted tennis courts, a gift shop, and conference rooms for up to 200. A restaurant serves three meals daily and has complete liquor service. A complete renovation was underway in late 1995. Pets are accepted with a $25 nonrefundable fee.

Holiday Inn Resort Hotel & Convention Center

850 S. Bluff St., St. George, UT 84770. ☎ **801/628-4235** or 800/457-9800. Fax 801/628-8157. 164 rms, including 7 suites. A/C TV TEL. Winter, $69–$89 double; summer, $110–$140 double. AE, CB, DC, DISC, JCB, MC, V.

With its Holidome recreation center, this is an excellent choice for travelers with kids or anyone who wants easy access to a large indoor-outdoor heated pool, whirlpool, lighted tennis court, putting green, weight room, pool table, Ping-Pong table, video arcade, and a separate children's play area. That should keep you busy, but if you find time to get to your room, you'll find it attractively decorated, with floral bedspreads on king- or queen-sized beds and solid wood furniture. Family rooms are slightly larger and come with hide-a-beds; king rooms have hair dryers and hot beverage makers in addition to the standard furnishings; and the luxury suites have individual whirlpool spas. The hotel offers a full range of services, and just off the beautiful cathedral-ceilinged lobby is a gift shop selling local crafts in addition to the standard magazines, T-shirts, and souvenirs. A formal dining room and coffee shop serve three meals daily, and full liquor service is available. Small pets may be accepted with management approval.

✪ Seven Wives Inn Bed & Breakfast

217 N. 100 West, St. George, UT 84770. ☎ **801/628-3737** or 800/600-3737. 12 units, including 1 suite. A/C TV TEL. $55–$125. Rates include full breakfast. AE, CB, DC, DISC, JCB, MC, V.

There are no polygamists hiding in the attic of Seven Wives Inn anymore—as they did in the 1880s after polygamy was outlawed—but it's still fun to imagine what things were like in those days. Innkeepers Jon and Alison Bowcutt will be happy to chat with you about the property's history. This bed-and-breakfast consists of two historic homes: the main house, built in 1873, is where polygamists hid; next door is the President's house, a four-square Victorian built 10 years later that played host to many of the Mormon church's early presidents. All of the dozen rooms have private baths, two with shower only. The honeymoon suite has a whirlpool tub for two. Many rooms have functioning fireplaces or wood-burning stoves, and the entire inn is decorated with antiques, mostly Victorian and Eastlake. Many of the rooms have decks or balconies. The inn is completely nonsmoking.

Singletree Inn

260 E. St. George Blvd., St. George, UT 84770. ☎ **801/673-6161** or 800/528-8890. Fax 801/673-7453. 48 units, including 2 family suites. A/C TV TEL. $50–$55 double; $60–$70 family suite. All rates include continental breakfast. AE, CB, DC, DISC, MC, V.

A few personal touches, such as dried-flower wall decorations, give this family-owned and -operated motel a homey feel; it's not institutional like many motels in this price category. Light-colored wallpaper is accented by the dark wood furnishings, and prints depicting area attractions hang on the walls. Rooms have either one king- or two queen-sized beds, there's an outdoor heated pool and whirlpool, and the motel's golf packages are better than most in the area. Small pets are accepted.

AN RV PARK

Settler's RV Park

1333 E. 100 South, St. George, UT 84770. ☎ **801/628-1624.** 155 sites. $16.90 with full hook-ups. MC, V. From I-15, take exit 8 (St. George Boulevard), go east one block, turn right onto River Road, then left onto 100 South.

Situated below a bluff just off I-15, this RV park is convenient for those seeing the area's attractions. The paved sites are fairly well-spaced, and once the trees grow a bit, they'll be at least partly shaded. The bath house is large and well-kept, there's a coin-operated laundry, and in addition to a heated pool and spa there are barbecues, a playground, a game room, shuffleboard, and horseshoes.

WHERE TO DINE

Andelin's Gable House Restaurant

290 E. St. George Blvd. ☎ **801/673-6796.** Reservations required spring and fall for prix fixe only. Main courses $4.50–$15.95; lunch $4.50–$9.95. Prix fixe dinner $25.95 for five courses, $21.95 for three courses. AE, DISC, MC, V. Mon–Sat 11:30am–10pm. From I-15, take exit 8 and head west on St. George Boulevard for about eight blocks. AMERICAN.

The Old English–garden decor, with lots of plants, flowered wallpaper, an eclectic display of antiques and collectibles, and a somewhat casually elegant atmosphere make the Gable House a popular special-occasion spot. At lunch you'll find croissant sandwiches, a good selection of salads, and chicken pot pie. Dinners include the very popular chicken pot pie again, with an especially flaky crust; slow-cooked beef brisket; and pink mountain trout, which is lightly floured and sautéed in butter. Among dinner entree salads, particularly recommended is the Oriental salad, with grilled chicken breast, Chinese noodles, Mandarin oranges, and almonds. The prix fixe dinners give you a choice of prime rib, roast rack of pork, or the fish of the day. No alcohol is served.

✪ Basila's Greek & Italian Cafe

Ancestor Square No. 38, 2 W. St. George Blvd. ☎ **801/673-7671.** Reservations for 6 or more only. Main courses $7.95–$16.95; lunch $3.75–$6.95. AE, DISC, MC, V. Tues–Sat 11:30am–2:30pm and 5–9pm. From I-15, take exit 8, head west on St. George Boulevard to Main Street; Ancestor Square is on the northwest corner. GREEK/ITALIAN.

Tucked away toward the back of Ancestor Square, Basila's is worth finding. You start off with crusty homemade bread and "Greek butter," a delightfully light mixture of olive oil and Balsamic vinegar. For lunch we had the four-cheese (ricotta, parmesan, romano, and feta) ravioli in marinara sauce, and a gyro with layers of seasoned lamb and beef on a bed of parsley and tomato with Tzatziki cucumber yogurt sauce; we highly recommend both. The spanakopeta, baked on the premises with thin layers of filo dough rolled with fresh spinach, ricotta, and parmesan cheese, and served with a lemon sauce, is a favorite at both lunch and dinner. For dessert, try the house favorite: Greek custard bread pudding. The tables are closely spaced in the fairly narrow, L-shaped dining room. There are plants in the windows, an eclectic collection of Mediterranean artwork arranged on high shelves around the exposed adobe walls, and slow-moving fans hanging from the open-beamed ceiling. There's also a small outdoor patio. Complete liquor service is available.

Bentley's Fine Dining

Greene Gate Village Bed & Breakfast, 76 W. Tabernacle St. ☎ **801/628-6999.** Reservations required. Five-course prix fixe $18. AE, DISC, MC, V. Thurs–Sat 6–9pm. Closed major holidays. From I-15, take exit 8, head west on St. George Boulevard to Main Street, turn left (south) on Main for one block to Tabernacle Street, then right (west) to the restaurant. AMERICAN.

Come to this handsome Victorian home for a quiet, romantic, elegant evening. A pianist plays quietly in the background as you dine, surrounded by antiques from the 1870s. Although the menu varies, you might have broiled filet mignon with sautéed mushrooms, chicken Cordon Bleu, or salmon poached in white wine. Desserts are always homemade, and include a variety of pies and cheesecakes. No alcoholic beverages are served.

Dick's Cafe

14 E. St. George Blvd. ☎ **801/673-3841.** Reservations required for groups and on holidays. Main courses $4.50–$10.95; breakfast $2.50–$7; lunch $3.25–$5.95. AE, DISC, MC, V. Daily 6am–9:30pm. From I-15 take exit 8, head west on St. George Boulevard for about 11 blocks and the cafe will be on your left. SOUTHWESTERN/AMERICAN.

Dick's, which claims to be the oldest eating establishment in St. George, opened in 1935. It's the sort of place you would expect to find in the Old West: a funky hometown cafe, with a long counter plus booths and tables, and regulars who specialize in drinking pots of coffee and swapping lies. You can get breakfast all day; all the American standards are available, plus a few spicy Mexican dishes that will really open your eyes. Lunches include sandwiches and burgers, salads and some other healthy stuff, and luncheon plates such as fresh roast turkey or liver and onions. At dinner, you can get more of the roast turkey and liver and onions, plus steaks, roast beef, grilled halibut, and fish-and-chips. Fans of chicken fried steak say Dick's is about the best around. Pies are fresh-baked on the premises. Children's and seniors' menus are available. No alcohol is served.

✪ Sullivan's Roccoco Steakhouse

511 S. Airport Rd. ☎ **801/673-3305.** Reservations accepted. Main courses $6.95–$25.95; lunch $3.50–$7.95. AE, DISC, MC, V. Mon–Fri 11am–10pm, Sat–Sun 5–10pm. From I-15, take exit 8, head west on St. George Boulevard to Bluff Street, cross over onto Airport Road, which immediately turns to the left and climbs the bluff; follow Airport Road to the restaurant. STEAK/SEAFOOD.

Excellent beef and the best views from any St. George restaurant make Sullivan's a great spot for special occasions. Sitting on a bluff overlooking the city, large glass windows take full advantage of a spectacular panorama of the city and surrounding red rock formations, especially as the sun begins to set and the city lights begin to twinkle below. Generous portions of prime rib and a variety of steaks are king here; the Roccoco is also considered the best spot in southwest Utah for lobster. All baking is done in-house, so try to save some room for a piece of pie—the shredded apple with caramel sauce and ice cream is spectacular. Those dropping by for lunch can choose from several sandwiches, including an extra special prime rib sandwich, burgers, and salads. The restaurant has full liquor service.

Tom's Delicatessen

175 West 900 S. Bluff. ☎ **801/628-1822.** Sandwiches $3.69–$6.19. MC, V. Tues–Sat 11am–6pm. From I-15, take exit 8, head west on St. George Boulevard to Bluff Street and turn left (south) for about two blocks. DELI.

Hidden in a narrow storefront in a small shopping center next to the Holiday Inn, Tom's quietly goes about its business of creating tasty, filling sandwiches. A St. George institution since 1978, Tom's offers 16 hot and 21 cold selections—just about all the basics: roast beef, turkey, pastrami. You can eat yours at one of the Formica tables along the wall, or carry it out for a picnic. No alcohol is served.

ST. GEORGE AFTER DARK

St. George, with its large non-drinking Mormon population, isn't one of the West's hot spots as far as the bar scene is concerned. Locals going out on the town will often attend a performing arts event (see below), and then stop in for a nightcap at one of the local restaurants that serves alcohol, such as Sullivan's Roccoco Steakhouse or Basila's Greek & Italian Cafe (see "Where to Dine," above). Keep in mind that these are not private clubs, so you'll need to buy something to eat in order to purchase a drink.

The Dixie Center, 425 S. 700 East (☎ 801/628-7003), is St. George's primary performing arts venue. The four-building complex hosts a wide range of events, from country and rock music to symphony, ballet, opera, and even sports.

Dixie College, 225 S. 700 East (☎ 801/673-4811), offers a variety of events throughout the school year. The Celebrity Concert Series, each October through April, has developed a strong following for programs such as *The Nutcracker* by the Nevada Dance Theatre, Ballet Hispanico, the BYU Folk Dance Ensemble, Joe Muscolino Little Big Band, the Utah Symphony Orchestra, and other solo and ensemble performers. Not to be outdone, the college's drama department offers its own series of five productions each year. There's usually a major musical in February; other productions will likely include dramas, comedies, a children's production, maybe even a Greek tragedy. Admission to college productions usually costs between $5 and $12 per person, and performances are presented at one of two theaters at the **College's Graff Fine Arts Center.** Call the box office (☎ 801/652-7800) to find out what's scheduled during your visit.

Music lovers will enjoy St. George's own **Southwest Symphonic Chorale and Southwest Symphony** (☎ 801/673-0700), the only full symphony orchestra between Provo and Las Vegas. Their repertoire includes classical, opera, and popular music. You'll want to get tickets early for the annual Christmas performance of Handel's *Messiah,* performed with the Dixie College Concert Choir, which usually sells out. Concerts are scheduled from October through early June, and tickets are in the $5 to $7 range.

The **St. George Tabernacle** (☎ 801/628-4072) presents free weekly concerts in a beautiful setting; see "Discovering Mormon History In & Around St. George," above, for further details.

For a spectacular outdoor musical drama that blends history, songs, drama, and dynamite special effects, take the short trip from St. George to the **Tuacahn Amphitheater & Center for the Arts,** 1100 Tuacahn Dr., Ivins (☎ 801/674-0012 or 800/746-9882 box office; fax 801/652-3227). Presented Monday through Saturday evenings at 8:30pm from mid-June through early October, ✪ *Utah!* depicts the settling of southern Utah by Mormon pioneers, particularly the life of Jacob Hamblin, known for his peacekeeping efforts with the Native Americans of the area. The musical, with live vocals but recorded instrumental accompaniment, comes to life with its state-of-the-art sound system and special effects, including lightning, a gigantic flood, and dazzling fireworks for the finale. Reservations are recommended. Tickets cost $14.50–$24.50 for adults, $9–$16 for children under 12. Free pre-show entertainment and backstage tours are offered, and Dutch oven dinners are served at $9 for adults and $7 for children under 12; call for details.

Zion National Park 13

by Don & Barbara Laine

So named by Mormon pioneers because it seemed to be a bit of heaven on earth, Zion National Park casts a spell over you as you gaze upon its sheer multicolored walls of sandstone, explore its narrow canyons, hunt for hanging gardens of wildflowers, or listen to the roar of the churning, tumbling Virgin River.

It's easy to conjure up a single defining image of the Grand Canyon or the delicately sculpted rock hoodoos of Bryce, but Zion is more difficult to pin down, a collage of images and secrets. It's not simply the towering Great White Throne, deep Narrows Canyon, or cascading waterfalls and emerald green pools. There's an entire smorgasbord of experiences, sights, and even smells here, from massive stone sculptures and monuments to lush forests and rushing rivers. Take time to walk its trails, visit viewpoints at different times of the day to see the changing light, and let the park work its magic on you.

Because of its extremes of elevation (from 3,800 feet to almost 9,000 feet) and climate (with temperatures soaring over 100°F in the summer and a landscape carpeted with snow in the winter), Zion harbors a vast array of plants and animals. About 800 native species of plants have been found: cactus, yucca, and mesquite in the hot, dry desert areas; ponderosa pine trees on the high plateaus; and cottonwoods and box elders along the rivers and streams. Of the 14 varieties of cactus that grow in the park, watch for the red claret cup, which has spectacular blooms in the spring. Wildflowers common in the park include the manzanita, with its tiny pink blossoms; buttercups; and the bright red hummingbird trumpet. Dubbed the "Zion Lily" because of its abundance in the park, the sacred datura has large funnel-shaped white flowers that open in the cool of night and are often closed by noon.

While exploring Zion, be sure to watch for "spring lines" and their hanging gardens, which you'll see clinging to the sides of cliffs. Because sandstone is porous, water can percolate down through it until it is stopped by a layer of harder rock. Then the water simply changes direction, moving horizontally to the rock face, where it oozes out, forming the "spring line" that provides life-giving nutrients to whatever seeds the wind delivers.

Speaking of living things, Zion National Park is a veritable zoo, with mammals ranging from pocket gophers to mountain lions, hundreds of birds (including golden eagles), lizards of all shapes and

How Nature Painted Zion's Landscape

Zion National Park is many things to many people: a day-hike down a narrow canyon, a rugged climb up the face of a massive stone monument, or the quiet appreciation of the red glow of sunset over majestic peaks. But at least to some degree, each of these experiences is possible because of rocks—their formation, uplifting, shifting, breaking, and eroding. The most important of Zion's nine rock layers in creating its colorful formations is Navajo sandstone, the thickest rock layer in the park, at up to 2,200 feet. This formation was created some 200 million years ago, during the Jurassic period, when North America was hot and dry. Movements in the earth's crust caused a shallow sea to cover windblown sand dunes, and minerals, including lime from the shells of sea creatures, glued sand particles together to form sandstone. Later crust movements caused the land to uplift, draining away the sea but leaving rivers that gradually carved the relatively soft sandstone into the spectacular shapes we see today.

So where do the colors come from? Essentially, from plain old rust. Most of the rocks at Zion are colored by iron, or hematite (iron oxide), either contained in the original stone or carried into the rocks by groundwater. Although iron often creates red and pink hues, seen in much of Zion's sandstone faces, it can also result in blacks, browns, yellows, and even greens. Sometimes the iron seeps into the rock, coloring it through, but it can also stain just the surface, often in vertical streaks. White streaks are frequently caused by deposits of salt left when water evaporates. Rocks can also be colored by bacteria that live on rock surfaces, ingest dust, and expel iron, manganese, and other minerals that stick to the rock and produce a shiny black, brown or reddish surface called desert varnish.

sizes, and a dozen species of snakes (only the western rattlesnake is poisonous, and they usually slither away from you faster than you can run from them). Mule deer are common, and although they're seldom seen, there are a few shy elk and bighorn sheep, plus foxes, coyote, ringtail cats, beaver, porcupines, skunks, and plenty of squirrels and bats. Practically every summer visitor sees lizards of some sort, often the colorful collared and whiptail lizards; and it's easy to hear the song of the canyon wren and the call of the piñon jay.

1 Just the Facts

Located in southwest Utah, at elevations ranging from 3,700 feet to 8,726 feet, Zion National Park has several sections: **Zion Canyon,** the main part of the park, where everyone goes, and the less-visited **Kolob Canyons.** The main east–west road through Zion Canyon is Utah 9, from which you can reach a 14-mile round-trip scenic drive/ tram route that provides access to most scenic overlooks and trailheads.

Getting There/Access Points St. George and Cedar City are the closest towns to Zion National Park with airport service. From either airport, it's easy to rent a car and drive to Zion (see chapter 12 for complete details). The park is located 42 miles northeast of St. George, and 56 miles south of Cedar City. From I-15 on the park's western side, the drive into Zion Canyon, the main part of the park—following Utah 9, or Utah 17 and Utah 9 to the south entrance—is easier but less scenic than the approach on the eastern side. Though the western approach is less scenic, it's the best route into the park; it's more direct, avoids possible delays at the Zion–Mt. Carmel

Tunnel, and delivers you to Springdale, just outside the park's southern entrance, where most of the area's lodging and restaurants are located. Outside Zion Canyon you'll find additional viewpoints and trailheads along Kolob Terrace Road, which starts just east of the park's southern entrance at the village of Virgin. This road is closed in the winter.

The Kolob Canyons section, in the park's northwest corner, is reached on the short Kolob Canyons Road off I-15.

From the east it's a spectacularly scenic 24-mile drive from Mt. Carmel on Utah 9, reached from either the north or south via U.S. 89. The park is 41 miles northwest of Kanab. However, be aware that this route into the park drops over 2,500 feet in elevation, passes through the mile-long Zion–Mt. Carmel Tunnel, and winds down six steep switchbacks. The tunnel is too small for two-way traffic that includes vehicles larger than standard passenger cars and pickup trucks. Buses, trucks, and most recreational vehicles must be driven down the center of the tunnel, and therefore all oncoming traffic must be stopped. This applies to all vehicles over 7'10" wide (including mirrors) or 11'4" tall (including luggage racks, etc.). From March through October, large vehicles are permitted in the tunnel only from 8am to 8pm daily; during other months arrangements can be made at park entrances or by calling park headquarters (☎ 801/772-3256). There is a $10 fee, good for two trips during a seven-day period, for affected vehicles. All vehicles over 13'1" tall and certain other particularly large vehicles are prohibited from driving anywhere on the park road between the east entrance and Zion Canyon.

From March to October, all vehicles over 21 feet long are prohibited from stopping at two parking areas: Weeping Rock (these vehicles may not enter the area) and the Temple of Sinawava (vehicles may be driven through but cannot park between 9am and 5pm).

You may also need to know that the park is 83 miles southwest of Bryce Canyon National Park, and 120 miles northwest of the north rim of Grand Canyon National Park in northern Arizona. It's 309 miles south of Salt Lake City and 158 miles northeast of Las Vegas, Nevada.

Information & Visitor Centers   For advance information on what to see in the park, hiking trails, camping, and lodging, contact Superintendent, **Zion National Park,** Springdale, UT 84767-1099 (☎ 801/772-3256). It's best to write at least a month before your planned visit, and specify what type of information you need. Officials request that those seeking trip-planning information write rather than call, leaving the phone lines open for those needing current and changeable information such as hiking trail conditions and closures.

If you want even more details to help plan your trip, you can order books, maps, and videos from the nonprofit **Zion Natural History Association, Zion National Park**, Springdale, UT 84767 (☎ 801/772-3264 or 800/635-3959). The association publishes several excellent books, including the colorful and informative 55-page *Zion National Park, Towers of Stone,* by J. L. Crawford, which sells for $9.50; and the easy-to-understand 22-page booklet *An Introduction to the Geology of Zion National Park,* by Al Warneke, which sells for $2.95. Some publications are available in foreign languages, and several videos can be purchased in either VHS or PAL formats. Major credit cards are accepted. Those wanting to help the nonprofit association can join ($15 single or $25 family annually) and get a 20% discount on purchases.

The park has two visitor centers. The more comprehensive **Zion Canyon Visitor Center** (☎ 801/772-3256), near the south entrance to the park, has a museum with exhibits on the geology and history of the area and presents an introductory slide

Zion National Park

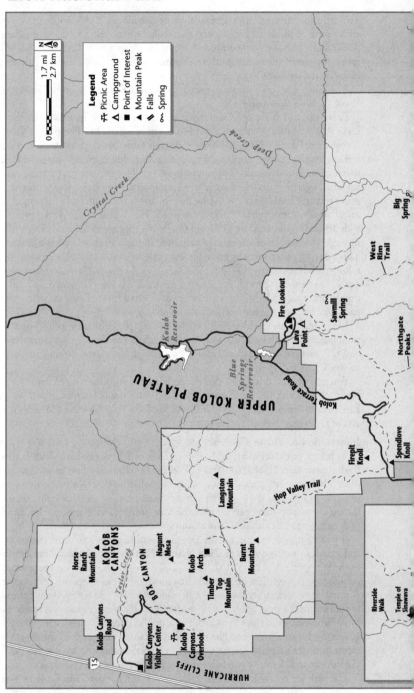

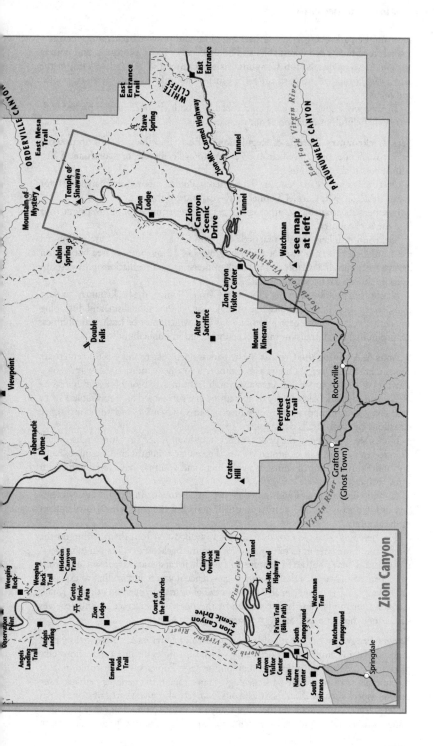

239

show on the park. Rangers can answer questions and provide backcountry permits, several free brochures are available, and books, maps, videos, postcards, and posters are sold. The smaller **Kolob Canyons Visitor Center** (☎ 801/586-9548), in the northwest corner of the park off I-15, can provide information, permits, books, and maps.

The Sentinel, a small free newspaper available at both visitor centers, is packed with extremely helpful information about the park.

Fees, Backcountry Permits & Regulations   Entry into the park (for up to seven days) costs $5 per private vehicle or $3 per motorcycle, bicycle, or pedestrian. A $15 annual pass is also available.

Oversized vehicles (see "Getting There/Access Points," above) are charged $10 for use of the Zion–Mt. Carmel Tunnel on the east side of the park.

Free permits, available at either visitor center, are required for all overnight trips into the backcountry.

Backcountry hikers should practice minimum impact techniques, are prohibited from building fires, and cannot travel in groups of 12 or more. A free booklet on backcountry travel, available at the visitor centers, lists all regulations plus descriptions of close to 20 backcountry trails.

Bicycles are prohibited in the Zion–Mt. Carmel Tunnel, the backcountry, and on trails, except the Pa'rus Trail. Feeding or molesting wildlife, vandalism, and disturbing any natural feature of the park is forbidden. Dogs, which must be leashed at all times, are prohibited on all trails, in the backcountry, and in public buildings.

Seasons & Avoiding the Crowds   The park is open year-round (visitor centers are closed Christmas Day), 24 hours a day, although weather conditions may limit some activities at certain times. For instance, you'll want to avoid long hikes in midsummer, when the park bakes under temperatures that can exceed an unbearable 110°F, or during and immediately after winter storms, when ice and snow at higher elevations can make trails dangerous.

If possible, try to avoid the peak summer months of June, July, and August, when Zion receives almost half its annual visitors. The quietest months are December, January, and February, but of course it's cold then, and you may have to contend with snow and ice.

A good compromise, if your schedule permits, is to visit in April, May, September, or October, when the weather is usually good but the park is less crowded than in the summer.

The best way to avoid crowds is simply to walk away from them, either on the longer and more strenuous hiking trails or into the backcountry. It's sad but true—most visitors never bother to venture far from their cars, and their loss can be your gain. You can have a wonderful solitary experience if you're just willing to expend a little energy to get it. You can also avoid hordes of tourists by spending time in Kolob Canyons, in the far northwest section of the park; it's spectacular and receives surprisingly little use, at least in comparison to Zion Canyon.

Ranger Programs   A variety of free programs and activities are presented by park rangers. Evening amphitheater programs, which sometimes include a slide show, take place most evenings at campground amphitheaters. Topics vary, but could include the animals or plants of the park, geology, man's role in the park, or perhaps some unique aspect such as Zion's slot canyons. Rangers also give short talks on similar subjects several times daily at the Zion Canyon Visitor Center and other locations. Ranger-guided hikes and walks, which may require reservations, might take you to little-visited areas of the park, on a trek to see wildflowers, or out at night for a hike under a full moon. Schedules of the various activities are posted on bulletin boards at the visitor centers, campgrounds, and other locations.

Kids from 6 to 12 years old can join the **Junior Rangers,** participate in a variety of programs, and earn certificates, badges, and patches. Morning and afternoon sessions, each lasting 2¹/₂ hours, are scheduled Tuesdays through Saturdays from Memorial Day through Labor Day, with children meeting at the Nature Center in the South Campground. There's a one-time fee of $1 per child, and the age range is strictly enforced.

Getting a Bird's-Eye View of the Park   Scenic Airlines (☎ 800/634-6801) offers combination air tours over Bryce Canyon and Zion national parks, plus the north rim of Grand Canyon National Park. Tours are given year-round, with prices starting at $275 for adults and $225 for children.

2 Seeing the Highlights

The best way to see Zion is to spend a week there, starting with the visitor center displays and programs, then a driving or guided tram tour, and gradually working from short hikes and walks to full-day and overnight treks into the backcountry. That's the ideal, but for most visitors, time and finances dictate a shorter visit.

If you have only a day or two at the park, we recommend starting at Zion Canyon Visitor Center for the slide show and exhibits, and then talking with a ranger about the amount of time you have, your abilities, and interests. Because Zion has such a variety of landscape and activities, each visitor can easily create a personalized itinerary. If your goal is to see as much of the park as possible in one full day we suggest the following:

After a quick stop at the visitor center, drive to **Zion Lodge** and take a ✪ **tram tour,** which hits the major roadside viewpoints and leaves the driving to someone else so that you can enjoy what you're seeing. It's a 1-hour ride that goes from the lodge to the Temple of Sinawava and back, with an informative and entertaining commentary by the tram driver, who points out prominent formations, historic sites, and things you might have missed on your own, such as daring climbers scaling the rock walls. There are several stops where passengers can get off for better views, or connect with trailheads, and then return to the lodge on a later tram. Cost is $2.95 for adults; $1.95 for children under 12, with tickets available at a window inside Zion Lodge. The tram operates daily from April to October, on the hour from 10am to 4pm.

Instead of staying on the tram all the way back to the lodge, we suggest you get off at the **Temple of Sinawava** and take the easy 2-mile round-trip **Riverside Walk,** which follows the Virgin River through a narrow canyon past hanging gardens. Then take the next tram back to the lodge (total time: 2- to 4-hours), where you might stop at the gift shop and possibly have lunch in the lodge restaurant. Near the lodge you'll find the trailhead for the **Emerald Pools.** Especially pleasant on hot days, this easy walk through a forest of oak, maple, fir, and cottonwood trees leads to a waterfall, hanging garden, and the shimmering lower pool. This part of the walk should take about an hour, round-trip, but those with a bit more ambition may want to add another hour and another mile to the loop by taking the moderately strenuous hike on a rocky, steeper trail to the upper pool. If time and energy remain, drive back toward the south park entrance and stop at **Watchman** (east of Watchman Campground), for the 2-mile, 2-hour round-trip moderately strenuous hike to a plateau with beautiful views of several rock formations and the town of Springdale. That evening, try to take in the campground amphitheater program.

3 Exploring Zion by Car

If you enter the park from the east, along the steep **Zion–Mt. Carmel Highway,** you'll travel 13 miles to the **Zion Canyon Visitor Center,** passing Checkerboard Mesa, a massive sandstone rock formation covered with horizontal and vertical lines that make it look like a huge fishing net. Continuing, you'll view a fairyland of fantastically shaped rocks of red, orange, tan, and white, as well as the Great Arch of Zion, carved high in a stone cliff.

Historically, almost all Zion National Park visitors have aimed their cars toward the 14-mile round-trip **Zion Canyon Scenic Drive,** which starts at the Zion Canyon Visitor Center. At this writing, visitors have the option of driving their own vehicles into the canyon, stopping at viewpoints and trailheads, and setting their own pace.

But that's expected to change. Traffic congestion, damage to roadside vegetation, noise, pollution, and a lack of parking are making the experience less and less pleasant, especially during the busy summer months, and park officials expect to have a mandatory shuttle bus service operating in Zion Canyon by 1998. In the meantime, motorists can still drive themselves, but be forewarned: especially in the summer, traffic is awful. Parking is hard to find, and you'll feel more like a Los Angeles or New York commuter than a national park visitor. We strongly recommend that you leave your car at the Zion Lodge parking lot and take the open-air tram.

You can take a much less crowded scenic drive in the northwest corner of the park. The ○ **Kolob Canyons Road** (about 45 minutes from Zion Canyon Visitor Center at I-15 Exit 40) runs 5 miles among spectacular red and orange rocks, ending at a high vista. Allow about 45 minutes round-trip, stopping at numbered viewpoints. Here's what you'll pass along the way:

Leaving **Kolob Canyons Visitor Center,** you'll drive along the Hurricane Fault to **Hurricane Cliffs,** a series of tall, gray cliffs composed of limestone, and onward to **Taylor Creek,** where a piñon-juniper forest clings to life on the rocky hillside, providing a home to the bright blue scrub jay. Your next stop is **Horse Ranch Mountain,** which, at 8,726 feet, is the national park's highest point. Passing a series of colorful rock layers, where you might be lucky enough to spot a golden eagle, your next stop is **Box Canyon,** along the south fork of Taylor Creek, with sheer rock walls soaring over 1,500 feet high. Next you'll see a multicolored layer of rock, pushed upward by tremendous forces from within the earth. Continue to a canyon, exposing a rock wall that likely began as a sand dune before being covered by an early sea and cemented into stone. Next stop is a side canyon, with large, arched alcoves boasting delicate curved ceilings. Head on to a view of **Timber Top Mountain,** which is a sagebrush-covered desert at its base, but is covered with stately fir and ponderosa pine at its peak. Watch for mule deer on the brushy hillsides, especially between October and March, when they might be spotted just after sunrise or before sunset. From here

Impressions

Nothing can exceed the wondrous beauty of Zion . . . in the nobility and beauty of the sculptures there is no comparison.

—Geologist Clarence Dutton, 1880

continue to **Rockfall Overlook;** a large scar on the mountainside marks the spot where a 1,000-foot chunk of stone crashed to the earth in July, 1983, the victim of erosion. And finally, stop to see the canyon walls themselves, colored orange-red by iron oxide and striped black by mineral-laden water running down the cliff faces.

More detail is provided in a road guide, which can be purchased for $1 at the Kolob Canyons Visitor Center.

4 Sports & Activities

For information as well as just about any piece of recreational equipment you might need, stop at **Bike Zion,** 445 Zion Park Blvd., Springdale (☎ 801/772-3929 or 800/4SLIKROK), and **Forest, Camping, and Hiking World,** at the same address and phone numbers.

BIKING & MOUNTAINBIKING

With one notable exception, bikes are prohibited on all trails, as well as forbidden to travel cross-country within the national park boundaries. This leaves only the park's established roads (except for the Zion–Mt. Carmel tunnel, where bikes are also prohibited), which are often clogged with motor vehicles.

But there's hope. The **Pa'rus Trail,** opened in late 1994, is the first phase of a new transportation plan for Zion National Park. It runs 2 miles along the Virgin River from the entrance to Watchman Campground to the beginning of the Zion Canyon Scenic Drive, crossing the river and several creeks, and providing good views of Watchman, West Temple, the Sentinel, and other lower canyon formations. The trail is paved, and open to bicyclists, pedestrians, and those with strollers or wheelchairs, but closed to cars. Plans call for allowing only shuttle buses, bicyclists, and hikers on the scenic drive, making the park truly bike-friendly.

Although mountainbikers will find they are generally not welcome in Zion National Park, outside the park, mostly on Bureau of Land Management property, they'll find numerous rugged jeep trails that are great for mountainbiking, plus slickrock cross-country trails and about 10 miles of single-track trails. Many are above the town of Springdale on Wire, Grafton, and Gooseberry Mesas, offering incredible high-country views across the national park. Talk with the knowledgeable staff at Bike Zion (see address above) about the best places for mountainbiking in the area. This full-service bike shop also offers maps, a full range of bikes and accessories, repairs, and rentals ($21 per day for a 21-speed mountainbike).

HIKING

Zion offers a wide variety of hiking trails, ranging from easy half-hour walks on paved paths, to grueling overnight hikes over rocky terrain along steep drop-offs. Following are our hiking suggestions; several free brochures on hiking trails are available at the visitor centers, and the **Zion Natural History Association** publishes a good 48-page booklet ($3.95) describing 18 trails (see "Information & Visitor Centers" earlier in this chapter). Hikers with a fear of heights should be especially careful when choosing trails; many include steep, dizzying drop-offs.

The **Weeping Rock Trail,** among the park's shortest and easiest rambles, is a half-mile round-trip walk from the Zion Canyon Scenic Drive to a rock alcove with a spring and hanging gardens of ferns and wildflowers. Although paved, the trail is not suitable for wheelchairs.

Another short hike is the ✪ **Emerald Pools Trail,** which can be an easy 1-hour walk or a moderately strenuous 2-hour hike, depending on how much of the loop you choose to do. A 0.6-mile paved path from the Emerald Pools Parking Area, through a forest of oak, maple, fir, and cottonwood, leads to a waterfall, hanging garden, and the Lower Emerald Pool, and is suitable for those in wheelchairs, with assistance. From here, a steeper, rocky trail (not appropriate for wheelchairs) continues past cactus, yucca, and juniper another half mile to Upper Emerald Pool, with another waterfall. A third pool, just above Lower Emerald Pool, offers impressive reflections of the cliffs. The pools are named for the green color of the water, which is caused by algae.

A particularly scenic hike is the **Hidden Canyon Trail,** a 2-mile moderately strenuous hike that takes about 3 hours. Starting at the Weeping Rock parking area, the trail climbs 1,000 feet through a narrow water-carved canyon, ending at the canyon's mouth. Those wanting to extend the hike can go another 0.6 mile to a small natural arch. Hidden Canyon Trail includes long drop-offs, and is not recommended for anyone with a fear of heights.

Another moderately strenuous but relatively short hike is the **Watchman Trail,** which starts by the service road east of Watchman Campground. This 2-mile round-trip hike, which takes about 2 hours, gets surprisingly light use, possibly because it can be very hot in the middle of the day. Climbing to a plateau near the base of the formation called The Watchman, it offers splendid views of lower Zion Canyon, the Towers of the Virgin, and West Temple formations.

For a strenuous, 4-hour, 5-mile hike—one that is most certainly not for anyone with even a mild fear of heights—take the **Angel's Landing Trail** to a summit that offers spectacular views into Zion Canyon. But be prepared: the final half mile follows a narrow, knife-edge trail along a steep ridge, where footing can be slippery even under the best of circumstances. Support chains have been set along parts of the trail.

✪ **Hiking the Narrows** is not hiking a trail at all, but walking or wading along the bottom of the Virgin River, through a spectacular 1,000-foot-deep chasm that, at 20 feet wide, definitely lives up to its name. Passing fancifully sculptured sandstone arches, hanging gardens, and waterfalls, this moderately strenuous hike can be completed in less than a day or in several days, depending on how much you want to do. However, the Narrows are subject to flash flooding, and may be closed. Signs indicating the Narrows' danger level are posted, and permits are required for full-day and overnight hikes (check with park rangers for details). Permits are not required for easy, short day hikes, with access just beyond the end of the Riverside Walk, a 2-mile trail that starts at the Temple of Sinawava parking area.

HORSEBACK RIDING

Guided rides in the park are available March through October from **Canyon Trail Rides,** P.O. Box 128, Tropic, UT 84776 (☎ 801/772-3967), with ticket sales and information at Zion Lodge. A 1-hour ride along the Virgin River costs $12.75 and a half-day ride on the Sand Beach Trail costs $37.10. Riders must weigh no more than 220 pounds, and children must be at least five years old for the 1-hour ride and eight years old for the half-day ride. Reservations are advised.

ROCK CLIMBING

Technical rock climbers like the sandstone cliffs in Zion Canyon, although rangers warn that much of the rock is loose, or "rotten," and climbing equipment and techniques suitable for granite are often less effective on sandstone. Free permits are required for overnight climbs, and because some routes may be closed at times, climbers should check at the visitor center before setting out.

WILDLIFE WATCHING

It's a rare visitor to Zion who doesn't spot a critter of some sort, from mule deer—often seen along roadways and in campgrounds—to the numerous varieties of lizards, including the park's largest, the chuckwalla, which can grow to 20 inches. The ringtail cat, a relative of the raccoon, prowls Zion Canyon at night, and is not above helping itself to your camping supplies. Along the Virgin River you'll see bank beaver, so named because they live in burrows instead of building dams. The park is also home to several types of squirrels, gophers, and pack rats. And if you're interested in spotting birds, you're in luck at Zion. The rare peregrine falcon, among the world's fastest birds, sometimes nests in the Weeping Rock area, where you're likely to see the dipper, winter wren, and white-throated swift. Also in the park you might see golden eagles, plus several species of hummingbirds, ravens, piñon jays, and possibly a roadrunner or two.

Snakes include the poisonous western rattler, found below 8,000 feet elevation, and there are also nonpoisonous kingsnakes and gopher snakes. Tarantulas, those large, usually slow-moving hairy spiders, are often seen in the late summer and fall. Contrary to popular belief, the tarantula's bite is not deadly, although it may be somewhat painful.

Remember, it's illegal to feed the wildlife; no matter how much you may want to befriend an animal by offering food, please remember that it's not healthy for the wildlife to eat human food or to get used to being fed this way.

5 Camping

The absolutely best places to camp are at one of the ✪ **national park campgrounds,** if you can find a site. Reservations are not accepted, and the campgrounds often fill by noon in the summer, so get there early in the day to claim a site. Some campers stay at nearby commercial campgrounds their first night in the area, then hurry into the park the next morning, circling like vultures until a site becomes available.

Both of Zion's main campgrounds, just inside the park's south entrance, have paved roads, well-spaced sites, lots of trees, and that national park atmosphere you came here to enjoy. There are restrooms with flush toilets but no showers, and no RV hookups. There is a dump station and public telephone, and sites for those with disabilities are available. The fee is $8 per night. **South Campground** has 141 sites, and is usually open from mid-March through mid-October only; **Watchman Campground** has 228 sites and is open year-round.

Lava Point, with only six sites, is located in Kolob Canyons. It has fire grates, tables, and toilets, but no water, and there is no fee. It is usually open from May through October.

If you can't get a site in the park, or if you prefer hot showers or complete RV hookups, there are several campgrounds in the surrounding area. The closest, **Zion Canyon Campground,** on Zion Park Boulevard a half mile south of the park entrance (P.O. Box 99), Springdale, UT 84767 (☎ 801/772-3237; fax 801/772-3844), has 180 sites, many shaded, and is open year-round. Although it's quite crowded in the summer, the campground is clean and well-maintained, and in addition to the usual showers and RV hookups, there's a self-service laundry, dump station, a store with groceries, souvenirs, and RV supplies, and a restaurant. Tenters are welcome; rates are from $13 to $20 for two people.

6 Accommodations

The only lodging actually in Zion National Park is at Zion Lodge (see below). The other properties listed here are all in Springdale, a village of some 350 people at the park's south entrance that has literally become the park's bedroom. Room tax is about 10% in Springdale; 9% in the park. Pets are not accepted unless otherwise noted.

You can also base yourself in St. George, which is 42 miles away; Kanab, which is 40 miles away; or Cedar City, 56 miles away.

Best Western Driftwood Lodge

1515 Zion Park Blvd., Springdale, UT 84767. ☎ **801/772-3262** or 800/528-1234. 47 units, including 2 family suites. A/C TV TEL. Apr–Oct $64–$76 double, $94–$102 family unit; Nov–Mar $54–$66 double, $84–$92 family unit. All rates include continental breakfast. AE, DC, DISC, MC, V.

This attractive, well-kept motel (extensively renovated in 1994) has beautiful lawns and gardens, offering a quiet, lush setting for sitting back and admiring the spectacular rock formations that practically surround the town. Spacious rooms have white walls and light wood-grain furnishings, and many have patios or balconies. Your room will have one queen, one king, or two king beds, and the two family suites each have one king-size and two queen beds. There's an outdoor heated pool with a sundeck, a Jacuzzi, and an art gallery and gift shop, but no restaurant on the premises. Pets are accepted at management discretion.

Bumbleberry Inn

897 Zion Park Blvd., Springdale, UT 84767. ☎ **801/772-3224** or 800/828-1534. Fax 801/772-3947. 23 rms. A/C TV TEL. Apr–Oct $54–$59 double; Nov–Mar $49–$54 double. DISC, MC, V.

Set back from the main highway, the Bumbleberry offers large, quiet rooms at a good price. Built in 1972, the motel was last renovated in 1991. Furnishings are simple but more than adequate, with a desk in addition to a table and two chairs, and decorated with art prints depicting the area's scenery. Most rooms have two queen-size beds and tub/shower combinations, although five rooms have one queen bed and shower only. There's a heated outdoor pool, picnic area, and an adjacent restaurant that serves three meals daily. Pets are accepted at the discretion of the management.

ⓢ Canyon Ranch Motel

668 Zion Park Blvd. (P.O. Box 175), Springdale, UT 84767. ☎ **801/772-3357.** 21 units. A/C TV. Mar–Oct $48–$68 double; Nov–Feb $38–$54 double. AE, DISC, MC, V.

Consisting of a series of two- and four-unit cottages set back from the highway, this place has the look of an old-fashioned auto camp on the outside while providing modern motel rooms inside. Rooms are either new or newly remodeled, and options include one queen- or king-size bed, two queens, or one queen and one double. Some rooms have showers only, while some have shower/tub combos, and there are no in-room telephones. Kitchen units are also available. Room 13, with two queen-size beds, offers spectacular views of the Zion National Park rock formations with several large picture windows, and views from most other rooms are almost as good. The units surround a lawn with trees and picnic tables, and there is an outdoor heated swimming pool and Jacuzzi. Pets are accepted at the discretion of the management.

Cliffrose Lodge & Gardens

281 Zion Park Blvd. (P.O. Box 510), Springdale, UT 84767. ☎ **801/772-3234** or 800/243-UTAH. Fax 801/772-3900. 36 units, including 6 suites. A/C TV TEL. Summer $109–$145 double. Lower rates in the winter. AE, DISC, MC, V.

With river frontage and 5 acres of lawns, shade trees, and flower gardens, the Cliffrose offers a beautiful setting just outside the entrance to Zion National Park. The modern well-kept rooms have all the standard motel appointments, with wood furnishings, floral-print bedspreads, and unusually large bathrooms with shower/tub combinations. On the lawns you'll find comfortable seating, including a lawn swing, plus there's a playground and large outdoor heated pool. Guests have use of a self-service laundry, and pets are accepted for a $10 fee.

✪ Flanigan's Inn

428 Zion Park Blvd. (P.O. Box 100), Springdale, UT 84767. ☎ **801/772-3244** or 800/765-RSVP. Fax 801/772-3396. 40 units. A/C TV TEL. Mid-Mar–Nov $69–$89 double; Dec–mid-Mar $49–$69 double. All rates include continental breakfast buffet. AE, DISC, MC, V.

A mountain lodge atmosphere pervades this very attractive complex of natural wood and rock, set among trees, lawns, and flowers just outside the entrance to Zion National Park. Parts of the inn date to 1947, but all rooms were completely renovated in the early 1990s, and have Southwest decor with wood furnishings and local art. Some units have whirlpool tubs and bidets, kitchenettes are available, and there is one room with a fireplace. This is a place where you might actually want to spend some time, unlike the other area options, which are just good places to sleep at the end of a long day spent exploring Zion. Flanigan's has its own nature trail leading to a hilltop vista, a heated outdoor swimming pool, a volleyball court, and a weight room. An on-site restaurant serves dinner, in addition to a continental breakfast for guests only (see "Dining," below). Summer reservations are often booked three to four months in advance.

Harvest House Bed & Breakfast at Zion

29 Canyonview Dr. (P.O. Box 125), Springdale, UT 84767. ☎ **801/772-3880.** Fax 801/772-3327. 4 rms. A/C. $75–$90 double. Rates include full breakfast. DISC, MC, V.

Even the smallest, least expensive room here is quite charming, with one queen-size bed, wicker furniture, and original paper art. Comfortable and quiet, this Utah territorial–style house was built in 1989; there's a cactus garden out front and a garden sitting area in back with a koi (Japanese carp) pond and spectacular views of the national park rock formations. We agree with owners Steven and Barbara Cooper, who call their decor "urban eclectic," with a smattering of collectibles, antiques of various periods, modern furnishings, original art, and photography. Two rooms have shower/tub combos, one has a tiled shower plus separate tub, and one has a shower only. Two rooms have decks, and all come with homemade cookies.

The homey living room—open to all—has a television and VCR with a collection of both new and classic movies, but the Coopers like to see their guests enjoying the great outdoors, and are anxious to share their knowledge of hiking and biking trails. Breakfasts are elegant and not at all run-of-the-mill, and might include selections such as homemade bagels with smoked salmon, frittatas, scrambled eggs with cheddar cheese, homemade granola, fruit, and yogurt. Facilities include an outdoor whirlpool. Children over six are welcome.

Zion Lodge

In Zion National Park. ☎ **801/586-7686.** Fax 801/586-3157. 120 units. A/C TEL. Motel rooms $75–$80 double; suites $113–$120 double; cabins $79–$85 double. AE, DISC, MC, V.

The motel units and cabins are nice enough, but then again, you don't come to Zion National Park to be indoors—you come for the scenery, and there's a pretty incredible view from the lobby's large picture windows. Sitting in a forest with spectacular views of the park's rock cliffs, the charming cabins each have a private porch, stone (gas-burning) fireplace, two double beds, pine board walls, and log beams. The comfortable motel units are basically just that—motel units—with two queen-sized beds and all the usual amenities except televisions. Motel suites each have one king-sized bed, a separate sitting room, and refrigerator. A gift shop offers everything from postcards to expensive silver-and-turquoise Native American jewelry.

Zion Park Inn

1215 Zion Park Blvd., Springdale, UT 84767. ☎ **801/772-3200** or 800/932-PARK. 120 rms. A/C TV TEL. $60–$80 double. AE, DC, DISC, JCB, MC, V.

Under construction when we went to press and scheduled to open in March 1996, this full-service hotel will be tied with Zion Lodge as the largest in the immediate Zion National Park area. There's a heated outdoor swimming pool, a restaurant serving American cuisine for three meals daily, and conference rooms with seating for up to 100. Pets are accepted with a deposit.

7 Dining

With the exception of Zion Lodge, which is in the park, these restaurants are all located on the main road through Springdale to the park.

Bit & Spur Saloon

1212 Zion Park Blvd., Springdale. ☎ **801/772-3498.** Reservations recommended. Main courses $8.50–$18. MC, V. Daily 5–10pm (beer bar open until 1am); brunch served mid-Mar–Oct Sat–Sun 8:30am–noon. Closed Dec–Jan. MEXICAN/SOUTHWESTERN.

This may look like an Old West–saloon, with its rough wood-and-stone walls and exposed beam ceiling, but it's an unusually clean saloon that also has a family dining room and patio dining. The food here is also a notch or two above what we expected, a bit closer to what you'd find in a good Santa Fe restaurant. The menu includes Mexican standards such as burritos, flautas, chile rellenos, and a traditional chile stew with pork; but you'll also find more creative dishes, including the pollo relleno—a grilled breast of chicken stuffed with cilantro pesto and goat cheese, and served with smoked pineapple chutney. Also good are the smokey chicken—a smoked, charbroiled game hen with sourdough stuffing and chipotle sauce—and the deep-dish chicken enchilada, with scallions, green chiles, and cheese. The Bit & Spur has a full liquor license and extensive wine list.

✪ Flanigan's Inn

428 Zion Park Blvd., Springdale. ☎ **801/772-3244.** Reservations recommended. Main courses $8.95–$19.95; pastas and salads $7.95–$11.95. AE, DISC, MC, V. Mon–Thurs 5–9:30pm; Fri–Sun until 10pm. Shorter hours in the winter. REGIONAL/WILD GAME.

With a greenhouse/garden atmosphere, this restaurant makes the most of the area's spectacular scenery with large windows for inside diners plus an outdoor patio. Specializing in southern Utah–style cooking, Flanigan's uses fresh local ingredients and herbs from the inn's garden whenever possible. The broiled salmon, served with a butter sauce and wild and brown rice, is always fresh; and the breast of chicken, served charbroiled, is free-range and chemical-free. Also popular are the Utah lamb chops, charbroiled and served with mint pear chutney and rice; the wild game plate with grilled elk, quail, and buffalo sausage, covered with a rich sauce and sprinkled with local pine nuts; and rabbit with mushrooms and sage—a commercially raised rabbit that is broiled and smothered in a traditional southern Utah sauce. Selections might also include a chicken curry salad or shrimp salad, and several pastas. Entrees are served with French country bread, the vegetable du jour, and a salad. A lighter menu, served until 6:30pm, is priced from $6.95. Microbrewery draft beers are available.

Zion Lodge

Zion National Park. ☎ **801/772-3213.** Dinner reservations required in the summer. Breakfast items $3.50–$5.95; lunch items $4.25–$6.95; main dinner courses $9.95–$15.95. AE, DC, DISC, MC, V. Daily 6:30–9:30am, noon–2:30pm, and 5:30–9pm. AMERICAN.

A mountain lodge atmosphere prevails here, complete with large windows that look out toward the park's magnificent rock formations from this spacious dining room above the Zion Lodge lobby. House specialties at dinner include an excellent slow-roasted prime rib au jus, and the very popular Utah red mountain trout. The menu also includes several chicken dishes, such as a skinless chicken breast basted with a spicy Caribbean sauce and served with a red onion relish. There are several vegetarian items on the menu, such as spinach linguini with roasted tomato sauce. Ask about the lodge's specialty ice creams and other exotic desserts. At lunch you'll find the trout and barbecued pork, plus burgers, sandwiches, and salads; and breakfasts offer all the usual American selections. The restaurant will pack lunches to go for hikers, and offers a children's menu and full liquor service.

Zion Pizza & Noodle

868 Zion Park Blvd., Springdale. ☎ **801/772-3815.** Reservations not accepted. Pizza $7.95–$10.95; pasta, calzone, and stromboli $6.95–$7.95; bagels 75¢–$3.95. No credit cards. President's Day–Thanksgiving noon–10pm; shorter hours in the winter. Bagels and espresso served 8am–3pm in the summer. Closed Jan–Feb. PIZZA/PASTA.

Located in a former LDS church with a turquoise steeple, this cafe has small, closely spaced tables and is decorated with black-and-white photos. Patrons order at the counter and help themselves at the beverage bar while waiting for their food to be delivered. The 12-inch pizzas are baked in a slate stone oven, and have lots of chewy crust. They're good, but New York–style pizza purists might be put off by oddly topped specialty pies, such as the southwestern burrito pizza or barbecue chicken pizza. But have no fear—you can get a basic cheese pizza, or add any of some 15 extra toppings from pepperoni to green chiles to pineapple. The noodle side of the menu offers a variety of pastas, such as fettuccini with roma tomatoes, fresh mushrooms, pesto sauce, cream, and grated parmesan; stromboli; and very often a locally popular nightly special of manicotti marinara. In the summer, bagel lovers will find plain or cream cheese–topped bagels plus several bagel sandwiches to munch with their espresso, latte, or cappuccino. The restaurant serves no alcohol. Take out and delivery are available.

8 Virtual Nature at Two Nearby Theaters

Just outside the south entrance to Zion National Park, in Springdale, are two worthwhile attractions.

"The Grand Circle: A National Park Odyssey," a multimedia production presented on a 24-by-40–foot screen in the outdoor Obert C. Tanner Amphitheater, is an excellent introduction to the national parks and monuments of southern Utah and northern Arizona. Using a state-of-the-art sound and projection system, and with the cliffs of Zion National Park in the background, the 1-hour program gives a brief look at the geology of the area, but devotes most of its time, sounds, and sights to the awe-inspiring scenery. Showings are scheduled at dusk nightly from late May through early September. Tickets cost $4 for adults, $3 for students and children under 12, or $10 per family.

The amphitheater, located just off Zion Park Boulevard, is also the venue for about a dozen **concerts** each summer, ranging from the annual Utah Symphony pops concert in late June or early July, to bluegrass, country, and acoustic. Tickets cost $5 to $9, depending on the performer. For information on the multimedia production or concert series contact **Dixie College in St. George** (☎ 801/652-7994).

You'll find an even bigger screen—some six stories high by 80 feet wide—at **Zion Canyon Theatre,** just outside the south entrance to Zion National Park at 145 Zion Park Blvd. (☎ 801/772-2400), where the 37-minute film "Treasure of the Gods" is presented year-round. There are thrilling scenes of the Zion National Park area, including a hair-raising flash flood through Zion Canyon's Narrows and some dizzying bird's-eye views, but don't take the history that's presented too literally—it's confusing at best. Admission costs $7 for adults; $4.50 for children 3 to 11. Shows begin hourly, 365 days a year; March through October from 9am to 9pm, and November through February from 11am to 7pm. The theater complex also includes a tourist information center, picnic area, gift and souvenir shops, a food emporium, a 30-minute photo processor, bookstore, and art gallery.

Index

FROMMER'S COMPLETE TRAVEL GUIDES

*(Comprehensive guides to destinations around the world, with
selections in all price ranges—from deluxe to budget)*

Acapulco/Ixtapa/Zihuatenjo
Alaska
Amsterdam
Arizona
Atlanta
Australia
Austria
Bahamas
Bangkok
Barcelona, Madrid &
   Seville
Belgium, Holland &
   Luxembourg
Berlin
Bermuda
Boston
Budapest & the Best of
   Hungary
California
Canada
Cancún, Cozumel & the
   Yucatán
Caribbean
Caribbean Cruises & Ports
   of Call
Caribbean Ports of Call
Carolinas & Georgia
Chicago
Colorado
Costa Rica
Denver, Boulder &
   Colorado Springs
Dublin
England

Florida
France
Germany
Greece
Hawaii
Hong Kong
Honolulu/Waikiki/Oahu
Ireland
Italy
Jamaica & Barbados
Japan
Las Vegas
London
Los Angeles
Maryland & Delaware
Maui
Mexico
Mexico City
Miami & the Keys
Montana & Wyoming
Montréal & Québec
   City
Munich & the Bavarian
   Alps
Nashville & Memphis
Nepal
New England
New Mexico
New Orleans
New York City
Northern New England
Nova Scotia, New
   Brunswick & Prince
   Edward Island

Paris
Philadelphia & the Amish
   Country
Portugal
Prague & the Best of the
   Czech Republic
Puerto Rico
Puerto Vallarta, Manzanillo
   & Guadalajara
Rome
San Antonio & Austin
San Diego
San Francisco
Santa Fe, Taos &
   Albuquerque
Scandinavia
Scotland
Seattle & Portland
South Pacific
Spain
Switzerland
Thailand
Tokyo
Toronto
U.S.A.
Utah
Vancouver & Victoria
Vienna
Virgin Islands
Virginia
Walt Disney World &
   Orlando
Washington, D.C.
Washington & Oregon

FROMMER'S FRUGAL TRAVELER'S GUIDES

*(The grown-up guides to budget travel, offering dream vacations
at down-to-earth prices)*

Australia from $45 a Day
Berlin from $50 a Day
California from $60 a Day
Caribbean from $60 a Day
Costa Rica & Belize from
   $35 a Day
Eastern Europe from
   $30 a Day

England from $50 a Day
Europe from $50 a Day
Florida from $50 a Day
Greece from $45 a Day
Hawaii from $60 a Day
India from $40 a Day
Ireland from $45 a Day
Italy from $50 a Day

Israel from $45 a Day
London from $60 a Day
Mexico from $35 a Day
New York from $70 a Day
New Zealand from $45 a Day
Paris from $60 a Day
Washington, D.C. from
   $50 a Day

FROMMER'S PORTABLE GUIDES

(Pocket-size guides for travelers who want everything in a nutshell)

Charleston & Savannah Las Vegas Washington, D.C. New Orleans San Francisco

FROMMER'S FAMILY GUIDES

(The complete guides for successful family vacations)

California with Kids New England with Kids San Francisco with Kids
Los Angeles with Kids New York City with Kids Washington, D.C. with Kids

FROMMER'S AMERICA ON WHEELS

(Everything you need for a successful road trip, including full-color road maps and ratings for every hotel)

California & Nevada	Midwest & the Great	Northwest & the	Southwest
Florida	Lake States	Great Plains States	Texas & the South-
Mid-Atlantic	New York & the New	Southeast	Central States
	England States		

FROMMER'S WALKING TOURS

(Memorable neighborhood strolls through the world's great cities)

Berlin	Montréal & Québec City	Spain's Favorite Cities
Chicago	New York	Tokyo
England's Favorite Cities	Paris	Venice
London	San Francisco	Washington, D.C.

SPECIAL-INTEREST TITLES

Arthur Frommer's Branson!
Arthur Frommer's New World of Travel
The Civil War Trust's Official Guide to the
    Civil War Discovery Trail
Frommer's America's 100 Best-Loved State
    Parks
Frommer's Caribbean Hideaways
Frommer's Complete Hostel Vacation Guide to
    England, Scotland & Wales
Frommer's Food Lover's Companion to France
Frommer's Food Lover's Companion to Italy
Frommer's Great European Driving Tours

Frommer's National Park Guide
Outside Magazine's Adventure Guide to New
    England
Outside Magazine's Adventure Guide to
    Northern California
Places Rated Almanac
Retirement Places Rated
USA Sports Traveler's and TV Viewer's
    Golf Tournament Guide
USA Sports Minor League Baseball Book
USA Today Golf Atlas
Wonderful Weekends from NYC

FROMMER'S IRREVERENT GUIDES

(Wickedly honest guides for sophisticated travelers)

Amsterdam	Manhattan	Paris	U.S. Virgin Islands
Chicago	Miami	San Francisco	Walt Disney World
London	New Orleans	Santa Fe	Washington, D.C.

UNOFFICIAL GUIDES

(Get the unbiased truth from these candid, value-conscious guides)

Atlanta	Euro Disneyland	Mini-Mickey
Branson, Missouri	The Great Smoky & Blue	Skiing in the West
Chicago	Ridge Mountains	Walt Disney World
Cruises	Las Vegas	Walt Disney World Companion
Disneyland	Miami & the Keys	Washington, D.C.

BAEDEKER
(With four-color photographs and a free pull-out map)

Amsterdam	Florence	London	Scotland
Athens	Florida	Mexico	Singapore
Austria	Germany	New York	South Africa
Bali	Great Britain	Paris	Spain
Belgium	Greece	Portugal	Switzerland
Budapest	Greek Islands	Prague	Thailand
California	Hawaii	Provence	Tokyo
Canada	Hong Kong	Rome	Turkish Coast
Caribbean	Ireland	San Francisco	Tuscany
China	Israel	St. Petersburg	Venice
Copenhagen	Italy	Scandinavia	Vienna
Crete	Lisbon		

FROMMER'S BY NIGHT GUIDES
(The series for those who know that life begins after dark)

Amsterdam	London	Miami	Paris
Chicago	Los Angeles	New Orleans	San Francisco
Las Vegas	Manhattan		

FROMMER'S BEST BEACH VACATIONS
(The top places to sun, stroll, shop, stay, play, party, and swim, with ratings for each beach)

California	Hawaii	New England
Carolinas & Georgia	Mid-Atlantic (from New	
Florida	York to Washington, D.C.)	

FROMMER'S BED & BREAKFAST GUIDES
(Selective guides with four-color photos and full descriptions of the best inns in each region)

California	Great American Cities	New England	The Rockies
Caribbean	Hawaii	Pacific Northwest	Southwest

FROMMER'S DRIVING TOURS
(Four-color photos and detailed maps outlining spectacular scenic driving routes)

Australia	France	Italy	Spain
Austria	Germany	Scandinavia	Switzerland
Britain	Ireland	Scotland	U.S.A.
Florida			

FROMMER'S BORN TO SHOP
(The ultimate guides for travelers who love to shop)

France	Hong Kong	Mexico
Great Britain	London	New York

TRAVEL & LEISURE GUIDES
(Sophisticated pocket-size guides for discriminating travelers)

Amsterdam	Hong Kong	New York	San Francisco
Boston	London	Paris	Washington, D.C.

WHEREVER YOU TRAVEL, *H*ELP IS NEVER FAR AWAY.

From planning your trip to providing travel assistance along the way, American Express® Travel Service Offices are always there to help.

> ## *Las Vegas*

American Express Travel Service
Caesar's Palace
3570 Las Vegas Blvd. South
Las Vegas
702/731-7705

Prestige Travel (R)
3870 East Flamingo Road
Suite A2
Las Vegas
702/731-2661

Mickey Cole Travel Service, Inc. (R)
Gold Coast Hotel & Casino
4000 W. Flamingo Road
Las Vegas
702/876-1410

Prestige Travel (R)
3504 Maryland Parkway
Las Vegas
702/794-2811

Travel

http://www.americanexpress.com/travel

**American Express Travel Service Offices
are located throughout Nevada.
For the office nearest you, call 1-800-AXP-3429.**